EDUCATION
MEETING AMERICA'S NEEDS?

ISSN 1557-7021

EDUCATION
MEETING AMERICA'S NEEDS?

Gina Giuliano

INFORMATION PLUS® REFERENCE SERIES
Formerly Published by Information Plus, Wylie, Texas

THOMSON
GALE

Detroit • New York • San Francisco • San Diego • New Haven, Conn. • Waterville, Maine • London • Munich

THOMSON

™

GALE

Education: Meeting America's Needs?
Gina Giuliano
Paula Kepos, Series Editor

Project Editor
John McCoy

Permissions
Margaret Abendroth, Edna Hedblad,
Emma Hull

Composition and Electronic Prepress
Evi Seoud

Manufacturing
Drew Kalasky

ISBN 0-7876-5103-6 (set)
ISBN 1-4144-0411-5
ISSN 1557-7021

This title is also available as an e-book.
ISBN 1-4144-1043-3 (set)
Contact your Thomson Gale sales representative for ordering information.

Printed in the United States of America
10 9 8 7 6 5 4 3 2 1

TABLE OF CONTENTS

degree-granting trends; persistence; faculty; rising costs and
financial assistance; distance education; and substance abuse
on campus.

Chapter 10 concerns public opinion on education, as reflected by
Phi Delta Kappa/Gallup polls that posed questions about public

school problems and quality, school reforms, reasons for student
failure, and the achievement gap between minority and white
children.

PREFACE

Education: Meeting America's Needs? is part of the *Information Plus Reference Series.* The purpose of each volume of the series is to present the latest facts on a topic of pressing concern in modern American life. These topics include today's most controversial and most studied social issues: abortion, capital punishment, care for the elderly, crime, the environment, health care, immigration, minorities, national security, social welfare, women, youth, and many more. Although written especially for the high school and undergraduate student, this series is an excellent resource for anyone in need of factual information on current affairs.

By presenting the facts, it is Thomson Gale's intention to provide its readers with everything they need to reach an informed opinion on current issues. To that end, there is a particular emphasis in this series on the presentation of scientific studies, surveys, and statistics. These data are generally presented in the form of tables, charts, and other graphics placed within the text of each book. Every graphic is directly referred to and carefully explained in the text. The source of each graphic is presented within the graphic itself. The data used in these graphics are drawn from the most reputable and reliable sources, in particular from the various branches of the U.S. government and from major independent polling organizations. Every effort has been made to secure the most recent information available. The reader should bear in mind that many major studies take years to conduct, and that additional years often pass before the data from these studies are made available to the public. Therefore, in many cases the most recent information available in 2006 dated from 2003 or 2004. Older statistics are sometimes presented as well if they are of particular interest and no more recent information exists.

Although statistics are a major focus of the *Information Plus Reference Series*, they are by no means its only content. Each book also presents the widely held positions and important ideas that shape how the book's subject is discussed in the United States. These positions are explained in detail and, where possible, in the words of their proponents. Some of the other material to be found in these books includes: historical background; descriptions of major events related to the subject; relevant laws and court cases; and examples of how these issues play out in American life. Some books also feature primary documents or have pro and con debate sections giving the words and opinions of prominent Americans on both sides of a controversial topic. All material is presented in an even-handed and unbiased manner; the reader will never be encouraged to accept one view of an issue over another.

HOW TO USE THIS BOOK

From escalating violence in the classroom to the production of high school graduates capable of competing in today's global marketplace, education is a hotly disputed topic in America. This book presents a snapshot of education in the United States. Areas covered include an overview of American education; primary, elementary, and secondary schools; public versus private schooling; special education; education of gifted children; testing and achievement of students at the primary, secondary, and college levels; national education goals; and "at-risk" students, including trends in dropout rates, drug use, and violence in schools. Also discussed are colleges and universities; issues such as home schooling, school choice, and vouchers; trends in teacher supply and demand; and public opinions about education.

Education: Meeting America's Needs? consists of ten chapters and three appendices. Each of the chapters is devoted to a particular aspect of education in the United States. For a summary of the information covered in each chapter, please see the synopses provided in the Table of Contents at the front of the book. Chapters generally begin with an overview of the basic facts and background information on the chapter's topic, then proceed to examine subtopics of particular interest. For example, Chapter 3, Education for Special School Populations, begins with the definition of disability and then goes on to discuss the numbers and characteristics of special education students, programs to meet their needs, and the transition from special education to higher education and the workforce. This is followed by a section on programs for gifted and talented students. The chapter concludes with a section on disadvantaged students and programs developed to meet their needs. Readers can find their way through a chapter by looking for the section and subsection headings, which are clearly set off from the text. They can also refer to the book's extensive Index if they already know what they are looking for.

Statistical Information

The tables and figures featured throughout *Education: Meeting America's Needs?* will be of particular use to the reader in learning about this issue. These tables and figures represent an extensive collection of the most recent and important statistics on education and related issues—for example, graphics in the book cover public elementary and secondary school revenue sources and amounts, student proficiency in reading, progress toward meeting requirements of the No Child Left Behind Act, public opinion on the use of vouchers, percentages of public school teachers without a major or minor in the fields in which they teach, percentages of those participating in adult education, and the number of college degrees conferred in various fields. Thomson Gale believes that making this information available to the reader is the most important way in which we fulfill the goal of this book: to help readers understand the issues and controversies surrounding education in the United States and reach their own conclusions.

Each table or figure has a unique identifier appearing above it for ease of identification and reference. Titles for the tables and figures explain their purpose. At the end of each table or figure, the original source of the data is provided.

In order to help readers understand these often complicated statistics, all tables and figures are explained in the text. References in the text direct the reader to the relevant statistics. Furthermore, the contents of all tables and figures are fully indexed. Please see the opening section of the Index at the back of this volume for a description of how to find tables and figures within it.

Appendices

In addition to the main body text and images, *Education: Meeting America's Needs?* has three appendices. The first is the Important Names and Addresses directory. Here the reader will find contact information for a number of government and private organizations that can provide further information on education. The second appendix is the Resources section, which can also assist the reader in conducting his or her own research. In this section the author and editors of *Education: Meeting America's Needs?* describe some of the sources that were most useful during the compilation of this book. The final appendix is the detailed Index, which facilitates reader access to specific topics in this book.

ADVISORY BOARD CONTRIBUTIONS

The staff of Information Plus would like to extend its heartfelt appreciation to the Information Plus Advisory Board. This dedicated group of media professionals provides feedback on the series on an ongoing basis. Their comments allow the editorial staff who work on the project to make the series better and more user-friendly. Our top priority is to produce the highest-quality and most useful books possible, and the Advisory Board's contributions to this process are invaluable.

The members of the Information Plus Advisory Board are:

- Kathleen R. Bonn, Librarian, Newbury Park High School, Newbury Park, California

- Madelyn Garner, Librarian, San Jacinto College—North Campus, Houston, Texas

- Anne Oxenrider, Media Specialist, Dundee High School, Dundee, Michigan

- Charles R. Rodgers, Director of Libraries, Pasco–Hernando Community College, Dade City, Florida

- James N. Zitzelsberger, Library Media Department Chairman, Oshkosh West High School, Oshkosh, Wisconsin

COMMENTS AND SUGGESTIONS

The editors of the *Information Plus Reference Series* welcome your feedback on *Education: Meeting America's Needs?* Please direct all correspondence to:

Editors
Information Plus Reference Series
27500 Drake Rd.
Farmington Hills, MI 48331-3535

CHAPTER 1
AN OVERVIEW OF AMERICAN EDUCATION

American education has always faced challenges. Debates about the purposes of schools, the benefits of education, the best approach to teaching and learning, and calls for reform of the system have been common in the history of education in the United States. Since the 1980s the nation has been working to resolve such critical issues as low academic performance, high dropout rates, and drug use and violence in schools. Parents worry about the escalating cost of a college education. Political and community leaders question the ability of U.S. schools to produce high school graduates capable of competing in an increasingly technical and international environment. Educational leaders raise concerns about the impacts of poverty on education, and about the adequacy of school resources. Voters and legislators debate the merits of alternative schools, including whether parents who educate their children in private schools should receive federal or state subsidies. Calls for school accountability are heard from both taxpayers and elected officials.

Despite these problems, the United States remains one of the most highly educated nations in the world. According to the U.S. Department of Education, in fall 2003 approximately 79.7 million Americans were involved either directly or indirectly in providing or receiving formal education. About 70.7 million students were enrolled in schools and colleges, and 4.2 million instructors were teaching at the elementary, secondary, or college level. Another 4.8 million people were professional, administrative, and support personnel at educational institutions. (See Table 1.1.)

EDUCATION LEVEL OF POPULATION HAS GROWN

The number of school years completed among Americans age twenty-five and older has been increasing. According to the U.S. Department of Education, in 1940 about one in four Americans (24.5%) twenty-five and older had completed four years or more of high school, but almost one in seven (13.7%) had completed fewer than five years of elementary school. By 2002 in the same age group, 84.1% of Americans had completed high school, while only 1.6% had fewer than five years of formal education. In 1940 less than 5% of the population twenty-five and older had completed four or more years of college; by 2002 about 26.7% had done so. (See Table 1.2 and Figure 1.1.)

Among people ages twenty-five to twenty-nine, 86.4% had completed four years of high school or more in 2002, while 29.3% had completed four or more years of college. White Americans were more likely than African-Americans or Hispanic Americans to have completed both high school and college. (See Table 1.2.)

SCHOOL ENROLLMENT

Virtually all American children five to seventeen years old are enrolled in school. According to the U.S. Department of Education, in 2001 more than 95% of all young people in this age group attended school. The enrollment of three- and four-year-olds has increased substantially since 1980, from 36.7% in that year to 52.4% in 2001. (See Table 1.3.)

The proportion of people enrolled in school drops sharply after age eighteen. By this age young people either graduate from or leave high school and may not immediately go on to any form of higher education. However, the proportion of older teens attending school has increased since 1980. According to the U.S. Department of Education, in 2001 the proportion of eighteen- and nineteen-year-olds enrolled in school reached 61%, up from 46.4% in 1980. (See Table 1.3.)

Enrollment Numbers Change

The number of students enrolled in elementary and secondary schools and in colleges is roughly proportional

TABLE 1.1

Projected number of participants in educational institutions, by level and control of institution, Fall 2003

[In millions]

Participants	All levels (elementary, secondary, and degree-granting)	Elementary and secondary schools			Degree-granting institutions		
		Total	Public	Private	Total	Public	Private
1	2	3	4	5	6	7	8
Total	**79.7**	**60.9**	**53.9**	**6.8**	**18.9**	**14.3**	**4.6**
Enrollment	70.7	54.3	48.0	6.3	16.4	12.5	3.8
Teachers and faculty	4.2	3.4	3.0	0.4	0.8	0.6	0.3
Other professional, administrative, and support staff	4.8	3.1	2.9	0.2	1.7	1.2	0.5

Note: Includes enrollments in local public school systems and in most private schools (religiously affiliated and nonsectarian). Excludes subcollegiate departments of institutions of higher education and federal schools. Elementary and secondary includes most kindergarten and some nursery school enrollment. Excludes preprimary enrollment in schools that do not offer first grade or above. Degree-granting institutions include full-time and part-time students enrolled in degree-credit and nondegree-credit programs in universities, other 4–year colleges, and 2–year colleges that participated in Title IV federal financial aid programs. Data for teachers and other staff in public and private elementary and secondary schools and colleges and universities are reported in terms of full-time equivalents. Detail may not sum to totals due to rounding.

SOURCE: Thomas D. Snyder, Alexandra G. Tan, and Charlene M. Hoffman, "Table 1. Projected Number of Participants in Educational Institutions, by Level and Control of Institution: Fall 2003," in *Digest of Education Statistics, 2003*, NCES 2005-025, U.S. Department of Education, National Center for Education Statistics, Washington, DC, December 2004, http://nces.ed.gov/programs/digest/d03/tables/dt001.asp (accessed July 26, 2005)

to the birth rates of the previous two decades. After World War II and the Korean conflict, the nation experienced a "baby boom" (1946–64) as returning soldiers settled down to start families. Consequently, school enrollment grew rapidly during the 1950s and 1960s as these babies matured to school age. According to the U.S. Department of Education, total enrollment peaked at sixty-one million in 1975, a number not attained again until 1991. Elementary enrollment, which includes the figures for public pre-kindergarten through grade eight and private kindergarten through grade eight, reached a record high of 36.7 million in 1969, and high school enrollment peaked at 15.7 million in 1976. (See Table 1.4.)

Birth rates declined as the baby boom waned, and so did school enrollments in the 1970s. An "echo effect" occurred in the 1980s, when those born during the baby boom started their own families. This increase in birth rates triggered an increase in school enrollment in the early 1990s. In 1991 the enrollment of students at schools of all levels was 61.7 million. In the years following 1991, school enrollment grew about 1% to 2% annually, to 69.8 million in 2001. (See Table 1.4.)

After a high of 36.7 million in 1969, elementary enrollment in public and private schools gradually declined and leveled off in the late 1980s at around thirty-three million. Elementary enrollment then rose through the 1990s to about thirty-nine million in 2001. It is expected to stay fairly stable through 2013. (See Table 1.4.)

Public high school enrollment, which began to decline in the late 1970s, started to increase again in the 1990s and is expected to continue to grow until 2008, after which it will decline slightly until 2013. College enrollments, unlike elementary and secondary enrollments, have risen consistently and are expected to reach almost 18.2 million by 2013. (See Table 1.4.)

EDUCATIONAL DIFFERENCES

Race and Ethnicity

The marked difference in educational attainment that once existed between whites and minorities has narrowed, although there are still significant gaps. According to the U.S. Department of Education, about 88.7% of white adults age twenty-five and older were high school graduates in 2002, while 79.2% of African-Americans and 57% of Hispanics were graduates. The most significant advances can be seen among young adults ages twenty-five to twenty-nine, where 93% of whites, 87.6% of African-Americans, and 62.4% of Hispanics were high school graduates in 2002, compared to 41.2% of whites and 12.3% of blacks and other races in 1940. (See Table 1.2.)

In 1940 white adults age twenty-five and older were 3.7 times more likely than African-Americans and other minorities to have completed four years of college (4.9% versus 1.3%). More than sixty years later, whites twenty-five and older were 1.7 times more likely to complete four years of college than African-Americans and 2.6 times more likely to complete four years of college than Hispanics. According to the U.S. Department of Education, in 2002, 29.4% of whites, 17.2% of African-Americans, and 11.1% of Hispanics completed four or more years of college. More than one-third of white

TABLE 1.2

Percent of persons age 25 and over, by years of school completed, race/ethnicity, and sex, selected years, 1910–2002

Age and year	Total			White, non-Hispanic[a]			Black, non-Hispanic[a]			Hispanic		
	Less than 5 years of elementary school	High school completion or higher[b]	4 or more years of college[c]	Less than 5 years of elementary school	High school completion or higher[b]	4 or more years of college[c]	Less than 5 years of elementary school	High school completion or higher[b]	4 or more years of college[c]	Less than 5 years of elementary school	High school completion or higher[b]	4 or more years of college[c]
1	2	3	4	5	6	7	8	9	10	11	12	13

25 and over

Males and females

Age and year	2	3	4	5	6	7	8	9	10	11	12	13
1910[d]	23.8	13.5	2.7	—	—	—	—	—	—	—	—	—
1920[d]	22.0	16.4	3.3	—	—	—	—	—	—	—	—	—
1930[d]	17.5	19.1	3.9	—	—	—	—	—	—	—	—	—
April 1940	13.7	24.5	4.6	10.9	26.1	4.9	41.8	7.7	1.3	—	—	—
April 1950	11.1	34.3	6.2	8.9	36.4	6.6	32.6	13.7	2.2	—	—	—
April 1960	8.3	41.1	7.7	6.7	43.2	8.1	23.5	21.7	3.5	—	—	—
March 1970	5.3	55.2	11.0	4.2	57.4	11.6	14.7	36.1	6.1	—	—	—
March 1975	4.2	62.5	13.9	2.6	65.8	14.9	12.3	42.6	6.4	18.2	38.5	6.6
March 1980	3.4	68.6	17.0	1.9	71.9	18.4	9.1	51.4	7.9	15.8	44.5	7.6
March 1985	2.7	73.9	19.4	1.4	77.5	20.8	6.1	59.9	11.1	13.5	47.9	8.5
March 1986	2.7	74.7	19.4	1.4	78.2	20.9	5.3	62.5	10.9	12.9	48.5	8.4
March 1987	2.4	75.6	19.9	1.3	79.0	21.4	4.9	63.6	10.8	11.9	50.9	8.6
March 1988	2.4	76.2	20.3	1.2	79.8	21.8	4.8	63.5	11.2	12.2	51.0	10.0
March 1989	2.5	76.9	21.1	1.2	80.7	22.8	5.2	64.7	11.7	12.2	50.9	9.9
March 1990	2.4	77.6	21.3	1.1	81.4	23.1	5.1	66.2	11.3	12.3	50.8	9.2
March 1991	2.4	78.4	21.4	1.1	82.4	23.3	4.7	66.8	11.5	12.5	51.3	9.7
March 1992	2.1	79.4	21.4	0.9	83.4	23.2	3.9	67.7	11.9	11.8	52.6	9.3
March 1993	2.1	80.2	21.9	0.8	84.1	23.8	3.7	70.5	12.2	11.8	53.1	9.0
March 1994	1.9	80.9	22.2	0.8	84.9	24.3	2.7	73.0	12.9	10.8	53.3	9.1
March 1995	1.8	81.7	23.0	0.7	85.9	25.4	2.5	73.8	13.3	10.6	53.4	9.3
March 1996	1.8	81.7	23.6	0.6	86.0	25.9	2.2	74.6	13.8	10.3	53.1	9.3
March 1997	1.7	82.1	23.9	0.6	86.3	26.2	2.0	75.3	13.3	9.4	54.7	10.3
March 1998	1.6	82.8	24.4	0.6	87.1	26.6	1.7	76.4	14.8	9.3	55.5	11.0
March 1999	1.6	83.4	25.2	0.6	87.7	27.7	1.7	77.4	15.5	9.0	56.1	10.9
March 2000	1.6	84.1	25.6	0.5	88.4	28.1	1.6	78.9	16.6	8.7	57.0	10.6
March 2001	1.6	84.3	26.1	0.5	88.7	28.6	1.3	79.5	16.1	9.3	56.5	11.2
March 2002	1.6	84.1	26.7	0.5	88.7	29.4	1.6	79.2	17.2	8.7	57.0	11.1

25 to 29

Age and year	2	3	4	5	6	7	8	9	10	11	12	13
1920[d]	5.9	38.1	—	12.9	22.0	4.5	44.6	6.3	1.2	—	—	—
April 1940	4.6	52.8	5.9	3.4	41.2	6.4	27.0	12.3	1.6	—	—	—
April 1950	2.8	60.7	7.7	3.3	56.3	8.2	16.1	23.6	2.8	—	—	—
April 1960	1.1	75.4	11.0	2.2	63.7	11.8	7.2	38.6	5.4	—	—	—
March 1970	1.0	83.1	16.4	0.9	77.8	17.3	2.2	58.4	10.0	—	—	—
March 1975	0.8	85.4	21.9	0.6	86.6	23.8	0.5	71.1	10.5	8.0	53.1	8.8
March 1980	0.7	86.1	22.5	0.3	89.2	25.0	0.6	76.7	11.6	6.7	58.0	7.7
March 1985	0.9	86.1	22.2	0.2	89.5	24.4	0.4	80.5	11.6	6.0	60.9	11.1
March 1986	0.9	86.0	22.4	0.4	89.6	25.2	0.5	83.5	11.8	5.6	59.1	9.0
March 1987	0.9	85.9	22.0	0.4	89.4	24.6	0.4	83.4	11.5	4.8	59.8	8.7
March 1988	1.0	85.5	22.7	0.3	89.7	25.1	0.3	80.9	12.0	6.0	62.3	11.3
March 1989	1.0	85.7	23.4	0.3	89.3	26.3	0.5	82.3	12.6	5.4	61.0	10.1
March 1990	1.2	85.4	23.2	0.3	90.1	26.4	1.0	81.7	13.4	7.3	58.2	8.1
March 1991	1.0	86.3	23.2	0.4	89.8	26.7	0.5	81.8	11.0	5.8	56.7	9.2
March 1992	0.9	86.7	23.6	0.3	90.7	27.2	0.8	80.9	11.0	5.2	60.9	9.5
March 1993	0.7	86.7	23.7	0.3	91.2	27.2	0.2	82.6	13.3	4.0	60.9	8.3
March 1994	0.8	86.1	23.3	0.2	91.1	27.1	0.6	84.1	13.6	3.6	60.3	8.0

TABLE 1.2

Percent of persons age 25 and over, by years of school completed, race/ethnicity, and sex, selected years, 1910–2002 [CONTINUED]

	Total			White, non-Hispanic[a]			Black, non-Hispanic[a]			Hispanic		
Age and year	Less than 5 years of elementary school	High school completion or higher[b]	4 or more years of college[c]	Less than 5 years of elementary school	High school completion or higher[b]	4 or more years of college[c]	Less than 5 years of elementary school	High school completion or higher[b]	4 or more years of college[c]	Less than 5 years of elementary school	High school completion or higher[b]	4 or more years of college[c]
1	2	3	4	5	6	7	8	9	10	11	12	13
March 1997	0.8	87.4	27.8	0.1	92.9	32.6	0.6	86.9	14.2	4.2	61.8	11.0
March 1998	0.7	88.1	27.3	0.1	93.6	32.3	0.4	88.2	15.8	3.7	62.8	10.4
March 1999	0.6	87.8	28.2	0.1	93.0	33.6	0.2	88.7	15.0	3.2	61.6	8.9
March 2000	0.7	88.1	29.1	0.1	94.0	34.0	*	86.8	17.8	3.8	62.8	9.7
March 2001	0.8	87.7	28.6	0.2	93.3	33.0	0.1	87.0	17.8	4.7	63.2	11.1
March 2002	1.1	86.4	29.3	0.1	93.0	35.9	0.6	87.6	18.0	4.7	62.4	8.9
Males												
25 and over												
April 1940	15.1	22.7	5.5	12.0	24.2	5.9	46.2	6.9	1.4	—	—	—
April 1950	12.2	32.6	7.3	9.8	34.6	7.9	36.9	12.6	2.1	—	—	—
April 1960	9.4	39.5	9.7	7.4	41.6	10.3	27.7	20.0	3.5	—	—	—
March 1970	5.9	55.0	14.1	4.5	57.2	15.0	17.9	35.4	6.8	—	—	—
March 1980	3.6	69.2	20.9	2.0	72.4	22.8	11.3	51.2	7.7	16.5	44.9	9.2
March 1990	2.7	77.7	24.4	1.3	81.6	26.7	6.4	65.8	11.9	12.9	50.3	9.8
March 1995	2.0	81.7	26.0	0.8	86.0	28.9	3.4	73.5	13.7	10.8	52.9	10.1
March 1996	1.9	81.9	26.0	0.7	86.1	28.8	2.9	74.6	12.5	10.1	53.0	10.3
March 1997	1.8	82.0	26.2	0.6	86.3	29.0	2.9	73.8	12.5	9.2	54.9	10.6
March 1998	1.7	82.8	26.5	0.7	87.1	29.3	2.3	75.4	14.0	9.3	55.7	11.1
March 1999	1.6	83.4	27.5	0.6	87.7	30.6	2.0	77.2	14.3	9.0	56.0	10.7
March 2000	1.6	84.2	27.8	0.6	88.5	30.8	2.1	79.1	16.4	8.2	56.6	10.7
March 2001	1.6	84.4	28.0	0.6	88.6	30.9	1.7	80.6	15.9	9.4	55.6	11.1
March 2002	1.7	83.8	28.5	0.5	88.5	31.7	1.9	79.0	16.5	9.0	56.1	11.0

TABLE 1.2

Percent of persons age 25 and over, by years of school completed, race/ethnicity, and sex, selected years, 1910–2002 [CONTINUED]

Age and year	Total			White, non-Hispanic[a]			Black, non-Hispanic[a]			Hispanic		
	Less than 5 years of elementary school	High school completion or higher[b]	4 or more years of college[c]	Less than 5 years of elementary school	High school completion or higher[b]	4 or more years of college[c]	Less than 5 years of elementary school	High school completion or higher[b]	4 or more years of college[c]	Less than 5 years of elementary school	High school completion or higher[b]	4 or more years of college[c]
1	2	3	4	5	6	7	8	9	10	11	12	13
25 and over												
						Females						
April 1940	12.4	26.3	3.8	9.8	28.1	4.0	37.5	8.4	1.2	—	—	—
April 1950	10.0	36.0	5.2	8.1	38.2	5.4	28.6	14.7	2.4	—	—	—
April 1960	7.4	42.5	5.8	6.0	44.7	6.0	19.7	23.1	3.6	—	—	—
March 1970	4.7	55.4	8.2	3.9	57.7	8.6	11.9	36.6	5.6	—	—	—
March 1980	3.2	68.1	13.6	1.8	71.5	14.4	7.4	51.5	8.1	15.3	44.2	6.2
March 1990	2.2	77.5	18.4	1.0	81.3	19.8	4.0	66.5	10.8	11.7	51.3	8.7
March 1995	1.7	81.6	20.2	0.6	85.8	22.1	1.7	74.1	13.0	10.4	53.8	8.4
March 1996	1.7	81.6	21.4	0.5	85.9	23.2	1.6	74.6	14.8	10.5	53.3	8.3
March 1997	1.6	82.2	21.7	0.5	86.3	23.7	1.3	76.5	14.0	9.5	54.6	10.1
March 1998	1.6	82.9	22.4	0.6	87.1	24.1	1.2	77.1	15.4	9.2	55.3	10.9
March 1999	1.5	83.3	23.1	0.5	87.6	25.0	1.5	77.5	16.5	9.0	56.3	11.0
March 2000	1.5	84.0	23.6	0.4	88.4	25.5	1.1	78.7	16.8	9.3	57.5	10.6
March 2001	1.5	84.2	24.3	0.4	88.8	26.5	1.0	78.6	16.3	9.1	57.4	11.3
March 2002	1.5	84.4	25.1	0.5	88.9	27.3	1.4	79.4	17.7	8.3	57.9	11.2

Note: Total includes other racial/ethnic groups not shown separately.

* Rounds to zero.

— Not available.

[a] Includes persons of Hispanic origin for years prior to 1980.

[b] Data for years prior to 1993 include all persons with at least 4 years of high school.

[c] Data for 1993 and later years are for persons with a bachelor's or higher degree.

[d] Estimates based on Bureau of the Census retrojection of 1940 Census data on education by age.

SOURCE: Thomas D. Snyder, Alexandra G. Tan, and Charlene M. Hoffman, "Table 8. Percent of Persons Age 25 and Over and 25 to 29, by Years of School Completed, Race/Ethnicity, and Sex: Selected Years, 1910–2002," in *Digest of Education Statistics, 2003*, NCES 2005-025, U.S. Department of Education, National Center for Education Statistics, Washington, DC, December 2004, http://nces.ed.gov/programs/digest/d03/tables/dt008.asp (accessed July 26, 2005)

FIGURE 1.1

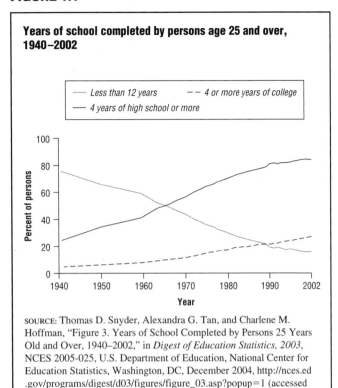

Years of school completed by persons age 25 and over, 1940–2002

SOURCE: Thomas D. Snyder, Alexandra G. Tan, and Charlene M. Hoffman, "Figure 3. Years of School Completed by Persons 25 Years Old and Over, 1940–2002," in *Digest of Education Statistics, 2003*, NCES 2005-025, U.S. Department of Education, National Center for Education Statistics, Washington, DC, December 2004, http://nces.ed .gov/programs/digest/d03/figures/figure_03.asp?popup=1 (accessed July 26, 2005)

25.1% in 2002. Nevertheless, the proportion of male students (28.5% in 2002) who completed four or more years of college was still higher. This does not hold true across race and ethnicity. White males (31.7%) were more likely than white females (27.3%) to have completed four or more years of college, but African-American and Hispanic males (16.5% and 11%, respectively) were less likely than African-American and Hispanic females (17.7% and 11.2%, respectively) to have completed four or more years of college in 2002. (See Table 1.2.)

PROJECTIONS TO 2013

The National Center for Education Statistics (NCES) estimates that the total public and private elementary and secondary enrollment will increase from 54.2 million in 2002 to 56.4 million in 2013. Enrollment in public pre-kindergarten through eighth grade was projected to hit its lowest level in 2005, and then begin a modest climb to 35.4 million. Public enrollment in grades nine through twelve is expected to rise through 2007, and then start to fall slightly. The number of people attending degree-granting institutions of higher learning is projected to increase from 16.1 million in 2002 to 18.2 million by 2013. (See Table 1.4.)

EDUCATION SPENDING

According to the U.S. Department of Education, expenditures for public and private education from pre-primary through graduate school rose to an estimated high of $780.1 billion for the 2001–02 school year. Expenditures for elementary and secondary schools reached $462.7 billion (59% of total education spending), and outlays for colleges and universities were estimated at $317.4 billion (41%). In 2001–02 the United States spent 7.7% of its gross domestic product (GDP—the total value of goods and services produced within the United States) on education. More than fifty years before, in the 1949–50 school year, the United States spent $8.9 billion, or 3.3% of its GDP, on education. (See Table 1.5.)

young adults (35.9%) aged twenty-five to twenty-nine were college graduates, compared to 18% of blacks and 8.9% of Hispanics in the same age group. (See Table 1.2.)

Gender

Traditionally, women were slightly more likely than men to complete high school but less likely to go on to college. In recent years the differences in high school graduation rates have disappeared. According to the U.S. Department of Education, in 2002 more than 84% of both women and men age twenty-five and older had completed four years of high school or more. The proportion of women age twenty-five and older graduating from college has increased steadily, from 3.8% in 1940 to

TABLE 1.3

Percent of the population ages 3 to 34 enrolled in school, by race/ethnicity, sex, and age, selected years, October 1980–October 2001

Year and age	Total				Males				Females			
	Total	White, non-Hispanic	Black, non-Hispanic	Hispanic origin	Total	White, non-Hispanic	Black, non-Hispanic	Hispanic origin	Total	White, non-Hispanic	Black, non-Hispanic	Hispanic origin
1	2	3	4	5	6	7	8	9	10	11	12	13
1980												
Total, 3 to 34 years	**49.7**	**48.8**	**54.0**	**49.8**	**50.9**	**50.0**	**56.2**	**49.9**	**48.5**	**47.7**	**52.1**	**49.8**
3 and 4 years	36.7	37.4	38.2	28.5	37.8	39.2	36.4	30.1	35.5	35.5	40.0	26.6
5 and 6 years	95.7	95.9	95.5	94.5	95.0	95.4	94.1	94.0	96.4	96.5	97.0	94.9
7 to 9 years	99.1	99.1	99.4	98.4	99.0	99.0	99.5	97.7	99.2	99.2	99.3	99.0
10 to 13 years	99.4	99.4	99.4	99.7	99.4	99.4	99.4	99.4	99.2	99.3	99.3	99.9
14 and 15 years	98.2	98.7	97.9	94.3	98.7	98.9	98.4	96.7	97.7	98.5	97.3	92.1
16 and 17 years	89.0	89.2	90.7	81.8	89.1	89.4	90.7	81.5	88.8	89.0	90.6	82.2
18 and 19 years	46.4	47.0	45.8	37.8	47.0	48.5	42.9	36.9	45.8	45.7	48.3	38.8
20 and 21 years	31.0	33.0	23.3	19.5	32.6	34.8	22.8	21.4	29.5	31.3	23.7	17.6
22 to 24 years	16.3	16.8	13.6	11.7	17.8	18.7	13.4	10.7	14.9	15.0	13.7	12.6
25 to 29 years	9.3	9.4	8.8	6.9	9.8	9.8	10.6	6.8	8.8	9.1	7.5	6.9
30 to 34 years	6.4	6.4	6.9	5.1	5.9	5.6	7.2	6.2	7.0	7.2	6.6	4.1
1985												
Total, 3 to 34 years	**48.3**	**47.8**	**50.8**	**47.7**	**49.2**	**48.7**	**52.6**	**47.5**	**47.4**	**46.9**	**49.2**	**47.9**
3 and 4 years	38.9	40.3	42.8	27.0	36.7	39.1	34.6	26.4	41.2	41.6	50.3	27.7
5 and 6 years	96.1	96.6	95.7	94.5	95.3	95.6	94.5	95.3	97.0	97.6	97.1	93.7
7 to 9 years	99.1	99.4	98.6	98.4	99.0	99.3	98.4	98.9	99.2	99.4	98.9	98.0
10 to 13 years	99.3	99.3	99.5	99.4	99.2	99.2	99.1	99.1	99.4	99.3	99.9	99.7
14 and 15 years	98.1	98.3	98.1	96.1	98.3	98.4	98.5	96.2	97.9	98.1	97.6	96.0
16 and 17 years	91.7	92.5	91.8	84.5	92.4	92.9	92.0	88.9	90.9	92.2	91.6	80.0
18 and 19 years	51.6	53.7	43.5	41.8	52.2	53.4	49.4	38.6	51.0	54.0	37.8	44.7
20 and 21 years	35.3	37.2	27.7	24.0	36.5	38.8	29.9	20.3	34.1	35.7	25.8	27.4
22 to 24 years	16.9	17.5	13.8	11.6	18.8	19.8	13.5	12.6	15.1	15.4	14.0	10.4
25 to 29 years	9.2	9.6	7.4	6.6	9.4	9.7	5.8	8.2	9.1	9.4	8.7	4.9
30 to 34 years	6.1	6.2	5.2	5.7	5.4	5.6	3.9	4.0	6.8	6.9	6.2	7.5
1990												
Total, 3 to 34 years	**50.2**	**49.8**	**52.2**	**47.2**	**50.9**	**50.4**	**54.3**	**46.8**	**49.5**	**49.2**	**50.3**	**47.7**
3 and 4 years	44.4	47.2	41.8	30.7	43.9	47.9	38.1	28.0	44.9	46.6	45.5	33.6
5 and 6 years	96.5	96.7	96.5	94.9	96.5	96.8	96.2	95.8	96.4	96.7	96.9	93.9
7 to 9 years	99.7	99.7	99.8	99.5	99.7	99.7	99.9	99.5	99.6	99.7	99.8	99.4
10 to 13 years	99.6	99.7	99.9	99.1	99.6	99.6	99.9	99.0	99.7	99.7	99.8	99.1
14 and 15 years	99.0	99.0	99.4	99.0	99.1	99.2	99.7	99.1	98.9	98.9	99.1	98.8
16 and 17 years	92.5	93.5	91.7	85.4	92.6	93.4	93.0	85.5	92.4	93.7	90.5	85.3
18 and 19 years	57.2	59.1	55.0	44.0	58.2	59.7	60.4	40.7	56.3	58.5	49.8	47.2
20 and 21 years	39.7	43.1	28.3	27.2	40.3	44.2	31.0	21.7	39.2	42.0	25.8	33.1
22 to 24 years	21.0	21.9	19.7	9.9	22.3	23.7	19.3	11.2	19.9	20.3	20.0	8.4
25 to 29 years	9.7	10.4	6.1	6.3	9.2	10.0	4.7	4.6	10.2	10.7	7.3	8.1
30 to 34 years	5.8	6.2	4.5	3.6	4.8	5.0	2.3	4.0	6.9	7.4	6.3	3.1

TABLE 1.3

Percent of the population ages 3 to 34 enrolled in school, by race/ethnicity, sex, and age, selected years, October 1980–October 2001 [CONTINUED]

Year and age	Total				Males				Females			
	Total	White, non-Hispanic	Black, non-Hispanic	Hispanic origin	Total	White, non-Hispanic	Black, non-Hispanic	Hispanic origin	Total	White, non-Hispanic	Black, non-Hispanic	Hispanic origin
1	2	3	4	5	6	7	8	9	10	11	12	13
1995												
Total, 3 to 34 years	**53.7**	**53.8**	**56.3**	**49.7**	**54.3**	**54.2**	**58.6**	**49.1**	**53.2**	**53.4**	**54.1**	**50.3**
3 and 4 years	48.7	52.2	47.8	36.9	49.4	51.1	52.4	40.8	48.1	53.5	43.4	32.7
5 and 6 years	96.0	96.6	95.4	93.9	95.3	95.9	94.6	93.6	96.8	97.4	96.3	94.3
7 to 9 years	98.7	98.9	97.7	98.5	98.9	99.0	98.1	98.5	98.5	98.9	97.2	98.2
10 to 13 years	99.1	99.0	99.2	99.2	99.1	99.0	99.5	98.8	99.0	98.9	98.9	99.5
14 and 15 years	98.9	98.8	99.0	98.9	99.0	98.9	99.6	98.4	98.8	98.7	98.3	99.4
16 and 17 years	93.6	94.4	93.0	88.2	94.5	95.0	95.6	88.4	92.6	93.8	90.3	88.0
18 and 19 years	59.4	61.8	57.5	46.1	59.5	61.9	59.2	47.4	59.2	61.8	56.1	44.8
20 and 21 years	44.9	49.7	37.8	27.1	44.7	50.0	36.7	24.8	45.1	49.3	38.7	29.2
22 to 24 years	23.2	24.4	20.0	15.6	22.8	24.1	20.6	18.2	23.6	24.8	19.5	16.6
25 to 29 years	11.6	12.3	10.0	7.1	11.0	12.2	6.3	7.4	12.2	12.3	13.0	8.7
30 to 34 years	5.9	5.7	7.7	4.7	5.4	5.0	6.9	5.6	6.5	6.3	8.3	4.9
2000												
Total, 3 to 34 years	**55.9**	**56.0**	**59.3**	**51.3**	**55.8**	**55.8**	**59.7**	**50.5**	**56.0**	**56.1**	**59.0**	**52.2**
3 and 4 years	52.1	54.6	59.8	35.9	50.8	54.1	58.0	31.9	53.4	55.2	61.8	40.0
5 and 6 years	95.6	95.5	96.7	94.3	95.1	94.5	96.0	95.4	96.1	96.4	97.5	93.1
7 to 9 years	98.1	98.4	97.5	97.5	98.0	98.1	98.2	96.6	98.2	98.6	96.7	98.4
10 to 13 years	98.3	98.5	98.5	97.4	98.3	98.2	98.8	98.4	98.3	98.8	98.1	96.4
14 and 15 years	98.7	98.9	99.6	96.2	98.7	98.8	99.6	96.9	98.6	99.0	99.6	95.4
16 and 17 years	92.8	94.0	91.7	87.0	92.7	94.7	88.9	85.7	92.9	93.3	94.6	88.3
18 and 19 years	61.2	63.9	57.2	49.5	58.3	61.2	51.5	48.0	64.2	66.7	62.2	51.1
20 and 21 years	44.1	49.2	37.4	26.1	41.0	45.8	31.3	24.2	47.3	52.7	42.3	28.1
22 to 24 years	24.6	24.9	24.0	18.2	23.9	25.0	22.0	15.2	25.3	24.8	25.8	21.6
25 to 29 years	11.4	11.1	14.5	7.4	10.0	10.5	11.6	5.1	12.7	11.8	16.7	9.5
30 to 34 years	6.7	6.1	9.9	5.6	5.6	4.7	8.5	5.7	7.7	7.4	11.2	5.5
2001												
Total, 3 to 34 years	**56.3**	**56.6**	**59.5**	**51.4**	**56.2**	**56.3**	**59.9**	**51.2**	**56.4**	**56.8**	**59.0**	**51.7**
3 and 4 years	52.4	55.2	60.5	39.9	51.7	54.5	56.7	43.0	53.1	56.0	64.3	36.6
5 and 6 years	95.3	95.3	95.9	93.6	95.2	94.8	95.5	94.8	95.4	95.9	96.4	92.3
7 to 9 years	98.2	98.5	97.9	97.4	98.5	98.8	98.6	97.9	97.8	98.3	97.1	96.9
10 to 13 years	98.4	98.8	96.9	98.3	98.1	98.4	95.9	98.6	98.8	99.1	98.0	98.1
14 and 15 years	98.1	98.2	97.9	97.8	98.1	97.8	99.1	98.5	98.1	98.6	96.7	97.2
16 and 17 years	93.4	94.6	92.0	88.3	93.0	94.0	92.9	87.8	93.9	95.3	90.9	88.9
18 and 19 years	61.0	64.0	60.4	45.6	58.8	62.4	58.7	39.8	63.2	65.7	62.1	51.3
20 and 21 years	46.0	50.7	37.2	28.0	44.8	49.2	36.7	24.2	47.2	52.3	37.5	31.8
22 to 24 years	25.4	25.6	27.1	15.6	24.0	23.8	23.6	14.6	26.7	27.4	30.2	16.7
25 to 29 years	11.8	11.7	11.8	7.9	10.5	10.9	7.5	6.7	13.0	12.5	15.3	9.2
30 to 34 years	6.9	6.4	11.7	4.4	5.8	5.4	8.6	3.5	7.9	7.4	14.3	5.3

Note: Includes enrollment in any type of graded public, parochial, or other private schools. Includes nursery schools, kindergartens, elementary schools, high schools, colleges, universities, and professional schools. Attendance may be on either a full-time or part-time basis and during the day or night. Enrollments in "special" schools, such as trade schools, business colleges, or correspondence schools, are not included. Begining 1995, preprimary enrollment was collected using new procedures. May not be comparable to figures for earlier years. Total includes persons from other racial/ethnic groups not shown separately.

SOURCE: Thomas D. Snyder, Alexandra G. Tan, and Charlene M. Hoffman, "Table 6. Percent of the Population 3 to 34 Years Old Enrolled in School, by Race/Ethnicity, Sex, and Age: Selected Years, October 1980 to October 2001," in *Digest of Education Statistics, 2003,* NCES 2005-025, U.S. Department of Education, National Center for Education Statistics, Washington, DC, December 2004, http://nces.ed.gov/programs/digest/d03/tables/dt006.asp (accessed July 26, 2005)

TABLE 1.4

Enrollment in educational institutions, by level and control of institution, selected years, 1869–70 to Fall 2013

[In thousands]

Year	Total enrollment, all levels	Elementary and secondary, total	Public elementary and secondary schools			Private elementary and secondary schools[a]			Degree-granting institutions[b]		
			Total	Prekindergarten through grade 8	Grades 9 through 12	Total	Prekindergarten through grade 8	Grades 9 through 12	Total	Public	Private
1	2	3	4	5	6	7	8	9	10	11	12
1869–70	—	—	6,872	6,792	80	—	—	—	52	—	—
1879–80	—	—	9,868	9,757	110	—	—	—	116	—	—
1889–90	14,491	14,334	12,723	12,520	203	1,611	1,516	95	157	—	—
1899–1900	17,092	16,855	15,503	14,984	519	1,352	1,241	111	238	—	—
1909–10	19,728	19,372	17,814	16,899	915	1,558	1,441	117	355	—	—
1919–20	23,876	23,278	21,578	19,378	2,200	1,699	1,486	214	598	—	—
1929–30	29,430	28,329	25,678	21,279	4,399	2,651	2,310	341	1,101	—	—
1939–40	29,539	28,045	25,434	18,832	6,601	2,611	2,153	458	1,494	797	698
1949–50	31,151	28,492	25,111	19,387	5,725	3,380	2,708	672	2,659	1,355	1,304
Fall 1959	44,497	40,857	35,182	26,911	8,271	5,675	4,640	1,035	3,640	2,181	1,459
Fall 1969	59,055	51,050	45,550	32,513	13,037	5,500[c]	4,200[c]	1,300[c]	8,005	5,897	2,108
Fall 1970	59,838	51,257	45,894	32,558	13,336	5,363	4,052	1,311	8,581	6,428	2,153
Fall 1971	60,220	51,271	46,071	32,318	13,753	5,200[c]	3,900[c]	1,300[c]	8,949	6,804	2,144
Fall 1972	59,941	50,726	45,726	31,879	13,848	5,000[c]	3,700[c]	1,300[c]	9,215	7,071	2,144
Fall 1973	60,047	50,445	45,445	31,401	14,044	5,000[c]	3,700[c]	1,300[c]	9,602	7,420	2,183
Fall 1974	60,297	50,073	45,073	30,971	14,103	5,000[c]	3,700[c]	1,300[c]	10,224	7,989	2,235
Fall 1975	61,004	49,819	44,819	30,515	14,304	5,000[c]	3,700[c]	1,300[c]	11,185	8,835	2,350
Fall 1976	60,490	49,478	44,311	29,997	14,314	5,167	3,825	1,342	11,012	8,653	2,359
Fall 1977	60,003	48,717	43,577	29,375	14,203	5,140	3,797	1,343	11,286	8,847	2,439
Fall 1978	58,897	47,637	42,551	28,463	14,088	5,086	3,732	1,353	11,260	8,786	2,474
Fall 1979	58,221	46,651	41,651	28,034	13,616	5,000[c]	3,700[c]	1,300[c]	11,570	9,037	2,533
Fall 1980	58,305	46,208	40,877	27,647	13,231	5,331	3,992	1,339	12,097	9,457	2,640
Fall 1981	57,916	45,544	40,044	27,280	12,764	5,500[c]	4,100[c]	1,400[c]	12,372	9,647	2,725
Fall 1982	57,591	45,166	39,566	27,161	12,405	5,600[c]	4,200[c]	1,400[c]	12,426	9,696	2,730
Fall 1983	57,432	44,967	39,252	26,981	12,271	5,715	4,315	1,400	12,465	9,683	2,782
Fall 1984	57,150	44,908	39,208	26,905	12,304	5,700[c]	4,300[c]	1,400[c]	12,242	9,477	2,765
Fall 1985	57,226	44,979	39,422	27,034	12,388	5,557	4,195	1,362	12,247	9,479	2,768
Fall 1986	57,709	45,205	39,753	27,420	12,333	5,452[c]	4,116[c]	1,336[c]	12,504	9,714	2,790
Fall 1987	58,253	45,487	40,008	27,933	12,076	5,479	4,232	1,247	12,767	9,973	2,793
Fall 1988	58,485	45,430	40,189	28,501	11,687	5,242[c]	4,036[c]	1,206[c]	13,055	10,161	2,894
Fall 1989	59,279	45,741	40,543	29,152	11,390	5,198[c]	4,035[c]	1,163[c]	13,539	10,578	2,961
Fall 1990	60,269	46,451	41,217	29,878	11,338	5,234	4,084	1,150	13,819	10,845	2,974
Fall 1991	61,681	47,322	42,047	30,506	11,541	5,275[c]	4,113[c]	1,162[c]	14,359	11,310	3,049
Fall 1992	62,633	48,145	42,823	31,088	11,735	5,322[c]	4,175[c]	1,147[c]	14,487	11,385	3,103
Fall 1993	63,118	48,813	43,465	31,504	11,961	5,348[c]	4,215[c]	1,132[c]	14,305	11,189	3,116
Fall 1994	63,888	49,609	44,111	31,898	12,213	5,498[c]	4,335[c]	1,163[c]	14,279	11,134	3,145
Fall 1995	64,764	50,502	44,840	32,341	12,500	5,662	4,465	1,197	14,262	11,092	3,169
Fall 1996	65,743	51,375	45,611	32,764	12,847	5,764[c]	4,551[c]	1,213[c]	14,368	11,120	3,247
Fall 1997	66,470	51,968	46,127	33,073	13,054	5,841	4,623	1,218	14,502	11,196	3,306
Fall 1998	66,982	52,475	46,539	33,346	13,193	5,937[c]	4,702[c]	1,235[c]	14,507	11,138	3,369
Fall 1999	67,667	52,876	46,857	33,488	13,369	6,018	4,765	1,254	14,791	11,309	3,482
Fall 2000	68,678	53,366	47,204	33,688	13,515	6,162[d]	4,875[d]	1,287[d]	15,312	11,753	3,560
Fall 2001	69,818	53,890	47,688	33,952	13,736	6,202[d]	4,880[d]	1,322[d]	15,928	12,233	3,695
Fall 2002[d]	70,260	54,158	47,918	33,942	13,976	6,241	4,885	1,356	16,102	12,354	3,749
Fall 2003[d]	70,657	54,296	48,040	33,843	14,198	6,256	4,876	1,379	16,361	12,546	3,814
Fall 2004[d]	70,923	54,455	48,175	33,669	14,506	6,279	4,871	1,408	16,468	12,627	3,841
Fall 2005[d]	71,294	54,615	48,304	33,534	14,770	6,311	4,878	1,433	16,679	12,786	3,893
Fall 2006[d]	71,794	54,907	48,524	33,589	14,936	6,383	4,933	1,449	16,887	12,942	3,945
Fall 2007[d]	72,069	55,049	48,640	33,654	14,986	6,409	4,950	1,458	17,020	13,042	3,978
Fall 2008[d]	72,292	55,124	48,690	33,791	14,899	6,434	4,975	1,459	17,168	13,153	4,015
Fall 2009[d]	72,597	55,223	48,761	33,994	14,767	6,461	5,001	1,461	17,374	13,308	4,066

TABLE 1.4

Enrollment in educational institutions, by level and control of institution, selected years, 1869–70 to Fall 2013 [CONTINUED]

[In thousands]

Year	Total enrollment, all levels	Elementary and secondary, total	Public elementary and secondary schools			Private elementary and secondary schools[a]			Degree-granting institutions[b]		
			Total	Prekindergarten through grade 8	Grades 9 through 12	Total	Prekindergarten through grade 8	Grades 9 through 12	Total	Public	Private
1	2	3	4	5	6	7	8	9	10	11	12
Fall 2010[d]	72,927	55,386	48,890	34,243	14,648	6,495	5,040	1,455	17,541	13,431	4,110
Fall 2011[d]	73,342	55,618	49,084	34,597	14,487	6,534	5,091	1,443	17,724	13,566	4,158
Fall 2012[d]	73,873	55,946	49,367	35,006	14,361	6,579	5,148	1,430	17,927	13,716	4,211
Fall 2013[d]	74,515	56,364	49,737	35,430	14,307	6,627	5,208	1,419	18,151	13,883	4,268

— Not available.

[a]Beginning in fall 1980, data include estimates for an expanded universe of private schools. Therefore, direct comparisons with earlier years should be avoided.

[b]Data for 1869–70 through 1949–50 include resident degree-credit students enrolled at any time during the academic year. Beginning in 1959, data include all resident and extension students enrolled at the beginning of the fall term.

[c]Estimated.

[d]Projected.

Note: Elementary and secondary enrollment includes pupils in local public school systems and in most private schools (religiously affiliated and nonsectarian), but generally excludes pupils in subcollegiate departments of colleges, federal schools, and home-schooled children. Based on the National Household Education Survey, the homeschooled children numbered approximately 850,000 in the spring of 1999. Public elementary enrollment includes most preprimary school pupils. Private elementary enrollment includes some preprimary students. Beginning in 1996–97, data are for degreegranting institutions. Degree-granting institutions are 2-year and 4-year institutions that were eligible to participate in Title IV federal financial aid programs. Data for degree-granting institutions for 1999 were imputed using alternative procedures. Some data have been revised from previously published figures. Detail may not sum to totals due to rounding.

SOURCE: Thomas D. Snyder, Alexandra G. Tan, and Charlene M. Hoffman, "Table 3. Enrollment in Educational Institutions, by Level and Control of Institution: Selected Years, 1869–70 to Fall 2013," in *Digest of Education Statistics, 2003*, NCES 2005-025, U.S. Department of Education, National Center for Education Statistics, Washington, DC, December 2004, http://nces.ed.gov/programs/digest/d03/tables/dt003.asp (accessed July 26, 2005)

TABLE 1.5

Total expenditures of educational institutions related to the GDP, selected years, 1929–30 to 2001–02

			Total expenditures for education (amounts in millions of current dollars)					
			All educational institutions		All elementary and secondary schools		All colleges and universities	
Year	Gross domestic product (in billions)	School year	Amount	As a percent of gross domestic product	Amount	As a percent of gross domestic product	Amount	As a percent of gross domestic product
1	2	3	4	5	6	7	8	9
1929	$103.7	1929–30	—	—	—	—	$632	0.6
1939	92.0	1939–40	—	—	—	—	758	0.8
1949	267.7	1949–50	$8,911	3.3	$6,249	2.3	2,662	1.0
1959	507.4	1959–60	23,860	4.7	16,713	3.3	7,147	1.4
1961	545.7	1961–62	28,503	5.2	19,673	3.6	8,830	1.6
1963	618.7	1963–64	34,440	5.6	22,825	3.7	11,615	1.9
1965	720.1	1965–66	43,682	6.1	28,048	3.9	15,634	2.2
1967	834.1	1967–68	55,652	6.7	35,077	4.2	20,575	2.5
1969	985.3	1969–70	68,459	6.9	43,183	4.4	25,276	2.6
1970	1,039.7	1970–71	75,741	7.3	48,200	4.6	27,541	2.6
1971	1,128.6	1971–72	80,672	7.1	50,950	4.5	29,722	2.6
1972	1,240.4	1972–73	86,875	7.0	54,952	4.4	31,923	2.6
1973	1,385.5	1973–74	95,396	6.9	60,370	4.4	35,026	2.5
1974	1,501.0	1974–75	108,664	7.2	68,846	4.6	39,818	2.7
1975	1,635.2	1975–76	118,706	7.3	75,101	4.6	43,605	2.7
1976	1,823.9	1976–77	126,417	6.9	79,194	4.3	47,223	2.6
1977	2,031.4	1977–78	137,042	6.7	86,544	4.3	50,498	2.5
1978	2,295.9	1978–79	148,308	6.5	93,012	4.1	55,296	2.4
1979	2,566.4	1979–80	165,627	6.5	103,162	4.0	62,465	2.4
1980	2,795.6	1980–81	182,849	6.5	112,325	4.0	70,524	2.5
1981	3,131.3	1981–82	197,801	6.3	120,486	3.8	77,315	2.5
1982	3,259.2	1982–83	212,081	6.5	128,725	3.9	83,356	2.6
1983	3,534.9	1983–84	228,597	6.5	139,000	3.9	89,597	2.5
1984	3,932.7	1984–85	247,657	6.3	149,400	3.8	98,257	2.5
1985	4,213.0	1985–86	269,485	6.4	161,800	3.8	107,685	2.6
1986	4,452.9	1986–87	291,974	6.6	175,200	3.9	116,774	2.6
1987	4,742.5	1987–88	313,375	6.6	187,999	4.0	125,376	2.6
1988	5,108.3	1988–89	346,883	6.8	209,377	4.1	137,506	2.7
1989	5,489.1	1989–90	381,525	7.0	230,970	4.2	150,555	2.7
1990	5,803.2	1990–91	412,652	7.1	248,930	4.3	163,722	2.8
1991	5,986.2	1991–92	432,987	7.2	261,255	4.4	171,732	2.9
1992	6,318.9	1992–93	456,070	7.2	274,335	4.3	181,735	2.9
1993	6,642.3	1993–94	477,237	7.2	287,507	4.3	189,730	2.9
1994	7,054.3	1994–95	503,925	7.1	302,400	4.3	201,525	2.9
1995	7,400.5	1995–96	529,596	7.2	318,246	4.3	211,350	2.9
1996	7,813.2	1996–97	562,771	7.2	339,151	4.3	223,620	2.9
1997	8,318.4	1997–98	594,849	7.2	361,415	4.3	233,434	2.8
1998	8,781.5	1998–99	634,232	7.2	384,038	4.4	250,194	2.8
1999	9,274.3	1999–2000	682,838	7.4	411,538	4.4	271,300	2.9
2000	9,824.6	a2000–01	737,918	7.5	442,618	4.5	295,300	3.0
2001	10,082.2	b2001–02	780,100	7.7	462,700	4.6	317,400	3.1

— Not available.
aPreliminary data for public elementary and secondary schools and estimates for colleges and universities.
bEstimated.
Note: Total expenditures for public elementary and secondary schools include current expenditures, interest on school debt, and capital outlay. Data for private elementary and secondary schools are estimated. Total expenditures for colleges and universities include current-fund expenditures and additions to plant value. Excludes expenditures of postsecondary institutions that do not confer associate or higher degrees. Data for 1995–96 and later years are for 4-year and 2-year degree-granting institutions that were eligible to participate in Title IV federal financial aid programs. Some data revised from previously published figures. Detail may not sum to totals due to rounding.

SOURCE: Thomas D. Snyder, Alexandra G. Tan, and Charlene M. Hoffman, "Table 29. Total Expenditures of Educational Institutions Related to the Gross Domestic Product, by Level of Institution: Selected Years, 1929–30 to 2001–02," in *Digest of Education Statistics, 2003*, NCES 2005-025, U.S. Department of Education, National Center for Education Statistics, Washington, DC, December 2004, http://nces.ed.gov/programs/digest/d03/tables/dt029.asp (accessed July 26, 2005)

CHAPTER 2
PREPRIMARY, ELEMENTARY, AND SECONDARY SCHOOLS

SCHOOL ENROLLMENTS

Preprimary, elementary, and secondary school enrollments reflect the number of births over a specific period. Because of the baby boom (1946–64), school enrollment grew rapidly during the 1950s and 1960s and then declined steadily during the 1970s and 1980s. According to the U.S. Department of Education, in 1985 public elementary and secondary school enrollment increased for the first time since 1971. Enrollment has grown slowly but steadily since the mid-1980s, reaching an estimated 47.9 million in public schools and 6.2 million in private schools in fall 2002. Slow but steady growth is projected to continue until 2010, when it most likely will decline slightly in 2011, rising again in 2013. (See Figure 2.1.)

Preprimary Growth

In contrast to the declining elementary and secondary school enrollment during the 1970s and early 1980s, preprimary enrollment showed substantial growth. According to the U.S. Department of Education, between 1970 and 1980 preprimary enrollment rose from 4.1 million to 4.9 million preschool-age children. While the overall population of three- to five-year-olds grew 29% between 1980 and 1993, enrollment in preprimary programs rose 35%, to 6.6 million. In 1994 new data collection methods indicated that 61% of the nation's 12.3 million three- to five-year-olds were enrolled in preprimary programs. These increases reflect the greater availability of and interest in preschool education. In 1965 only 27.1% of the 12.5 million children in this age group were enrolled in nursery school or kindergarten. By October 2001, 63.9% of the 11.9 million preschool-age children in the United States were enrolled in preprimary programs. Note that because of the change in data collection methods, figures prior to 1994 may not be comparable to later years. (See Table 2.1.)

As the proportion of working mothers has grown, the proportion of young children in full-day preprimary programs has also increased. In 2001 more than half (51.8%) of children in preprimary programs attended school all day, compared to 31.8% in 1980 and 17% in 1970. (See Table 2.1.)

Geographic Shifts

There have been significant changes in regional school enrollment. According to the U.S. Department of Education, between 1970 and 1980, school enrollment in forty-one states and the District of Columbia dropped, with most of the decline occurring at the elementary level. Between fall 1996 and fall 2001, thirteen states increased enrollment by 5% or more, while sixteen other states reported increases of less than 5%. Decreases in school enrollment were reported in twenty-one states and the District of Columbia. (See Figure 2.2.)

During the 2001–02 school year, according to the U.S. Department of Education, 32,695 of the 91,759 public elementary and secondary schools in the United States were located in urban fringe areas (that is, outside the central city but within the metropolitan area). That figure represented 36% of all American public schools. Rural areas of the country contained another 27% (24,565). Public schools within large (10,746) and midsized cities (10,813) combined to account for 23.5% of the total. (See Table 2.2.)

School Size

According to the U.S. Department of Education, in 2001–02 the average enrollment at public schools was 520 students per school—477 in elementary schools and 718 in secondary schools. Most (70.4%) public school students attended schools with enrollments of 500 students or more. More than a fifth (20.3%) were enrolled at schools with between 300 and 499 students, and 9.3% of public school students attended schools with enrollments of less than 300 students. (See Table 2.3.)

FIGURE 2.1

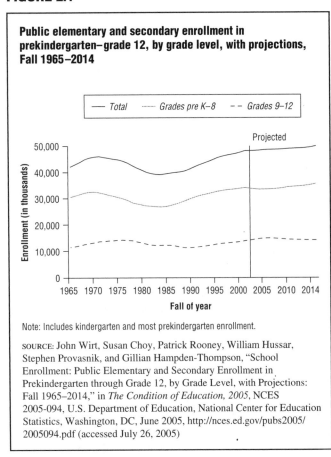

Public elementary and secondary enrollment in prekindergarten–grade 12, by grade level, with projections, Fall 1965–2014

Note: Includes kindergarten and most prekindergarten enrollment.

SOURCE: John Wirt, Susan Choy, Patrick Rooney, William Hussar, Stephen Provasnik, and Gillian Hampden-Thompson, "School Enrollment: Public Elementary and Secondary Enrollment in Prekindergarten through Grade 12, by Grade Level, with Projections: Fall 1965–2014," in *The Condition of Education, 2005*, NCES 2005-094, U.S. Department of Education, National Center for Education Statistics, Washington, DC, June 2005, http://nces.ed.gov/pubs2005/2005094.pdf (accessed July 26, 2005)

Racial and Ethnic Diversity

Public school enrollment has become more racially and ethnically diverse, reflecting the nation's changing demographics. According to the U.S. Department of Education, between 1991 and 2001 the proportion of non-Hispanic white students declined from 67.4% to 60.3%, while the proportion of non-Hispanic African-American students increased slightly, from 16.4% to 17.2%. The proportion of Hispanic students rose from 11.8% to 17.1%; Asian or Pacific Islander students increased from 3.4% to 4.2%; and the percentage of Native American/Alaska Native students rose from 1% to 1.2%. (See Table 2.4.)

THE SCHOOL-AGE POPULATION

According to the U.S. Census Bureau in *Statistical Abstract of the United States: 2004–2005*, the U.S. population included 61.4 million elementary- and secondary-age children (ages five to nineteen) in 2003. About 21% of the total U.S. population were school-age children.

Poor School-Age Children

According to the U.S. Census Bureau, in 2003, 12.5% of Americans were living in poverty. Among children under age eighteen the proportion living in poverty was 17.6% in 2003. (See Table 2.5.) Poverty

remains a persistent problem for the nation and its schools. Children who are poor are more likely to be undernourished, subject to frequent illnesses, and generally much less ready for learning.

Poverty rates vary widely by race and ethnicity, as well as by the type of household in which a child lives. In 2003 the proportion of whites (of all age groups) living in poverty was 10.5%, compared to 24.4% of African-Americans and 22.5% of Hispanics. Families living in households headed by a female with no spouse present were more likely to be poor (28%) than families that were headed by a married couple (5.4%). (See Table 2.5.)

FINANCING THE SCHOOLS
Sources of Funding

Public schools obtain funds from three sources: local, state, and federal governments. Typically, local governments rely on property taxes to finance education, while state governments use revenues from sales taxes and, in some instances, income taxes, lotteries, excise taxes (such as gasoline taxes), motor vehicle fees, and other taxes that are sometimes referred to as "sin" taxes (alcohol and tobacco). Local and state governments have traditionally been the primary sources of revenue for elementary and secondary schools, with the federal government contributing a relatively small proportion. (See Figure 2.3.)

At the beginning of the twentieth century, education funding was primarily the responsibility of the local entities. For example, according to the National Center for Education Statistics (NCES) in *Digest of Education Statistics Tables and Figures 2003*, during the 1919–20 school year, a full 83.2% of school revenues were derived from local sources, while 16.5% came from the state and 0.3% were contributed by the federal government. Throughout most of the twentieth century, a dramatic shift in funding methods raised the federal government portion of school revenues to 9.8% during the school years 1978–79 and 1979–80. At the same time, local and state contributions became nearly equal in proportion. In 1978–79, for instance, the states provided 45.6% of public education funding, while local sources provided 44.6%. After 1980 the federal proportion dropped, hitting about 6% in 1990, with state and local sources continuing to divide the remainder. By the 2000–01 school year, federal government funding had increased slightly to 7.3%. State governments in 2000–01 provided 49.7% of education revenues, and local governments about 43%. Figure 2.3 compares revenue sources for public elementary and secondary schools since 1970.

The dependence on state and local revenues has significant meaning for school funding. State revenues, which rely on sales and income taxes, are tied to business

TABLE 2.1

Enrollment of 3-, 4-, and 5-year-old children in preprimary programs, selected years, October 1965–October 2001

[In thousands]

Year and age	Total population, 3 to 5 years old	Enrollment by level and control						Enrollment by attendance		
		Total	Percent enrolled	Nursery school		Kindergarten		Full-day	Part-day	Percent full-day
				Public	Private	Public	Private			
1	2	3	4	5	6	7	8	9	10	11
Total, 3 to 5 years old										
1965	12,549	3,407	27.1	127	393	2,291	596	—	—	—
1970	10,949	4,104	37.5	332	762	2,498	511	698	3,405	17.0
1975	10,185	4,955	48.7	570	1,174	2,682	528	1,295	3,659	26.1
1980	9,284	4,878	52.5	628	1,353	2,438	459	1,551	3,327	31.8
1985	10,733	5,865	54.6	846	1,631	2,847	541	2,144	3,722	36.6
1987	10,872	5,931	54.6	819	1,736	2,842	534	2,090	3,841	35.2
1988	10,993	5,978	54.4	851	1,770	2,875	481	2,044	3,935	34.2
1989	11,039	6,026	54.6	930	1,894	2,704	497	2,238	3,789	37.1
1990	11,207	6,659	59.4	1,199	2,180	2,772	509	2,577	4,082	38.7
1991	11,370	6,334	55.7	996	1,828	2,967	543	2,408	3,926	38.0
1992	11,545	6,402	55.5	1,073	1,783	2,995	550	2,410	3,992	37.6
1993	11,954	6,581	55.1	1,205	1,779	3,020	577	2,642	3,939	40.1
1994[a]	12,328	7,514	61.0	1,848	2,314	2,819	534	3,468	4,046	46.2
1995[a]	12,518	7,739	61.8	1,950	2,381	2,800	608	3,689	4,051	47.7
1996[a]	12,378	7,580	61.2	1,830	2,317	2,853	580	3,562	4,019	47.0
1997[a]	12,121	7,860	64.9	2,207	2,231	2,847	575	3,922	3,939	49.9
1998[a]	12,078	7,788	64.5	2,213	2,299	2,674	602	3,959	3,829	50.8
1999[a]	11,920	7,844	65.8	2,209	2,298	2,777	560	4,154	3,690	53.0
2000[a]	11,858	7,592	64.0	2,146	2,180	2,701	565	4,008	3,584	52.8
2001[a]	11,899	7,602	63.9	2,164	2,201	2,724	512	3,940	3,662	51.8
3 years old										
1965	4,149	203	4.9	41	153	5	4	—	—	—
1970	3,516	454	12.9	110	322	12	10	142	312	31.3
1975	3,177	683	21.5	179	474	11	18	259	423	37.9
1980	3,143	857	27.3	221	604	16	17	321	536	37.5
1985	3,594	1,035	28.8	278	679	52	26	350	685	33.8
1987	3,569	1,022	28.6	264	703	24	31	378	644	37.0
1988	3,719	1,027	27.6	298	678	24	26	369	658	35.9
1989	3,713	1,005	27.1	277	707	3	18	390	615	38.8
1990	3,692	1,205	32.6	347	840	11	7	447	758	37.1
1991	3,811	1,074	28.2	313	702	38	22	388	687	36.1
1992	3,905	1,081	27.7	336	685	26	34	371	711	34.3
1993	4,053	1,097	27.1	369	687	20	20	426	670	38.9
1994[a]	4,081	1,385	33.9	469	887	19	9	670	715	48.4
1995[a]	4,148	1,489	35.9	511	947	15	17	754	736	50.6
1996[a]	4,045	1,506	37.2	511	947	22	26	657	848	43.7
1997[a]	3,947	1,528	38.7	643	843	25	18	754	774	49.4
1998[a]	3,989	1,498	37.6	587	869	27	14	735	763	49.1
1999[a]	3,862	1,505	39.0	621	859	13	12	773	732	51.3
2000[a]	3,929	1,541	39.2	644	854	27	16	761	779	49.4
2001[a]	3,985	1,538	38.6	599	901	14	23	715	823	46.5
4 years old										
1965	4,238	683	16.1	68	213	284	118	—	—	—
1970	3,620	1,007	27.8	176	395	318	117	230	776	22.8
1975	3,499	1,418	40.5	332	644	313	129	411	1,008	29.0
1980	3,072	1,423	46.3	363	701	239	120	467	956	32.8
1985	3,598	1,766	49.1	496	859	276	135	643	1,123	36.4
1987	3,597	1,717	47.7	431	881	280	125	548	1,169	31.9
1988	3,598	1,768	49.1	481	922	261	104	519	1,249	29.4
1989	3,692	1,882	51.0	524	1,055	202	100	592	1,290	31.4
1990	3,723	2,087	56.1	695	1,144	157	91	716	1,371	34.3
1991	3,763	1,994	53.0	584	982	287	140	667	1,326	33.5
1992	3,807	1,982	52.1	602	971	282	126	632	1,350	31.9
1993	4,044	2,178	53.9	719	957	349	154	765	1,413	35.1
1994[a]	4,202	2,532	60.3	1,020	1,232	198	82	1,095	1,438	43.3
1995[a]	4,145	2,553	61.6	1,054	1,208	207	84	1,104	1,449	43.3
1996[a]	4,148	2,454	59.2	1,029	1,168	180	77	1,034	1,420	42.1
1997[a]	4,033	2,665	66.1	1,197	1,169	207	92	1,161	1,505	43.5
1998[a]	4,002	2,666	66.6	1,183	1,219	210	53	1,179	1,487	44.2
1999[a]	4,021	2,769	68.9	1,212	1,227	207	122	1,355	1,414	48.9
2000[a]	3,940	2,556	64.9	1,144	1,121	227	65	1,182	1,374	46.2
2001[a]	3,927	2,608	66.4	1,202	1,121	236	49	1,255	1,354	48.1

TABLE 2.1

Enrollment of 3-, 4-, and 5-year-old children in preprimary programs, selected years, October 1965–October 2001 [CONTINUED]

[In thousands]

Year and age	Total population, 3 to 5 years old	Enrollment by level and control						Enrollment by attendance		
		Total	Percent enrolled	Nursery school		Kindergarten		Full-day	Part-day	Percent full-day
				Public	Private	Public	Private			
1	2	3	4	5	6	7	8	9	10	11
5 years old[b]										
1965	4,162	2,521	60.6	18	27	2,002	474	—	—	—
1970	3,814	2,643	69.3	45	45	2,168	384	326	2,317	12.3
1975	3,509	2,854	81.3	59	57	2,358	381	625	2,228	21.9
1980	3,069	2,598	84.7	44	48	2,183	322	763	1,835	29.4
1985	3,542	3,065	86.5	73	94	2,519	379	1,151	1,914	37.6
1987	3,706	3,192	86.1	124	152	2,538	378	1,163	2,028	36.4
1988	3,676	3,184	86.6	72	170	2,590	351	1,155	2,028	36.3
1989	3,633	3,139	86.4	129	132	2,499	378	1,255	1,883	40.0
1990	3,792	3,367	88.8	157	196	2,604	411	1,414	1,953	42.0
1991	3,796	3,267	86.0	100	143	2,642	382	1,354	1,913	41.4
1992	3,832	3,339	87.1	135	127	2,688	390	1,408	1,931	42.2
1993	3,857	3,306	85.7	116	136	2,651	403	1,451	1,856	43.9
1994[a]	4,044	3,597	88.9	359	194	2,601	442	1,704	1,893	47.4
1995[a]	4,224	3,697	87.5	385	226	2,578	507	1,830	1,867	49.5
1996[a]	4,185	3,621	86.5	290	202	2,652	477	1,870	1,750	51.7
1997[a]	4,141	3,667	88.5	368	219	2,616	465	2,007	1,660	54.7
1998[a]	4,087	3,624	88.7	442	211	2,437	535	2,044	1,579	56.4
1999[a]	4,037	3,571	88.4	376	212	2,557	426	2,027	1,544	56.8
2000[a]	3,989	3,495	87.6	359	206	2,447	484	2,065	1,431	59.1
2001[a]	3,987	3,456	86.7	363	179	2,474	440	1,970	1,485	57.0

— Not available.

[a]Data collected using new procedures. May not be comparable with figures prior to 1994.
[b]Enrollment data include only those students in preprimary programs.
Note: Data are based on sample surveys of the civilian noninstitutional population. Although cells with fewer than 75,000 children are subject to wide sampling variation, they are included in the table to permit various types of aggregations. Detail may not sum to totals due to rounding.

SOURCE: Thomas D. Snyder, Alexandra G. Tan, and Charlene M. Hoffman, "Table 43. Enrollment of 3-, 4-, and 5-Year-Old Children in Preprimary Programs, by Level and Control of Program and by Attendance Status: Selected Years, October 1965 to October 2001 (in Thousands)," in *Digest of Education Statistics, 2003*, NCES 2005-025, U.S. Department of Education, National Center for Education Statistics, Washington, DC, June 2003, http://nces.ed.gov/programs/digest/d03/tables/dt043.asp (accessed July 26, 2005)

cycles. Local school funding is usually linked to property taxes. When a recession occurs or businesses close or move away, causing property values to decline, school funding is directly affected. Also, per capita income and property values are typically lower in rural areas, and local taxes may not be enough to fund the district's schools. In these cases, states must find ways to fill the gap.

To try to resolve these problems, many states now use complex formulas for distributing state education funds to equalize the per-pupil expenditure statewide—that is, they give proportionately more state funds per student to poor districts than to wealthy districts.

Another issue is the adequacy of the education the state offers children. According to *Overview and Inventory of State Education Reforms: 1990 to 2000* (David Hurst, Alexandra Tan, Anne Meek, and Jason Sellers, U.S. Department of Education, National Center for Education Statistics, Washington, DC, July 2003), disparities in spending between wealthy and impoverished school districts led to legal challenges during the 1970s and 1980s. Some state courts have found that state education finance systems failed to deliver an

acceptable level of educational services. States have started to focus on determining educational adequacy rather than requiring equity.

Education experts are developing standards—what it takes in terms of teachers, curriculum, and expenditures—to achieve an adequate education. The definition of adequacy differs from state to state. Each state is examining what a core education means and how much it costs.

In *Financing Education So That No Child Is Left Behind: Determining the Costs of Improving Student Performance*, by Andrew Reschovsky and Jennifer Imazeki (in William J. Fowler, Jr., ed., *Developments in School Finance: 2003*, U.S. Department of Education, National Center for Education Statistics, Washington, DC, August 2004), the authors state that, prior to the recent court cases, the focus of most school funding reform efforts has been on resources rather than on the link between educational finance and student performance. The study found that the amount of money required for student performance standards varies across school districts due to factors beyond the school districts' control. Some districts have to pay higher salaries in

FIGURE 2.2

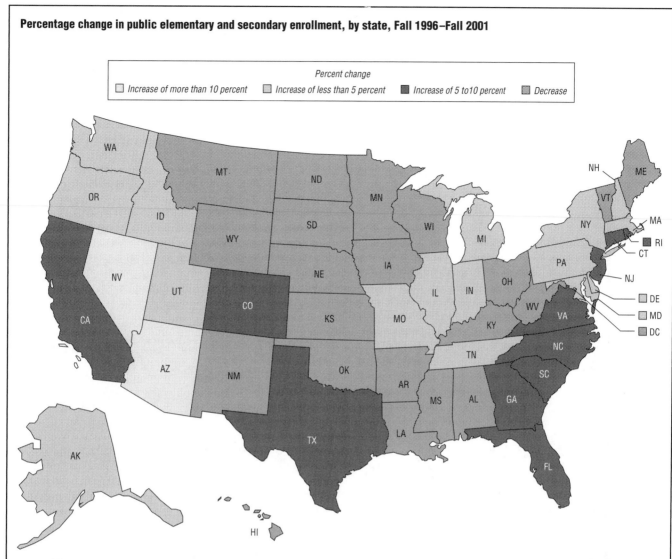

Percentage change in public elementary and secondary enrollment, by state, Fall 1996–Fall 2001

Percent change

☐ Increase of more than 10 percent ☐ Increase of less than 5 percent ■ Increase of 5 to 10 percent ▨ Decrease

SOURCE: Thomas D. Snyder, Alexandra G. Tan, and Charlene M. Hoffman, "Figure 9. Percentage Change in Public Elementary and Secondary Enrollment, by State: Fall 1996 to Fall 2001," in *Digest of Education Statistics, 2003*, NCES 2005-025, U.S. Department of Education, National Center for Education Statistics, Washington, DC, December 2004, http://nces.ed.gov/programs/digest/d03/figures/figure_09.asp?popup=1 (accessed July 26, 2005)

order to attract teachers; others have large numbers of economically disadvantaged students, or students from families where English is not the first language, and these schools need extra resources.

Revenues

According to the U.S. Department of Education, in the 2000–01 school year revenues for public elementary and secondary schools totaled $401 billion. State (49.7%) and local authorities (40.8%) provided most of the revenues, with less than 7.3% coming from the federal government and 2.3% from private sources. The proportions of federal, state, and local funding varied by state. In Hawaii the state provided 89.8% of revenue, while in Nevada the state provided only 28.6%. The federal government supplied 15.8% of the school

revenue for Alaska and 3.9% for New Jersey. Local and intermediate sources accounted for 88.1% of school revenue in the District of Columbia, and less than 0.5% in Hawaii. (See Table 2.6.)

Expenditures

According to the U.S. Department of Education in *A Guide to Education and No Child Left Behind*, federal, state, and local government spending for public elementary and secondary education amounted to $591.3 billion during the 2003–04 school year. (See Figure 2.4.)

The NCES estimates that per-pupil spending in 2002–03, the last year for which figures have been released, averaged $8,041. Figure 2.5 offers a graphic depiction of the dramatic rise in public schools' expenditures

TABLE 2.2

Characteristics of public elementary and secondary enrollment and finances, by type of locale, 2000–01 and 2001–02

Characteristic	Total[a]	Large city[b]	Midsize city[c]	Urban fringe of a large city[d]	Urban fringe of midsize city[e]	Large town[f]	Small town[g]	Rural outside an MSA[h]	Rural within an MSA[i]
1	2	3	4	5	6	7	8	9	10
Schools, enrollment, and teachers, 2001–02									
Enrollment, in thousands	47,061	7,336	6,006	15,405	5,002	608	4,539	4,345	3,817
Schools	91,759	10,746	10,813	23,669	9,026	1,298	11,284	16,397	8,168
Average school size[j]	515	683	556	651	555	469	403	265	468
Pupil/teacher ratio[k]	16.2	17.0	16.0	17.0	16.4	15.9	15.4	14.2	16
Enrollment (percent distribution)	100.0	15.6	12.8	32.7	10.6	1.3	9.6	9.2	8.1
Schools (percent distribution)	100.0	11.7	11.8	25.8	9.8	1.4	12.3	17.9	8.9
Revenues and expenditures, 2000–01									
Total revenue, in millions of dollars	**$406,508**	**$66,320**	**$51,964**	**$136,530**	**$39,127**	**$4,580**	**$35,271**	**$35,623**	**$32,347**
Federal	28,417	6,408	4,390	6,409	2,372	382	2,904	3,115	1,397
Impact aid	873	47	90	178	57	5	109	339	29
Bilingual education	64	12	11	17	2	1	5	10	2
Indian education	56	5	5	5	2	2	11	24	2
Children with disabilites	4,285	672	583	1,248	381	52	329	268	232
Eisenhower science awards	154	28	25	40	15	2	14	12	7
Drug free schools	247	46	44	70	21	4	22	16	13
Chapter 2 (block grants)	757	133	127	190	69	11	90	79	46
Vocational education	534	112	80	106	52	8	56	45	23
Title I	6,232	1,682	1,065	1,152	562	88	693	674	281
Other and unclassified	15,216	3,670	2,360	3,403	1,210	211	1,576	1,648	761
State	200,153	32,328	28,069	60,026	19,755	2,518	19,641	20,274	16,148
State school lunch programs	377	60	52	117	41	4	39	36	28
Local	177,938	27,583	19,505	70,094	17,000	1,679	12,726	12,234	14,803
Property tax[l]	108,061	14,579	11,242	46,153	10,150	1,072	8,217	7,287	8,618
Parent government contribution[l]	29,727	7,996	3,557	10,281	2,897	141	1,007	1,393	2,422
Lunch sales	5,761	517	640	2,084	684	74	578	563	615
Transportation	66	2	6	38	5	1	4	3	4
Other	34,322	4,489	4,058	11,539	3,265	392	2,920	2,987	3,144
Total revenue (percent distribution)	100.0	100.0	100.0	100.0	100.0	100.0	100.0	100.0	100.0
Federal	7.0	9.7	8.4	4.7	6.1	8.3	8.2	8.7	4.3
State	49.2	48.7	54.0	44.0	50.5	55.0	55.7	56.9	49.9
Local	43.8	41.6	37.5	51.3	43.4	36.7	36.1	34.3	45.8
Total expenditures, in millions of dollars	**$564,187**	**$93,780**	**$69,804**	**$192,173**	**$53,851**	**$6,190**	**$47,444**	**$47,984**	**$45,736**
Current expenditures for schools	415,162	69,938	52,020	139,778	39,585	4,630	35,527	35,688	33,197
Instruction	343,859	57,735	44,257	114,304	32,655	3,962	30,287	30,158	26,748
Operation and maintenance	206,904	35,922	26,545	68,401	19,869	2,381	18,339	17,969	16,054
Food service	32,802	5,770	4,223	11,010	3,085	389	2,854	2,826	2,485
Other	13,414	2,299	1,763	3,768	1,422	178	1,425	1,492	1,052
Other current expenditures	90,738	13,744	11,726	31,123	8,280	1,015	7,669	7,871	7,158
Interest on school debt	9,536	1,545	987	3,481	999	89	729	637	1,048
Capital outlay	48,751	8,553	5,070	17,790	4,987	457	3,519	3,788	4,332

TABLE 2.2

Characteristics of public elementary and secondary enrollment and finances, by type of locale, 2000–01 and 2001–02 [CONTINUED]

Characteristic	Total[a]	Large city[b]	Midsize city[c]	Urban fringe of a large city[d]	Urban fringe of midsize city[e]	Large town[f]	Small town[g]	Rural outside an MSA[h]	Rural within an MSA[i]
1	2	3	4	5	6	7	8	9	10
Current expenditures (percent distribution)	100.0	100.0	100.0	100.0	100.0	100.0	100.0	100.0	100.0
Instruction	60.2	62.2	60.0	59.8	60.8	60.1	60.6	59.6	60.0
Operation and maintenance	9.5	10.0	9.5	9.6	9.4	9.8	9.4	9.4	9.3
Food service	3.9	4.0	4.0	3.3	4.4	4.5	4.7	4.9	3.9
Other	26.4	23.8	26.5	27.2	25.4	25.6	25.3	26.1	26.8
Current expenditure per student (in dollars)	7,372	7,902	7,409	7,572	6,612	6,499	6,638	6,895	7,118
Instruction expenditure per student (in dollars)	4,436	4,916	4,444	4,531	4,023	3,906	4,019	4,108	4,272

[a]The total column includes data for 126 LEAs (local education agencies) with unknown locale codes.
[b]Central city of a consolidated metropolitan statistical area (CMSA) or metropolitan statistical area (MSA) with the city having a population greater than or equal to 250,000.
[c]Central city of a CMSA or an MSA with the city having a population of less than 250,000.
[d]Any incorporated place, census designated place, or non-place territory within a CMSA or an MSA of a large city and defined as urban by the Census Bureau.
[e]Any incorporated place, census designated place, or non-place territory within a CMSA or an MSA of a mid-size city and defined as urban by the Census Bureau.
[f]Place not within an MSA but with population of 25,000 or more.
[g]Place not within an MSA with a population of at least 2,500, but less than 25,000.
[h]Place with a population of less than 2,500 outside a CMSA or an MSA, and designated as rural by the Census Bureau.
[i]Place with a population of less than 2,500 within a CMSA or an MSA and designated as rural by the Census Bureau.
[j]Average for schools reporting enrollment.
[k]Ratio for schools reporting both full-time-equivalent teachers and fall enrollment data.
[l]Property tax and parent government contributions are determined on the basis of independence or dependence of the local school system and are mutually exclusive.
Note: Detail may not sum to totals due to rounding.

SOURCE: Thomas D. Snyder, Alexandra G. Tan, and Charlene M. Hoffman, "Table 88. Public Elementary and Secondary Students, Schools, Pupil to Teacher Ratios, and Finances, by Type of Locale: 2000–01 and 2001–02," in Digest of Education Statistics, 2003, NCES 2005-025, U.S. Department of Education, National Center for Education Statistics, Washington, DC, December 2004, http://nces.ed.gov/programs/digest/d03/tables/dt088.asp (accessed July 26, 2005)

TABLE 2.3

Public elementary and secondary schools and enrollment, by type and size of school, 2001–02

Enrollment size of school	Number of schools, by type						Enrollment, by type of school[a]					
			Secondary[d]						Secondary[d]			
	Total[b]	Elementary[c]	All schools	Regular schools[f]	Combined elementary/ secondary[e]	Other[b]	Total[b]	Elementary[c]	All schools	Regular schools[f]	Combined elementary/ secondary[e]	Other[b]
1	**2**	**3**	**4**	**5**	**6**	**7**	**8**	**9**	**10**	**11**	**12**	**13**
Total	**94,112**	**65,228**	**22,180**	**18,382**	**5,288**	**1,416**	**47,518,623**	**30,945,876**	**15,215,033**	**14,737,809**	**1,275,287**	**82,427**
Percent[g]	100.00	100.00	100.00	100.00	100.00	100.00	100.00	100.00	100.00	100.00	100.00	100.00
Under 100	10.76	6.21	15.63	8.34	45.31	58.53	0.94	0.64	1.00	0.59	6.36	18.57
100 to 199	9.77	8.73	11.18	10.20	16.27	21.07	2.81	2.77	2.28	1.86	8.82	21.59
200 to 299	11.52	12.85	8.14	8.34	8.66	9.03	5.59	6.83	2.83	2.59	7.93	15.91
300 to 399	13.32	15.67	7.73	8.32	7.22	4.52	8.96	11.50	3.75	3.60	9.38	11.22
400 to 499	13.14	15.89	6.73	7.39	5.36	3.85	11.34	14.95	4.20	4.11	8.93	12.11
500 to 599	10.94	13.11	6.04	6.66	4.34	0.84	11.51	15.03	4.63	4.54	8.80	3.30
600 to 699	8.13	9.43	5.48	6.19	3.09	0.50	10.11	12.78	4.95	4.97	7.40	2.36
700 to 799	5.76	6.38	4.80	5.45	2.25	0.50	8.27	9.98	5.01	5.06	6.18	2.80
800 to 999	6.92	6.90	8.08	9.19	2.97	0.33	11.82	12.79	10.07	10.20	9.73	2.10
1,000 to 1,499	6.07	4.18	12.67	14.40	2.99	0.50	13.95	10.23	21.64	21.89	13.22	4.49
1,500 to 1,999	2.15	0.53	7.40	8.52	0.95	0.00	7.08	1.87	17.78	18.20	6.08	0.00
2,000 to 2,999	1.27	0.12	5.01	5.77	0.36	0.33	5.74	0.57	16.49	16.90	3.09	5.55
3,000 or more	0.27	0.01	1.09	1.25	0.23	0.00	1.87	0.07	5.37	5.49	4.07	0.00
Average enrollment[g]	520	477	718	807	270	138	520	477	718	807	270	138

[a]These enrollment data should be regarded as approximations only. Totals differ from those reported in other tables because this table represents data reported by schools rather than by states or school districts. Percentage distribution and average enrollment calculations exclude data for schools not reporting enrollment.

[b]Includes special education, alternative, and other schools not classified by grade span.

[c]Includes schools beginning with grade 6 or below and with no grade higher than 8.

[d]Includes schools with no grade lower than 7.

[e]Includes schools beginning with grade 6 or below and ending with grade 9 or above.

[f]Excludes special education schools, vocational schools, and alternative schools.

[g]Data are for schools reporting their enrollment size.

Note: Detail may not sum to totals due to rounding.

SOURCE: Thomas D. Snyder, Alexandra G. Tan, and Charlene M. Hoffman, "Table 93. Public Elementary and Secondary Schools and Enrollment, by Type and Size of School: 2001–02," in *Digest of Education Statistics, 2003*, NCES 2005-025, U.S. Department of Education, National Center for Education Statistics, Washington, DC, December 2004, http://nces.ed.gov/programs/digest/d03/tables/dt093.asp (accessed July 26, 2005)

TABLE 2.4

Enrollment in public elementary and secondary schools, by race/ethnicity, Fall 1991 and Fall 2001

State of jurisdiction	Percentage distribution, Fall 1991						Percentage distribution, Fall 2001					
	Total	White*	Black*	Hispanic	Asian or Pacific Islander	American Indian/ Alaska Native	Total	White*	Black*	Hispanic	Asian or Pacific Islander	American Indian/ Alaska Native
1	2	3	4	5	6	7	8	9	10	11	12	13
United States	100.0	67.4	16.4	11.8	3.4	1.0	100.0	60.3	17.2	17.1	4.2	1.2
Alabama	100.0	62.8	35.5	0.3	0.5	0.9	100.0	60.5	36.5	1.5	0.8	0.7
Alaska	100.0	66.9	4.4	2.2	3.9	22.6	100.0	60.4	4.7	3.6	5.9	25.5
Arizona	100.0	62.4	4.2	25.0	1.5	6.9	100.0	51.3	4.7	35.3	2.1	6.6
Arkansas	100.0	74.5	24.0	0.6	0.6	0.3	100.0	71.1	23.3	4.2	0.9	0.5
California	100.0	44.5	8.6	35.3	10.8	0.8	100.0	35.0	8.4	44.5	11.2	0.9
Colorado	100.0	74.9	5.2	16.6	2.3	1.0	100.0	66.8	5.7	23.3	3.0	1.2
Connecticut	100.0	74.3	12.8	10.4	2.2	0.2	100.0	69.2	13.8	13.7	3.0	0.3
Delaware	100.0	67.3	27.8	3.1	1.6	0.2	100.0	59.6	31.1	6.6	2.4	0.3
District of Columbia	100.0	4.0	89.5	5.3	1.1	#	100.0	4.6	84.4	9.4	1.6	#
Florida	100.0	61.2	24.2	12.9	1.6	0.2	100.0	52.5	24.9	20.4	1.9	0.3
Georgia	100.0	60.7	37.9	0.6	0.8	#	100.0	53.8	38.2	5.5	2.4	0.2
Hawaii	100.0	23.9	2.6	5.2	67.9	0.3	100.0	20.3	2.4	4.5	72.3	0.4
Idaho	100.0	92.6	0.3	4.9	0.8	1.3	100.0	85.4	0.8	11.2	1.3	1.3
Illinois	100.0	65.4	21.4	10.3	2.8	0.1	100.0	59.0	21.2	16.2	3.5	0.2
Indiana	100.0	86.4	10.9	1.9	0.7	0.1	100.0	83.0	11.8	3.9	1.0	0.2
Iowa	100.0	94.0	2.9	1.4	1.4	0.4	100.0	89.6	4.1	4.0	1.7	0.5
Kansas	100.0	84.6	8.1	4.7	1.7	0.9	100.0	77.8	8.9	9.8	2.2	1.3
Kentucky	100.0	89.8	9.4	0.2	0.5	#	100.0	87.7	10.3	1.1	0.7	0.2
Louisiana	100.0	52.7	44.7	1.0	1.2	0.4	100.0	48.7	47.8	1.6	1.3	0.7
Maine	100.0	98.3	0.5	0.2	0.8	0.2	100.0	96.2	1.4	0.6	1.1	0.7
Maryland	100.0	60.4	33.2	2.5	3.6	0.3	100.0	52.4	37.2	5.4	4.6	0.4
Massachusetts	100.0	80.5	7.8	8.1	3.5	0.2	100.0	75.7	8.6	10.8	4.5	0.3
Michigan	100.0	78.2	17.2	2.4	1.3	1.0	100.0	73.4	20.0	3.6	2.0	1.0
Minnesota	100.0	89.9	3.6	1.4	3.2	1.8	100.0	82.0	7.0	3.8	5.2	2.0
Mississippi	100.0	48.3	50.7	0.1	0.5	0.4	100.0	47.3	51.0	0.9	0.7	0.2
Missouri	100.0	82.5	15.7	0.8	0.9	0.2	100.0	79.0	17.5	2.0	1.2	0.3
Montana	100.0	88.4	0.4	1.3	0.7	9.2	100.0	85.9	0.6	1.9	1.0	10.6
Nebraska	100.0	89.4	5.5	2.9	1.1	1.1	100.0	81.8	6.9	8.2	1.6	1.6
Nevada	100.0	73.2	9.0	12.1	3.7	2.0	100.0	54.5	10.3	27.4	6.1	1.7
New Hampshire	100.0	97.0	0.8	1.0	1.0	0.2	100.0	95.0	1.2	2.1	1.5	0.2
New Jersey	100.0	64.4	18.6	12.2	4.7	0.1	100.0	59.4	17.9	16.0	6.6	0.2
New Mexico	100.0	41.2	2.3	45.3	0.9	10.4	100.0	34.3	2.4	51.0	1.1	11.3
New York	100.0	59.4	20.1	15.8	4.4	0.3	100.0	54.8	19.9	18.6	6.2	0.4
North Carolina	100.0	66.4	30.2	0.9	1.0	1.6	100.0	60.0	31.3	5.2	1.9	1.5
North Dakota	100.0	91.2	0.7	0.6	0.7	6.8	100.0	88.7	1.1	1.3	0.8	8.1
Ohio	100.0	83.6	14.1	1.3	0.9	0.1	100.0	80.1	16.7	1.9	1.2	0.1
Oklahoma	100.0	73.5	10.0	3.0	1.1	12.4	100.0	63.7	10.8	6.5	1.5	17.5
Oregon	100.0	88.1	2.4	4.9	2.9	1.8	100.0	79.1	3.0	11.5	4.2	2.2
Pennsylvania	100.0	82.2	13.2	2.9	1.7	0.1	100.0	77.7	15.3	4.8	2.1	0.1
Rhode Island	100.0	82.7	6.5	7.2	3.1	0.4	100.0	73.4	8.1	14.8	3.2	0.6
South Carolina	100.0	57.7	41.1	0.5	0.6	0.1	100.0	54.7	41.7	2.4	1.0	0.2
South Dakota	100.0	90.6	0.5	0.6	0.7	7.6	100.0	86.2	1.3	1.4	1.0	10.2
Tennessee	100.0	76.6	22.2	0.3	0.7	0.1	100.0	71.8	24.8	2.1	1.2	0.2
Texas	100.0	49.0	14.3	34.4	2.1	0.2	100.0	40.9	14.4	41.7	2.8	0.3
Utah	100.0	91.9	0.7	4.0	1.9	1.4	100.0	84.7	1.0	9.9	2.8	1.5
Vermont	100.0	97.9	0.6	0.3	0.7	0.6	100.0	95.8	1.2	1.0	1.5	0.5
Virginia	100.0	72.6	23.7	1.0	2.6	0.1	100.0	62.8	27.1	5.5	4.3	0.3
Washington	100.0	81.4	4.2	6.1	5.8	2.5	100.0	73.5	5.4	10.9	7.5	2.6
West Virginia	100.0	95.5	3.9	0.2	0.4	0.1	100.0	94.5	4.4	0.4	0.6	0.1
Wisconsin	100.0	85.2	8.8	2.7	2.1	1.3	100.0	80.1	10.2	5.0	3.4	1.4
Wyoming	100.0	89.6	0.9	6.0	0.7	2.8	100.0	87.3	1.4	7.2	0.9	3.2

since 1960. Adjusted for inflation, expenditures per student have risen more than 60% since 1980, according to the NCES.

International Comparisons of Expenditures per Student

One method of measuring a country's commitment to education is to examine what portion of its gross domestic product (GDP, the total value of goods and services produced in the nation) goes to educating its people. In 2000, according to the U.S. Department of Education, public expenditures for education in the United States totaled 5% of GDP—3.5% for primary and secondary education, and another 1.1% for higher education. (See Figure 2.6 and Table 2.7.) Of the selected countries listed in Table 2.7, Denmark spent the highest proportion (8.4%) of GDP on education, and Russia spent the lowest proportion (3%) in 2000. For primary and secondary education, Sweden and New Zealand tied

TABLE 2.4

Enrollment in public elementary and secondary schools, by race/ethnicity, Fall 1991 and Fall 2001 [CONTINUED]

State of jurisdiction	Percentage distribution, Fall 1991						Percentage distribution, Fall 2001					
	Total	White*	Black*	Hispanic	Asian or Pacific Islander	American Indian/ Alaska Native	Total	White*	Black*	Hispanic	Asian or Pacific Islander	American Indian/ Alaska Native
1	2	3	4	5	6	7	8	9	10	11	12	13
Bureau of Indian Affairs	—	—	—	—	—	—	100.0	0.0	0.0	0.0	0.0	100.0
Department of Defense dependents schools												
Overseas schools	—	—	—	—	—	—	100.0	61.6	19.1	9.3	9.1	·1.0
Domestic schools	—	—	—	—	—	—	100.0	51.6	25.8	18.5	3.5	0.6
Outlying areas												
American Samoa	100.0	0.0	0.0	0.0	100.0	0.0	100.0	0.0	0.0	0.0	100.0	0.0
Guam	100.0	10.3	1.6	0.3	87.8	0.0	100.0	1.5	0.3	0.2	97.9	0.1
Northern Marianas	100.0	0.1	0.0	0.0	99.9	0.0	100.0	0.4	0.1	0.0	99.5	0.0
Puerto Rico	—	—	—	—	—	—	100.0	0.0	0.0	100.0	0.0	0.0
Virgin Islands	100.0	0.9	86.8	11.8	0.5	0.0	—	—	—	—	—	—

— Not available.
Rounds to zero.
*Excludes persons of Hispanic origin.
Note: Percentage distribution based upon students for whom race/ethnicity was reported, which may be less than the total number of students in the state. Detail may not sum to totals due to rounding.

SOURCE: Adapted from Thomas D. Snyder, Alexandra G. Tan, and Charlene M. Hoffman, "Table 42. Percentage Distribution of Enrollment in Public Elementary and Secondary Schools, by Race/Ethnicity and State or Jurisdiction: Fall 1991 and Fall 2001," in *Digest of Education Statistics, 2003*, NCES 2005-025, U.S. Department of Education, National Center for Education Statistics, Washington, DC, December 2004, http://nces.ed.gov/programs/digest/d03/tables/dt042.asp (accessed July 26, 2005)

for the highest proportion of GDP (4.9%), and Russia spent the lowest proportion (1.7%). The percentage of GDP that the United States spent on public education in 2000 increased by 0.3% from 1985, when it was 4.7%. The largest increase during this time (from data available) was in Denmark, from 6.2% to 8.4% of GDP.

Another way to examine international expenditures for education is by comparing how much money countries spend per student in relation to GDP per capita. In general, those countries with the highest GDP per capita spent the most on education. According to the U.S. Department of Education, the United States had GDP per capita of $34,602 in 2000 and spent $7,397 per elementary and secondary student. Mexico had GDP per capita of $9,117 and spent $1,415 in that year, while Switzerland had GDP per capita of $29,617 and spent $8,187 per elementary and secondary student. (See Table 2.8.) Total education expenditures, including postsecondary, as a percentage of GDP were highest in the United States (6.6%), Korea (6.6%), and Canada (6.2%).

PRIVATE SCHOOLS

According to the U.S. Department of Education, about 5.3 million students attended private elementary and secondary schools throughout the country in 2001–02. (See Table 2.9.)

Characteristics

The U.S. Department of Education notes that most enrollment (nearly four million) in private schools in 2001–02 existed at the elementary level, while 1.3 million students were enrolled in private high schools. (See Table 2.9.)

In 2001–02 more students in the South were enrolled in private schools than in any other region of the country. More than 1.6 million students in the South, about 1.4 million students in the Midwest, another 1.3 million in the Northeast, and one million students in the West were enrolled in private schools. (See Table 2.9.)

Most private school students attend Catholic schools. According to the U.S. Department of Education, in 2001–02 nearly half (47%) of students who attended private schools were enrolled in a Catholic school, while 36% attended schools that were affiliated with another religion, and 17% attended a nonsectarian private school (schools that do not have a religious orientation or purpose). (See Figure 2.7.)

TEACHERS IN PUBLIC AND PRIVATE SCHOOLS

In fall 2002 there were nearly three million teachers in public elementary and secondary schools and 385,000 in private schools. The average ratio of students to teachers was 16.1 pupils to every teacher. Public schools had almost the same pupil/teacher ratios (16.1) as private

TABLE 2.5

People and families in poverty, by selected characteristics, 2002 and 2003

[Numbers in thousands. People as of March of the following year.]

Characteristic	2002 below poverty		2003 below poverty		Change in poverty (2003 less 2002)[a]	
	Number	Percentage	Number	Percentage	Number	Percentage
People						
Total	34,570	12.1	35,861	12.5	1,291	0.3
Family status						
In families	24,534	10.4	25,684	10.8	1,150	0.4
Householder	7,229	9.6	7,607	10.0	378	0.4
Related children under 18	11,646	16.3	12,340	17.2	694	0.9
Related children under 6	4,296	18.5	4,654	19.8	358	1.4
In unrelated subfamilies	417	33.7	464	38.6	46	4.9
Reference person	167	31.7	191	37.6	25	5.8
Children under 18	241	35.4	271	41.7	31	6.3
Unrelated individual	9,618	20.4	9,713	20.4	95	—
Male	4,023	17.7	4,154	18.0	131	0.3
Female	5,595	22.9	5,559	22.6	−36	−0.2
Race[b] and Hispanic origin						
White alone or in combination	24,074	10.3	24,950	10.6	876	0.3
White alone[c]	23,466	10.2	24,272	10.5	806	0.3
White alone, not Hispanic	15,567	8.0	15,902	8.2	335	0.2
Black alone or in combination	8,884	23.9	9,108	24.3	224	0.4
Black alone[d]	8,602	24.1	8,781	24.4	180	0.3
Asian alone or in combination	1,243	10.0	1,527	11.8	284	1.9
Asian alone[e]	1,161	10.1	1,401	11.8	240	1.8
Hispanic origin (of any race)	8,555	21.8	9,051	22.5	497	0.6
Age						
Under 18 years	12,133	16.7	12,866	17.6	733	0.9
18 to 64 years	18,861	10.6	19,443	10.8	582	0.2
65 years and older	3,576	10.4	3,552	10.2	−24	−0.2
Nativity						
Native	29,012	11.5	29,965	11.8	952	0.3
Foreign born	5,558	16.6	5,897	17.2	339	0.6
Naturalized citizen	1,285	10.0	1,309	10.0	24	—
Not a citizen	4,273	20.7	4,588	21.7	315	1.0
Region						
Northeast	5,871	10.9	6,052	11.3	182	0.4
Midwest	6,616	10.3	6,932	10.7	316	0.5
South	14,019	13.8	14,548	14.1	529	0.3
West	8,064	12.4	8,329	12.6	265	0.2
Residence						
Inside metropolitan areas	27,096	11.6	28,367	12.1	1,271	0.4
Inside central cities	13,784	16.7	14,551	17.5	767	0.8
Outside central cities	13,311	8.9	13,816	9.1	504	0.2
Outside metropolitan areas	7,474	14.2	7,495	14.2	20	—
Work experience						
All workers (16 years and older)	8,954	5.9	8,820	5.8	−134	−0.1
Worked full-time year-round	2,635	2.6	2,636	2.6	1	—
Not full-time year-round	6,318	12.4	6,183	12.2	−135	−0.3
Did not work at least one week	14,647	21.0	15,446	21.5	799	0.4

schools (16.2). These ratios were considerably lower than they had been during the 1950s, '60s, and '70s. (See Table 2.10.)

SUPPORTIVE PROGRAMS AND SERVICES

The type of supportive programs and services available to schools and school districts is one indicator of the access students have to educational opportunities. Although individual schools can apply directly for these programs and services, the school district (especially in public schools) usually decides whether the programs and services will be provided in its schools.

Schools offer a variety of student services, such as free or reduced-price lunches financed by public funds, services for disabled students, remedial programs, programs for gifted and talented students, programs under Chapter I (federal funds designated for special educational programs for disadvantaged children) of the Elementary and Secondary Education Act of 1965 (P.L. 89-10), drug and alcohol prevention programs,

TABLE 2.5

People and families in poverty, by selected characteristics, 2002 and 2003 [CONTINUED]

[Numbers in thousands. People as of March of the following year.]

Characteristic	2002 below poverty		2003 below poverty		Change in poverty (2003 less 2002)[a]	
	Number	Percentage	Number	Percentage	Number	Percentage
Families						
Total	7,229	9.6	7,607	10.0	378	0.4
Type of family						
Married-couple	3,052	5.3	3,115	5.4	63	0.1
Female householder, no husband present	3,613	26.5	3,856	28.0	243	1.4
Male householder, no wife present	564	12.1	636	13.5	73	1.4

— Represents zero or round to zero.
[a]Details may not sum to total because of rounding.
[b]Data for American Indians and Alaska Natives, and Asian, Native Hawaiian and Other Pacific Islanders are not shown separately.
[c]White alone refers to people who reported white and did not report any other race category. The use of this single-race population does not imply that it is the preferred method of presenting or analyzing data. The Census Bureau uses a variety of approaches. About 2.6 percent of people reported more than one race in Census 2000.
[d]Black alone refers to people who reported black and did not report any other race category.
[e]Asian alone refers to people who reported Asian and did not report any other race category.

SOURCE: Carmen DeNavas-Walt, Bernadette D. Proctor, and Robert J. Mills, "Table 3. People and Families in Poverty by Selected Characteristics: 2002 and 2003," in *Income, Poverty, and Health Insurance Coverage in the United States: 2003*, Current Population Reports P60-226, U.S. Department of Commerce, Economics and Statistics Administration, U.S. Census Bureau, Washington, DC, August 2004, http://www.census.gov/prod/2004pubs/p60-226.pdf (accessed July 26, 2005)

FIGURE 2.3

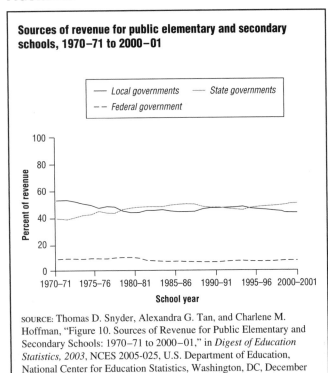

Sources of revenue for public elementary and secondary schools, 1970–71 to 2000–01

SOURCE: Thomas D. Snyder, Alexandra G. Tan, and Charlene M. Hoffman, "Figure 10. Sources of Revenue for Public Elementary and Secondary Schools: 1970–71 to 2000–01," in *Digest of Education Statistics, 2003*, NCES 2005-025, U.S. Department of Education, National Center for Education Statistics, Washington, DC, December 2004, http://nces.ed.gov/programs/digest/d03/figures/figure_10.asp?popup=1 (accessed July 26, 2005)

English as a second language (ESL) programs, and bilingual programs.

Of the $8,041 schools spent per student in 2002–03, most of this expenditure was for instruction (61%); 39% was for support services and noninstructional costs. Among the fifty states and the District of Columbia, New Jersey had the highest per-student expenditure ($12,568) and Utah the lowest ($4,838). (See Table 2.11.)

Prekindergarten and Kindergarten

Most public and private schools provide prekindergarten and kindergarten programs. According to the Council of Chief State School Officers (CCSSO), twenty-six states (54%) required half-day kindergarten programs in 2002, fourteen (29%) required full-day programs, and eight (17%) had no statewide policy. (See Figure 2.8.) Kindergarten attendance is now nearly universal in the United States, and the majority of primary school children have had at least one organized group experience (day care center or nursery school) prior to starting first grade.

According to the U.S. Department of Education, in 2000–01 there were 822,000 children in prekindergarten. Nearly one-quarter (23%) were age three or younger, 68.3% were age four, and 8.7% were five years of age or older. Almost half (48.6%) were white, 22.6% were African-American, and 24% were Hispanic. Less than half (46.8%) of the children in prekindergarten programs in the Northeast and slightly more than half (50.7%) in the Central region of the country were low income, meaning they were eligible for a free or reduced lunch. The percentage of low-income prekindergarten students in the Southeast was 70.7% and in the West was 69.8%. (See Table 2.12.)

TABLE 2.6

Revenues for public elementary and secondary schools, by source, 2000–01

State or jurisdiction	Total, in thousands	Federal			State		Local and intermediate		Private[c]	
		Amount, in thousands	Per student	Percent of total	Amount, in thousands	Percent of total	Amount, in thousands	Percent of total	Amount, in thousands	Percent of total
1	2	3	4	5	6	7	8	9	10	11
United States	$400,919,024	$29,086,413	$616	7.3	$199,146,586	49.7	$163,479,177	40.8	$9,206,847	2.3
Alabama	4,812,302	453,817	613	9.4	2,881,224	59.9	1,227,512	25.5	249,749	5.2
Alaska	1,370,271	215,921	1,619	15.8	782,348	57.1	333,592	24.3	38,410	2.8
Arizona	5,797,151	616,976	703	10.6	2,525,390	43.6	2,506,856	43.2	147,929	2.6
Arkansas	2,812,169	260,705	579	9.3	1,676,138	59.6	820,201	29.2	55,125	2.0
California	51,007,510	4,159,513	677	8.2	31,392,549	61.5	14,929,920	29.3	525,528	1.0
Colorado	5,349,899	299,576	413	5.6	2,222,083	41.5	2,576,924	48.2	251,315	4.7
Connecticut	6,460,491	276,427	492	4.3	2,553,180	39.5	3,527,302	54.6	103,583	1.6
Delaware	1,112,519	87,904	767	7.9	732,599	65.9	277,769	25.0	14,247	1.3
District of Columbia	1,042,711	115,527	1,676	11.1	a	a	918,793	88.1	8,391	0.8
Florida	17,866,868	1,599,259	657	9.0	8,695,213	48.7	6,917,556	38.7	654,841	3.7
Georgia	12,191,113	783,487	542	6.4	5,963,337	48.9	5,249,268	43.1	195,020	1.6
Hawaii	1,682,330	140,951	765	8.4	1,511,317	89.8	9,105	0.5	20,957	1.2
Idaho	1,593,966	128,646	525	8.1	977,438	61.3	461,605	29.0	26,278	1.6
Illinois	18,217,079	1,421,519	694	7.8	6,124,183	33.6	10,301,826	56.6	369,551	2.0
Indiana	9,033,180	464,489	470	5.1	4,833,954	53.5	3,477,771	38.5	256,967	2.8
Iowa	3,954,178	248,689	502	6.3	1,943,708	49.2	1,556,878	39.4	204,902	5.2
Kansas	3,597,726	231,473	492	6.4	2,198,216	61.1	1,074,216	29.9	93,820	2.6
Kentucky	4,509,893	448,073	673	9.9	2,702,932	59.9	1,258,841	27.9	100,047	2.2
Louisiana	5,060,133	580,356	781	11.5	2,497,875	49.4	1,921,174	38.0	60,729	1.2
Maine	1,934,178	153,100	739	7.9	863,295	44.6	880,399	45.5	37,384	1.9
Maryland	7,846,891	477,463	560	6.1	2,928,715	37.3	4,178,103	53.2	262,611	3.3
Massachusetts	10,148,498	511,198	524	5.0	4,420,622	43.6	5,052,863	49.8	163,816	1.6
Michigan	16,358,532	1,116,374	649	6.8	10,603,606	64.8	4,276,902	26.1	361,649	2.2
Minnesota	7,873,549	370,648	434	4.7	4,765,802	60.5	2,497,149	31.7	239,951	3.0
Mississippi	2,903,534	400,804	805	13.8	1,607,126	55.4	804,183	27.7	91,421	3.1
Missouri	7,102,501	491,233	538	6.9	2,661,904	37.5	3,680,122	51.8	269,242	3.8
Montana	1,140,168	131,299	848	11.5	542,692	47.6	418,700	36.7	47,477	4.2
Nebraska	2,307,804	168,036	587	7.3	805,419	34.9	1,210,412	52.4	123,937	5.4
Nevada	2,393,494	122,360	359	5.1	683,605	28.6	1,497,331	62.6	90,198	3.8
New Hampshire	1,714,147	77,365	371	4.5	884,875	51.6	712,119	41.5	39,788	2.3
New Jersey	15,967,075	628,834	479	3.9	6,669,858	41.8	8,351,731	52.3	316,652	2.0
New Mexico	2,426,705	338,213	1,056	13.9	1,725,551	71.1	316,268	13.0	46,674	1.9
New York	34,266,171	1,961,653	681	5.7	15,818,051	46.2	16,187,387	47.2	299,080	0.9
North Carolina	9,262,181	670,380	518	7.2	6,144,449	66.3	2,216,699	23.9	230,653	2.5
North Dakota	767,798	102,697	940	13.4	299,089	39.0	324,794	42.3	41,216	5.4
Ohio	16,649,361	1,007,370	549	6.1	7,187,325	43.2	7,840,209	47.1	614,457	3.7
Oklahoma	4,034,825	410,681	659	10.2	2,386,216	59.1	1,035,597	25.7	202,332	5.0
Oregon	4,564,408	336,992	617	7.4	2,566,099	56.2	1,528,766	33.5	132,551	2.9
Pennsylvania	17,053,891	1,107,864	611	6.5	6,443,673	37.8	9,176,463	53.8	325,901	1.9
Rhode Island	1,545,675	90,634	576	5.9	652,723	42.2	781,753	50.6	20,566	1.3
South Carolina	5,459,399	446,838	660	8.2	2,941,097	53.9	1,873,403	34.3	198,061	3.6
South Dakota	885,229	107,532	836	12.1	312,880	35.3	438,651	49.6	26,167	3.0
Tennessee	5,711,950	524,351	577	9.2	2,532,336	44.3	2,493,439	43.7	161,824	2.8
Texas	30,469,570	2,656,951	654	8.7	12,855,241	42.2	14,246,504	46.8	710,874	2.3
Utah	2,745,656	204,939	426	7.5	1,608,249	58.6	867,784	31.6	64,683	2.4
Vermont	1,035,679	60,523	593	5.8	732,563	70.7	226,175	21.8	16,418	1.6
Virginia	9,313,330	520,773	455	5.6	3,939,548	42.3	4,649,755	49.9	203,253	2.2
Washington	8,058,875	625,231	622	7.8	5,072,388	62.9	2,101,004	26.1	260,253	3.2
West Virginia	2,375,788	243,131	849	10.2	1,450,453	61.1	654,155	27.5	28,049	1.2
Wisconsin	8,327,255	418,472	476	5.0	4,424,429	53.1	3,295,254	39.6	189,099	2.3
Wyoming	803,414	69,176	769	8.6	403,020	50.2	317,995	39.6	13,223	1.6

SCHOOL ATTENDANCE
Days in Attendance

The Council of Chief State School Officers (CCSSO) reported that in 2002 thirty-four states required 180 or more days of school per year, and eight states required between 175 and 179 days. (See Figure 2.9.) The remaining states required a set number of hours rather than days, or had variations based on student grade level. The number of required hours per day ranged from three to seven, with thirty states requiring five or more hours per day.

The CCSSO reported in *Key State Education Policies on PK–12 Education* (2005) that the number of states requiring at least 180 days of school had increased to thirty-five by 2004, with six states mandating between 175 and 179 days of school per year. Kansas, with 186 days, had the longest school year in 2004, followed by Illinois and Michigan, both with 185. Of states that required a fixed number of days in 2004, Colorado, Idaho, and South Dakota had the least (170).

TABLE 2.6

Revenues for public elementary and secondary schools, by source, 2000–01 [CONTINUED]

State or jurisdiction	Total, in thousands	Federal			State		Local and intermediate		Private[c]	
		Amount, in thousands	Per student	Percent of total	Amount, in thousands	Percent of total	Amount, in thousands	Percent of total	Amount, in thousands	Percent of total
1	2	3	4	5	6	7	8	9	10	11
Outlying areas										
American Samoa	58,262	45,822	2,918	78.6	10,551	18.1	1,801	3.1	89	0.2
Guam	—	—	—	—	—	—	—	—	—	—
Northern Marianas	55,164	17,619	1,761	31.9	37,230	67.5	255	0.5	60	0.1
Puerto Rico	2,331,691	671,870	1,097	28.8	1,658,907	71.1	98	b	815	b
Virgin Islands	165,801	28,256	1,452	17.0	0	0.0	137,400	82.9	146	0.1

— Not available.
[a]Not applicable.
[b]Rounds to zero.
[c]Includes revenues from gifts, and tuition and fees from patrons.
Note: Excludes revenues for state education agencies. Detail may not sum to totals due to rounding.

SOURCE: Thomas D. Snyder, Alexandra G. Tan, and Charlene M. Hoffman, "Table 157. Revenues for Public Elementary and Secondary Schools, by Source and State or Jurisdiction: 2000–01," in *Digest of Education Statistics, 2003*, NCES 2005-025, U.S. Department of Education, National Center for Education Statistics, Washington, DC, December 2004, http://nces.ed.gov/programs/digest/d03/tables/dt157.asp (accessed July 26, 2005)

FIGURE 2.4

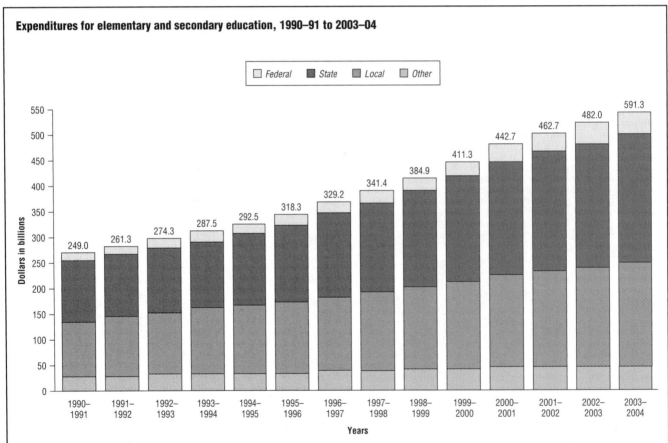

Expenditures for elementary and secondary education, 1990–91 to 2003–04

SOURCE: U.S. Department of Education, "Expenditures for Elementary and Secondary Education," in *A Guide to Education and No Child Left Behind*, U.S. Department of Education, Office of the Secretary, Office of Public Affairs, Washington DC, 2004, http://www.ed.gov/nclb/overview/intro/guide/guide_pg11.html#spending (accessed July 26, 2005)

Compulsory Attendance

Most industrialized Western nations require children to attend school for about ten years. According to the CCSSO, in 2004 nearly all U.S. states required students to attend school starting between ages five and eight and continuing through ages sixteen to eighteen. In 2004,

FIGURE 2.5

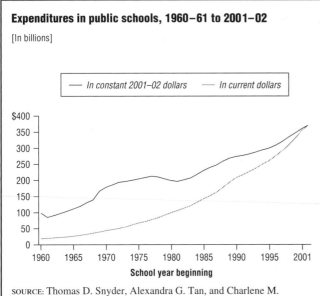

Expenditures in public schools, 1960–61 to 2001–02

[In billions]

SOURCE: Thomas D. Snyder, Alexandra G. Tan, and Charlene M. Hoffman, "Figure 7. Enrollment, Number of Teachers, Pupil/Teacher Ratios, and Expenditures in Public Schools: 1960–61 to 2001–02," in *Digest of Education Statistics, 2003*, NCES 2005-025, U.S. Department of Education, National Center for Education Statistics, Washington, DC, December 2004, http://nces.ed.gov/programs/digest/d03/figures/figure_07.asp?popup=1 (accessed July 26, 2005)

eight states required students to be enrolled by age six; twenty-two states required students to enter school before age seven; and nineteen states required students to begin school by age eight.

The CCSSO reported in *Key State Education Policies on PK–12 Education: 2004* that thirty-one states required students to remain enrolled until age sixteen, and seven established seventeen as the minimum age for leaving school. The District of Columbia and eleven states mandated students to remain enrolled until age eighteen. New Mexico law required students to gain the "age of majority" or meet other requirements.

GRADUATING FROM HIGH SCHOOL

According to the U.S. Department of Education, in 1899–1900 only 6.4% of seventeen-year-olds had graduated from high school. By 1929–30 this proportion had risen to 29%, and by 1949–50 it had grown to 59%. The proportion peaked at 77.1% in 1968–69 and then dropped to 71.4% in 1979–80. The proportion fluctuated between 71% and 74% throughout much of the 1980s and the early 1990s, and dropped to between 69% and 70% until 1998–99. At the end of the 2002–03 school year, three million students graduated from high school. (See Table 2.13.) High school graduates are not the same as high school completers—students who finish their high school education through alternative pro-

grams, such as the General Educational Development (GED) program.

General Educational Development (GED) Diplomas

The General Educational Development (GED) diploma is an alternative way for young people who have left school to get equivalency credit for high school graduation. According to the U.S. Department of Education, about one million people took the GED test in 2001. The number of those getting GED diplomas rose sharply from 340,000 in 1975 to 489,000 in 1981. The number gaining a GED diploma generally dropped during the 1980s, falling to 357,000 in 1989, but by 2001 it had again increased to 648,000. (See Table 2.14.) The American Council on Education (ACE) reported on its Web site (http://www. acenet.edu/) that 412,044 adults passed GED tests in 2003. According to ACE, one in seven high school diplomas in the United States is issued on the basis of GED testing.

CAREER AND TECHNICAL EDUCATION

Career and technical education, also known as vocational education, includes such study areas as office administration, automotive technology, carpentry and construction, medical technology, agricultural production, culinary arts, transportation, electronics, and computer graphics. For much of the twentieth century, most high schools had a two-track educational system—an academic curriculum that centered on traditional subjects and prepared students for college, and a vocational curriculum that focused on career skills and prepared students to enter the workforce. However, today's high-skill job market requires all high school graduates to have both academic knowledge and workplace skills and training. Professional careers now demand technical skills and the ability to work in teams; technical careers require the ability to diagnose and analyze problems.

The integration of academic and vocational education, emphasizing a curriculum that makes connections between knowledge development and its application in the workplace, is mandated in the United States under the Carl D. Perkins Vocational and Applied Technology Education Act of 1990 (P.L. 101-392). Speaking during a Perkins Act reauthorization hearing in May 2004, Representative Mike Castle (R-Delaware) noted that "66% of all public secondary schools have one or more vocational and technical education programs, with approximately 96% of high school students taking at least one vocational and technical course during their secondary studies." Both the Senate and the House of Representatives voted to reauthorize the Perkins Act in 2005.

Developments in Vocational Education Programs

According to the U.S. Department of Education, successful career and technical education should encourage

FIGURE 2.6

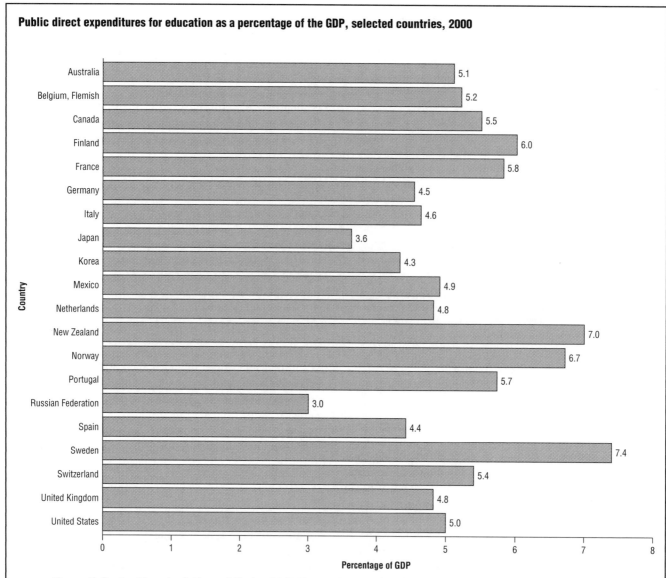

Public direct expenditures for education as a percentage of the GDP, selected countries, 2000

SOURCE: Thomas D. Snyder, Alexandra G. Tan, and Charlene M. Hoffman, "Figure 28. Public Direct Expenditures for Education as a Percentage of the Gross Domestic Product: Selected Countries, 2000," in *Digest of Education Statistics, 2003*, NCES 2005-025, U.S. Department of Education, National Center for Education Statistics, Washington, DC, December 2004, http://nces.ed.gov/programs/digest/d03/figures/figure_28.asp?popup=1 (accessed July 26, 2005)

links between high schools and postsecondary institutions, include a challenging academic core, offer nonduplicative technical courses leading to a degree or certificate, and focus on career pathways that are in demand and lead to economic self-sufficiency. The Office of Vocational and Adult Education, a division of the Department of Education, has identified several areas crucial to the future of technical education, including:

- Incorporating both school- and work-based learning
- Increasing business partnerships within the community
- Preparing students for continuing education
- Establishing partnerships with postsecondary institutions, including colleges and universities; and
- Taking advantage of higher technology and the Internet

TABLE 2.7

Public expenditures on education as a percentage of the GDP, by level and country, selected years, 1985–2000

Country	All institutions[a]					Primary and secondary institutions					Higher education institutions				
	1985	1990	1995	1999	2000	1985	1990	1995	1999	2000	1985	1990	1995	1999	2000
1	2	3	4	5	6	7	8	9	10	11	12	13	14	15	16
Average for year	5.3	4.9	4.9	5.1	5.2	3.7	3.5	3.4	3.5	3.5	1.1	1.0	0.9	1.2	1.2
Average for countries reporting data for all years	5.4	5.2	5.3	5.6	5.4	3.7	3.7	3.6	3.7	3.6	1.1	1.1	1.1	1.4	1.4
Australia	5.4	4.3	4.5	5.0	5.1	3.5	3.2	3.2	3.8	3.9	1.7	1.0	1.2	1.2	1.2
Austria	5.6	5.2	5.3	6.3	5.8	3.7	3.6	3.8	4.1	3.8	1.0	1.0	0.9	1.7	1.4
Belgium[b]	6.3	4.8	5.0	5.5	5.2	4.0	3.4	3.4	3.5	3.4	1.0	0.8	0.9	1.5	1.3
Canada	6.1	5.4	5.8	5.7	5.5	4.1	3.7	4.0	3.5	3.3	2.0	1.5	1.5	1.9	2.0
Czech Republic	—	—	4.8	4.4	4.4	—	—	3.4	3.0	3.0	—	—	0.7	0.8	0.8
Denmark	6.2	6.2	6.5	8.1	8.4	4.7	4.4	4.2	4.8	4.8	1.2	1.3	1.3	2.4	2.5
Finland	5.8	6.4	6.6	6.2	6.0	—	4.3	4.2	3.8	3.6	—	1.2	1.7	2.1	2.0
France	—	5.1	5.8	6.0	5.8	—	3.7	4.1	4.2	4.1	—	0.8	1.0	1.1	1.0
Germany[c]	4.6	—	4.5	4.7	4.5	2.8	—	2.9	3.0	3.0	1.0	—	1.0	1.1	1.1
Greece	—	—	3.7	3.6	3.8	—	—	2.8	2.4	2.7	—	—	0.8	1.1	0.9
Hungary	—	5.0	4.9	4.7	4.9	—	3.5	3.3	2.9	3.1	—	0.8	0.8	0.9	1.0
Iceland	—	4.3	4.5	—	6.0	—	3.3	3.4	—	4.7	—	0.6	0.7	—	1.1
Ireland	5.6	4.7	4.7	4.3	4.4	4.0	3.3	3.3	3.1	3.0	0.9	0.9	0.9	1.2	1.3
Italy	4.7	5.8	4.5	4.5	4.6	3.2	4.1	3.2	3.2	3.2	0.6	1.0	0.7	0.8	0.8
Japan	—	3.6	3.6	3.5	3.6	—	2.9	2.8	2.7	2.7	—	0.4	0.4	0.5	0.5
Korea, Republic of	—	—	3.6	4.1	4.3	—	—	3.0	3.2	3.3	—	—	0.3	0.6	0.7
Luxembourg	—	—	4.3	—	—	—	—	4.2	—	—	—	—	0.1	—	—
Mexico	—	3.2	4.6	4.4	4.9	—	2.2	3.4	3.1	3.4	—	0.7	0.8	0.8	0.9
Netherlands	6.2	5.7	4.6	4.8	4.8	4.1	3.6	3.0	3.1	3.2	1.5	1.6	1.1	1.3	1.3
New Zealand	—	5.5	5.3	6.3	7.0	—	3.9	3.8	4.8	4.9	—	1.2	1.1	1.2	1.7
Norway	5.1	6.2	6.8	7.4	6.7	4.0	4.1	4.1	4.3	3.9	0.7	1.1	1.5	2.0	1.7
Poland	—	—	5.2	5.2	5.2	—	—	3.3	3.6	3.8	—	—	0.8	0.8	0.8
Portugal	—	—	5.4	5.7	5.7	—	—	4.1	4.2	4.2	—	—	1.0	1.0	1.0
Russian Federation	—	—	3.4	3.0[d]	3.0	—	—	1.9	—	1.7	—	—	0.7	—	0.5
Spain	3.6	4.2	4.8	4.5	4.4	2.9	3.2	3.5	3.3	3.1	0.4	0.7	0.8	0.9	1.0
Sweden	—	5.3	6.6	7.7	7.4	—	4.4	4.4	5.1	4.9	—	1.0	1.6	2.1	2.0
Switzerland	4.9	5.0	5.5	5.5	5.4	4.0	3.7	4.1	4.0	3.9	0.9	1.0	1.1	1.2	1.2
Turkey	—	3.2	2.2	4.0	3.5	—	2.3	1.4	2.9	2.4	—	0.9	0.8	1.1	1.1
United Kingdom	4.9	4.3	4.6	4.7	4.8	3.1	3.5	3.8	3.3	3.4	1.0	0.7	0.7	1.1	1.0
United States	4.7	5.3	5.0	5.2	5.0	3.2	3.8	3.5	3.5	3.5	1.3	1.4	1.1	1.4	1.1

— Not available.

[a]Includes preprimary and other expenditures not classified by level.

[b]Data are for Flemish Belgium only.

[c]Data for 1985 are for the former West Germany.

[d]Data are for 2000.

Note: Direct public expenditure on educational services includes both amounts spent directly by governments to hire educational personnel and to procure other resources, and amounts provided by governments to public or private institutions, or households. Figures for 1985 also include transfers and payments to private entities, and thus are not strictly comparable with later figures. Some data revised from previously published figures.

SOURCE: Thomas D. Snyder, Alexandra G. Tan, and Charlene M. Hoffman, "Table 416. Total Public Direct Expenditures on Education as a Percentage of the Gross Domestic Product, by Level and Country: Selected Years, 1985 to 2000," in *Digest of Education Statistics, 2003*, NCES 2005-025, U.S. Department of Education, National Center for Education Statistics, Washington, DC, December 2004, http://nces.ed.gov/programs/digest/d03/tables/dt416.asp (accesssed July 26, 2005)

TABLE 2.8

Annual expenditures on public and private institutions per student and as a percentage of GDP for OECD countries, by level of education, 2000

Country	Expenditures on public and private institutions per student[a]		Expenditures on public and private institutions as a percentage of GDP			GDP per capita (in equivalent U.S. dollars converted using PPPs)[b]
	Elementary and secondary[c]	Post-secondary[d]	Elementary and secondary[c]	Post-secondary[d]	Total[e]	
OECD mean	$5,162	$9,509	3.6	1.3	4.9	$23,317
Australia	5,867	12,854	4.3	1.6	5.9	26,325
Austria[f]	7,851	10,851	3.8	1.2	5.1	28,070
Belgium	5,732	10,771	3.6	1.3	4.9	26,392
Canada	5,947	14,983	3.6	2.6	6.2	28,130
Czech Republic	2,541	5,431	3.0	0.9	4.0	13,806
Denmark	7,467	11,981	4.2	1.6	5.7	28,755
Finland	5,292	8,244	3.5	1.7	5.2	25,357
France	6,214	8,373	4.2	1.1	5.4	25,090
Germany	5,779	10,898	3.4	1.0	4.6	26,139
Greece	3,696	3,402	2.8	0.9	3.8	15,885
Hungary	2,352	7,024	2.8	1.1	3.9	12,204
Iceland	6,293	7,994	—	0.9	5.8	28,143
Ireland	3,976	11,083	2.9	1.5	4.5	28,285
Italy	6,506	8,065	3.2	0.9	4.1	25,095
Japan	5,971	10,914	2.9	1.1	4.0	26,011
Korea	3,644	6,118	4.0	2.6	6.6	15,186
Luxembourg	—	—	—	—	—	48,239
Mexico	1,415	4,688	3.8	1.1	4.9	9,117
Netherlands	5,138	11,934	3.1	1.2	4.3	27,316
New Zealand	—	—	4.5	0.9	5.5	20,372
Norway[f]	7,399	13,353	3.7	1.3	4.9	36,242
Poland	1,988	3,222	3.7	0.8	4.5	9,547
Portugal[f]	—	4,766	4.1	1.1	5.2	16,780
Slovak Republic	1,732	4,949	2.8	0.8	3.6	11,278
Spain	4,636	6,666	3.3	1.2	4.5	20,195
Sweden	6,337	15,097	4.3	1.7	6.0	26,161
Switzerland	8,187	18,450	4.2	1.2	5.5	29,617
Turkey	—	4,121	2.4	1.0	3.4	6,211
United Kingdom	4,844	9,657	3.8	1.0	4.8	24,964
United States	7,397	20,358	3.9	2.7	6.6	34,602

— Not available.

[a]Per student expenditures are calculated based on public and private full-time-equivalent (FTE) enrollment figures for the 1999–2000 school year and on current expenditures and capital outlays from both public and private sources where data are available.

[b]GDP adjusted to national financial year.

[c]Includes postsecondary nontertiary data (International Standard Classification of Education [ISCED] level 4) for Belgium, Finland, Japan, Norway, Poland, Slovak Republic, Spain, and the United Kingdom.

[d]Includes all tertiary level data. Also, includes postsecondary nontertiary data for Canada, Japan, and the United States.

[e]Total includes elementary/secondary, postsecondary, and postsecondary nontertiary expenditures.

[f]Data are for full- and part-time students.

Note: Educational expenditures are from public and private revenue sources. Purchasing Power Parity (PPP) indices are used to convert other currencies to U.S. dollars. Within-country consumer price indices are used to adjust the PPP indices to account for inflation because the fiscal year has a different starting date in different countries. Includes all institutions, public and private, with the exception of Greece, Hungary, Iceland, Italy, Norway, Poland, Switzerland, and Turkey, which include public institutions only.

SOURCE: John Wirt, Susan Choy, Stephen Provasnik, Patrick Rooney, Anindita Sen, and Richard Tobin, "Table 36–1. Annual Expenditures on Public and Private Institutions Per Student and as a Percentage of GDP for OECD Countries, by Level of Education: 2000," in *The Condition of Education, 2004*, NCES 2004-077, U.S. Department of Education, National Center for Education Statistics, Washington, DC, June 2004, http://nces.ed.gov/programs/coe/2004/section6/table.asp?tableID=92 (accessed July 26, 2005)

TABLE 2.9

Private elementary and secondary school enrollment and as a percentage of total enrollment in public and private schools, by region and grade level, selected years, 1989–90 to 2001–02

[Totals in thousands]

School year and grade level	Total enrollment		Northeast		Midwest		South		West	
	Total	Percent of total enrollment	Total	Percent of total Northeast enrollment	Total	Percent of total Midwest enrollment	Total	Percent of total South enrollment	Total	Percent of total West enrollment
Grades K–12										
1989–90	4,838	10.7	1,346	15.7	1,368	12.2	1,280	8.1	844	8.7
1991–92	4,890	10.4	1,324	15.2	1,353	11.8	1,304	8.0	909	8.7
1993–94	4,836	10.0	1,276	14.3	1,309	11.3	1,386	8.2	865	8.0
1995–96	5,032	10.1	1,289	14.0	1,349	11.4	1,445	8.2	949	8.4
1997–98	5,076	9.9	1,287	13.7	1,346	11.2	1,510	8.4	933	8.0
1999–2000	5,163	9.9	1,295	13.6	1,345	11.1	1,576	8.6	947	7.9
2001–02	5,342	10.1	1,337	13.9	1,355	11.2	1,641	8.7	1,008	8.1
Grades K–8*										
1989–90	3,588	11.0	947	15.7	1,052	13.1	949	8.2	639	9.0
1991–92	3,657	10.7	935	15.0	1,059	12.8	974	8.1	689	9.1
1993–94	3,641	10.4	907	14.2	1,021	12.2	1,048	8.4	664	8.4
1995–96	3,760	10.4	911	13.9	1,042	12.3	1,086	8.4	721	8.8
1997–98	3,781	10.3	911	13.6	1,036	12.1	1,126	8.6	708	8.4
1999–2000	3,849	10.3	917	13.6	1,035	12.1	1,177	8.8	720	8.3
2001–02	3,951	10.4	935	13.8	1,039	12.1	1,223	8.9	754	8.5
Grades 9–12*										
1989–90	1,126	9.0	362	14.6	288	9.2	291	6.8	185	7.1
1991–92	1,126	8.9	346	13.6	276	8.9	302	7.0	203	7.3
1993–94	1,102	8.4	328	13.1	273	8.5	315	7.1	186	6.4
1995–96	1,160	8.5	334	13.0	286	8.5	330	7.1	209	6.8
1997–98	1,181	8.3	330	12.5	292	8.5	353	7.2	206	6.3
1999–2000	1,225	8.4	338	12.6	297	8.6	375	7.5	214	6.3
2001–02	1,293	8.6	364	13.0	302	8.6	389	7.5	239	6.8

*Grades K–8 and 9–12 do not include ungraded students and therefore these two categories do not sum to grades K–12.
Note: Detail may not sum to totals because of rounding.

SOURCE: John Wirt, Susan Choy, Patrick Rooney, William Hussar, Stephen Provasnik, and Gillian Hampden-Thompson, "Table 2–2. Private Elementary and Secondary School Enrollment and as a Percentage of Total Enrollment in Public and Private Schools, by Region and Grade Level: Various School Years, 1989–90 through 2001–02," in *The Condition of Education, 2005*, NCES 2005-094, U.S. Department of Education, National Center for Education Statistics, Washington, DC, June 2005, http://nces.ed.gov/programs/coe/2005/section1/table.asp?tableID=225 (accessed July 26, 2005)

FIGURE 2.7

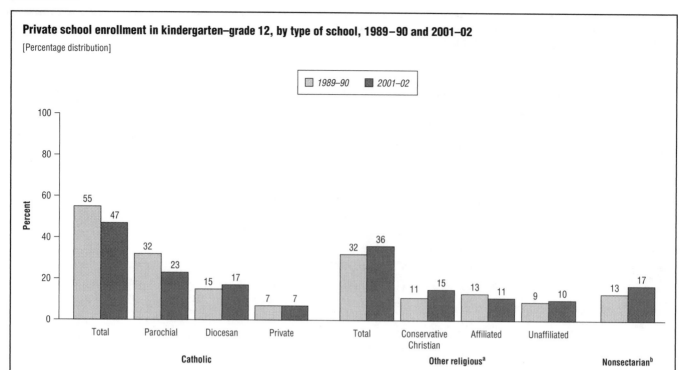

Private school enrollment in kindergarten–grade 12, by type of school, 1989–90 and 2001–02

[Percentage distribution]

[a]Other religious schools have a religious orientation or purpose, but are not Roman Catholic. Conservative Christian schools are those with membership in at least one of four associations: Accelerated Christian Education, American Association of Christian Schools, Association of Christian Schools International, or Oral Roberts University Education Fellowship. Affiliated schools are those with membership in one of 11 associations: Association of Christian Teachers and Schools, Christian Schools International, Council of Islamic Schools in North America, Evangelical Lutheran Education Association, Friends Council on Education, General Conference of the Seventh-Day Adventist Church, National Association of Episcopal Schools, National Christian School Association, National Society for Hebrew Day Schools, Solomon Schechter Day Schools, Southern Baptist Association of Christian Schools or indicating membership in "other religious school associations." Unaffiliated schools are those that have a religious orientation or purpose, but are not classied as Conservative Christian or afliated.
[b]Nonsectarian schools do not have a religious orientation or purpose.
Note: Detail may not sum to totals because of rounding.

SOURCE: John Wirt, Susan Choy, Patrick Rooney, William Hussar, Stephen Provasnik, and Gillian Hampden-Thompson, "Private School Enrollment: Percentage Distribution of Private School Students in Kindergarten through Grade 12, by Type of School: 1989–90 and 2001–02," in *The Condition of Education, 2005*, NCES 2005-094, U.S. Department of Education, National Center for Education Statistics, Washington, DC, June 2005, http://nces .ed.gov/pubs2005/2005094.pdf (accessed July 26, 2005)

TABLE 2.10

Public and private elementary and secondary teachers, enrollment, and pupil to teacher ratios, selected years, Fall 1955–Fall 2002

Year	Elementary and secondary teachers, in thousands			Elementary and secondary enrollment, in thousands			Elementary and secondary pupil/teacher ratio		
	Total	Public	Private	Total	Public	Private	Total	Public	Private
1	2	3	4	5	6	7	8	9	10
1955	1,286	1,141	145[a]	35,280	30,680	4,600[a]	27.4	26.9	31.7[a]
1960	1,600	1,408	192[a]	42,181	36,281	5,900[a]	26.4	25.8	30.7[a]
1965	1,933	1,710	223	48,473	42,173	6,300	25.1	24.7	28.3
1970	2,292	2,059	233	51,257	45,894	5,363	22.4	22.3	23.0
1971	2,293	2,063	230[a]	51,271	46,071	5,200[a]	22.4	22.3	22.6[a]
1972	2,337	2,106	231[a]	50,726	45,726	5,000[a]	21.7	21.7	21.6[a]
1973	2,372	2,136	236[a]	50,446	45,446	5,000[a]	21.3	21.3	21.2[a]
1974	2,410	2,165	245[a]	50,073	45,073	5,000[a]	20.8	20.8	20.4[a]
1975	2,453	2,198	255[a]	49,819	44,819	5,000[a]	20.3	20.4	19.6[a]
1976	2,457	2,189	268	49,478	44,311	5,167	20.1	20.2	19.3
1977	2,488	2,209	279	48,717	43,577	5,140	19.6	19.7	18.4
1978	2,479	2,207	272	47,635	42,550	5,085	19.2	19.3	18.7
1979	2,461	2,185	276[a]	46,651	41,651	5,000[a]	19.0	19.1	18.1[a]
1980	2,485	2,184	301	46,208	40,877	5,331	18.6	18.7	17.7
1981	2,440	2,127	313[a]	45,544	40,044	5,500[a]	18.7	18.8	17.6[a]
1982	2,458	2,133	325[a]	45,165	39,566	5,600[a]	18.4	18.6	17.2[a]
1983	2,476	2,139	337	44,967	39,252	5,715	18.2	18.4	17.0
1984	2,508	2,168	340[a]	44,908	39,208	5,700[a]	17.9	18.1	16.8[a]
1985	2,549	2,206	343	44,979	39,422	5,557	17.6	17.9	16.2
1986	2,592	2,244	348[a]	45,205	39,753	5,452[a]	17.4	17.7	15.7[a]
1987	2,631	2,279	352	45,487	40,008	5,479	17.3	17.6	15.6
1988	2,668	2,323	345[a]	45,430	40,189	5,242[a]	17.0	17.3	15.2[a]
1989	2,734	2,357	377	45,741	40,543	5,198	16.7	17.2	13.8
1990	2,753	2,398	355[a]	46,451	41,217	5,234[a]	16.9	17.2	14.7[a]
1991	2,787	2,432	355	47,322	42,047	5,275	17.0	17.3	14.9
1992	2,822	2,459	363[a]	48,145	42,823	5,322[a]	17.1	17.4	14.7[a]
1993	2,870	2,504	366	48,813	43,465	5,348	17.0	17.4	14.6
1994	2,926	2,552	374[a]	49,609	44,111	5,498[a]	17.0	17.3	14.7[a]
1995	2,978	2,598	380	50,502	44,840	5,662	17.0	17.3	14.9
1996	3,054	2,667	387[a]	51,375	45,611	5,764[a]	16.8	17.1	14.9[a]
1997	3,134	2,746	388	51,968	46,127	5,841	16.6	16.8	15.1
1998	3,221	2,830	391[a]	52,476	46,539	5,937[a]	16.3	16.4	15.2[a]
1999	3,306	2,911	395	52,875	46,857	6,018	16.0	16.1	15.2
2000	3,332	2,941	390[a]	53,366	47,204	6,162[a]	16.0	16.0	15.8[a]
2001	3,388	2,998	390	53,890	47,688	6,202[a]	15.9	15.9	15.9[a]
2002[b]	3,369	2,983	385	54,158	47,918	6,241	16.1	16.1	16.2

[a]Estimated.
[b]Projected.
Note: Data for teachers are expressed in full-time equivalents. Data for private schools includes kindergarten and a relatively small number of nursery school teachers and students. Ratios for public schools reflect totals reported by states and differ from totals reported for schools by states or school districts. Some data have been revised from previously published figures. Detail may not sum to totals due to rounding.

SOURCE: Thomas D. Snyder, Alexandra G. Tan, and Charlene M. Hoffman, "Table 64. Public and Private Elementary and Secondary Teachers, Enrollment, and Pupil to Teacher Ratios: Selected Years, Fall 1955 to Fall 2002," in *Digest of Education Statistics, 2003*, NCES 2005-025, U.S. Department of Education, National Center for Education Statistics, Washington, DC, December 2004, http://nces.ed.gov/programs/digest/d03/tables/dt064.asp (accessed July 26, 2005)

TABLE 2.11

Current expenditures per pupil for public elementary and secondary schools, by function, state, and outlying areas, 2002–03

[In dollars]

State	Fall 2002 student membership	Current expenditures per pupil in membership			
		Total	Instruction	Support services	Noninstruction
United States	48,201,032[a]	8,041[a,b]	4,932[a,b]	2,780[a]	329[a]
Alabama	739,366[a]	6,300[a]	3,812[a]	2,058[a]	430[a]
Alaska	134,364	9,870	5,740	3,798	332
Arizona	937,755	6,282	3,765	2,221	296
Arkansas	450,985	6,482	3,961	2,196	325
California	6,353,667[a]	7,552[a]	4,591[a]	2,678[a]	283[a]
Colorado	751,862	7,384	4,230	2,900	254
Connecticut	570,023	11,057	7,052	3,612	394
Delaware	116,342	9,693	5,965	3,276	452
District of Columbia	76,166	11,847	6,216	5,331	300
Florida	2,539,929	6,439	3,786	2,338	315
Georgia	1,496,012	7,774	4,925	2,459	391
Hawaii	183,829	8,100	4,833	2,839	428
Idaho	248,604	6,081	3,721	2,098	262
Illinois	2,084,187	8,287	4,952	3,068	268
Indiana	1,003,875	8,057	4,932	2,797	329
Iowa	482,210	7,574	4,508	2,511	554
Kansas	470,957	7,454	4,413	2,697	345
Kentucky	660,782	6,661	4,066	2,233	362
Louisiana	730,464	6,922	4,203	2,291	428
Maine	204,337	9,344	6,269	2,774	300
Maryland	866,743	9,153	5,693	3,042	418
Massachusetts	982,989	10,460	6,656	3,486	318
Michigan	1,785,160	8,781	5,002	3,509	269
Minnesota	846,891	8,109	5,201	2,536	372
Mississippi	492,645	5,792	3,466	1,966	360
Missouri	924,445	7,349[b]	4,481[b]	2,551	317
Montana	149,995	7,496	4,606	2,583	307
Nebraska	285,402	8,074	5,151	2,360	563
Nevada	369,498	6,092	3,812	2,080	200
New Hampshire	207,671	8,579	5,569	2,746	264
New Jersey	1,367,438	12,568	7,424	4,757	387
New Mexico	320,234	7,125	3,953	2,842	329
New York	2,888,233	11,961	8,213	3,459	290
North Carolina	1,335,954	6,562	4,173	2,023	366
North Dakota	104,225	6,870	4,102	2,230	538
Ohio	1,838,285	8,632	4,956	3,390	286
Oklahoma	624,548	6,092	3,528	2,160	404
Oregon	554,071	7,491	4,438	2,798	255
Pennsylvania	1,816,747	8,997	5,557	3,088	352
Rhode Island	159205[a]	10,349	6,685	3,396	267
South Carolina	694,389	7,040	4,199	2,464	376
South Dakota	130,048	6,547	3,836	2,361	349
Tennessee	927,608[a]	6,118[a,b]	3,933[a,b]	1,885[a]	300[a]
Texas	4,259,823	7,136	4,307	2,469	360
Utah	489,262	4,838	3,103	1,461	273
Vermont	99,978	10,454	6,713	3,458	283
Virginia	1,177,229	7,822	4,809	2,705	308
Washington	1,014,798	7,252[b]	4,317[b]	2,582	353
West Virginia	282,455	8,319	5,115	2,742	463
Wisconsin	881,231	9,004	5,566	3,149	289
Wyoming	88,116	8,985	5,381	3,317	287

TABLE 2.11

Current expenditures per pupil for public elementary and secondary schools, by function, state,and outlying areas, 2002–03 [CONTINUED]

[In dollars]

State	Fall 2002 student membership	Current expenditures per pupil in membership			
		Total	Instruction	Support services	Noninstruction
Outlying areas					
American Samoa	15,984	2,976	1,543	893	540
Guam	—	—	—	—	—
Northern Marianas	11,251	4,519	3,871	437	211
Puerto Rico	596,502	4,260	3,145	606	509
Virgin Islands	18,333	6,840	4,459	2,168	213

— Not available.
Note: Detail may not sum to totals because of rounding. National totals do not include outlying areas. Both the District of Columbia and Hawaii have only one school district each; therefore, neither is comparable to other states.
[a]Prekindergarten students were imputed, affecting total student count and per pupil expenditure calculation. In Tennessee, prekindergarten students were imputed and tuition expenditures (included in instruction) were redistributed.
[b]Value affected by redistribution of reported expenditure values to correct for missing data items.

SOURCE: Jason Hill and Frank Johnson, "Table 5. Student Membership and Current Expenditures Per Pupil in Membership for Public Elementary and Secondary Schools, by Function, State, and Outlying Areas: School Year 2002–03," in *Revenues and Expenditures for Public Elementary and Secondary Education: School Year 2002–03*, NCES 2005-353, U.S. Department of Education, National Center for Education Statistics, Washington, DC, April 2005, http://nces.ed.gov/ccd/pubs/npefs03/table_5.asp?popup=1 (accessed July 26, 2005)

FIGURE 2.8

FIGURE 2.9

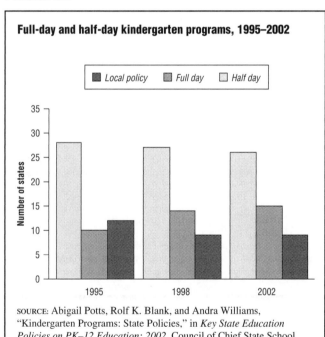

Full-day and half-day kindergarten programs, 1995–2002

SOURCE: Abigail Potts, Rolf K. Blank, and Andra Williams, "Kindergarten Programs: State Policies," in *Key State Education Policies on PK–12 Education: 2002*, Council of Chief State School Officers, Washington, DC, 2002. Reproduced with permission.

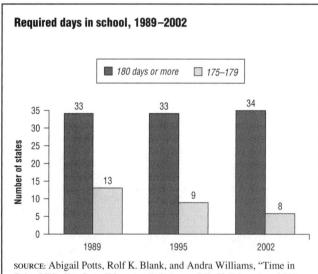

Required days in school, 1989–2002

SOURCE: Abigail Potts, Rolf K. Blank, and Andra Williams, "Time in School," in *Key State Education Policies on PK–12 Education: 2002*, Council of Chief State School Officers, Washington, DC, 2002. Reproduced with permission.

TABLE 2.12

Number and percentage distribution of prekindergarten children in public elementary schools, by selected student and school characteristics, 2000–01

School characteristic	Number of children in pre-kindergarten	Age			Race/ethnicity[a]					Student characteristic		
		3 or younger	4	5 or older	American Indian	Asian	Black	White	Hispanic	LEP[b]	Low income[c]	IEP[d]
Total	822,000	23.0	68.3	8.7	1.9	2.7	22.6	48.6	24.0	15.1	61.1	29.7
Enrollment												
Less than 300	193,000	28.7	61.4	9.9	2.6	2.6	17.7	60.8	16.2	9.7	54.4	32.7
300–499	233,000	21.0	69.1	9.9	2.0	2.4	21.9	56.2	17.4	11.4	58.2	27.9
500–699	211,000	22.6	69.6	7.8	1.3	2.8	28.9	44.8	22.1	13.4	62.3	31.3
700 or more	184,000	20.0	73.1	7.0	1.6	3.1	21.7	30.6	43.0	27.4	70.1	27.1
Location												
Central city	310,000	23.8	68.4	7.8	1.0	3.6	33.1	27.6	34.6	21.6	72.3	26.2
Urban fringe/large town	279,000	24.3	67.9	7.8	1.2	3.3	20.1	51.1	24.2	15.6	54.6	31.7
Rural/small town	233,000	20.3	68.8	10.8	3.9	0.8	11.7	73.7	9.9	5.7	53.2	32.1
Region												
Northeast	137,000	24.9	70.0	5.1	0.8*	4.7	22.4	52.6	19.5	8.7	46.8	28.1
Southeast	191,000	19.4	72.8	7.8	1.7	1.7	38.0	49.3	9.2	6.5	70.7	33.5
Central	230,000	27.0	59.6	13.3	0.9	2.0	20.5	63.4	13.0	8.5	50.7	31.1
West	264,000	21.1	71.8	7.1	3.4	3.0	13.4	33.3	46.8	30.3	69.8	26.6
Percent minority												
Less than 10	181,000	24.8	63.2	11.9	1.7	0.9	1.9	92.6	2.9	0.9	34.5	37.0
10–24	109,000	30.2	60.5	9.2	1.6	2.9	9.8	77.8	7.8	4.1	47.3	39.0
25–49	150,000	19.4	72.8	7.8	2.4	4.0	18.8	56.5	17.9	13.1	54.0	29.4
50–75	106,000	24.9	65.7	9.4	3.1	5.8	29.9	34.9	26.3	12.3	70.3	29.2
75 or more	267,000	20.1	73.8	6.1	1.4	1.8	41.5	7.6	47.7	31.2	82.4	20.6
Percent of students eligible for free or reduced-price lunch												
Less than 15	87,000	29.6	59.0	11.5	1.4	6.0	4.2	80.7	7.7	6.6	11.1	39.5
15–29	75,000	24.8	62.5	12.7	1.3	2.5	9.4	76.8	9.8	4.8	27.4	45.6
30–49	129,000	22.8	65.8	11.3	1.7	2.8	13.6	68.3	13.2	8.7	37.6	34.8
50–74	207,000	21.3	71.8	6.8	2.6	3.3	20.2	54.0	19.9	11.2	62.9	30.3
75 or more	318,000	21.5	71.7	6.8	1.7	1.6	36.3	21.7	38.7	24.9	86.7	19.6
Percent of students limited English proficient												
Less than 1	409,000	23.4	66.2	10.3	2.4	1.3	25.2	62.1	8.9	#	55.3	33.9
1–10	141,000	25.3	65.4	9.3	1.6	3.0	26.8	55.9	12.1	4.2	53.1	30.0
More than 10	263,000	20.7	73.7	5.6	1.3	4.6	17.0	22.5	54.6	44.4	74.1	23.3

\# Rounds to zero.

*Interpret data with caution (estimates are unstable).

[a]American Indian includes Alaska Native, Asian includes Pacific Islander and Native Hawaiian, black includes African American, and Hispanic includes Latino. Racial categories exclude Hispanic origin.

[b]LEP refers to limited English proficient students, or "English language learners."

[c]Low income is defined as eligible for free or reduced-price lunch.

[d]IEP refers to students with Individualized Education Programs and includes children in special education and general education classes.

Note: Detail may not sum to totals because of rounding. Data on some of the variables in this table are missing for some cases.

SOURCE: John Wirt, Susan Choy, Stephen Provasnik, Patrick Rooney, Anindita Sen, and Richard Tobin, "Table 2–2. Number and Percentage Distribution of Prekindergarten Children in Public Elementary Schools, by Age, Race/Ethnicity, and Selected Student and School Characteristics: 2000–01," in *The Condition of Education, 2004*, NCES 2004-077, U.S. Department of Education, National Center for Education Statistics, Washington, DC, June 2004, http://nces.ed.gov/programs/coe/2004/section1/table.asp?tableID=33 (accessed July 26, 2005)

TABLE 2.13

High school graduates compared with population age 17, selected years, 1869–70 to 2002–03

[Numbers in thousands]

School year	Population 17 years old[a]	Total[b]	Male	Female	Public[c]	Private[d]	Graduates as a ratio of 17-year-old population
			High school graduates				
			Sex		Control		
1	2	3	4	5	6	7	8
1869–70	815	16	7	9	—	—	2.0
1879–80	946	24	11	13	—	—	2.5
1889–90	1,259	44	19	25	22	22	3.5
1899–1900	1,489	95	38	57	62	33	6.4
1909–10	1,786	156	64	93	111	45	8.8
1919–20	1,855	311	124	188	231	80	16.8
1929–30	2,296	667	300	367	592	75	29.0
1939–40	2,403	1,221	579	643	1,143	78	50.8
1947–48	2,261	1,190	563	627	1,073	117	52.6
1949–50	2,034	1,200	571	629	1,063	136	59.0
1951–52	2,086	1,197	569	627	1,056	141	57.4
1953–54	2,135	1,276	613	664	1,129	147	59.8
1955–56	2,242	1,415	680	735	1,252	163	63.1
1956–57	2,272	1,434	690	744	1,270	164	63.1
1957–58	2,325	1,506	725	781	1,332	174	64.8
1958–59	2,458	1,627	784	843	1,435	192	66.2
1959–60	2,672	1,858	895	963	1,627	231	69.5
1960–61	2,892	1,964	955	1,009	1,725	239	67.9
1961–62	2,768	1,918	938	980	1,678	240	69.3
1962–63	2,740	1,943	956	987	1,710	233	70.9
1963–64	2,978	2,283	1,120	1,163	2,008	275	76.7
1964–65	3,684	2,658	1,311	1,347	2,360	298	72.1
1965–66	3,489	2,665	1,323	1,342	2,367	298	76.4
1966–67	3,500	2,672	1,328	1,344	2,374	298	76.3
1967–68	3,532	2,695	1,338	1,357	2,395	300	76.3
1968–69	3,659	2,822	1,399	1,423	2,522	300	77.1
1969–70	3,757	2,889	1,430	1,459	2,589	300	76.9
1970–71	3,872	2,938	1,454	1,484	2,638	300	75.9
1971–72	3,973	3,002	1,487	1,515	2,700	302	75.6
1972–73	4,049	3,035	1,500	1,535	2,729	306	75.0
1973–74	4,132	3,073	1,512	1,561	2,763	310	74.4
1974–75	4,256	3,133	1,542	1,591	2,823	310	73.6
1975–76	4,272	3,148	1,552	1,596	2,837	311	73.7
1976–77	4,272	3,152	1,548	1,604	2,837	315	73.8
1977–78	4,286	3,127	1,531	1,596	2,825	302	73.0
1978–79	4,327	3,101	1,517	1,584	2,801	300	71.7
1979–80	4,262	3,043	1,491	1,552	2,748	295	71.4
1980–81	4,212	3,020	1,483	1,537	2,725	295	71.7
1981–82	4,134	2,995	1,471	1,524	2,705	290	72.4
1982–83	3,962	2,888	1,437	1,451	2,598	290	72.9
1983–84	3,784	2,767	—	—	2,495	272	73.1
1984–85	3,699	2,677	—	—	2,414	263	72.4
1985–86	3,670	2,643	—	—	2,383	260	72.0
1986–87	3,754	2,694	—	—	2,429	265	71.8
1987–88	3,849	2,773	—	—	2,500	273	72.0
1988–89	3,842	2,744	—	—	2,459	285	71.4
1989–90	3,505	2,589	—	—	2,320	269	73.9
1990–91	3,418	2,493	—	—	2,235	258	72.9
1991–92	3,399	2,478	—	—	2,226	252	72.9
1992–93	3,449	2,480	—	—	2,233	247	71.9
1993–94	3,443	2,464	—	—	2,221	243	71.6
1994–95	3,636	2,520	—	—	2,274	246	69.3
1995–96	3,640	2,518	—	—	2,273	245	69.2
1996–97	3,792	2,612	—	—	2,358	254	68.9
1997–98	4,008	2,704	—	—	2,439	265	67.5
1998–99	3,918	2,759	—	—	2,486	273	70.4

TABLE 2.13

High school graduates compared with population age 17, selected years, 1869–70 to 2002–03 [CONTINUED]

[Numbers in thousands]

School year	Population 17 years old[a]	High school graduates					Graduates as a ratio of 17-year-old population
		Total[b]	Sex		Control		
			Male	Female	Public[c]	Private[d]	
1	2	3	4	5	6	7	8
1999–2000	4,057	2,831	—	—	2,554	277	69.8
2000–01	4,006	2,852	—	—	2,569	283	71.2
2001–02[e]	4,052	2,917	—	—	2,630	287	72.0
2002–03[e]	—	2,986	—	—	2,685	301	—

— Not available.

[a]For years 1869–70 through 1989–90, 17-year-old population is an estimate of the October 17-year-old population based on July data. Data for 1990–91 and later years are October estimates prepared by the Census Bureau.

[b]Includes graduates of public and private schools.

[c]Data for 1929–30 and preceding years are from statistics of public high schools and exclude graduates from high schools that failed to report to the Office of Education.

[d]For most years, private school data have been estimated based on periodic private school surveys.

[e]Public high school graduates based on state estimates.

Note: Includes graduates of regular day school programs. Excludes graduates of other programs, when separately reported, and recipients of high school equivalency certificates. Some data have been revised from previously published figures. Detail may not sum to totals due to rounding.

SOURCE: Thomas D. Snyder, Alexandra G. Tan, and Charlene M. Hoffman, "Table 102. High School Graduates Compared with Population 17 Years of Age, by Sex of Graduates and Control of School: Selected Years, 1869–70 to 2002–03," in *Digest of Education Statistics, 2003*, NCES 2005-025, U.S. Department of Education, National Center for Education Statistics, Washington, DC, December 2004, http://nces.ed.gov/programs/digest/d03/tables/dt102.asp (accessed July 26, 2005)

TABLE 2.14

GED test takers and credentials issued, by age, 1971–2001

Year	Number of test takers, in thousands[a]	Number completing test battery, in thousands[b]	Number of credentials issued, in thousands[c]	Percentage distribution of credentials issued,[d] by age				
				19 years old or less	20- to 24-year-olds	25- to 29-year-olds	30- to 34-year-olds	35 years old or over
1	2	3	4	5	6	7	8	9
1971[e]	377	—	227	—	—	—	—	—
1972[e]	419	—	245	—	—	—	—	—
1973[e]	423	—	249	—	—	—	—	—
1974	—	—	294	35	27	13	9	17
1975	—	—	340	33	26	14	9	18
1976	—	—	333	31	28	14	10	17
1977	—	—	332	40	24	13	8	14
1978	—	—	381	31	27	13	10	18
1979	—	—	426	37	28	12	13	11
1980	—	—	479	37	27	13	8	15
1981	—	—	489	37	27	13	8	14
1982	—	—	486	37	28	13	8	15
1983	—	—	465	34	29	14	8	15
1984	—	—	427	32	28	15	9	16
1985	—	—	413	32	26	15	10	16
1986	—	—	428	32	26	15	10	17
1987	—	—	444	33	24	15	10	18
1988	—	—	410	35	22	14	10	18
1989	632	541	357	35	24	13	—	—
1990	714	615	410	36	25	13	10	15
1991	755	657	462	33	28	13	10	16
1992	739	639	457	33	28	13	9	17
1993	746	651	469	33	27	13	10	16
1994	774	668	491	36	25	13	9	15
1995	787	682	504	38	25	13	9	15
1996	824	716	488	39	25	13	9	14
1997	785	681	460	43	24	12	8	13
1998	776	673	481	44	24	11	7	13
1999	808	702	498	44	25	11	7	13
2000	811	699	487	45	25	11	7	13
2001	1,016	928	648	41	26	11	8	14

— Not available.

[a]Number of people taking the GED tests (one or more subtests).

[b]Number of people completing the entire GED battery of five tests.

[c]Number of people receiving high school equivalency credentials based on the GED tests.

[d]Data for 1988 and prior years are for number of test takers and may not be comparable to later years.

[e]Includes outlying areas.

Note: Except where indicated, data are for United States only and exclude outlying areas. Detail may not sum to totals due to rounding. Some data have been revised from previously published figures.

SOURCE: Thomas D. Snyder, Alexandra G. Tan, and Charlene M. Hoffman, "Table 105. General Educational Development (GED) Test Takers and Credentials Issued, by Age: 1971 to 2001," in *Digest of Education Statistics, 2003*, NCES 2005-025, U.S. Department of Education, National Center for Education Statistics, Washington, DC, December 2004, http://nces.ed.gov/programs/digest/d03/tables/dt105.asp (accessed July 26, 2005)

CHAPTER 3
EDUCATION FOR SPECIAL SCHOOL POPULATIONS

The right to public education is guaranteed to all children in the United States. For many children, however, acquiring an education that fits their special needs is not always easy. For the mentally or physically disabled, gifted or talented, or significantly disadvantaged, preparation for adulthood requires extra effort on the part of both the children and the education system.

DISABLED CHILDREN

In 1975 Congress passed the Education for All Handicapped Children Act (P.L. 94-142, amended in 1983 by P.L. 98-199), which required schools to develop programs for disabled children. In 1992 the Act was renamed the Individuals with Disabilities Education Act (IDEA). It defines disabled children as those who are:

> mentally retarded, hard of hearing, deaf, orthopedically impaired, other health impaired, speech and language impaired, visually impaired, seriously emotionally disturbed, children with specific learning disabilities who, by reason thereof, require special education and related services (20 U.S.C. 1401 [a][1]).

In its 1993 report *To Assure the Free Appropriate Public Education of All Children with Disabilities*, the U.S. Department of Education Office of Special Education Programs (OSEP) stated the purposes of IDEA:

- To help states develop early intervention services for infants and toddlers with disabilities and their families.

- To assure a free appropriate public education to all children and youth with disabilities.

- To protect the rights of disabled children and youth from birth to age twenty-one and their families.

- To help provide early intervention services and the education of all children with disabilities.

- To assess and assure the effectiveness of efforts to provide early intervention services and education of children with disabilities.

Change in the Number Served

As a result of IDEA, an increasing number of students have been served in programs for the disabled. According to the U.S. Department of Education, during 2001–02, about 6.4 million disabled children and youth ages three through twenty-one were served. Between 1976–77 and 2001–02 the number of students participating in these programs rose by more than 2.7 million, a 73% increase. Between 1991–92 and 2001–02, the largest change was in the number of students with autism or traumatic brain injury from 5,000 to 118,000, a 2,360% increase. (See Table 3.1.)

Prior to the 1991–92 school year, students with autism or traumatic brain injury were distributed among several categories, but primarily "other health impairments." Even with the removal of students with autism or traumatic brain injury, the category "other health impairments," which includes students who have attention deficit/hyperactivity disorder (ADHD), increased by 481% between 1991–92 and 2001–02, from 58,000 to 337,000. The number of deaf-blind students decreased from 3,000 in 1980–81 to 2,000 in 2001–02, a 33% reduction. The proportion of children and youth with disabilities, as a percentage of public school enrollment, has risen steadily from 8.3% in 1976–77 to 13.4% in 2001–02. (See Table 3.1.) Some of this increase may reflect more effective identification of people with disabilities.

The majority of students with disabilities who were served in federally supported programs in 2001–02 were those identified as having specific learning disabilities (44.4%), speech or language impairments (16.9%), mental retardation (9.2%), emotional disturbance (7.4%), or

TABLE 3.1

Students ages 3–21 served in federally supported programs for the disabled, by type of disability, selected years, 1976–77 to 2001–02

Type of disability	1976–77	1980–81	1989–90	1990–91	1991–92	1992–93	1993–94	1994–95	1995–96	1996–97	1997–98	1998–99	1999–2000	2000–01	2001–02
1	2	3	4	5	6	7	8	9	10	11	12	13	14	15	16
						Number served in thousands									
All disabilities	3,694	4,144	4,594	4,710	4,875	5,036	5,216	5,378	5,573	5,730	5,903	6,055	6,190	6,296	6,407
Specific learning disabilities	796	1,462	2,047	2,129	2,232	2,351	2,408	2,489	2,579	2,649	2,725	2,789	2,830	2,843	2,846
Speech or language impairments	1,302	1,168	971	985	996	994	1,014	1,015	1,022	1,043	1,056	1,068	1,078	1,084	1,084
Mental retardation	961	830	547	535	537	518	536	555	570	579	589	597	600	599	592
Emotional disturbance	283	347	380	390	399	400	414	427	438	445	453	462	468	473	476
Hearing impairments	88	79	57	58	60	60	64	64	67	68	69	70	70	70	70
Orthopedic impairments	87	58	48	49	51	52	56	60	63	66	67	69	71	72	73
Other health impairments	141	98	52	55	58	65	82	106	133	160	190	221	254	292	337
Visual impairments	38	31	22	23	24	23	24	24	25	25	25	26	26	25	25
Multiple disabilities	—	68	86	96	97	102	108	88	93	98	106	106	111	121	127
Deaf-blindness	—	3	2	1	1	1	1	1	1	1	1	2	2	1	2
Autism and traumatic brain injury	—	—	—	—	5	19	24	29	39	44	54	67	80	94	118
Developmental delay	—	—	—	—	—	—	—	—	—	—	4	12	19	28	45
Preschool disabled[a]	—	—	381	390	416	450	486	519	544	552	564	568	582	592	612
						Percentage distribution of children served									
All disabilities	100.0	100.0	100.0	100.0	100.0	100.0	100.0	100.0	100.0	100.0	100.0	100.0	100.0	100.0	100.0
Specific learning disabilities	21.5	35.3	44.6	45.2	45.8	46.7	46.2	46.3	46.3	46.2	46.2	46.1	45.7	45.2	44.4
Speech or language impairments	35.2	28.2	21.1	20.9	20.4	19.7	19.4	18.9	18.3	18.2	17.9	17.6	17.4	17.2	16.9
Mental retardation	26.0	20.0	11.9	11.4	11.0	10.3	10.3	10.3	10.2	10.1	10.0	9.9	9.7	9.5	9.2
Emotional disturbance	7.7	8.4	8.3	8.3	8.2	7.9	7.9	7.9	7.9	7.8	7.7	7.6	7.6	7.5	7.4
Hearing impairments	2.4	1.9	1.2	1.2	1.2	1.2	1.2	1.2	1.1	1.2	1.1	1.1	1.1	1.1	1.1
Orthopedic impairments	2.4	1.4	1.0	1.0	1.0	1.0	1.1	1.1	1.1	1.2	1.1	1.1	1.1	1.1	1.1
Other health impairments	3.8	2.4	1.1	1.2	1.2	1.3	1.6	2.0	2.4	2.8	3.2	3.6	4.1	4.6	5.3
Visual impairments	1.0	0.7	0.5	0.5	0.5	0.5	0.5	0.4	0.4	0.4	0.4	0.4	0.4	0.4	0.4
Multiple disabilities	—	1.6	1.9	2.0	2.0	2.0	2.1	1.6	1.7	1.7	1.8	1.8	1.8	1.9	2.0
Deaf-blindness	—	0.1	*	*	*	*	*	*	*	*	*	*	*	*	*
Autism and traumatic brain injury	—	—	—	—	0.1	0.4	0.5	0.5	0.7	0.8	0.9	1.1	1.3	1.5	1.8
Developmental delay	—	—	—	—	—	—	—	—	—	—	0.1	0.2	0.3	0.4	0.7
Preschool disabled[a]	—	—	8.3	8.3	8.5	8.9	9.3	9.7	9.8	9.6	9.6	9.4	9.4	9.4	9.6

TABLE 3.1

Students ages 3–21 served in federally supported programs for the disabled, by type of disability, selected years, 1976–77 to 2001–02 [CONTINUED]

Type of disability	1976–77	1980–81	1989–90	1990–91	1991–92	1992–93	1993–94	1994–95	1995–96	1996–97	1997–98	1998–99	1999–2000	2000–01	2001–02
1	2	3	4	5	6	7	8	9	10	11	12	13	14	15	16
						Number served as a percent of total enrollment[b]									
All disabilities	8.3	10.1	11.3	11.4	11.6	11.8	12.0	12.2	12.4	12.6	12.8	13.0	13.2	13.3	13.4
Specific learning disabilities	1.8	3.6	5.0	5.2	5.3	5.5	5.5	5.6	5.8	5.8	5.9	6.0	6.0	6.0	6.0
Speech or language impairments	2.9	2.9	2.4	2.4	2.4	2.3	2.3	2.3	2.3	2.3	2.3	2.3	2.3	2.3	2.3
Mental retardation	2.2	2.0	1.3	1.3	1.3	1.2	1.2	1.3	1.3	1.3	1.3	1.3	1.3	1.3	1.2
Emotional disturbance	0.6	0.8	0.9	0.9	0.9	0.9	1.0	1.0	1.0	1.0	1.0	1.0	1.0	1.0	1.0
Hearing impairments	0.2	0.2	0.1	0.1	0.1	0.1	0.1	0.1	0.1	0.1	0.1	0.2	0.1	0.2	0.1
Orthopedic impairments	0.2	0.1	0.1	0.1	0.1	0.1	0.1	0.1	0.1	0.1	0.1	0.1	0.2	0.2	0.2
Other health impairments	0.3	0.2	0.1	0.1	0.1	0.2	0.2	0.2	0.3	0.4	0.4	0.5	0.5	0.6	0.7
Visual impairments	0.1	0.1	0.1	0.1	0.1	0.1	0.1	0.1	0.1	0.1	0.1	0.1	0.1	0.1	0.1
Multiple disabilities	—	0.2	0.2	0.2	0.2	0.2	0.2	0.2	0.2	0.2	0.2	0.2	0.2	0.3	0.3
Deaf-blindness	—	*	*	*	*	*	*	*	*	*	*	*	*	*	*
Autism and traumatic brain injury	—	—	—	—	*	*	0.1	0.1	0.1	0.1	0.1	0.1	0.2	0.2	0.2
Developmental delay	—	—	—	—	—	—	—	—	—	—	#	#	#	0.1	0.1
Preschool disabled[a]	—	—	0.9	0.9	1.0	1.1	1.1	1.2	1.2	1.2	1.2	1.2	1.2	1.3	1.3

— Not available.

*Rounds to zero.

[a]Includes preschool children 3–5 years served under Chapter I and IDEA, Part B. Prior to 1987–88, these students were included in the counts by disability condition. Beginning in 1987–88, states were no longer required to report preschool children (0–5 years) by disability condition.

[b]Based on the total enrollment in public schools, kindergarten through 12th grade, including a relatively small number of prekindergarten students.

Note: Includes students served under Chapter I and Individuals with Disabilities Education Act (IDEA), formerly the Education of the Handicapped Act. Prior to October 1994, children and youth with disabilities were served under the Individuals with Disabilities Education Act, Part B, and Chapter 1 of the Elementary and Secondary Education Act. In October 1994, Congress passed the Improving America's Schools Act in which funding for children and youth with disabilities was consolidated under IDEA, Part B. Data reported in this table for years prior to 1993–94 include children ages 0–21 served under Chapter 1. Counts are based on reports from the 50 states and the District of Columbia only (i.e., figures from outlying areas are not included). Increases since 1987–88 are due in part to new legislation enacted in fall 1986, which mandates public school special education services for all disabled children ages 3 through 5, in addition to age groups previously mandated. Some data have been revised from previously published figures. Detail may not sum to totals due to rounding.

SOURCE: Thomas D. Snyder, Alexandra G. Tan, and Charlene M. Hoffman, "Table 52. Children 3 to 21 Years Old Served in Federally Supported Programs for the Disabled,by Type of Disability: Selected Years, 1976–77 to 2001–02," in Digest of Education Statistics, 2003, NCES 2005-025, U.S. Department of Education, National Center for Education Statistics, Washington, DC, December 2004, http://nces.ed.gov/programs/digest/d03/tables/dt052.asp (accessed July 26, 2005)

other health impairments (5.3%). Students with multiple disabilities, hearing impairments, orthopedic impairments, autism or traumatic brain injury, visual impairments, and deaf-blindness, each made up about 2% or less of students with disabilities. Disabled preschool children (those aged three to five) made up 9.6% of students with disabilities in 2001–02. (See Table 3.1.)

Learning Disabilities

The Education for All Handicapped Children Act defines a learning disability (LD) as "a disorder in one or more of the basic psychological processes involved in understanding or using language, spoken or written, which may manifest itself in an imperfect ability to listen, think, speak, read, write, or do mathematical calculations."

The law includes perceptual handicaps, brain injury, minimal brain dysfunction, dyslexia, and developmental aphasia (inability to use words) as learning disabilities. The LD category does not include learning problems that are primarily the result of visual, hearing, or motor handicaps; mental retardation; or environmental, cultural, or economic disadvantage. To be categorized as learning disabled, a student must also show a severe discrepancy between potential, as measured by Intelligence Quotient (IQ), and current ability level, as measured by achievement tests. A student who has problems in school and needs remedial education but does not fit into any other category may be labeled as having a learning disability.

According to the U.S. Department of Education, in 2001–02, 2.8 million students were classified with specific learning disabilities, 3.6 times the 796,000 students identified in 1976–77. In 1976–77, LD students made up fewer than one-quarter (21.5%) of all those with disabilities, compared to almost half (44.4%) in 2001–02. (See Table 3.1.) Better understanding and diagnosis of learning disabilities may explain part of the increase. The growth also may reflect the problem of fitting students into a category, as mentioned above.

Characteristics of Special Education Students

According to the *24th Annual Report to Congress on the Implementation of the Individuals with Disabilities Act* (U.S. Department of Education, Washington, DC, 2002), males are disproportionately represented among students in special education programs. More than two-thirds of all special education students are male. In 2000–01 males made up about 68% of all secondary school students with disabilities. Several theories have been proposed to explain the disproportion of males in various disability categories. Some evidence suggests that boys have a greater vulnerability than girls do to certain genetic maladies and are more prone to developmental lags because of physiological or maturational differences. Some researchers have reported a higher degree of reading disabilities in boys than in girls, although others failed to find similar problems among males in other countries. Still others have suggested gender bias in the diagnosis and classification of students with disabilities.

According to the U.S. Department of Education, 62.3% of the disabled population ages six through twenty-one in 2000–01 was white. White students made up a slightly smaller percentage of the special education population than their representation in the general population (62.9%). African-American students, who accounted for 14.8% of the general population, comprised 19.8% of the disabled population, while the proportion of Hispanic students in special education was 14.5%, less than their representation in the general population (17.5%). Of the remainder of the disabled population, 1.9% were Asian/Pacific Islander and 1.5% were Native American.

These racial and ethnic percentages varied slightly in 2003, according to the National Center for Education Statistics (NCES) in *Data Tables for OSEP State Reported Data*. The total number of students served under IDEA increased to 6.6 million in 2003. Of this number, more than four million (60.8%) were classified as non-Hispanic whites, and 1.3 million (20.1%) were African-Americans. Hispanic children, at approximately one million, made up another 15.6% of those served, along with 137,544 Asian/Pacific Islander students (2.1% of program participants) and 90,349 Native American/Alaska Natives (1.4%).

Serving Disabled Students

Public Law 94-142 states that an Individual Education Plan (IEP) must be developed for each child who receives special education services. It must include a statement of the student's current performance as well as long-term (annual) goals and short-term objectives. It must also describe the nature and duration of the instructional services designed to meet the goals. Finally, it must describe the methods of evaluation that will be used to monitor the child's progress and to determine whether the objectives are being met.

According to the U.S. Department of Education, in 2002–03 there were more than 6.4 million students in the United States who had an IEP. Rhode Island had the highest proportion, at 20.4%, and Colorado had the lowest, at 10.1%. (See Table 3.2.)

Inclusion Programs

An ongoing debate has developed over where and how disabled students should be taught. For years, many disabled children were taught at home or in special classrooms or schools. Now, however, many parents, educators, and specialists believe that including disabled

TABLE 3.2

Number and percentage of public school students participating in select programs, 2002–03

State	Number of students with IEPs	Percent of students with IEPs	Number of students receiving ELL services	Percent of students receiving ELL services	Number of students receiving migrant services during school year[a]	Number of students receiving migrant services during summer	Number of students eligible for free or reduced-price meals	Percent of all students eligible for free or reduced-price meals
Reporting states[b]	6,449,904	13.4	4,029,340	8.4	—	—	16,955,477	35.2
Alabama	94,343	12.9	10,568	1.4	7,825	2,630	364,226	50.1
Alaska	18,131	13.5	16,378	12.2	10,220	1,369	34,846	25.9
Arizona	101,648	10.6	143,744	14.9	2,094	8,635	c	c
Arkansas	57,185	12.7	15,146	3.4	8,813	1,558	218,277	48.4
California	673,935	10.8	1,599,542	25.6	230,478	151,112	3,002,890	48.1
Colorado	75,585	10.1	86,128	11.5	12,653	3,026	214,115	28.5
Connecticut	74,020	12.9	22,651	4.0	4,551	2,206	145,017	25.4
Delaware	16,723	14.4	3,449	3.0	291	170	41,319	35.5
District of Columbia	12,400	16.3	5,798	7.6	814	115	47,189	62.0
Florida	389,632	15.3	203,712	8.0	49,091	4,357	1,148,685	45.4
Georgia	177,608	11.9	70,464	4.7	9,539	3,671	674,800	45.1
Hawaii	22,814	12.4	12,853	7.0	1,520	271	80,630	43.9
Idaho	28,904	11.6	18,747	7.5	8,347	4,284	90,447	36.4
Illinois	305,970	14.7	168,727	8.1	—	2,441	741,954	35.6
Indiana	166,414	16.6	42,629	4.2	4,538	833	325,856	32.5
Iowa	73,123	15.2	13,961	2.9	12,526	3,444	137,404	28.5
Kansas	63,845	13.6	17,942	3.8	14,801	4,873	168,744	36.0
Kentucky	100,294	15.2	6,343	1.0	4,077	3,443	434,012	69.0
Louisiana	99,729	13.7	11,108	1.5		2,730	443,102	60.7
Maine	33,763	16.1	2,632	1.3	348	900	62,047	30.4
Maryland	106,299	12.3	27,311	3.2	2,203		265,989	30.7
Massachusetts	150,551	15.3	51,622	5.3	c	c	257,359	26.2
Michigan	238,273	13.3	c	c	987	3,326	553,124	31.0
Minnesota	111,960	13.2	51,275	6.1	2,405	950	231,450	27.3
Mississippi	63,738	12.9	2,250	0.5	4,616	485	321,712	65.3
Missouri	143,383	15.5	13,121	1.4			333,964	36.2
Montana	19,162	12.8	6,642	4.4	13,419	3,382	47,877	31.9
Nebraska	45,018	15.8	13,803	4.8	548	40	92,423	32.4
Nevada	42,504	11.5	58,753	15.9	155		125,660	34.1
New Hampshire	29,238	14.1	3,270	1.6	868	1,298	32,132	15.5
New Jersey	218,533	16.0	57,548	4.2	1,924	583	371,392	27.2
New Mexico	63,593	19.9	65,317	20.4	—		182,469	57.0
New York	420,274	14.4	178,909	6.1	15,132	9,021	c	c
North Carolina	190,146	14.2	59,849	4.5	291	438	452,486	33.9
North Dakota	13,653	13.1	883	0.8	c		29,270	28.1
Ohio	248,127	13.5	25,782	1.4		631	535,072	29.2
Oklahoma	91,184	14.6	40,192	6.4	20,394	5,105	320,600	51.3
Oregon	71,433	12.9	52,331	9.4	8,768	7,446	211,674	38.5
Pennsylvania	242,837	13.4					528,011	29.1
Rhode Island	32,500	20.4	10,087	6.3			53,084	33.4
South Carolina	109,423	15.8	7,467	1.1	518	1,022	343,810	49.6
South Dakota	17,241	13.5	4,524	3.5	2,265	245	38,800	30.3
Tennessee	142,566	15.8			—			
Texas	502,700	11.8	630,686	14.8	108,649	3,485	1,968,976	46.2
Utah	56,085	11.6	43,299	8.9	4,105	411	149,728	30.9
Vermont	13,765	13.8	1,057	1.1	858		25,501	25.5
Virginia	169,237	14.4	49,845	4.2	1,273	569	355,212	30.2

TABLE 3.2

Number and percentage of public school students participating in select programs, 2002–03 [CONTINUED]

State	Number of students with IEPs	Percent of students with IEPs	Number of students receiving ELL services	Percent of students receiving ELL services	Number of students receiving migrant services during school year[a]	Number of students receiving migrant services during summer	Number of students eligible for free or reduced-price meals	Percent of all students eligible for free or reduced-price meals
Department of Defense (DoD) dependents schools, Bureau of Indian Affairs, and outlying areas								
DoDDS: DoDs Overseas	6,056	8.3	6,140	8.4	—	—	—	—
DDESS: DoDs Domestic	3,212	10.0	1,892	5.9	—	—	—	—
Bureau of Indian Affairs	—	—	—	—	—	—	—	—
American Samoa	867	5.4	15,447	96.6	—	—	15,891	99.4
Guam	—	—	—	—	—	—	—	—
Northern Marianas	542	4.8	—	—	1,030	1,199	11,070	98.4
Puerto Rico	69,327	11.6	—	—	14,128	c	484,069	81.2
Virgin Islands	1,497	8.2	1,223	6.7	—	—	—	—

— Not available.

[a]Migrant students include those who were enrolled at any time during the previous (2001–02) regular school year. They are reported for each school in which they enrolled; because this is a duplicated count, the table does not show migrants as a percentage of all students.

[b]Reporting states total includes the 50 states and the District of Columbia. It is suppressed if data were missing for 15 percent or more of all school or agencies. State totals exclude states for which data were missing for 20 percent or more of the schools or agencies.

[c]Data were missing for more than 20 percent of schools or districts.

Note: IEP is the acronym for individualized education program. ELL is the acronym for English language learner. Some data items were more likely to be missing from charter schools than from other schools. Free lunch data were missing for 459 of 2,575 charter schools in the 50 states and District of Columbia and migrant student data were missing for 417. Data on ELL students were missing for 248 of the total 1,241 operational charter school districts in the 50 states and District of Columbia. Percentages are based on schools and agencies reporting. Detail may not sum to totals because of rounding.

SOURCE: Lee Hoffman, Jennifer Sable, Julia Naum, and Dell Gray, "Table 3. Number and Percentage of Public School Students Participating in Selected Programs: United States and Other Jurisdictions, School Year 2002–03," *Public Elementary and Secondary Students, Staff, Schools, and School Districts: School Year 2002–03*, NCES 2005-314, U.S. Department of Education, National Center for Education Statistics, Institute for Education Sciences, Washington, DC, February 2005, http://nces.ed.gov/pubs2005/2005314.pdf (accessed July 26, 2005)

TABLE 3.3

Disabled persons ages 6–21 receiving education services, by educational environment and type of disability, 1999–2001

[Percentage distribution]

Type of disability	All environments	Regular school, outside regular class			Separate public school facility	Separate private school facility	Public residential facility	Private residential facility	Homebound/ hospital placement
		Less than 21 percent	21–60 percent	More than 60 percent					
1	2	3	4	5	6	7	8	9	10
1999–2000									
All persons, 6 to 21 years old	100.0	47.3	28.3	20.3	1.9	1.0	0.4	0.3	0.5
Specific learning disabilities	100.0	45.3	37.9	15.8	0.4	0.3	0.1	0.1	0.2
Speech or language impairments	100.0	87.5	6.7	5.3	0.2	0.2	*	*	0.1
Mental retardation	100.0	14.1	29.5	50.5	4.1	0.9	0.4	0.2	0.4
Emotional disturbance	100.0	25.8	23.4	32.8	7.5	5.5	1.5	2.0	1.5
Hearing impairments	100.0	40.3	19.3	24.5	5.4	1.6	8.0	0.6	0.2
Orthopedic impairments	100.0	44.4	21.9	27.7	3.5	0.7	0.1	0.1	1.6
Other health impairments	100.0	44.9	33.2	17.2	0.9	0.7	0.1	0.2	2.7
Visual impairments	100.0	49.1	19.5	17.7	4.6	1.1	6.5	0.9	0.6
Multiple disabilities	100.0	11.2	18.8	43.0	15.0	6.8	1.3	1.4	2.5
Deaf-blindness	100.0	14.8	10.1	39.7	13.8	3.4	12.2	4.2	1.7
Autism	100.0	20.7	14.5	49.9	7.9	5.4	0.2	1.1	0.5
Traumatic brain injury	100.0	31.0	26.6	31.6	2.6	4.6	0.4	0.9	2.3
Developmental delay	100.0	44.7	29.7	24.2	0.8	0.2	*	*	0.3
2000–01									
All persons, 6 to 21 years old	100.0	46.5	29.8	19.5	1.9	1.1	0.4	0.3	0.5
Specific learning disabilities	100.0	44.3	40.3	14.4	0.3	0.3	0.1	0.1	0.2
Speech or language impairments	100.0	85.6	8.4	5.1	0.2	0.6	*	*	0.1
Mental retardation	100.0	13.2	29.1	51.7	4.2	0.9	0.3	0.2	0.4
Emotional disturbance	100.0	26.8	23.4	31.8	7.7	5.4	1.6	2.0	1.3
Hearing impairments	100.0	42.3	20.0	22.5	4.4	1.9	8.3	0.6	0.2
Orthopedic impairments	100.0	46.4	23.4	24.3	3.5	0.7	0.1	0.1	1.6
Other health impairments	100.0	45.1	33.9	16.7	0.8	0.8	0.2	0.2	2.4
Visual impairments	100.0	50.5	20.1	16.0	4.7	1.2	5.9	0.9	0.7
Multiple disabilities	100.0	12.1	16.0	45.5	14.6	6.9	1.3	1.3	2.3
Deaf-blindness	100.0	18.1	9.9	34.2	14.5	4.5	12.5	4.4	1.9
Autism	100.0	24.3	15.3	46.4	7.2	5.2	0.3	0.9	0.4
Traumatic brain injury	100.0	32.3	27.9	29.4	2.8	4.2	0.3	0.9	2.2
Developmental delay	100.0	46.4	29.9	22.3	0.6	0.4	*	0.1	0.2

*Rounds to zero.
Note: Data by disability condition are only reported for 6- to 21-year-old students. Detail may not sum to totals due to rounding.

SOURCE: Thomas D. Snyder, Alexandra G. Tan, and Charlene M. Hoffman, "Table 53. Percentage Distribution of Disabled Persons 6 to 21 Years Old Receiving Education Services for the Disabled, by Educational Environment and Type of Disability: United States and Outlying Areas, 1999–2000," in *Digest of Education Statistics, 2003*, NCES 2005-025, U.S. Department of Education, National Center for Education Statistics, Washington, DC, December 2004, http://nces.ed.gov/programs/digest/d03/tables/dt053.asp (accessed July 26, 2005)

students in regular classrooms benefits both disabled and nondisabled students.

In this inclusion model of instruction, the special education student spends part of the day in the regular classroom. The student spends the rest of the day in a resource room with a special education teacher, where the student receives help in subjects such as reading or mathematics. According to the U.S. Department of Education, during the 2000–01 school year, 96% of disabled students ages six through twenty-one received most of their educational and related services in school settings with nondisabled students. Spending most of the time in the regular classroom and less than 21% of the time outside of the regular classroom was the most common instructional environment (46.5%). An additional 29.8% of students received special education and related

services by spending between 21% and 60% of the school day outside of regular classes. Another 19.5% were served most of the time in separate classrooms within a regular education building, spending more than 60% of the day outside of the regular classroom. Almost nine out of every ten speech or language impaired children (85.6%) were educated primarily in regular classrooms, and more than half (51.7%) of those with mental retardation received special education mostly outside of regular classrooms. (See Table 3.3.)

According to the U.S. Department of Education, in the 2003–04 school year, 50% of all students with disabilities were in regular classrooms 80% or more of the day. White students (55%) were more likely to spend 80% or more of their day in regular classrooms than African-American (39%), Hispanic (46%), Native

FIGURE 3.1

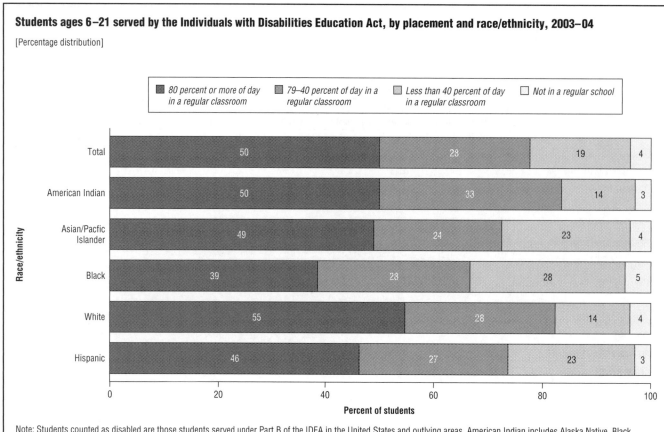

Students ages 6–21 served by the Individuals with Disabilities Education Act, by placement and race/ethnicity, 2003–04

[Percentage distribution]

Legend:
- 80 percent or more of day in a regular classroom
- 79–40 percent of day in a regular classroom
- Less than 40 percent of day in a regular classroom
- Not in a regular school

Race/ethnicity	80%+	79–40%	<40%	Not in regular school
Total	50	28	19	4
American Indian	50	33	14	3
Asian/Pacfic Islander	49	24	23	4
Black	39	28	28	5
White	55	28	14	4
Hispanic	46	27	23	3

Percent of students (0 to 100)

Note: Students counted as disabled are those students served under Part B of the IDEA in the United States and outlying areas. American Indian includes Alaska Native, Black includes African American, Pacific Islander includes Native Hawaiian, and Hispanic includes Latino. Race categories exclude Hispanic origin unless specfied. Detail may not sum to totals because of rounding.

SOURCE: John Wirt, Susan Choy, Patrick Rooney, William Hussar, Stephen Provasnik, and Gillian Hampden-Thompson, "Students with Disabilities: Percentage Distribution of Students Ages 6–21 Served by the Individuals with Disabilities Education Act, by Placement in Educational Environment and Race/Ethnicity: 2003–04," in *The Condition of Education, 2005*, NCES 2005-094, U.S. Department of Education, National Center for Education Statistics, Washington, DC, June 2005, http://nces.ed.gov/pubs2005/2005094.pdf (accessed July 26, 2005)

American (50%), or Asian/Pacific Islander (49%) students. (See Figure 3.1.)

Public Opinion about Standards for Special Education Students

In "The 36th Annual Phi Delta Kappa/Gallup Poll of the Public's Attitude toward the Public Schools" (Lowell C. Rose and Alec M. Gallup, *Phi Delta Kappan*, September 2004), the public was asked if students enrolled in special education should be required to meet the same standards as all other students in the school. Almost two-thirds (61%) of participants believed that special education students should not be held to the same standards as all other students, while 36% believed special education students should be required to meet the same standards as all other students in school. The percentage of public school parents who felt that special education students should not be held to the same standards as all other students was slightly higher (63%), while respondents with no children in school were less likely to feel this way (59%). (See Table 3.4.)

TABLE 3.4

Public opinion on whether students enrolled in special education should be required to meet the same standards as all other students, 2004

IN YOUR OPINION, SHOULD STUDENTS ENROLLED IN SPECIAL EDUCATION BE REQUIRED TO MEET THE SAME STANDARDS AS ALL OTHER STUDENTS IN THE SCHOOL?

	National totals		No children in school		Public school parents	
	'04 %	'03 %	'04 %	'03 %	'04 %	'03 %
Yes, should	36	31	37	31	35	31
No, should not	61	67	59	66	63	68
Don't know	3	2	4	3	2	1

SOURCE: Lowell C. Rose and Alec M. Gallup, "Table 15. In your opinion, should students enrolled in special education be required to meet the same standards as all other students in the school?," in "The 36th Annual Phi Delta Kappa/Gallup Poll of the Public's Attitudes Toward the Public Schools," *Phi Delta Kappan*, September 2004. Reproduced with permission.

TABLE 3.5

Public opinion on whether a school should be designated in need of improvement if special education students fail to make state goals, 2004

IN YOUR OPINION, SHOULD A SCHOOL BE DESIGNATED IN NEED OF IMPROVEMENT IF THE SPECIAL EDUCATION STUDENTS ARE THE ONLY GROUP IN THAT SCHOOL THAT FAILS TO MAKE STATE GOALS OR NOT?

	National totals %	No children in school %	Public school parents %
Yes, should	39	40	39
No, should not	56	54	58
Don't know	5	6	3

SOURCE: Lowell C. Rose and Alec M. Gallup, "Table 17. In your opinion, should a school be designated in need of improvement if the special education students are the only group in that school that fail to make state goals or not?," in "The 36th Annual Phi Delta Kappa/Gallup Poll of the Public's Attitudes Toward the Public Schools," *Phi Delta Kappan*, September 2004. Reproduced with permission.

Under the No Child Left Behind Act (NCLB; see Chapter 5), student scores on standardized tests are used to determine if a school is in need of improvement. The Phi Delta Kappa/Gallup Poll asked the public whether a school should be designated as in need of improvement if special education students are the only group in the school that fails to make state goals. More than half (56%) of the public responded that the school should not be considered in need of improvement if scores of special education students are the only group in the school that fails to make state goals; however, 39% believed that the school should be considered in need of improvement. (See Table 3.5.)

Trends in Special Education

In 1986 Congress highlighted the importance of the preschool years by amending the Education of the Handicapped Act through Public Law 99-457, which lowered the age at which children were eligible for special education and related services to three years old. The amendments also established the Handicapped Infants and Toddlers Program to assist children and their families from birth to age three. Having children with special needs receive educational services at younger ages builds the foundation for learning the skills they will need in elementary school. For many disabled children, early education programs can reduce or even eliminate the need for intensive services later.

In addition, special education has helped to eliminate the myth that disabled individuals, even the severely disabled, are unwilling or unable to work. Schools are assessing the abilities and talents of students with handicaps and matching them with potential occupations. Disabled students are receiving more training in vocational skills, as well as in making the transition from school to community life and work.

Exiting from Special Education

According to the U.S. Government Accountability Office (GAO), only twenty-one states routinely collect data on students with disabilities who leave school. (See Figure 3.2.) In 1984–85, the Office of Special Education Programs began collecting data on students aged fourteen and older who left the education system. According to the U.S. Department of Education, in 2000–01, 582,791 students exited special education. Of this number, nearly one-third of exiting students with disabilities graduated with diplomas, 33,427 (6%) received attendance certificates, and 5,959 (1%) reached the maximum age for services, which varies by state. The remainder either no longer were receiving special education services (12%) or left the educational system for other reasons (including death). (See Table 3.6.)

According to the GAO, the overall completion rate for students with disabilities was 68% and the dropout rate was 29% in 2000–01. Students with emotional disturbances were most likely to drop out; in 2000–01 more than half (53%) dropped out of school. Those with sensory impairments, however, with an 83% completion rate, were most likely to finish their education with either a diploma or alternative credential. (See Table 3.7.)

Transition of Students with Disabilities to Higher Education and Employment

The U.S. Department of Education provides funding through Title I of the Workforce Investment Act of 1998 for state-level vocational rehabilitation programs to provide employment and training-related services for individuals with disabilities, giving priority to those who are significantly disabled. Assistance offered includes employment, training, educational, and support services. Colleges and universities are required by the Americans with Disabilities Act of 1990 (P.L. 101-336) to make education accessible to students with disabilities. Services include alternative examination formats, readers, interpreters, and ramps for wheelchair access.

GIFTED AND TALENTED STUDENTS
Defining Giftedness

For more than a century, researchers, scientists, and educators have tried to define the term "gifted." Historically, the term was closely associated with the concept of genius. After IQ tests were developed, people who scored poorly were labeled retarded, and those who scored extremely well were considered geniuses. Currently some observers criticize the use of IQ tests as the single measure of intelligence. They believe the tests are biased in favor of the white middle and upper classes and penalize those from different cultural backgrounds. Also, many researchers and educators believe that giftedness is more than high intellectual ability. It also involves creativity,

FIGURE 3.2

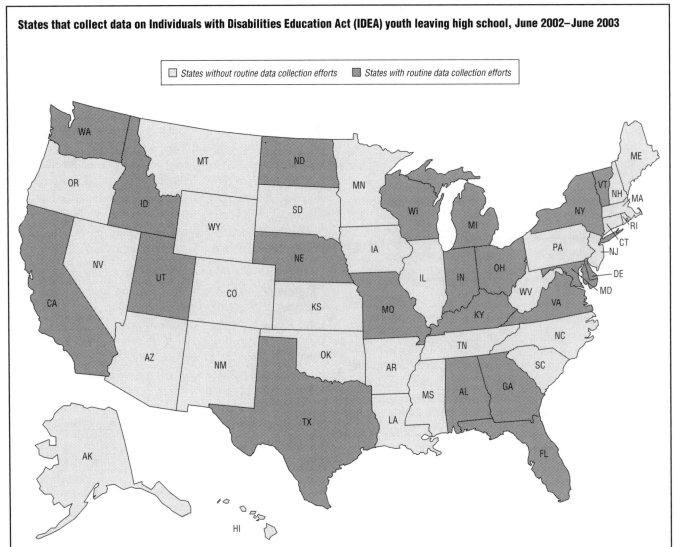

States that collect data on Individuals with Disabilities Education Act (IDEA) youth leaving high school, June 2002–June 2003

☐ *States without routine data collection efforts* ■ *States with routine data collection efforts*

SOURCE: Lacinda Ayers and Tranchau Nguyen, "Figure 3. States That Collect Data on IDEA Youth Leaving High School," in *Special Education: Federal Actions Can Assist States in Improving Postsecondary Outcomes for Youth*, GAO-03-773, U.S. General Accounting Office, Washington, DC, July 2003, http://www.gao.gov/new.items/d03773.pdf (accessed July 26, 2005)

memory, motivation, physical dexterity, social adeptness, and aesthetic sensitivity—qualities needed to succeed in life but not measured by IQ tests.

Researchers and educators generally agree that intelligence takes many forms and that multiple criteria are necessary for measurement. Educators are learning to identify outstanding talent by evaluating student abilities in different settings, rather than relying solely on test scores. The following definition, based on that in the Jacob K. Javits Gifted and Talented Students Education Act of 1988 (P.L. 100-297), reflects the current knowledge and thinking.

- Children and youth with outstanding talent perform or show the potential for performing at remarkably high levels of accomplishment when compared with others of their age, experience, or environment.

- These children and youth exhibit high performance capability in intellectual, creative, and/or artistic areas, possess an unusual leadership capacity, or excel in specific academic fields. They require services or activities not ordinarily provided by the schools.

- Outstanding talents are present in children and youth from all cultural groups, across all economic strata, and in all areas of human endeavor.

Identifying Gifted Students

Most states and localities have developed definitions of gifted and talented students based on the 1972 Marland Report to Congress (P.L. 91-230, section 806). This definition identified such areas as general intellectual ability, specific academic aptitude, creative or productive thinking, leadership ability, visual and performing artistic talent,

TABLE 3.6

Number of students with disabilities exiting special education, by basis of exit, age, and type of disability, 2000–01

Age and type of disability	Total exiting special education	Graduated with diploma	Received a certificate of attendance	Reached maximum age[a]	No longer receives special education	Died	Moved, known to continue	Moved, not known to continue	Dropped out[b]
1	2	3	4	5	6	7	8	9	10
Age group									
14 to 21 and over	582,791	173,523	33,427	5,959	70,448	1,791	148,031	59,940	89,672
14	64,541	17	29	5	15,438	245	34,655	10,897	3,255
15	71,433	77	34	4	16,583	312	35,087	12,219	7,117
16	81,222	1,170	213	8	14,995	337	32,715	12,743	19,041
17	121,070	42,432	4,668	48	12,790	336	25,024	11,194	24,578
18	144,146	79,878	12,914	777	7,390	262	13,831	7,293	21,801
19	66,264	37,095	8,789	418	2,298	137	4,576	3,258	9,693
20	19,258	8,286	3,418	904	620	77	1,450	1,429	3,074
21 and over	14,857	4,568	3,362	3,795	334	85	693	907	1,113
Type of disability for 14- to 21-year-olds and over									
All disabilities	582,791	173,523	33,427	5,959	70,448	1,791	148,031	59,940	89,672
Specific learning disabilities	340,511	117,645	14,813	1,558	41,069	580	79,863	33,692	51,291
Mental retardation	67,062	16,735	11,820	2,472	2,729	380	16,536	5,791	10,599
Emotional disturbance	94,794	15,032	2,342	579	8,038	169	34,806	13,721	20,107
Speech or language impairments	23,267	4,685	579	97	10,582	32	3,734	1,673	1,885
Multiple disabilities	9,686	2,742	1,184	652	420	249	2,678	775	986
Other health impairments	27,763	8,815	905	107	5,691	202	6,351	2,717	2,975
Hearing impairments	6,503	2,747	604	76	605	14	1,340	517	600
Orthopedic impairments	5,882	2,295	403	123	775	101	1,107	441	637
Visual impairments	2,498	1,161	170	35	219	25	516	178	194
Autism	2,563	740	422	215	157	15	649	216	149
Deaf-blindness	182	54	27	10	7	10	44	17	13
Traumatic brain injury	2,080	872	158	35	156	14	407	202	236

[a]The upper age mandate for providing special education and related services as defined by state law, practice, or court order.
[b]Dropped out is defined as the total who were enrolled at some point in the reporting year, were not enrolled at the end of the report year, and did not exit through any of the other bases described. This category includes dropouts, runaways, GED recipients, expulsions, status unknown, and other exiters.

SOURCE: Thomas D. Snyder, Alexandra G. Tan, and Charlene M. Hoffman, "Table 109. Number of Students with Disabilities Exiting Special Education, by Basis of Exit, Age, and Type of Disability: United States and Outlying Areas: 2000–01," in *Digest of Education Statistics, 2003*, NCES 2005-025, U.S. Department of Education, National Center for Education Statistics, Washington, DC, December 2004, http://nces.ed.gov/programs/digest/d03/tables/dt109.asp (accessed July 26, 2005)

and psychomotor ability, and estimated that gifted students represent at least 3% to 5% of the student population. However, the methods used by most districts to identify gifted students lag far behind the Marland definition.

Serving Gifted Students

According to the *National Survey on the State Governance of K12 Gifted and Talented Education* (Michael Swanson, Tennessee Initiative for Gifted Education Reform, August 2002), identification of gifted students is mandated in thirty-two states. In some states gifted programming is mandated, and in others both identification and service are mandated. Twenty-four states do not have a full-time director of gifted education. Not all states and localities collect data in the same way, so it is difficult to determine the exact number of students served in gifted and talented programs.

When the Jacob K. Javits Gifted and Talented Students Education Act was reauthorized in 1994, a small federal contribution was established. This program supports grants, research, and the development of national leadership abilities. The Act gives funding priority to programs that support gifted and talented students who are economically disadvantaged, speak limited English, or have disabilities. Under the 2001 reauthorization of the Elementary and Secondary Education Act (ESEA; also known as the No Child Left Behind Act), grants for gifted and talented education are awarded under two priorities. The first priority supports the development of models that serve students who are underrepresented in gifted and talented programs, and the second priority supports state and local efforts to improve services for gifted and talented students. Authorized appropriations under the Javits Gifted and Talented Students Education Program for fiscal year 2005 totaled more than $11 million, an increase of nearly 70% from the $6.5 million appropriated in 2000.

DISADVANTAGED STUDENTS

Children who are disadvantaged economically and socially often lag behind their peers. Statistically, they start preschool education later or miss it entirely and thus are less ready to start school. They have more learning

TABLE 3.7

High school completion and dropout rates by disability type, 2000–01

| Disability | Completion rate | | | Dropout rate |
	Diploma	Alternative credential	Total completion rate	
All IDEA students	57	11	68	29
Emotional disturbances	39	6	45	53
Learning disabilities	64	8	71	27
Mental retardation	40	28	68	25
Other cognitive disabilities	57	20	77	13
Speech/language impairments	64	8	72	26
Orthopedic impairments	64	11	76	18
Sensory impairments	69	14	83	14
Other health impairments	68	7	75	23
Multiple disabilities	48	20	68	17

Notes: Total completion rate may not equal the sum of diploma and alternative credential rates because of rounding errors.
Total completion and dropout rates do not add to 100 because a small percentage of students aged out of high school or died.

SOURCE: Lacinda Ayers and Tranchau Nguyen, "Table 1. High School Completion and Dropout Rates by Disability Type, 2000–01 School Year," in *Special Education: Federal Actions Can Assist States in Improving Postsecondary Outcomes for Youth*, GAO-03-773, U.S. General Accounting Office, Washington, DC, July 2003, http://www.gao.gov/new.items/d03773 .pdf (accessed July 26, 2005)

disabilities, are more likely to be held back a grade, and ultimately have higher dropout rates. Among the disadvantaged groups defined by educators and observers are children from families with very low incomes; children who are linguistically isolated (LI) or have limited English proficiency (LEP), usually because they are members of immigrant families; and children who change schools frequently—for example, children of seasonal farm workers or homeless parents.

Table 3.8 shows the 1960–2001 dropout rates for sixteen- to twenty-four-year-olds. The table displays what statisticians refer to as the "status dropout" rate: those who were not enrolled in school but were not high school graduates. According to the U.S. Department of Education, in 2001 minority students (African-American, 10.9%; Hispanic, 27%) were more likely than white students (7.3%) to drop out. (See Table 3.8.) Since the Department of Education began tracking the dropout rate of Hispanic students in 1972, Hispanics have consistently dropped out of high school at a higher rate than white or African-American students. (See Figure 3.3.)

The Title I (formerly Chapter 1) education program is the major federal program designed to help states and schools meet the special educational needs of disadvantaged students. Title I originated as part of the Elementary and Secondary Education Act of 1965 (P.L. 89-10) and was amended by the Improving America's Schools Act of 1994 (P.L. 103-382). Title I provides funds for programs and resources so that schools can improve

learning for at-risk students. In particular, schools with high concentrations of low-income children are targeted.

States and school districts can apply for Title I funds for a variety of programs aimed at improving the performance of disadvantaged students. According to the U.S. Department of Education, appropriations for Title I in fiscal year 2005 were more than $12.7 billion. Typically, states with higher numbers of poor, immigrant, and/or migrant students apply for and receive more federal funds.

According to the U.S. Department of Education, there were 49,829 Title I–eligible schools in the nation in 2002–03. California had the most Title I–eligible schools (5,489), followed by Texas (4,799), New York (2,716), Ohio (2,615), Illinois (2,412), and Pennsylvania (2,178). Nearly half (49.8%) of all students in the country attended a Title I–eligible school. More than 84% of students in the District of Columbia and 80% of students in Montana attended a school that was Title I–eligible in 2002–03. In Utah 19% of students attended a Title I–eligible school that year. (See Table 3.9.) Michigan data was incomplete at the time Table 3.9 was prepared, but the NCES reported in 2005 that 17.1% of Michigan students attended a school receiving Title I funds (http:// nces.ed.gov/nationsreportcard/states/).

According to the U.S. Department of Education, Title I appropriations totaled $8.5 billion in 2000–01. California ($1.1 billion), New York ($769.9 million), and Texas ($743.6 million), which are the largest states and have the largest proportions of poor children, accounted for more than 30% of the available Title I funding in 2000–01. Vermont ($19.6 million) and Wyoming ($19.3 million), which have small populations and very small proportions of poor children, each received less than 0.25% each of available Title I funding. (See Table 3.10.) By fiscal year 2004 total appropriations of Title I reached more than $14.3 billion, according to the NCES in *Digest of Education Statistics, 2004* (http://nces.ed.gov/programs/digest/ d04/tables/dt04_370.asp). California continued to receive the largest share of the funds, $2.1 billion, followed by New York ($1.4 billion) and Texas ($1.3 billion).

Free Lunch Eligibility

Students from families with low incomes are eligible for free or reduced-price meals at school. To determine allocations of funds under Title I, public schools are annually ranked according to the number of children eligible for free and reduced-price school meals as an indicator of the socioeconomic status of the school population. According to the U.S. Department of Education, in 2002–03, almost seventeen million students were eligible for a free or reduced-price lunch—more than 35% of all students in the United States. Kentucky (69%) had the highest rate of eligible students among the fifty states

TABLE 3.8

Percent of high school dropouts among persons ages 16–24, by sex and race/ethnicity, selected years, April 1960–October 2001

Year	All races	White, non-Hispanic	Black, non-Hispanic	Hispanic origin	All races	White, non-Hispanic	Black, non-Hispanic	Hispanic origin	All races	White, non-Hispanic	Black, non-Hispanic	Hispanic origin
		Total				Male				Female		
1	2	3	4	5	6	7	8	9	10	11	12	13
1960[a]	27.2	—	—	—	27.8	—	—	—	26.7	—	—	—
1967[b]	17.0	15.4	28.6	—	16.5	14.7	30.6	—	17.3	16.1	26.9	—
1968[b]	16.2	14.7	27.4	—	15.8	14.4	27.1	—	16.5	15.0	27.6	—
1969[b]	15.2	13.6	26.7	—	14.3	12.6	26.9	—	16.0	14.6	26.7	—
1970[b]	15.0	13.2	27.9	—	14.2	12.2	29.4	—	15.7	14.1	26.6	—
1971[b]	14.7	13.4	23.7	—	14.2	12.6	25.5	—	15.2	14.2	22.1	—
1972	14.6	12.3	21.3	34.3	14.1	11.6	22.3	33.7	15.1	12.8	20.5	34.8
1973	14.1	11.6	22.2	33.5	13.7	11.5	21.5	30.4	14.5	11.8	22.8	36.4
1974	14.3	11.9	21.2	33.0	14.2	12.0	20.1	33.8	14.3	11.8	22.1	32.2
1975	13.9	11.4	22.9	29.2	13.3	11.0	23.0	26.7	14.5	11.8	22.9	31.6
1976	14.1	12.0	20.5	31.4	14.1	12.1	21.2	30.3	14.2	11.8	19.9	32.3
1977	14.1	11.9	19.8	33.0	14.5	12.6	19.5	31.6	13.8	11.2	20.0	34.3
1978	14.2	11.9	20.2	33.3	14.6	12.2	22.5	33.6	13.9	11.6	18.3	33.1
1979	14.6	12.0	21.1	33.8	15.0	12.6	22.4	33.0	14.2	11.5	20.0	34.5
1980	14.1	11.4	19.1	35.2	15.1	12.3	20.8	37.2	13.1	10.5	17.7	33.2
1981	13.9	11.3	18.4	33.2	15.1	12.5	19.9	36.0	12.8	10.2	17.1	30.4
1982	13.9	11.4	18.4	31.7	14.5	12.0	21.2	30.5	13.3	10.8	15.9	32.8
1983	13.7	11.1	18.0	31.6	14.9	12.2	19.9	34.3	12.5	10.1	16.2	29.1
1984	13.1	11.0	15.5	29.8	14.0	11.9	16.8	30.6	12.3	10.1	14.3	29.0
1985	12.6	10.4	15.2	27.6	13.4	11.1	16.1	29.9	11.8	9.8	14.3	25.2
1986	12.2	9.7	14.2	30.1	13.1	10.3	15.0	32.8	11.4	9.1	13.5	27.2
1987	12.6	10.4	14.1	28.6	13.2	10.8	15.0	29.1	12.1	10.0	13.3	28.1
1988	12.9	9.6	14.5	35.8	13.5	10.3	15.0	36.0	12.2	8.9	14.0	35.4
1989	12.6	9.4	13.9	33.0	13.6	10.3	14.9	34.4	11.7	8.5	13.0	31.6
1990	12.1	9.0	13.2	32.4	12.3	9.3	11.9	34.3	11.8	8.7	14.4	30.3
1991	12.5	8.9	13.6	35.3	13.0	8.9	13.5	39.2	11.9	8.9	13.7	31.1
1992[c]	11.0	7.7	13.7	29.4	11.3	8.0	12.5	32.1	10.7	7.4	14.8	26.6
1993[c]	11.0	7.9	13.6	27.5	11.2	8.2	12.6	28.1	10.9	7.6	14.4	26.9
1994[c]	11.4	7.7	12.6	30.0	12.3	8.0	14.1	31.6	10.6	7.5	11.3	28.1
1995[c]	12.0	8.6	12.1	30.0	12.2	9.0	11.1	30.0	11.7	8.2	12.9	30.0
1996[c]	11.1	7.3	13.0	29.4	11.4	7.3	13.5	30.3	10.9	7.3	12.5	28.3
1997[c]	11.0	7.6	13.4	25.3	11.9	8.5	13.3	27.0	10.1	6.7	13.5	23.4
1998[c]	11.8	7.7	13.8	29.5	13.3	8.6	15.5	33.5	10.3	6.9	12.2	25.0
1999[c]	11.2	7.3	12.6	28.6	11.9	7.7	12.1	31.0	10.5	6.9	13.0	26.0
2000[c]	10.9	6.9	13.1	27.8	12.0	7.0	15.3	31.8	9.9	6.9	11.1	23.5
2001[c]	10.7	7.3	10.9	27.0	12.2	7.9	13.0	31.6	9.3	6.7	9.0	22.1

— Not available.

[a]Based on the April 1960 decennial census.

[b]White and black include persons of Hispanic origin.

[c]Because of changes in data collection procedures, data may not be comparable with figures for earlier years.

Note: All races includes other racial/ethnic groups not shown separately. "Status" dropouts are 16- to 24-year-olds who are not enrolled in school and who have not completed a high school program regardless of when they left school. People who have received GED credentials are counted as high school completers. All data except for 1960 are based on October counts. Data are based upon sample surveys of the civilian noninstitutionalized population.

SOURCE: Thomas D. Snyder, Alexandra G. Tan, and Charlene M. Hoffman, "Table 107. Percent of High School Dropouts (Status Dropouts) Among Persons 16 to 24 Years Old, by Sex and Race/Ethnicity: Selected Years, April 1960 to October 2001," in *Digest of Education Statistics, 2003*, NCES 2005-025, U.S. Department of Education, National Center for Education Statistics, Washington, DC, December 2004, http://nces.ed.gov/programs/digest/d03/tables/dt107.asp (accessed July 26, 2005)

during the 2002–03 school year, while New Hampshire (15.5%) had the lowest. (See Table 3.2.)

LEP Students

Students with Limited English Proficiency (LEP) are those for whom English is not their first language. They are served by English as a Second Language (ESL) programs, which are sometimes known as English Language Learner (ELL) programs. The primary purpose of ESL programs is to teach students English so that they can learn the content of instruction in English.

According to the U.S. Department of Education, in 2002–03 there were more than four million students in the United States receiving ELL services. California (1.6 million), Texas (630,686), Florida (203,712), New York (178,909) and Illinois (168,727) had the largest numbers of ELL students. The states with the largest proportions of their students receiving ELL services were California (25.6%), New Mexico (20.4%), Nevada (15.9%) and Texas (14.8%). (See Table 3.2.)

Students on the Move

Children who move frequently during their school years are more likely to have emotional or behavioral problems, to repeat a grade, or to be suspended or expelled from school. Experts theorize that these children

FIGURE 3.3

Dropout rates of 16- to 24-year-olds, by race/ethnicity, October 1972–2002

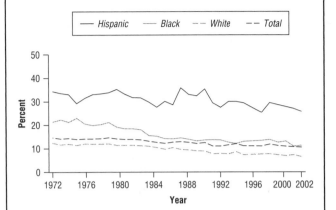

Note: The status dropout rate reported in this indicator is one of a number of rates reporting on high school dropout and completion behavior in the United States. Due to small sample sizes for most or all of the years shown in the figure, American Indians/Alaska Natives and Asians/Pacific Islanders are included in the total but are not shown separately. The erratic nature of the Hispanic status dropout rates reflects, in part, the historically small sample size of Hispanics. Black includes African American and Hispanic includes Latino. Race categories exclude Hispanic origin unless specied.

SOURCE: John Wirt, Susan Choy, Patrick Rooney, William Hussar, Stephen Provasnik, and Gillian Hampden-Thompson, "Status Dropouts: Dropout Rates of 16- through 24-Year-Olds, by Race/Ethnicity: October 1972–2002," in *The Condition of Education, 2005*, NCES 2005-094, U.S. Department of Education, National Center for Education Statistics, Washington, DC, June 2005, http://nces.ed.gov/pubs2005/2005094.pdf (accessed July 26, 2005)

TABLE 3.9

Number of Title I eligible schools and percentage of students served, 2002–03

State	Title I eligible schools	
	Number of Title I eligible schools[a]	Percent of all students in these schools
Reporting states[b]	**49,829**	**49.8**
Alabama	874	56.3
Alaska	318	41.0
Arizona	984	54.2
Arkansas	814	65.7
California	5,489	61.9
Colorado	859	44.7
Connecticut	466	39.2
Delaware	105	49.4
District of Columbia	166	84.2
Florida	1,409	38.8
Georgia	963	40.7
Hawaii	143	44.6
Idaho	478	63.7
Illinois	2,412	58.4
Indiana	1,045	47.2
Iowa	709	38.3
Kansas	647	35.2
Kentucky	1,037	74.6
Louisiana	931	54.4
Maine	530	67.2
Maryland	466	25.9
Massachusetts	1,131	54.3
Michigan	(c)	*
Minnesota	980	41.8
Mississippi	675	68.8
Missouri	1,322	49.8
Montana	691	80.4
Nebraska	497	36.1
Nevada	226	40.5
New Hampshire	264	47.4
New Jersey	1,368	54.0
New Mexico	525	55.8
New York	2,716	60.1
North Carolina	1,125	38.7
North Dakota	443	67.6
Ohio	2,615	59.9
Oklahoma	1,187	59.3
Oregon	581	37.8
Pennsylvania	2,178	63.0
Rhode Island	149	40.5
South Carolina	529	40.4
South Dakota	346	43.3
Tennessee	817	40.9
Texas	4,799	60.0
Utah	218	19.4

experience stress in the loss of old friends and familiar surroundings. Children may not understand the reasons for moving or may see the moves as a loss of autonomy. In addition, frequent moves may be a symptom of a stressed, chaotic family, a characteristic known to be related to emotional and school problems.

MIGRANT CHILDREN. With frequent moves, low incomes, and limited English skills, migrant children are at high risk for developing school-related problems. They often live in substandard housing and are frequently poor and alienated from other children at school. They may experience exposure to harmful agricultural chemicals and receive inadequate health care. These factors can make getting an education very difficult. The Title I Migrant Education Program (MEP), authorized under the Hawkins-Stafford Elementary and Secondary School Improvement Amendments of 1968 (P.L. 100-297), provides funding for state education agencies to meet the special needs of migrant children.

The term "migrant children" may refer to independent children who move often, perhaps from family to family, or to children of migrant workers who move frequently to secure jobs in farming, fishing, timber, or dairy industries. The MEP serves current and former (for up to three years) migrant children ages three through twenty-one. Most migrant education programs include preschool services, testing, regular academic or remedial instruction, bilingual education, vocational education, guidance and counseling, and health services.

According to the U.S. Department of Education, California (230,478), Texas (108,649) and Florida (49,091) had the largest number of students receiving migrant services during the 2001–02 school year. (See Table 3.2; although Table 3.2 is for 2002–03, data for migrant children were reported based on the prior school year.)

TABLE 3.9

Number of Title I eligible schools and percentage of students served, 2002–03 [CONTINUED]

	Title I eligible schools	
State	Number of Title I eligible schools[a]	Percent of all students in these schools
Vermont	216	56.9
Virginia	780	29.6
Washington	913	39.0
West Virginia	427	44.0
Wisconsin	1,083	44.7
Wyoming	183	36.5

— Not available.
*Not applicable.
[a]Number of Title I eligible schools includes those with and without schoolwide Title I programs.
[b]Reporting states total includes the 50 states and the District of Columbia. It is suppressed if data were missing for 15 percent or more of all school or agencies. State totals exclude states for which data were missing for 20 percent or more of the schools or agencies.
[c]Data were missing for more than 20 percent of schools.
Note: Percentages are based on all schools reporting in a state. Numbers of schools include those not reporting students in membership.

SOURCE: Adapted from Lee Hoffman, Jennifer Sable, Julia Naum, and Dell Gray, "Table 10. Number of Title I and Magnet Schools and Percentage of Students Served: United States and Other Jurisdictions, School Year 2002–03," *Public Elementary and Secondary Students, Staff, Schools, and School Districts: School Year 2002–03*, NCES 2005-314, U.S. Department of Education, National Center for Education Statistics, Institute for Education Sciences, Washington, DC, February 2005, http://nces.ed.gov/pubs2005/2005314.pdf (accessed July 26, 2005)

HOMELESS CHILDREN. The U.S. Department of Education estimates that approximately 800,000 children and youth experience homelessness at some point during each year. The McKinney-Vento Homeless Assistance Act of 1987 provides funding to facilitate the enrollment, attendance, and success in school of homeless children and youth. Changing schools significantly impedes a student's academic and social growth. The Act requires school districts to keep students in their school of origin, if at all possible, unless doing so is contrary to the wishes of the parents or guardians. According to the latest estimate available from the Department of Education, 87% of homeless children were attending school in 2001, up from 55% in 1996.

The McKinney-Vento Act was reauthorized under the NCLB Act of 2001. Under the law, schools cannot segregate homeless children in a separate program within a school based on homelessness alone. Also, schools must immediately enroll homeless students even if the students are unable to produce the educational records normally required for enrollment. In addition, states and their school districts must ensure that homeless children are provided transportation to and from the school they attended prior to becoming homeless, if their parents or guardians request it, and school districts must designate a local liaison for homeless children and youths. For fiscal year 2005, the federal government authorized $62.5 million in McKinney-Vento education grants for programs serving homeless children and youth.

Head Start

The Head Start program, established as part of the Economic Opportunity Act of 1964 (P.L. 88-452), has been one of the most durable federal programs for at-risk children. Because disadvantaged children tend to be less prepared for an academic environment, Head Start operates where it is needed most—in early childhood, up to age five. Most children enter the program at ages three or four. In the past, not many children under age three were served by Head Start projects, but the 1994 reauthorization of Head Start (P.L. 103-252) established a companion program, Early Head Start (EHS), to serve infants and toddlers.

According to the U.S. Department of Health and Human Services, 9% of the 905,851 children enrolled in Head Start preschool programs in 2004 were two years old or younger, 34% were three years old, and 52% were four years old. Hispanic children accounted for 31.2% of enrollees; 31.1% were African-American; 26.9% were white; 5% were multiracial; 3.1% were Native American or Alaska Native; 1.8% were Asian; and less than 1% were Hawaiian/Pacific Islanders. (See Table 3.11.)

Head Start appropriations increased substantially during the final two decades of the twentieth century. According to the U.S. Department of Health and Human Services, in 1980, the program served 376,300 students and had appropriations of $735 million. By 2000, 761,844 children were enrolled in Head Start, and funding reached $4.5 billion. More than $5.6 billion in Head Start funds were allocated in 2002. (See Table 3.12.) The Department of Health and Human Services reported on the Head Start Web site (http://www.acf.hhs.gov/programs/hsb/research/2005.htm) that since its inception in 1965, more than twenty-two million students have participated in Head Start programs.

In September 2005 the House of Representatives approved a bill that would strengthen the Head Start program. The bill was not without controversy, however, as it would allow Head Start programs run by religious organizations to discriminate against potential teachers based on their religious beliefs. Under the bill, qualified teachers could be fired or not hired if they do not share the same religious beliefs as the groups running the Head Start programs, and parent volunteers could be banned from participating in classrooms because of their religious beliefs ("Discrimination in Head Start," *New York Times*, September 28, 2005).

TABLE 3.10

Appropriations for Title I and Title IV, Elementary and Secondary Education Act (ESEA), 1999–2000 and 2000–01

[In thousands]

State or other area	Title I total, school year 1999–2000[a]	Title I,[b] school year 2000–01[c] Total	Local education grants Total[f]	Basic grants	Concentration grants	Neglected and delinquent children	Migrant children	Other[e]	Title VI[d] 1999 appropriations for 1999–2000	Title VI[d] 2000 appropriations for 2000–01
1	2	3	4	5	6	7	8	9	10	11
Total[g]	$8,289,582	$8,500,086	$7,807,397	$6,578,695	$1,146,813	$42,000	$354,689	$296,000	$375,000	$365,750
Alabama	133,972	137,037	129,133	108,479	20,655	506	2,921	4,477	5,520	5,266
Alaska	27,672	26,916	19,089	16,079	3,011	170	6,628	1,029	1,862	1,816
Arizona	130,818	134,330	121,897	101,967	19,930	1,715	6,343	4,375	6,408	6,443
Arkansas	85,004	86,627	79,071	67,442	11,629	274	4,485	2,797	3,443	3,278
California	1,065,523	1,119,928	972,870	833,272	139,598	3,522	107,211	36,325	44,575	43,634
Colorado	78,218	80,052	71,304	60,668	10,636	315	6,052	2,381	5,258	5,280
Connecticut	74,468	76,604	70,351	59,917	10,434	883	2,804	2,566	4,078	4,144
Delaware	22,269	22,764	21,268	16,44700	4,822	109	319	1,066	1,862	1,816
District of Columbia	26,910	27,684	25,547	21,837	3,710	356	443	1,338	1,862	1,816
Florida	391,594	401,481	363,366	309,157	54,209	1,266	23,565	13,284	17,857	17,779
Georgia	218,637	226,462	210,268	180,821	29,447	2,337	6,253	7,604	10,131	10,030
Hawaii	21,021	22,149	20,158	17,291	2,867	102	834	1,055	1,862	1,816
Idaho	28,500	28,904	23,516	19,861	3,655	108	4,164	1,115	1,862	1,816
Illinois	337,019	341,790	326,711	278,814	47,897	1,747	1,621	11,712	16,090	15,647
Indiana	122,821	125,342	116,422	101,953	14,469	750	4,051	4,120	7,726	7,575
Iowa	55,659	56,614	53,287	47,051	6,236	343	1,121	1,862	3,838	3,647
Kansas	67,096	69,683	56,306	48,828	7,478	359	10,995	2,023	3,604	3,495
Kentucky	141,131	142,853	127,790	108,142	19,649	646	9,934	4,484	4,992	4,798
Louisiana	198,517	201,813	191,236	161,738	29,498	909	2,842	6,826	6,216	5,949
Maine	36,798	37,596	31,963	27,453	4,511	133	4,238	1,262	1,862	1,816
Maryland	105,879	108,414	102,604	87,769	14,834	1,678	472	3,660	6,531	6,538
Massachusetts	159,039	162,717	153,374	126,656	26,718	935	2,703	5,706	7,456	7,311
Michigan	351,442	356,370	334,366	278,187	56,179	732	9,612	11,660	13,123	12,948
Minnesota	92,688	93,893	87,986	76,903	11,083	224	2,538	3,145	6,625	6,454
Mississippi	128,450	130,421	124,796	106,154	18,642	316	1,005	4,304	3,907	3,739
Missouri	138,513	142,176	134,785	114,383	20,403	866	1,581	4,944	7,367	7,040
Montana	27,542	28,302	26,320	22,393	3,927	62	744	1,176	1,862	1,816
Nebraska	37,699	38,392	32,207	28,851	3,356	224	4,621	1,340	2,342	2,235
Nevada	23,883	24,814	23,322	20,455	2,867	154	232	1,107	2,217	2,367
New Hampshire	20,503	21,100	19,698	15,856	3,842	256	100	1,047	1,862	1,816
New Jersey	182,896	187,507	177,216	148,612	28,604	2,245	1,589	6,456	10,135	9,916
New Mexico	68,112	70,054	66,240	56,467	9,773	297	1,070	2,447	2,590	2,474
New York	751,931	769,871	731,360	621,037	110,323	2,574	7,977	27,959	23,004	21,917
North Carolina	155,311	163,038	150,973	131,039	19,934	948	5,690	5,427	9,598	9,555
North Dakota	20,736	21,194	19,821	16,447	3,374	44	263	1,067	1,862	1,816
Ohio	312,305	317,133	302,372	257,785	44,587	2,239	2,034	10,488	14,810	14,290
Oklahoma	99,005	101,976	96,338	82,527	13,811	208	2,014	3,417	4,622	4,411
Oregon	83,282	84,506	68,819	59,765	9,054	1,230	12,070	2,388	4,237	4,129
Pennsylvania	352,608	357,840	335,858	283,187	52,671	679	8,470	12,833	15,064	14,538
Rhode Island	25,943	26,323	24,654	21,229	3,425	345	108	1,215	1,862	1,816
South Carolina	101,870	105,883	100,734	86,321	14,413	1,089	459	3,601	4,972	4,771
South Dakota	21,417	21,892	19,734	16,677	3,057	253	846	1,058	1,862	1,816
Tennessee	137,269	140,149	134,693	112,564	22,129	520	365	4,570	6,822	6,616
Texas	727,313	743,579	665,787	567,427	98,360	2,764	50,946	24,082	28,121	27,710
Utah	38,152	38,550	35,293	29,501	5,792	461	1,479	1,317	3,489	3,375
Vermont	19,294	19,630	17,739	15,146	2,593	193	678	1,021	1,862	1,816
Virginia	119,224	124,366	118,413	102,850	15,563	1,055	656	4,241	8,445	8,247
Washington	125,513	127,592	108,940	93,186	15,753	733	14,218	3,702	7,571	7,447
West Virginia	75,111	76,445	73,480	61,854	11,626	307	124	2,535	2,184	2,056
Wisconsin	129,977	132,030	125,862	113,863	11,999	1,032	630	4,506	7,165	6,904
Wyoming	18,553	19,251	17,754	14,887	2,867	317	167	1,013	1,862	1,816

TABLE 3.10

Appropriations for Title I and Title IV, Elementary and Secondary Education Act (ESEA), 1999–2000 and 2000–01 [CONTINUED]

[In thousands]

State or other area	Title I total, school year 1999–2000[a]	Title I,[b] school year 2000–01[c]							Title VI[d]	
			Local education grants			Neglected and delinquent children	Migrant children	Other[e]	1999 appropriations for 1999–2000	2000 appropriations for 2000–01
		Total	Total[f]	Basic grants	Concentration grants					
1	2	3	4	5	6	7	8	9	10	11
Other activities										
Bureau of Indian Affairs	50,205	51,343	51,343	0	0	0	0	0	0	0
Migrant coordination activities	8,500	8,500	0	0	0	0	8,500	0	0	0
Even Start migrant, Indian, and territory (set-aside)	6,200	7,500	0	0	0	0	0	7,500	0	0
Even Start evaluation/ technical assistance	3,720	3,000	0	0	0	0	0	3,000	0	0
Even Start/state literacy initiative	1,000	0	0	0	0	0	0	0	0	0
Competitive grants	9,054	5,000	5,000	0	0	0	0	0	0	0
Other non state allocations	0	2,500	2,500	0	0	0	0	0	0	0
Outlying areas										
American Samoa	5,355	5,572	5,572	0	0	0	0	0	451	440
Guam	5,023	5,023	5,023	0	0	0	0	0	1,051	250
Northern Marianas	2,848	2,964	2,964	0	0	0	0	0	257	1,025
Puerto Rico	273,453	277,159	262,416	221,502	40,914	472	3,903	10,369	6,040	5,629
Virgin Islands	9,118	9,487	9,487	0	0	0	0	0	866	845

[a]Data are based on fiscal year 2000 budget authorizations. Excludes $6,977,000 for Title I evaluation.
[b]Formerly Chapter 1.
[c]Data are based on fiscal year 2001 budget authorizations. Excludes $8,900,000 for Title I evaluation.
[d]Formerly Chapter 2.
[e]Includes capital expenses, Even Start grants, and accountability grants.
[f]Includes other programs not shown separately.
[g]Total includes other activities and outlying areas.
Note: Elementary and Secondary Education Act was most recently revised through the Improving America's Schools Act (IASA) of 1994. Detail may not sum to totals due to rounding.

SOURCE: Thomas D. Snyder and Charlene M. Hoffman, "Table 369. Appropriations for Title I and Title IV, Elementary and Secondary Education Act (ESEA) of 1994, by State or Other Area and Type of Appropriation: 1999–2000 and 2000–01," in *Digest of Education Statistics, 2001*, NCES 2002-130, U.S. Department of Education, National Center for Education Statistics, Washington, DC, February 2002, http://nces.ed.gov/programs/digest/d01/dt369.asp (accessed July 26, 2005)

TABLE 3.11

Head Start enrollment, 2004

Enrollment	905,851
Ages	
Number of 5 year olds and older	5%
Number of 4 year olds	52%
Number of 3 year olds	34%
Number under 3 years of age	9%
Racial/ethnic composition	
American Indian-Alaska Native	3.10%
Hispanic	31.20%
Black	31.10%
White	26.90%
Asian	1.80%
Hawaiian/Pacific Islander	0.90%
Multi-racial/other	5.00%
Number of grantees	1,604
Number of classrooms	48,260
Number of centers	20,050
Average cost per child	$7,222
Paid staff	211,950
Volunteers	1,353,000

SOURCE: U.S. Department of Health and Human Services, "Head Start Program Fact Sheet," U.S. Department of Health and Human Services, Administration for Children and Families, Head Start Bureau, 2004, http://www.acf.hhs.gov/programs/hsb/research/2005.htm (accessed July 26, 2005)

TABLE 3.12

U.S. Department of Health and Human Services allocations for Head Start and enrollment in Head Start, 1999–2002

	1999		2000		2001		2002	
State or jurisdiction	Head Start allocations (in thousands)	Head Start enrollment[a]	Head Start allocations (in thousands)	Head Start enrollment[b]	Head Start allocations (in thousands)	Head Start enrollment[c]	Head Start allocations (in thousands)	Head Start enrollment[d]
1	2	3	4	5	6	7	8	9
United States[e]	$4,021,476	729,697	$4,546,132	761,844	$5,346,145	804,598	$5,627,581	810,472
Alabama	71,983	15,263	82,414	15,823	95,374	16,498	100,154	16,529
Alaska	8,786	1,281	9,738	1,297	11,656	1,586	12,104	1,839
Arizona	62,444	11,127	73,697	11,882	89,629	12,865	96,913	13,297
Arkansas	43,449	10,097	48,379	10,316	57,381	10,818	61,024	10,930
California	554,366	86,459	642,512	95,280	758,591	97,667	801,430	98,687
Colorado	46,602	9,135	52,226	9,333	61,805	9,826	65,716	9,872
Connecticut	37,906	6,825	41,674	6,857	47,931	7,207	49,985	7,224
Delaware	8,873	2,126	9,820	2,119	11,831	2,243	12,286	2,231
District of Columbia	19,201	3,279	20,926	3,345	23,203	3,343	24,091	3,403
Florida	169,996	30,792	195,696	32,389	236,056	34,657	252,370	35,610
Georgia	112,040	21,121	126,281	21,580	151,340	23,140	161,740	23,414
Hawaii	15,786	2,799	18,199	2,916	21,166	3,073	21,977	3,073
Idaho	14,121	2,266	16,098	2,387	20,158	2,890	21,663	3,347
Illinois	192,580	35,211	214,965	37,767	248,855	39,805	259,780	39,619
Indiana	65,226	13,057	72,467	13,323	85,241	14,256	88,667	14,145
Iowa	36,038	7,003	40,714	7,235	47,381	7,689	49,495	7,620
Kansas	32,958	7,000	37,061	7,447	44,951	7,897	47,909	8,013
Kentucky	76,409	15,281	85,198	15,701	99,054	16,419	103,473	16,190
Louisiana	100,196	20,703	110,318	20,975	128,484	21,969	135,048	22,136
Maine	18,695	3,618	20,378	3,631	24,770	3,958	26,661	4,002
Maryland	54,966	9,626	61,920	9,968	71,713	10,487	74,929	10,527
Massachusetts	78,544	12,094	85,917	12,250	99,675	13,004	104,182	13,040
Michigan	171,121	33,422	186,842	33,769	215,873	35,112	225,290	35,269
Minnesota	51,740	9,630	56,401	9,715	65,523	10,164	69,643	10,331
Mississippi	117,375	25,091	129,843	25,455	149,606	26,624	155,259	26,742
Missouri	78,622	16,191	93,475	16,574	108,305	17,718	113,256	17,646
Montana	13,839	2,678	15,267	2,703	18,944	2,971	20,117	2,982
Nebraska	23,890	4,518	26,660	4,571	32,142	4,982	34,580	5,252
Nevada	11,484	2,035	12,369	2,035	18,367	2,694	19,786	2,754
New Hampshire	9,114	1,425	9,838	1,425	12,388	1,632	12,861	1,632
New Jersey	94,945	14,443	104,743	14,567	120,245	15,329	125,176	15,262
New Mexico	35,363	7,108	38,374	7,135	45,919	7,618	49,185	7,749
New York	304,283	45,040	342,136	46,805	398,522	48,952	418,239	49,493
North Carolina	93,979	17,394	104,684	17,808	124,580	18,991	132,667	19,202
North Dakota	10,561	2,002	11,973	2,042	15,750	2,287	16,036	2,307
Ohio	178,271	36,454	196,684	38,261	226,942	38,072	236,999	38,081
Oklahoma	54,422	12,217	61,555	12,655	72,190	13,228	76,910	13,460
Oregon	40,118	5,480	46,071	5,771	54,785	9,129	57,105	9,199
Pennsylvania	165,674	29,124	181,844	29,650	209,346	31,104	219,115	30,986
Rhode Island	15,330	2,817	17,378	2,952	20,412	3,150	21,184	3,150
South Carolina	56,280	11,207	64,060	11,604	74,963	12,184	78,507	12,248
South Dakota	12,708	2,485	14,045	2,587	17,513	2,925	18,079	2,827
Tennessee	81,387	14,753	92,040	15,747	107,146	16,344	112,344	16,507
Texas	299,891	58,173	361,846	63,171	429,075	67,572	454,292	67,664
Utah	23,185	4,679	27,840	5,079	35,858	5,403	36,270	5,527
Vermont	9,691	1,438	10,514	1,438	12,553	1,573	13,023	1,573
Virginia	66,246	12,243	74,487	12,652	89,890	13,612	95,366	13,772
Washington	69,601	9,831	78,359	10,287	92,257	11,106	97,247	11,167
West Virginia	36,062	7,043	39,842	7,144	46,713	7,590	48,625	7,650
Wisconsin	67,582	13,113	72,177	12,953	83,337	13,478	86,941	13,489
Wyoming	7,546	1,500	8,187	1,468	10,760	1,757	11,882	1,803

TABLE 3.12

U.S. Department of Health and Human Services allocations for Head Start and enrollment in Head Start, 1999–2002 [CONTINUED]

State or jurisdiction	1999 Head Start allocations (in thousands)	Head Start enrollment[a]	2000 Head Start allocations (in thousands)	Head Start enrollment[b]	2001 Head Start allocations (in thousands)	Head Start enrollment[c]	2002 Head Start allocations (in thousands)	Head Start enrollment[d]
1	2	3	4	5	6	7	8	9
Other activities								
Migrant programs	178,122	38,132	206,391	31,607	246,905	33,355	257,815	33,850
Support activities	—	*	—	*	—	*	210,255	*
American Indian/Alaska Native programs	130,191	21,237	144,768	22,391	171,289	23,632	181,794	23,837
Outlying areas	172,634	40,889	205,616	41,812	240,376	43,650	259,125	44,290
Puerto Rico	155,526	33,470	185,563	34,393	216,476	35,894	234,304	36,920
Pacific territories	10,297	5,989	12,356	5,989	14,381	6,209	14,943	6,209
Virgin Islands	6,811	1,430	7,697	1,430	9,519	1,547	9,878	1,161

— Not available.

*Not applicable.

[a]The distribution of enrollment by age was: 6 percent were 5 years old and over; 59 percent were 4-year-olds; 31 percent were 3-year-olds; and 4 percent were under 3 years of age. Handicapped children accounted for 13 percent in Head Start programs. The racial/ethnic composition was: American Indian/Alaska Native, 3 percent; Hispanic, 27 percent; Black, 35 percent; White, 31 percent; and Asian, 3 percent.

[b]The distribution of enrollment by age was: 5 percent were 5 years old and over; 56 percent were 4-year-olds; 33 percent were 3-year-olds; and 6 percent were under 3 years of age. Handicapped children accounted for 13 percent in Head Start programs. The racial/ethnic composition was: American Indian/Alaska Native, 3 percent; Hispanic, 29 percent; Black, 35 percent; White, 30 percent; Asian, 2 percent, and Hawaiian/Pacific Islander, 1 percent.

[c]The distribution of enrollment by age was: 4 percent were 5 years old and over; 54 percent were 4-year-olds; 35 percent were 3-year-olds; and 7 percent were under 3 years of age. Handicapped children accounted for 13 percent in Head Start programs. The racial/ethnic composition was: American Indian/Alaska Native, 4 percent; Hispanic, 30 percent; Black, 34 percent; White, 30 percent; Asian, 2 percent, and Hawaiian/Pacific Islander, 1 percent.

[d]The distribution of enrollment by age was: 5 percent were 5 years old and over; 52 percent were 4-year-olds; 36 percent were 3-year-olds; and 7 percent were under 3 years of age. Handicapped children accounted for 13 percent in Head Start programs. The racial/ethnic composition was: American Indian/Alaska Native, 3 percent; Hispanic, 30 percent; Black, 33 percent; White, 28 percent; Asian, 2 percent, and Hawaiian/Pacific Islander, 1 percent.

[e]Excludes other activities and outlying areas.

Note: Detail may not sum to totals due to rounding.

SOURCE: Thomas D. Snyder, Alexandra G. Tan, and Charlene M. Hoffman, "Table 374. U.S. Department of Health and Human Services Allocations for Head Start and Enrollment in Head Start, by State or Jurisdiction: Fiscal Years 1999 to 2002," in *Digest of Education Statistics, 2003*, NCES 2005-025, U.S. Department of Education, National Center for Education Statistics, Washington, DC, December 2004, http://nces.ed.gov/programs/digest/d03/tables/dt374.asp (accessed July 26, 2005)

CHAPTER 4
TESTING AND ACHIEVEMENT

STANDARDS AND ASSESSMENTS

Content standards provide a framework for the knowledge and skills that students are expected to acquire. Performance standards determine how well students should be able to perform relative to the content standards. Assessments provide information regarding the attainment of standards. Elementary, secondary, and special education programs rely on state standards-based assessment systems to evaluate the effectiveness of federal programs. According to federal expectations for Title I (the federal program that helps states and schools meet special education needs), academic standards must be rigorous and exceed minimum competencies. They must be fair, valid, and reliable, and include all students. Assessment results should be reported for schools and districts, and they must include demographic categories (gender, race and ethnicity, English proficiency, disability, migrant status, and low income status). Title I legislation specifies that performance standards must provide information for at least three levels of performance.

NATIONAL ASSESSMENT OF EDUCATIONAL PROGRESS

The National Assessment of Educational Progress (NAEP) has conducted assessments of American students since 1969. The federally funded NAEP is the only regular national survey of educational achievement at the elementary, middle, and high school levels. It is authorized by Congress and administered by the National Center for Education Statistics (NCES). The Augustus F. Hawkins–Robert T. Stafford Elementary and Secondary School Improvement Amendments of 1988 (P.L. 100-290) established the National Assessment Governing Board (NAGB) to formulate policy guidelines for NAEP. The NAGB determines which subjects will be assessed and how they will be assessed.

According to the U.S. Department of Education, the NAEP has two major goals: to discover what American students know and can do in key subject areas and to measure educational progress over long periods of time. Designed as a measure of the nation's educational system, the NAEP is a series of reading, writing, mathematics, science, history, civics, and geography tests. The tests are given periodically to randomly selected samples of youth ages nine (grade four), thirteen (grade eight), and seventeen (grade twelve) attending both public and private schools. Student performance in all grade levels is measured on a proficiency scale of zero to five hundred. This allows a comparison of younger students with older ones, as well as an assessment of progress from year to year. Table 4.1 shows the schedule from 1990 to 2010 for assessing individual subjects and releasing long-term trend data. (See Table 4.1.)

Beginning with the 1990 assessments, the NAGB also developed achievement levels for each subject at each grade level in an effort to measure the match between students' actual achievement and their desired achievement. A panel of teachers, education specialists, and other members of the general public categorized these levels into basic, proficient, and advanced. Basic level was defined as "partial mastery of prerequisite knowledge and skills that are fundamental for proficient work at each grade." Proficient level was defined as "solid academic performance for each grade assessed. Students reaching this level have demonstrated competency over challenging subject matter, including subject-matter knowledge, application of such knowledge to real-world situations, and analytical skills appropriate to the subject matter." The advanced level was defined as "superior performance." Achievement levels provide another way to report assessment results, allowing comparisons between percentages of students who achieve a particular level on one assessment with the percentage who achieve that level the next time that subject is assessed. They are also used to make comparisons between states and the nation.

TABLE 4.1

Schedule of NAEP assessments, 1990–2010

Year	Main NAEP		
	National	State	Long-term trend
1990	Mathematics Science Reading	Mathematics (8)	Mathematics Science Reading Writing
1992	Mathematics Reading Writing	Mathematics (4,8) Reading (4)	Mathematics Science Reading Writing
1994	Geography U.S. History Reading	Reading (4)	Mathematics Science Reading Writing
1996	Mathematics Science	Mathematics (4,8) Science (8)	Mathematics Science Reading Writing
1997	Arts (8)		
1998	Reading Writing Civics	Reading (4,8) Writing (8)	
1999			Mathematics Science Reading
2000	Mathematics Science Reading (4)	Mathematics (4,8) Science (4,8)	
2001	U.S. History Geography		
2002	Reading Writing	Reading (4,8) Writing (4,8)	
2003	Reading (4,8) Mathematics (4,8)	Reading (4,8) Mathematics (4,8)	
2004			Mathematics Reading
2005	Reading Mathematics Science	Reading (4,8) Mathematics (4,8) Science (4,8)	
2006	U.S. History Economics (12) Civics		
2007	Reading (4,8) Mathematics (4,8) Writing (8,12)	Reading (4,8) Mathematics (4,8) Writing (8)	
2008	Arts (8)		Mathematics Reading
2009	Reading Mathematics Science	Reading (4,8) Mathematics (4,8) Science (4,8)	
2010	World History (12) Geography		

Note: Grades tested are 4, 8, and 12 in main NAEP (National Assessment for Educational Progress) and ages 9, 13, and 17 in Long-term Trend NAEP unless otherwise indicated. NAEP assessment schedules are subject to change.

SOURCE: National Assessment Governing Board, "Schedule of NAEP Assessments," in *The Nation's Report Card: An Introduction to the National Assessment for Educational Progress (NAEP)*, NCES 2005-454 Revised, U.S. Department of Education, National Center for Educational Statistics, Institute for Education Sciences, Washington, DC, n.d., http://nces.ed.gov/nationsreportcard/pdf/about/2005454.pdf (accessed July 26, 2005).

READING PERFORMANCE

The ability to read is fundamental to virtually all aspects of the education process. If students cannot read well, they usually cannot succeed in other subject areas. Eventually, they may have additional problems in a society that requires increasingly sophisticated job skills.

The NAEP assesses proficiency in three different types of reading: reading for literary experience, reading for information, and reading to perform a task. The first type of reading involves various genres of creative writing, including fiction, poetry, drama, biography, myths, legends, and folktales, and students are asked to explore such literary features as characters, plots, and themes. "Reading for information" assesses students' ability to use magazines, newspapers, textbooks, and essays to gain knowledge about the world. The third type of reading assessment addresses students' capacity to use what they learn from such informational sources as train schedules, instruction manuals, game directions, and maps. This component is not part of fourth-grade assessments. Overall, the NAEP reading assessments examine students' ability to understand and interpret the material they read, to make connections between the material and their own experiences, and to evaluate the structure and content of what they have read.

NAEP reading performance is described in terms of the percentage of students attaining the three achievement levels—basic, proficient, and advanced. A 300 score indicates relative proficiency in understanding complicated literary and informational material.

According to the National Center for Education Statistics, long-term trend data from 1971 to 2004 indicate that the average reading scale score for nine-year-olds increased from 208 in 1971 to 219 in 2004. Reading scores of nine-year-olds went up from 212 in 1999 to 219 in 2004. The reading scores of thirteen-year-olds went up four points between 1971 and 2004, from 255 to 259, but the score stayed the same between 1999 and 2004 (259). For seventeen-year-olds, reading scores were the same in 2004 as in 1971 (285), and showed a three-point decrease after 1999, when the average reading scale score was 288. (See Figure 4.1.)

Prior to 1998, administration procedures for the NAEP reading assessment did not permit the use of accommodations such as extra time or individual (rather than group) administration for special needs students. In 1998 administration procedures were introduced that allowed students with disabilities and limited English proficiency to use such accommodations.

The NAEP defines an accommodation as a change in testing conditions that removes barriers to participation but does not alter what is being tested. Examples of accommodations include extended time to complete the test, testing in small group or one-on-one sessions, use of a scribe to write the student's answers, and reading the instructions aloud. Bilingual test booklets can be used for subjects other than reading assessments.

FIGURE 4.1

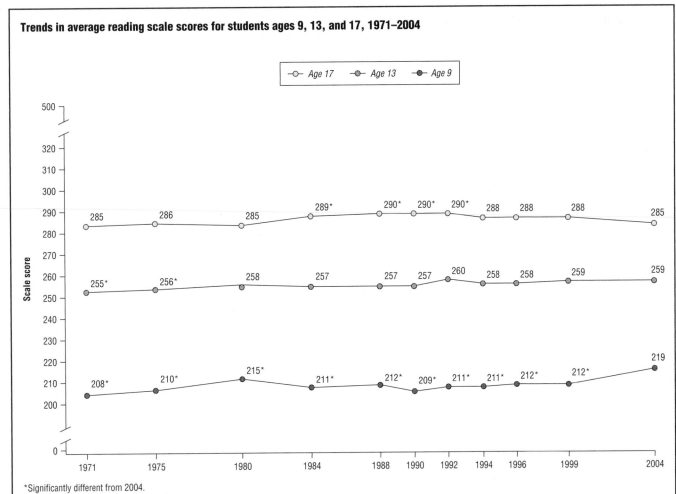

Trends in average reading scale scores for students ages 9, 13, and 17, 1971–2004

*Significantly different from 2004.

SOURCE: National Assessment Governing Board, "Figure 1. Trends in Average Reading Scale Scores for Students Ages 9, 13, and 17: 1971–2004," in *NAEP 2004 Trends in Academic Progress: Three Decades of Student Performance in Reading and Mathematics Findings in Brief*, NCES 2005-463, U.S. Department of Education, National Center for Education Statistics, Institute of Education Sciences, Washington, DC, July 2005, http://nces.ed.gov/nationsreportcard/pdf/main2005/2005463.pdf (accessed July 26, 2005)

Long-Term Trend Reading Scores of Nine-Year-Olds

Scores of nine-year-olds increased for all ethnic groups and both genders between 1971 and 2004, and the average reading score of nine-year-olds in 2004 was higher than in any previous assessment. The achievement gap between scores of white and African-American nine-year-olds decreased between 1971 and 2004. Between white and Hispanic students at age nine, the achievement gap decreased from 1975 to 1999, but it stayed the same from 1999 to 2004. (See Table 4.2.) On average, females scored higher than males in reading in 2004. Among nine-year-olds, the gender gap between females and males decreased from thirteen points in 1971 to five points in 2004. The score gap between white and African-American students decreased eighteen points from 1971 to 2004 and nine points between 1999 and 2004.

Long-Term Trend Reading Scores of Thirteen-Year-Olds

Scores of thirteen-year-olds increased for all ethnic groups and both genders from 1971 to 1999, but in 2004

the average scores were not statistically different from those in 1999. The achievement gap between scores of white and African-American students decreased from 1971 to 2004, but has stayed about the same since 1999. The gap between white and Hispanic thirteen-year-olds stayed about the same from 1975 to 2004. (See Table 4.3.) Among thirteen-year-olds, there was only a small change in the gender gap between males and females from 1971 to 2004; on average, in 1971 females scored eleven points higher than males in reading, in 1999 females scored twelve points higher, and in 2004 females scored ten points higher than males in reading. The score gap between white and African-American students at age thirteen decreased seventeen points from 1971 to 2004.

Long-Term Trend Reading Scores of Seventeen-Year-Olds

On average, scores of all seventeen-year-olds showed no statistically significant difference from 1971 to 2004.

TABLE 4.2

Summary of trends in average reading and mathematics scale scores and score gaps for students age 9, 1971–2004

Reading	Change from 1971*	Change from 1999
Overall	↑	↑
Male	↑	↑
Female	↑	↑
White	↑	↑
Black	↑	↑
Hispanic	↑	↑
Mathematics	**Change from 1973**	**Change from 1999**
Overall	↑	↑
Male	↑	↑
Female	↑	↑
White	↑	↑
Black	↑	↑
Hispanic	↑	↑
Racial/ethnic gaps: reading	**Change from 1971***	**Change from 1999**
White-black	↓	↓
White-Hispanic	↓	↔
Racial/ethnic gaps: mathematics	**Change from 1973**	**Change from 1999**
White-black	↓	↔
White-Hispanic	↔	↓

↑ Average score or score gap increased.
↓ Average score or score gap decreased.
↔ Any change in average score or score gap was not statistically significant.
*Data for Hispanic students are included in the overall national results but not reported as a separate racial/ethnic category in 1971. Therefore, the results for Hispanic students are from 1975.

SOURCE: National Assessment Governing Board, "Figure 3. Summary of Trends in Average Reading and Mathematics Scale Scores and Score Gaps for Students Age 9: 1971–2004," in *NAEP 2004 Trends in Academic Progress: Three Decades of Student Performance in Reading and Mathematics Findings in Brief*, NCES 2005-463, U.S. Department of Education, National Center for Education Statistics, Institute of Education Sciences, Washington, DC, July 2005, http://nces.ed.gov/nationsreportcard/pdf/main2005/2005463.pdf (accessed July 26, 2005)

TABLE 4.3

Summary of trends in average reading and mathematics scale scores and score gaps for students age 13, 1971–2004

Reading	Change from 1971*	Change from 1999
Overall	↑	↔
Male	↑	↔
Female	↑	↔
White	↑	↔
Black	↑	↔
Hispanic	↑	↔
Mathematics	**Change from 1973**	**Change from 1999**
Overall	↑	↑
Male	↑	↑
Female	↑	↑
White	↑	↑
Black	↑	↑
Hispanic	↑	↑
Racial/ethnic gaps: reading	**Change from 1971***	**Change from 1999**
White-black	↓	↔
White-Hispanic	↔	↔
Racial/ethnic gaps: mathematics	**Change from 1973**	**Change from 1999**
White-black	↓	↔
White-Hispanic	↓	↔

↑ Average score or score gap increased.
↓ Average score or score gap decreased.
↔ Any change in average score or score gap was not statistically significant.
*Data for Hispanic students are included in the overall national results but not reported as a separate racial/ethnic category in 1971. Therefore, the results for Hispanic students are from 1975.

SOURCE: National Assessment Governing Board, "Figure 6. Summary of Trends in Average Reading and Mathematics Scale Scores and Score Gaps for Students Age 13: 1971–2004," in *NAEP 2004 Trends in Academic Progress: Three Decades of Student Performance in Reading and Mathematics Findings in Brief*, NCES 2005-463, U.S. Department of Education, National Center for Education Statistics, Institute of Education Sciences, Washington, DC, July 2005, http://nces.ed.gov/nationsreportcard/pdf/main2005/2005463.pdf (accessed July 26, 2005)

However, scores of African-American students increased from 1971 to 1999. For Hispanic students they increased from 1975 to 1999, and for both groups they stayed about the same from 1999 to 2004. The achievement gap between scores of white and African-American students decreased from 1971 to 1999. They also decreased between white and Hispanic students from 1975 to 1999, but there was no significant difference in scores for either group from 1999 to 2004. (See Table 4.4.) Among seventeen-year-olds, there were only small differences in the gender gap between males and females from 1971 to 2004; on average, in 1971 females scored twelve points higher than males in reading, in 1999 females scored thirteen points higher, and in 2004 females scored fourteen points higher than males in reading. The score gap between white and African-American students at age seventeen decreased twenty-four points from 1971 to 2004.

Early Childhood Factors Associated with Reading Performance

According to the National Center for Education Statistics, children whose family members read to them eventually demonstrate higher reading performance and do better in school. In 2001–02, one-third (33%) of children about nine months of age were read to by a relative on a daily basis; even fewer (27%) were told stories. These numbers compared unfavorably with those for other activities, including nearly three-quarters (74%) who were sung to, 68% who played peek-a-boo, 64% who were taken on errands, and nearly half (47%) who played outside every day. (See Table 4.5; while totals in Table 4.5 reflect percentages for children nine months of age, children were assessed as young as six months and as old as twenty-two months.)

More nine-month-old white children (41%) than African-American (23%), Hispanic (21%), Asian/Pacific Islander (26%), or Native American (18%) children were read to every day. Nearly half (48%) of children whose mothers have a bachelor's degree or higher were read to daily. Poor children (22%) were less likely to be read to than nonpoor children (36%). In terms of other literary activities, three-quarters (75%) of white children were sung to every day, which was not much different from African-American (73%), Hispanic (70%), or Asian/Pacific Islander (71%). About 64% of Native American children were sung

TABLE 4.4

Summary of trends in average reading and mathematics scale scores and score gaps for students age 17, 1971–2004

Reading	Change from 1971*	Change from 1999
Overall	↔	↔
Male	↔	↔
Female	↔	↔
White	↔	↔
Black	↑	↔
Hispanic	↑	↔
Mathematics	**Change from 1973**	**Change from 1999**
Overall	↔	↔
Male	↔	↔
Female	↑	↔
White	↑	↔
Black	↑	↔
Hispanic	↑	↔
Racial/ethnic gaps: reading	**Change from 1971***	**Change from 1999**
White-black	↓	↔
White-Hispanic	↓	↔
Racial/ethnic gaps: mathematics	**Change from 1973**	**Change from 1999**
White-black	↓	↔
White-Hispanic	↓	↔

↑ Average score or score gap increased.

↓ Average score or score gap decreased.

↔ Any change in average score or score gap was not statistically significant.

*Data for Hispanic students are included in the overall national results but not reported as a separate racial/ethnic category in 1971. Therefore, the results for Hispanic students are from 1975.

SOURCE: National Assessment Governing Board, "Figure 9. Summary of Trends in Average Reading and Mathematics Scale Scores and Score Gaps for Students Age 17: 1971–2004," in *NAEP 2004 Trends in Academic Progress: Three Decades of Student Performance in Reading and Mathematics Findings in Brief*, NCES 2005-463, U.S. Department of Education, National Center for Education Statistics, Institute of Education Sciences, Washington, DC, July 2005, http://nces.ed.gov/nationsreportcard/pdf/main2005/2005463.pdf (accessed July 26, 2005)

to every day. Children ages fourteen to twenty-two months were more likely to be read stories every day than younger children. Nearly half (44%) of children in this age group were read stories on a daily basis. (See Table 4.5.)

Another way to look at the early development of children is by the number of family risk factors. Risk factors include living in a household that is below the poverty level, having a language other than English spoken as the primary language at home, having a mother whose highest education was less than a high school diploma or equivalent, and living in a single-parent household. According to the National Center for Education Statistics, 41% of nine-month-old children who had no family risk factors were read to on a daily basis, while 25% of those with one risk factor and 20% of those with two or more risk factors were read to daily in 2001–02. (See Figure 4.2.)

Homework Habits and Reading Performance

The NAEP asked students background questions about their school and home experiences. One question asked was how much time they spent on homework the day before. Possible responses included that no homework was assigned; that homework was assigned but the student did not do it; less than one hour was spent on homework; one to two hours were spent on homework; or more than two hours were spent on homework. The National Center for Education Statistics then analyzed the responses of students by age, and how they scored on the assessment. Nine-year-old students in 2004 who did not have homework assigned the day before had average reading scores of 217; those who had homework but did not do it had average scores of 204; students who spent less than one hour on homework or one to two hours on homework had average scores of 221; and those who spent more than two hours on homework had average scores of 204.

For thirteen-year-olds, the 2004 average reading scale scores for those who did not have homework assigned the day before was 248; students who had homework but did not do it scored 245; those who spent less than one hour on homework scored 261 on average; students who spent one to two hours on homework the day before scored 268; and those who spent more than two hours on homework achieved an average score of 272.

Among seventeen-year-olds in 2004, students who did not have homework the day before scored 270, on average, in reading. Those who had homework assigned but did not do it scored 279. Students who spent less than one hour on homework the day before scored 287, and those who spent one to two hours on homework scored 295. The average reading scale scores of students who spent more than two hours on homework the day before were 304 in 2004.

Daily Reading and Reading Performance

Students at all three ages were asked about the number of pages per day they read in school and for homework. According to the National Center for Education Statistics, nine-year-olds who reported reading five or fewer pages per day had average reading scale scores of 211 in 2004. The score was 220 for students who read six to ten pages per day, 222 for students who read eleven to fifteen pages per day, 223 for students who read sixteen to twenty pages per day, and 222 for students who read more than twenty pages per day. (See Figure 4.3.)

Among thirteen-year-olds, the average reading scale score in 2004 for students who read five or fewer pages per day was 249. For students who read six to ten pages per day, the score was 260. It was 262 for students who reported reading eleven to fifteen pages or sixteen to twenty pages per day, and 263 for students who read more than twenty pages per day. (See Figure 4.3.)

TABLE 4.5

Percentage of babies who engaged in selected activities with a family member daily, by child and family characteristics, 2001–02

Child and family characteristic	Read stories	Told stories	Sung to	Taken on errands	Played peek-a-boo	Played outside
Total	33	27	74	64	68	47
Age						
Less than 10 months	31	26	73	63	68	46
11–13 months	32	27	73	65	69	47
14–22 months	44	37	73	70	64	59
Sex						
Male	32	27	73	64	68	48
Female	33	27	74	64	68	46
Race/ethnicity[a]						
American Indian	18	23	64	75	64	46
Asian/Pacific Islander	26	25	71	38	73	43
Black	23	24	73	63	61	45
White	41	31	75	65	72	47
Hispanic	21	21	70	64	64	48
Birth weight[b]						
Normal	33	27	73	64	68	47
Low	29	28	76	58	70	44
Very low	27	28	73	51	66	38
Poverty status						
Poor	22	24	67	64	64	48
Nonpoor	36	28	75	64	70	47
Mother's education						
Less than high school	22	22	66	64	65	50
High school diploma or equivalent	27	25	72	67	70	44
Some college	35	29	78	65	69	44
Bachelor's degree or higher	48	33	79	59	70	48
Family type						
Two parents, with other siblings	31	25	71	63	65	46
Two parents, without other siblings	38	32	78	62	75	48
One parent, with other siblings	24	25	72	62	65	46
One parent, without other siblings	29	27	73	71	70	48
Primary language spoken in the home						
English	36	29	75	65	70	46
Other than English	18	19	67	57	63	49
Mother's employment						
35 hours or more	29	26	73	59	67	41
Less than 35 hours	36	27	75	66	69	46
Unemployed	27	26	75	68	71	50
Not in labor force	34	28	73	65	68	51
Number of family risk factors[c]						
Zero	41	31	77	64	70	46
One	25	25	73	64	67	47
Two or more	20	20	65	63	64	51

[a]American Indian includes Alaska Native, black includes African American, Pacific Islander includes Native Hawaiian, and Hispanic includes Latino. Race categories exclude Hispanic origin unless specified.

[b]Normal birth weight is more than 5.5 pounds; low birthweight is more than 3.3 to 5.5 pounds; and very low birthweight is 3.3 pounds or less.

[c]Family risk factors include living below the poverty level, living in a household where the primary language was not English, having a mother whose highest education was less than a high school diploma or equivalent, and living in a single-parent household.

Note: While the Early Childhood Longitudinal Study, Birth Cohort was designed to collect information on children about 9 months of age (i.e., 8 to 10 months), children were assessed as young as 6 months and as old as 22 months. Seventy-two percent of the children were between 8 and 10 months at the time of the assessment and 84 percent were between 8 and 11 months.

SOURCE: John Wirt, Susan Choy, Patrick Rooney, William Hussar, Stephen Provasnik, and Gillian Hampden-Thompson, "Table 35–1. Percentage of Children About 9 Months of Age Who Engaged in Selected Activities with a Family Member Daily in a Typical Week, by Child and Family Characteristics: 2001–02," in *The Condition of Education, 2005*, NCES 2005-094, U.S. Department of Education, National Center for Education Statistics, Washington, DC, June 2005, http://nces.ed.gov/programs/coe/2005/section6/table.asp?tableID=301 (accessed July 26, 2005)

In 2004 seventeen-year-olds who read five or fewer pages per day had average reading scale scores of 268. The scores were 282 for students who read six to ten pages per day, 287 for those who read eleven to fifteen pages per day, 293 for students who reported reading sixteen to twenty pages per day, and 297 for students who read more than twenty pages per day. (See Figure 4.3.)

Students were asked how often they read for fun. According to the National Center for Education Statistics,

FIGURE 4.2

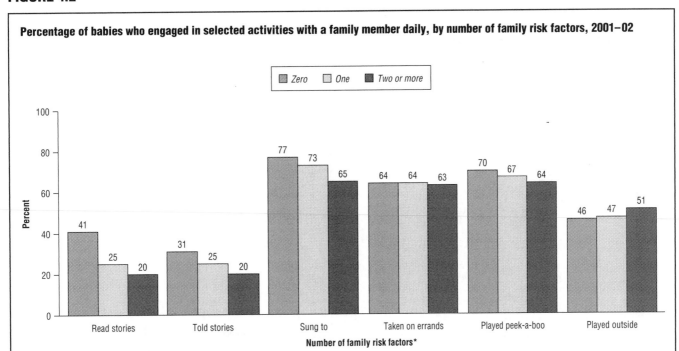

Percentage of babies who engaged in selected activities with a family member daily, by number of family risk factors, 2001–02

Legend: ▨ Zero ▢ One ▦ Two or more

*Family risk factors include living below the poverty level, living in a household where the primary language was not English, having a mother whose highest education was less than a high school diploma or equivalent, and living in a single-parent household.
Note: While the Early Childhood Longitudinal Study, Birth Cohort (ECLS–B) was designed to collect information on children about 9 months of age (i.e., 8 to 10 months), children were assessed as young as 6 months and as old as 22 months. Seventy-two percent of the children were between 8 and 10 months at the time of the assessment, and 84 percent were between 8 and 11 months.

SOURCE: John Wirt, Susan Choy, Patrick Rooney, William Hussar, Stephen Provasnik, and Gillian Hampden-Thompson, "Parent–Child Interactions: Percentage of Children About 9 Months of Age who Engaged in Selected Activities with a Family Member Daily in a Typical Week, by Number of Family Risk Factors: 2001–02," in *The Condition of Education, 2005*, NCES 2005-094, U.S. Department of Education, National Center for Education Statistics, Washington, DC, June 2005, http://nces.ed.gov/pubs2005/2005094.pdf (accessed July 26, 2005)

among nine-year-olds, those who read for fun almost every day had average reading scale scores of 220 in 2004. Those who reported reading for fun once or twice per week scored 224 on average. The scores were 216 for students who read for fun once or twice per month, 209 for those who read for fun a few times per year, and 203 for students who reported that they never or hardly ever read for fun. (See Figure 4.4.)

The average reading scale score was 271 for thirteen-year-olds who reported reading for fun almost every day. The score was 261 for students who read for fun once or twice per week, 256 for those who read for fun once or twice per month, and 236 for students who never or hardly ever read for fun. Too few students responded that they read for fun only a few times per year for a reliable estimate of the average reading scale score to be reported for this group. (See Figure 4.4.)

For seventeen-year-olds who reported reading for fun almost every day the average reading scale score was 305 in 2004. It was 288 for students who reported reading for fun once or twice a week, 287 for those who read for fun once or twice a month, 272 for those who read for fun a few times a year, and 268 for students who never or hardly ever read for fun. (See Figure 4.4.)

MATHEMATICS PERFORMANCE

Since 1973 the NAEP has assessed the mathematics performance of nine-, thirteen-, and seventeen-year-olds. The 2005 NAEP mathematics framework specifies five content areas to be assessed: number properties and operations; measurement; geometry; data analysis and probability; and algebra. According to the National Center for Education Statistics, on the 2003 mathematics assessment, 39% of all grade eight students scored at the basic level, 23% at the proficient level, and 5% at the advanced level. The remaining students were categorized as below basic level.

Long-term trend data for 1973 to 2004 from the National Center for Education Statistics indicate that the average mathematics scale scores for nine-year-olds increased from 219 in 1973 to 241 in 2004. Between 1999 and 2004 mathematics scores of nine-year-olds went up nine points from 232 to 241. The mathematics scores of thirteen-year-olds rose fifteen points between 1973 and 2004, from 266 to 281, with an increase of five points from 1999 to 2004 (276 to 281). For seventeen-year-olds, mathematics scores were not much different in 2004 (307) from the 1973 level (304). However, the 2004 scores represented a slight decline from 1999, when

FIGURE 4.3

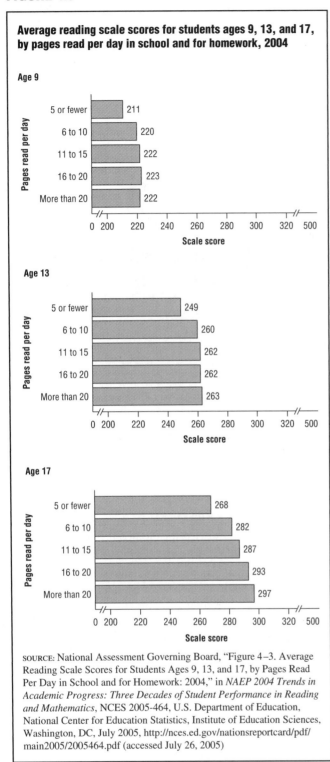

Average reading scale scores for students ages 9, 13, and 17, by pages read per day in school and for homework, 2004

Age 9

Pages read per day

5 or fewer	211
6 to 10	220
11 to 15	222
16 to 20	223
More than 20	222

Scale score

Age 13

Pages read per day

5 or fewer	249
6 to 10	260
11 to 15	262
16 to 20	262
More than 20	263

Scale score

Age 17

Pages read per day

5 or fewer	268
6 to 10	282
11 to 15	287
16 to 20	293
More than 20	297

Scale score

SOURCE: National Assessment Governing Board, "Figure 4–3. Average Reading Scale Scores for Students Ages 9, 13, and 17, by Pages Read Per Day in School and for Homework: 2004," in *NAEP 2004 Trends in Academic Progress: Three Decades of Student Performance in Reading and Mathematics*, NCES 2005-464, U.S. Department of Education, National Center for Education Statistics, Institute of Education Sciences, Washington, DC, July 2005, http://nces.ed.gov/nationsreportcard/pdf/ main2005/2005464.pdf (accessed July 26, 2005)

FIGURE 4.4

Average reading scale scores for students ages 9, 13, and 17, by frequency of reading for fun, 2004

Age 9

Frequency of reading for fun

Almost every day	220
Once or twice a week	224
Once or twice a month	216
A few times a year	209
Never or hardly ever	203

Scale score

Age 13

Frequency of reading for fun

Almost every day	271
Once or twice a week	261
Once or twice a month	256
A few times a year*	
Never or hardly ever	236

Scale score

Age 17

Frequency of reading for fun

Almost every day	305
Once or twice a week	288
Once or twice a month	287
A few times a year	272
Never or hardly ever	268

Scale score

*Reporting standards not met. Sample size is insufficient to permit a reliable estimate.

SOURCE: National Assessment Governing Board, "Figure 4–5. Average Reading Scale Scores for Students Ages 9, 13, and 17, by Frequency of Reading for Fun: 2004," in *NAEP 2004 Trends in Academic Progress: Three Decades of Student Performance in Reading and Mathematics*, NCES 2005-464, U.S. Department of Education, National Center for Education Statistics, Institute of Education Sciences, Washington, DC, July 2005, http://nces.ed.gov/nationsreportcard/pdf/main2005/2005464 .pdf (accessed July 26, 2005)

scores for seventeen-year-olds had reached an all-time high of 308. (See Figure 4.5.)

Since 1996 schools have been encouraged to make testing accommodations on the mathematics NAEP for students with disabilities or limited English proficiency. According to the National Center for Education Statistics, average mathematics scores increased for grade four

students from 213 in 1990 to 235 in 2003. In 1996 students in grade four who had testing accommodations scored the same as students who did not have testing accommodations (224). In 2000 grade four students with accommodations scored slightly lower (226) on average than students who did not have accommodations (228).

FIGURE 4.5

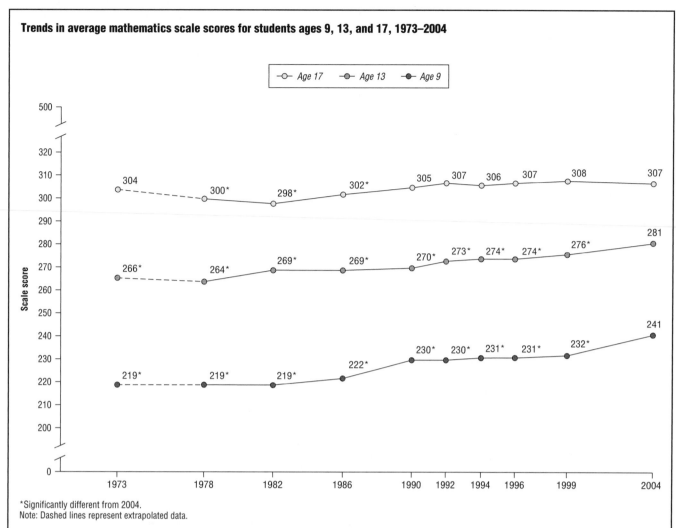

Trends in average mathematics scale scores for students ages 9, 13, and 17, 1973–2004

*Significantly different from 2004.
Note: Dashed lines represent extrapolated data.

SOURCE: National Assessment Governing Board, "Figure 2. Trends in Average Mathematics Scale Scores for Students Ages 9, 13, and 17: 1973–2004," in *NAEP 2004 Trends in Academic Progress: Three Decades of Student Performance in Reading and Mathematics Findings in Brief*, NCES 2005-463, U.S. Department of Education, National Center for Education Statistics, Institute of Education Sciences, Washington, DC, July 2005, http://nces.ed.gov/nationsreportcard/pdf/main2005/2005463.pdf (accessed July 26, 2005)

Among students in grade eight, scores increased from 263 in 1990 to 278 in 2003. In 1996 students with accommodations scored 270, while those without accommodations scored 272. There was a two-point difference between the scores again in 2000, when students with accommodations scored 273, and those without accommodations scored 275. Since there were no significant differences between scores of students with and without accommodations, after 2000 the data for all students was reported in only a single category, with accommodations. (See Figure 4.6.)

**Long-Term Trend Mathematics Scores
of Nine-Year-Olds**

According to the National Center for Education Statistics, scores of nine-year-olds increased for all ethnic groups and both genders from 1973 to 1999 and from 1999 to 2004. The achievement gap between mathematics scores

of white and African-American nine-year-olds narrowed between 1973 and 1999, but it stayed about the same from 1999 to 2004. Between white and Hispanic students at age nine, the achievement gap in mathematics stayed about the same from 1975 to 1999, but it decreased from 1999 to 2004. (See Table 4.2.) Although there has been a small score gap since 1973 and a three-point gap in the 2004 mathematics scores of male and female nine-year-olds, it was not considered statistically significant. The score gap between white and African-American students decreased twelve points from 1973 to 2004.

**Long-Term Trend Mathematics Scores
of Thirteen-Year-Olds**

The National Center for Education Statistics reports that the scores of thirteen-year-olds increased for all ethnic groups and both genders from 1973 to 1999, as well as from 1999 to 2004. The achievement gap between

FIGURE 4.6

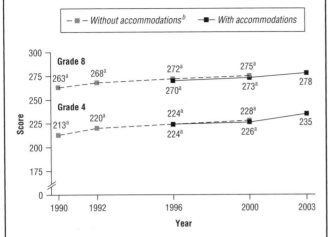

Average mathematics scores for 4th- and 8th-graders, selected years, 1990–2003

[a]Significantly different from 2003.

[b]Testing accommodations (e.g., extended time, small group testing) for children with disabilities and limited-English-proficient students were not permitted.

Note: In addition to allowing for accommodations, the accommodations-permitted results (1996–2003) differ slightly from previous years' results, and from previously reported results for 1996 and 2000, due to changes in sample weighting procedures. The NAEP national sample in 2003 was obtained by aggregating the samples from each state, rather than by obtaining an independently selected national sample. As a consequence, the size of the national sample increased, and smaller differences between years or between types of students were found to be statistically significant than would have been detected in previous assessments. The 2003 mathematics assessment did not include students in grade 12.

SOURCE: John Wirt, Susan Choy, Patrick Rooney, William Hussar, Stephen Provasnik, and Gillian Hampden-Thompson, "Mathematics Performance: Average Mathematics Scores for 4th- and 8th-Graders: Selected Years, 1990–2003," in *The Condition of Education, 2005,* NCES 2005-094, U.S. Department of Education, National Center for Education Statistics, Washington, DC, June 2005, http://nces.ed.gov/pubs2005/2005094.pdf (accessed July 26, 2005)

mathematics scores of white and African-American students decreased from 1973 to 1999 but stayed about the same between 1999 and 2004. The gap between white and Hispanic thirteen-year-olds also decreased from 1975 to 1999 and stayed about the same from 1999 to 2004. (See Table 4.3.) Among thirteen-year-olds, there was only a small change in the gender gap from 1973 to 2004; on average, in 1973 females scored two points higher than males in mathematics; in 1999 males scored two points higher; and in 2004 males scored four points higher than females in mathematics. The mathematics score gap between white and African-American students at age thirteen narrowed nineteen points between 1973 and 2004.

Long-Term Trend Mathematics Scores of Seventeen-Year-Olds

According to the National Center for Education Statistics, on average, mathematics scores of seventeen-year-olds showed no statistically significant difference from 1973 to 2004. However, scores of female, white, and African-American students increased between 1973 and 1999, and scores of Hispanic students improved from 1975 to 1999. Between 1999 and 2004 there were no statistically significant changes in scores for any group. The achievement gap between mathematics scores of white and African-American students decreased from 1973 to 1999, but it stayed about the same from 1999 to 2004. The gap also decreased between white and Hispanic students from 1975 to 1999, but it showed no significant difference from 1999 to 2004. (See Table 4.4.) Among seventeen-year-olds, the mathematics gender gap between males and females decreased five points from 1973 to 1999; on average, in 1973 males scored eight points higher than females in mathematics, while in 1999 males scored three points higher. No change was seen in the mathematics gender gap between 1999 and 2004. The score gap between white and African-American students at age seventeen decreased twelve points from 1973 to 2004.

Mathematics Instruction and Math Performance

Students taking the mathematics NAEP were asked several background questions related to course taking, homework, television watching, and computer use. Each of these factors was analyzed to see how it related to performance in mathematics.

At age thirteen, students were asked what kind of mathematics class they were in that year. According to the National Center for Education Statistics, thirteen-year-olds who were in regular mathematics had average scale scores of 269 in 2004. Those in pre-algebra scored 284, and those in algebra scored 296. Students who were taking another mathematics course scored 279. The sample of students who reported that they were not taking mathematics was too small to provide a reliable estimate of an average score. (See Figure 4.7.)

At age seventeen, students were asked whether they were currently taking, or had ever taken, any course in a list of mathematics courses. Students who were taking or had taken pre-algebra (or less) as their highest-level mathematics course scored 270 on average in 2004. According to the National Center for Education Statistics, those who were taking or had taken first-year algebra as their highest course scored 282, and those for whom geometry was the highest mathematics course scored 296. Second-year algebra students scored 310, while students who had taken or were taking calculus scored 336. The sample of students who reported that they had taken another course, such as trigonometry or general mathematics, was too small to provide a reliable estimate of an average score. (See Figure 4.8.)

Students age seventeen were asked about the frequency with which they did mathematics homework. According to the National Center for Education Statistics, students who reported doing mathematics homework often

FIGURE 4.7

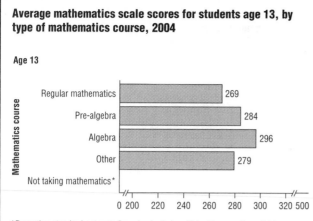

Average mathematics scale scores for students age 13, by type of mathematics course, 2004

*Reporting standard not met. Sample size is insufficient to permit a reliable estimate.

SOURCE: National Assessment Governing Board, "Figure 4–7. Average Mathematics Scale Scores for Students Age 13, by Type of Mathematics Course: 2004," in *NAEP 2004 Trends in Academic Progress: Three Decades of Student Performance in Reading and Mathematics*, NCES 2005-464, U.S. Department of Education, National Center for Education Statistics, Institute of Education Sciences, Washington, DC, July 2005, http://nces.ed.gov/nationsreportcard/pdf/main2005/2005464 .pdf (accessed July 26, 2005)

FIGURE 4.8

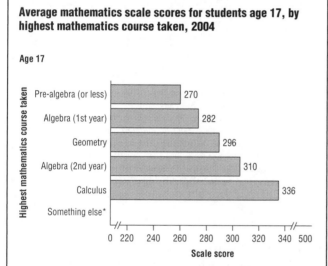

Average mathematics scale scores for students age 17, by highest mathematics course taken, 2004

*Reporting standards not met. Sample size is insufficient to permit a reliable estimate.

SOURCE: National Assessment Governing Board, "Figure 4–9. Average Mathematics Scale Scores for Students Age 17, by Highest Mathematics Course Taken: 2004," in *NAEP 2004 Trends in Academic Progress: Three Decades of Student Performance in Reading and Mathematics*, NCES 2005-464, U.S. Department of Education, National Center for Education Statistics, Institute of Education Sciences, Washington, DC, July 2005, http://nces.ed.gov/nationsreportcard/pdf/main2005/2005464 .pdf (accessed July 26, 2005)

FIGURE 4.9

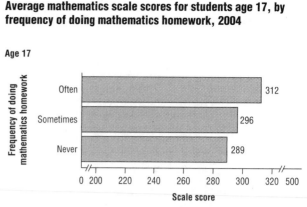

Average mathematics scale scores for students age 17, by frequency of doing mathematics homework, 2004

SOURCE: National Assessment Governing Board, "Figure 4–15. Average Mathematics Scale Scores for Students Age 17, by Frequency of Doing Mathematics Homework: 2004," in *NAEP 2004 Trends in Academic Progress: Three Decades of Student Performance in Reading and Mathematics*, NCES 2005-464, U.S. Department of Education, National Center for Education Statistics, Institute of Education Sciences, Washington, DC, July 2005, http://nces.ed.gov/nationsreportcard/pdf/ main2005/2005464.pdf (accessed July 26, 2005)

At ages thirteen and seventeen, students were asked about their use of computers for mathematics work. According to the National Center for Education Statistics, thirteen-year-olds who reported receiving computer instruction had average scale scores of 283 in 2004, while those who did not receive computer instruction scored 280. Students age thirteen who had access to a computer in school for mathematics scored 283, and those who did not have access in school scored 282. Those who used a computer to solve mathematical problems scored 283, while those who did not use a computer scored 278 on average in 2004. (See Figure 4.10.)

According to the National Center for Education Statistics, seventeen-year-olds who reported receiving computer instruction had average mathematics scale scores of 307, which was the same as for those who did not receive computer instruction in 2004. Students at age seventeen who had access to a computer in school for mathematics scored 308, and those who did not have access in school scored 303. Those who used a computer to solve mathematical problems scored 309, while those who did not use a computer scored 303 on average in 2004. (See Figure 4.10.)

Television Viewing Habits and Mathematics Scores

Students at all three ages (nine, thirteen, and seventeen) were asked how much television they watched every day. According to the National Center for Education Statistics, among nine-year-olds, students who reported watching zero to two hours of television per day had average mathematics scale scores of 244 in 2004. Those who watched three to five hours of television daily scored 245, while those who reported watching

had average scale scores of 312 in 2004. Among those reporting that they did mathematics homework sometimes, the score was 296, and students who never did math homework scored 289 on average. (See Figure 4.9.)

FIGURE 4.10

FIGURE 4.11

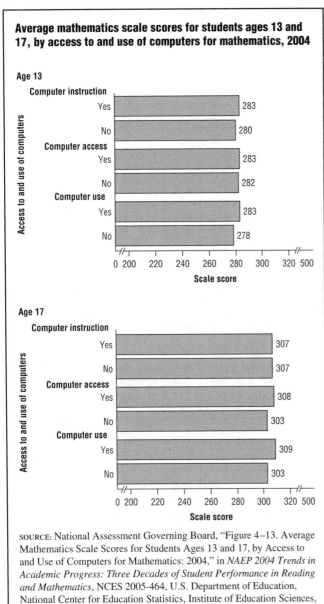

Average mathematics scale scores for students ages 13 and 17, by access to and use of computers for mathematics, 2004

SOURCE: National Assessment Governing Board, "Figure 4–13. Average Mathematics Scale Scores for Students Ages 13 and 17, by Access to and Use of Computers for Mathematics: 2004," in *NAEP 2004 Trends in Academic Progress: Three Decades of Student Performance in Reading and Mathematics*, NCES 2005-464, U.S. Department of Education, National Center for Education Statistics, Institute of Education Sciences, Washington, DC, July 2005, http://nces.ed.gov/nationsreportcard/pdf/main2005/2005464.pdf (accessed July 26, 2005)

Average mathematics scale scores for students ages 9, 13, and 17, by amount of daily television watching, 2004

Age 9

Number of hours watched per day
- 0 to 2 hours: 244
- 3 to 5 hours: 245
- 6 or more hours: 229

Age 13

Number of hours watched per day
- 0 to 2 hours: 288
- 3 to 5 hours: 279
- 6 or more hours: 264

Age 17

Number of hours watched per day
- 0 to 2 hours: 313
- 3 to 5 hours: 300
- 6 or more hours: 286

SOURCE: National Assessment Governing Board, "Figure 4–17. Average Mathematics Scale Scores for Students Ages 9, 13, and 17, by Amount of Daily Television Watching: 2004," in *NAEP 2004 Trends in Academic Progress: Three Decades of Student Performance in Reading and Mathematics*, NCES 2005-464, U.S. Department of Education, National Center for Education Statistics, Institute of Education Sciences, Washington, DC, July 2005, http://nces.ed.gov/nationsreportcard/pdf/main2005/2005464.pdf (accessed July 26, 2005)

six or more hours of television every day had scores of 229 on average. (See Figure 4.11.)

According to the National Center for Education Statistics, thirteen-year-olds who reported watching zero to two hours of television per day had average mathematics scale scores of 288 in 2004. Those who watched three to five hours of television on a daily basis scored 279, while students who reported watching six or more hours of television every day had scores of 264 on average. (See Figure 4.11.)

According to the National Center for Education Statistics, seventeen-year-olds who reported watching zero to two hours of television per day had average mathematics scale scores of 313 in 2004. Those who

watched three to five hours of television daily scored 300, while students who reported watching six or more hours of television every day had scores of 286 on average. (See Figure 4.11.)

SCIENCE PERFORMANCE

Since 1977 the NAEP has assessed the science performance of students at age nine, thirteen, and seventeen. According to the NAEP Web site (http://nces.ed.gov/nationsreportcard/science/whatmeasure.asp), the science assessment addresses students' knowledge of facts in areas of earth, physical, and life sciences and measures their ability to "use the tools, procedures, and reasoning processes of science to develop an increased understanding of the natural world." The most recent results that have been released reflect the assessments conducted in 2000.

In general, the 2000 NAEP assessments indicated that science performance has remained stable since 1996. High-performing eighth-grade students increased their science scale scores between 1996 and 2000, while those of middle-performing twelfth-graders decreased. NAEP science assessments were again conducted in 2005, with results to be made public in 2006.

According to the National Center for Education Statistics, average scores on the NAEP science assessment were not significantly different overall in 2000 from 1996 levels. However, Native American students in all three grades and twelfth-grade white students had lower scores in 2000 than they did in 1996. Eighth-grade male students' average science score was higher in 2000 than it was in 1996. Twelfth-grade males and females scored lower in 2000, on average, than they had in 1996.

WRITING PERFORMANCE

In 2002 NAEP administered a writing assessment to students in grades four, eight, and twelve. Students were asked to write narrative, informative, and persuasive essays based on a variety of materials, including photographs, cartoons, and poems. They were asked to draft, revise, and edit their work, which was measured at three achievement levels: basic, proficient, and advanced. The basic level means partial mastery of the knowledge and skills that are fundamental for proficient work at a given grade. The proficient level represents solid academic performance; students reaching this level demonstrate competency in challenging subject matter. The advanced level indicates mastery of both the basic and proficient levels and represents superior performance. The next writing assessment is scheduled for 2007. (See Table 4.1.)

Writing scores at each grade level ranged from 0 to 300. Basic level achievement scores in grade four ranged from 115 to 175; proficient level ranged from 176 to 224; and advanced level scores ranged from 225 to 300. Basic level achievement scores in grade eight ranged from 114 to 172; proficient level scores from 173 to 223; and advanced level scores from 224 to 300. Basic level achievement scores in grade twelve ranged from 122 to 177; proficient level scores from 178 to 229; and advanced level scores from 230 to 300. Performance is scaled separately, so average scale scores cannot be compared across grades.

Comparisons between 1998 and 2002

According to the National Center for Education Statistics, all the 2002 writing results for grade four, and some of the eighth and twelfth grade results, were significantly different from the 1998 assessment. The proportion of grade four students who scored below the basic

TABLE 4.6

Percentage of students by writing achievement level, grades 4, 8, and 12, 1998 and 2002

	Below basic	At basic	At proficient	At advanced	At or above basic	At or above proficient
Grade 4						
1998	16*	61*	22*	1*	84*	23*
2002	14	58	26	2	86	28
Grade 8						
1998	16	58*	25*	1*	84	27*
2002	15	54	29	2	85	31
Grade 12						
1998	22*	57*	21	1*	78*	22
2002	26	51	22	2	74	24

*Significantly different from 2002.
Note: Percentages within each writing achievement level range may not add to 100, or to the exact percentages at or above achievement levels, due to rounding.

SOURCE: Hilary R. Persky, Mary C. Daane, and Ying Jin, "Table 2.1. Percentage of Students by Writing Achievement Level, Grades 4, 8, and 12: 1998 and 2002," in *The Nation's Report Card: Writing 2002*, NCES 2003-529, U.S. Department of Education, National Center for Education Statistics, Washington, DC, July 2003, http://nces.ed.gov/nationsreportcard/pdf/main2002/2003529.pdf (accessed July 26, 2005)

level was 16% in 1998, while in 2002 it had dropped to 14%. (See Table 4.6.) Another 61% of fourth-graders scored at the basic level of writing achievement in 1998, while 58% were at this level of achievement in 2002. Proficient students increased from 22% in 1998 to 26% in 2002, and advanced students increased from 1% in 1998 to 2% in 2002. Among eighth-grade students, 58% scored at the basic level in 1998; this decreased to 54% in 2002. Students writing at the proficient level increased from 25% in 1998 to 29% in 2002, and advanced students increased from 1% in 1998 to 2% in 2002. The proportion of grade twelve students at the basic level decreased from 57% in 1998 to 51% in 2002. Students in grade twelve scoring at the advanced level increased from 1% in 1998 to 2% in 2002. The only statistically significant change that showed decreased writing proficiency was between the proportion of seniors scoring below basic in 1998 (22%) and in 2002 (26%).

Results by Race/Ethnicity

According to the National Center for Education Statistics, fourth-grade Asian/Pacific Islander students had the highest average writing scores of all racial and ethnic groups in 2002 at 167, followed by white students (161), Hispanic students (141), and African-American students (140). At grade eight, white and Asian/Pacific Islander students both scored an average of 161 on the assessment, followed by Hispanic students (137) and African-American students (135). White twelfth-graders scored highest among racial and ethnic groups at that level in 2002 (154), followed by Asian/Pacific Islander students (151), Hispanic students (136), and African-American students

(130). The National Center for Education Statistics indicated that average scores were not available for Native American/Alaska Native students because the sample size was too small to ensure the accuracy of results.

Results by Gender

At all three grade levels, females had higher average writing scores than males in 2002. Fourth-grade females scored an average 163, compared to 146 for males. Eighth-grade girls scored 164, compared to 143 for boys, and twelfth-grade girls scored 160, compared to 136 for boys. Average writing scale scores increased five points for fourth-grade girls between 1998 and 2002 and four points for fourth-grade boys. Writing scores for eighth-graders also showed improvement, with girls' scores rising four points between 1998 and 2002 and boys' scores increasing an average of three points. However, average writing scale scores did not show improvement among twelfth-graders between 1998 and 2002. The average score for female students edged up slightly from 159 to 160, but the scores for male students declined by four points from 140 to 136.

GEOGRAPHY PERFORMANCE

In 2001 NAEP administered a geography assessment to students in grades four, eight, and twelve, measuring performance at three achievement levels: basic, proficient, and advanced. The Geography NAEP measures students' knowledge, understanding, and ability to apply knowledge about "space and place"; "environment and society"; and "spatial dynamics and connections." For example, students must *know* where the world's largest tropical rain forest is located, *understand* why it is located near the equator, and *apply* that knowledge in support of the conclusion that tropical rain forests promote wide species variation.

Comparisons between 1994 and 2001 Scores

According to the National Center for Education Statistics, at grade four the percentage of students performing at the basic or proficient levels in geography increased from 70% in 1994 to 74% in 2001. The percentage of eighth-grade students performing at or above the basic level increased from 71% in 1994 to 74% in 2001. The percentage of twelfth-graders achieving at least a basic level of proficiency rose slightly from 70% in 1994 to 71% in 2001.

At all three grade levels, white students achieved the highest average scores in 2001: white fourth-graders averaged 222, eighth-graders averaged 273, and twelfth-graders averaged 291. Asian/Pacific Islander students had the second-highest averages at fourth grade (212) and eighth grade (266), but were edged out by Native American students in twelfth grade (286 and 288). Hispanic students had higher average scores than African-American students in all three grades. However, the average scores of African-American fourth-graders improved dramatically from 168 in 1994 to 181 in 2001 and almost closed the gap with Hispanic fourth-graders, who averaged 184.

In 2001 male students at all three grade levels had higher average scale scores than females, but there were no significant changes in the scores of males and females from 1994 to 2001. The next geography assessment is scheduled for 2010. (See Table 4.1.)

U.S. HISTORY PERFORMANCE

In 2001 NAEP administered a U.S. history assessment to students in grades four, eight, and twelve, measuring performance at three achievement levels: basic, proficient, and advanced. According to the NAEP Web site (http://nces.ed.gov/nationsreportcard/ushistory/whatmeasure.asp), the test focused on several themes in American history, including:

1. "Change and continuity in American democracy: ideas, institutions, practices, and controversies;

2. The gathering and interactions of peoples, cultures, and ideas;

3. Economic and technological changes and their relation to society, ideas, and the environment; and

4. The changing role of America in the world."

The NAEP U.S. history assessments evaluated students' knowledge and understanding of historical events, concepts, and movements and measured their ability to analyze and interpret historical issues, patterns, and relationships.

Comparisons between 1994 and 2001 Scores

According to the National Center for Educational Statistics, in grade four the percentage of students performing at the basic level or above increased from 64% in 1994 to 67% in 2001, but there were no significant differences in the percentages performing at the proficient or advanced levels. In grade eight, the percentage of students who performed at the basic level remained steady at 48% between 1994 and 2001, but increases were noted in those achieving the proficient level (from 13% in 1994 to 15% in 2001) and the advanced level (from 1% to 2%). In grade twelve there were no significant changes in performance at any level of proficiency. More than half of twelfth-graders (57%) failed to achieve even the basic level of proficiency. About one-third of twelfth-graders scored in the basic range in 2001, 10% reached the proficient ranking, and 1% were advanced.

Average Scores by Race/Ethnicity

At all three grade levels, white students had higher scale scores than African-American, Hispanic, and Native American students. Asian/Pacific Islanders ranked second behind white students in both the fourth and eighth grades but had the highest average scores among twelfth graders.

African-American students achieved significantly higher average scores in 2001 (188) than they had in 1994 (177). The average for white fourth-grade students also showed improvement from 215 in 1994 to 220 in 2001. Eighth-grade white students scored a higher average in 2001 (271) than they had in 1994 (267), and twelfth-grade Hispanic students increased their average scores significantly in 2001 (274) from 1994 (267).

Results by Gender

Male fourth graders improved significantly from 203 in 1994 to 209 in 2001, matching the average reached by female fourth-grade students in 2001. Male students in eighth grade averaged 264 in 2001, which was three points above the average for female students in the same grade. Among twelfth-graders in 2001, male students surpassed the female average, with male students measuring 288 to the female students' 286. The next U.S. history assessment will be in 2006. (See Table 4.1.)

Computer Use and U.S. History Performance

Students and teachers answered questions for the 2001 NAEP U.S. history assessment related to the ways in which they use computers at school in history and social studies classes. According to the National Center for Education Statistics, about one-quarter of students in grade four and one-third of students in grades eight and twelve reported that they use computers for social studies at least once every few weeks. At all three grades, students who used computers every day in class had lower average scale scores than students who used computers less frequently.

INTERNATIONAL COMPARISONS

In 2003 the Trends in International Mathematics and Science Study (TIMSS, formerly known as the Third International Mathematics and Science Study) compared the mathematics and science performance of fourth-graders in twenty-five countries and eighth-graders in forty-five countries around the world. This comparison with students in other countries allows the United States to monitor its progress toward the goal of being first in the world in mathematics and science achievement.

According to the National Center for Educational Statistics, at grade eight U.S. mathematics scores increased from 1995 to 2005, but there was no significant difference in average scores between 1999 and 2003, so the gain was made between 1995 and 1999. The TIMSS indicated that in 2003 U.S. students in grades four and eight scored above the international average in mathematics. On average, grade four students scored higher than students in thirteen countries and lower than students in eleven countries. The average score of U.S. students in grade eight in mathematics was higher than students in thirty countries, but students in thirteen countries outperformed U.S. eighth graders. (See Table 4.7.)

TABLE 4.7

Average mathematics scores of 8th-grade students, by country, 2003

Average score relative to the United States	Country	Score
Significantly higher	Singapore	605
	Korea, Republic of	589
	Hong Kong SAR[a,b]	586
	Chinese Taipei	585
	Japan	570
	Belgium-Flemish	537
	Netherlands[b]	536
	Estonia	531
	Hungary	529
Not significantly different	Malaysia	508
	Latvia	508
	Russian Federation	508
	Slovak Republic	508
	Australia	505
	United States[c]	504
	Lithuania[d]	502
	Sweden	499
	Scotland[b]	498
	Israel[c]	496
	New Zealand	494
Significantly lower	Slovenia	493
	Italy	484
	Armenia	478
	Serbia	477
	Bulgaria	476
	Romania	475
	International average	466
	Norway	461
	Moldova, Republic of	460
	Cyprus	459
	Macedonia, Republic of[c]	435
	Lebanon	433
	Jordan	424
	Iran, Islamic Republic of	411
	Indonesia[d]	411
	Tunisia	410
	Egypt	406
	Bahrain	401
	Palestinian National Authority	390
	Chile	387
	Morocco[c]	387
	Philippines	378
	Botswana	366
	Saudi Arabia	332
	Ghana	276
	South Africa	264

[a]Hong Kong is a Special Administrative Region (SAR) of the People's Republic of China.
[b]Met international guidelines for participation rates only after replacement schools were included.
[c]Country did not meet international sampling or other guidelines.
[d]National desired population does not cover all of the international desired population.
Note: Countries were required to sample students in the upper of the two grades that contained the larger number of 9- and 13-year-olds. In the United States and most countries, this corresponds to grades 4 and 8.

SOURCE: John Wirt, Susan Choy, Patrick Rooney, William Hussar, Stephen Provasnik, and Gillian Hampden-Thompson, "International Mathematics Performance: Average Mathematics Scores of 8th-Grade Students, by Country: 2003," in *The Condition of Education, 2005,* NCES 2005-094, U.S. Department of Education, National Center for Education Statistics, Washington, DC, June 2005, http://nces.ed.gov/pubs2005/2005094.pdf (accessed July 26, 2005)

The National Center for Education Statistics reports that in 2003 students in the United States in grades four and eight scored, on average, above the international average in science. At grade four, U.S. students outperformed students in sixteen countries, while students in three countries scored higher than U.S. students. At grade eight, students in the United States outperformed students in thirty-six countries, while students in eight countries scored higher than U.S. eighth graders. (See Table 4.8.)

CARNEGIE UNITS AND HIGH SCHOOL COURSE AVAILABILITY

In response to the recommendations of the National Education Goals Panel (see Chapter 5), many state legislatures, local school boards, and departments of education have attempted to strengthen high school graduation requirements. While state-mandated standards cannot necessarily measure activities in the classroom, they tend to indicate a state's desire to improve its schools.

The District of Columbia and most states have established minimum Carnegie units (one unit equals an academic year course of two semesters) required for high school graduation. According to the Council of Chief State School Officers (CCSSO), as of 2002, thirty-eight states required four credits in English (see Figure 4.12), twenty-five states required 2.5 or more credits in mathematics (see Figure 4.13), twenty-two states required 2.5 or more credits in science (see Figure 4.14), and thirty-six states required 2.5 or more credits in social studies. (See Figure 4.15.)

Table 4.9 shows the average Carnegie units earned by high school graduates in various subject fields in 2000. According to the National Center for Education Statistics, the average number of Carnegie units earned by public high school graduates in 2000 was just over twenty-six. Students earned an average of 4.4 credits in English, 3.8 in history/social studies, 3.6 in mathematics, 3.2 in science, 2 in foreign language, 2 in art, 4.2 in vocational education, and 0.8 in computer science.

In "The 36th Annual Phi Delta Kappa/Gallup Poll of the Public's Attitude toward the Public Schools" (Lowell C. Rose and Alec M. Gallup, *Phi Delta Kappan*, September 2004), those polled were asked whether they favored or opposed requiring high school students to take four years of English, mathematics, and science to graduate from high school in their community. More than three-quarters (78%) favored this requirement. Twenty percent opposed requiring four years of English, mathematics, and science for high school graduation. (See Table 4.10.)

According to the National Center for Education Statistics, since 1982 the proportion of students taking

TABLE 4.8

Average science scores of 8th-grade students, by country, 2003

Average score relative to the United States	Country	Score
Significantly higher	Singapore	578
	Chinese Taipei	571
	Korea, Republic of	558
	Hong Kong SAR[a,b]	556
	Estonia	552
	Japan	552
	Hungary	543
Not significantly different	Netherlands[b]	536
	United States[c]	527
	Australia	527
	Sweden	524
	Slovenia	520
	New Zealand	520
Significantly lower	Lithuania[d]	519
	Slovak Republic	517
	Belgium-Flemish	516
	Russian Federation	514
	Latvia	512
	Scotland[b]	512
	Malaysia	510
	Norway	494
	Italy	491
	Israel[c]	488
	Bulgaria	479
	Jordan	475
	International average	473
	Moldova, Republic of	472
	Romania	470
	Serbia	468
	Armenia	461
	Iran, Islamic Republic of	453
	Macedonia, Republic of[c]	449
	Cyprus	441
	Bahrain	438
	Palestinian National Authority	435
	Egypt	421
	Indonesia[d]	420
	Chile	413
	Tunisia	404
	Saudi Arabia	398
	Morocco[c]	396
	Lebanon	393
	Philippines	377
	Botswana	365
	Ghana	255
	South Africa	244

[a]Hong Kong is a Special Administrative Region (SAR) of the People's Republic of China.
[b]Met international guidelines for participation rates only after replacement schools were included.
[c]Country did not meet international sampling or other guidelines.
[d]National desired population does not cover all of the international desired population.
Note: Countries were required to sample students in the upper of the two grades that contained the larger number of 9- and 13-year-olds. In the United States and most countries, this corresponds to grades 4 and 8.

SOURCE: John Wirt, Susan Choy, Patrick Rooney, William Hussar, Stephen Provasnik, and Gillian Hampden-Thompson, "International Science Performance: Average Science Scores of 8th-Grade Students, by Country: 2003," in *The Condition of Education, 2005*, NCES 2005-094, U.S. Department of Education, National Center for Education Statistics, Washington, DC, June 2005, http://nces.ed.gov/pubs2005/2005094.pdf (accessed July 26, 2005)

FIGURE 4.12

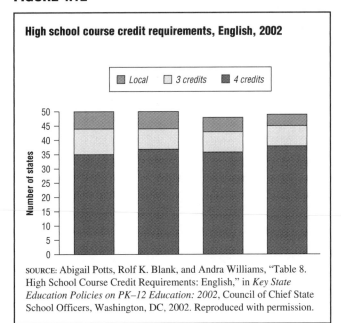

High school course credit requirements, English, 2002

SOURCE: Abigail Potts, Rolf K. Blank, and Andra Williams, "Table 8. High School Course Credit Requirements: English," in *Key State Education Policies on PK–12 Education: 2002*, Council of Chief State School Officers, Washington, DC, 2002. Reproduced with permission.

FIGURE 4.14

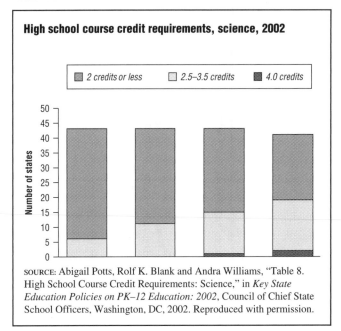

High school course credit requirements, science, 2002

SOURCE: Abigail Potts, Rolf K. Blank and Andra Williams, "Table 8. High School Course Credit Requirements: Science," in *Key State Education Policies on PK–12 Education: 2002*, Council of Chief State School Officers, Washington, DC, 2002. Reproduced with permission.

FIGURE 4.13

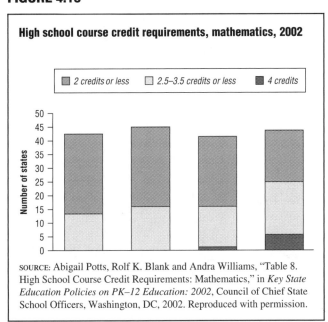

High school course credit requirements, mathematics, 2002

SOURCE: Abigail Potts, Rolf K. Blank and Andra Williams, "Table 8. High School Course Credit Requirements: Mathematics," in *Key State Education Policies on PK–12 Education: 2002*, Council of Chief State School Officers, Washington, DC, 2002. Reproduced with permission.

FIGURE 4.15

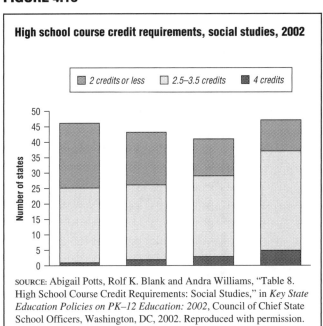

High school course credit requirements, social studies, 2002

SOURCE: Abigail Potts, Rolf K. Blank and Andra Williams, "Table 8. High School Course Credit Requirements: Social Studies," in *Key State Education Policies on PK–12 Education: 2002*, Council of Chief State School Officers, Washington, DC, 2002. Reproduced with permission.

advanced coursework in mathematics, English, science, and foreign language has increased. However, advanced courses are not offered in all schools. In 2000 schools in a central city, schools in the Northeast and Southeast, and schools with twelfth-grade enrollment of 450 or more were more likely to offer advanced courses. More than two-fifths (43%) of large schools (twelfth-grade enrollment of 450 or more), 31% of schools in the Northeast, and nearly a third (32%) of schools in central cities offered at least four advanced courses each in mathematics, English, science, and foreign language. (See Figure 4.16.)

GRADUATION REQUIREMENTS AND HIGH SCHOOL EXIT EXAMS

According to *Key State Education Policies on PK–12 Education: 2004* (Council of Chief State School Officers, Washington, DC, 2004), seventeen states reported requiring specific mathematics courses, and twenty-three states reported requiring specific science courses for high school graduates in 2004. Algebra, required by seventeen states, was the most common mathematics course required, and biology, required by fourteen states, was the most common science course. Health was required in twenty-eight states in 2004; thirty-three states required

TABLE 4.9

Average number of Carnegie units earned by public high school graduates in various subject fields, by selected student characteristics, selected years, 1982–2000

Graduation year and selected student characteristic	Total	English	History/ social studies	Mathematics			Science					Foreign languages	Arts	Vocational education[a]	Personal use[b]	Computer related[c]
				Total	Less than algebra	Algebra or higher	Total	General science	Biology	Chemistry	Physics					
1	2	3	4	5	6	7	8	9	10	11	12	13	14	15	16	17
2000 graduates	26.05	4.39	3.83	3.56	0.61	2.95	3.20	0.85	1.29	0.69	0.36	1.95	2.03	4.21	2.88	0.83
Sex																
Male	25.91	4.31	3.76	3.53	0.68	2.86	3.16	0.88	1.20	0.65	0.40	1.71	1.75	4.60	3.09	0.93
Female	26.17	4.46	3.89	3.58	0.55	3.03	3.25	0.82	1.36	0.73	0.33	2.18	2.30	3.82	2.69	0.74
Race/ethnicity																
White, non-Hispanic	26.21	4.32	3.86	3.56	0.58	2.98	3.24	0.84	1.30	0.70	0.38	1.98	2.12	4.34	2.79	0.81
Black, non-Hispanic	25.76	4.43	3.75	3.54	0.72	2.82	3.13	0.91	1.26	0.65	0.27	1.70	1.95	4.29	2.98	0.85
Hispanic	25.47	4.69	3.77	3.42	0.74	2.68	2.87	0.85	1.19	0.58	0.24	1.90	1.77	3.83	3.21	0.89
Asian/Pacific Islander	26.21	4.57	3.77	3.96	0.35	3.61	3.71	0.71	1.36	0.96	0.65	2.51	1.79	2.82	3.09	0.92
American Indian/ Alaska Native	25.11	4.12	3.75	3.29	0.91	2.38	2.88	0.98	1.25	0.45	0.19	1.40	1.99	4.79	2.89	0.96
Academic track																
Academic[d]	25.57	4.47	3.93	3.70	0.49	3.21	3.39	0.81	1.35	0.80	0.42	2.32	2.52	2.28	2.96	0.54
Vocational[e]	23.44	3.33	2.62	2.11	1.28	0.82	1.61	0.84	0.65	0.06	0.05	0.15	0.57	9.56	3.50	1.17
Both[f]	26.81	4.33	3.76	3.45	0.74	2.71	3.04	0.89	1.24	0.59	0.30	1.56	1.47	6.46	2.74	1.20
Neither[g]	21.58	3.50	1.86	2.27	1.76	0.51	1.59	1.04	0.48	0.04	0.02	0.20	0.93	5.52	5.72	0.29

[a]Includes nonoccupational vocational education, vocational general introduction, agriculture, business, marketing, health, occupational home economics, trade and industry, and technical courses.

[b]Includes personal and social courses, religion and theology, and courses not included in the other subject fields.

[c]Though shown separately here, computer-related courses are also included in the mathematics and vocational categories.

[d]Includes students who complete at least 12 Carnegie units in academic courses, but less than 3 Carnegie units in any specific labor market preparation field.

[e]Includes students who complete at least 3 Carnegie units in a specific labor market preparation field, but less than 12 Carnegie units in academic courses.

[f]Includes students who complete at least 12 Carnegie units in academic courses and at least 3 Carnegie units in a specific labor market preparation field.

[g]Includes students who complete less than 12 Carnegie units in academic courses and less than 3 Carnegie units in a specific labor market preparation field.

Note: The Carnegie unit is a standard of measurement that represents one credit for the completion of a 1-year course. Data differ slightly from figures appearing in other NCES reports because of differences in taxonomies and case exclusion criteria. Detail may not sum to totals due to rounding.

SOURCE: Adapted from Thomas D. Snyder, Alexandra G. Tan, and Charlene M. Hoffman, "Table 137. Average Number of Carnegie Units Earned by Public High School Graduates in Various Subject Fields, by Selected Student Characteristics: Selected Years, 1982 to 2000," in *Digest of Education Statistics, 2003*, NCES 2005-025, U.S. Department of Education, National Center for Education Statistics, Washington, DC, December 2004, http://nces.ed.gov/programs/digest/d03/tables/dt137.asp (accessed July 26, 2005)

TABLE 4.10

Public opinion on whether four years of English, math, and science should be a high school graduation requirement, 2004

SOME STATES ARE NOW REQUIRING THAT HIGH SCHOOL STUDENTS COMPLETE FOUR YEARS OF ENGLISH, MATH, AND SCIENCE IN ORDER TO GRADUATE FROM HIGH SCHOOL. WOULD YOU FAVOR OR OPPOSE THIS REQUIREMENT IN THE PUBLIC SCHOOLS IN YOUR COMMUNITY?

	National totals	No children in school	Public school parents
	%	%	%
Favor	78	79	76
Oppose	20	20	22
Don't know	2	1	2

SOURCE: Lowell C. Rose and Alec M. Gallup, "Table 34. Some states are now requiring that high school students complete four years of English, math, and science in order to graduate from high school. Would you favor or oppose this requirement in the public schools in your community?," in "The 36th Annual Phi Delta Kappa/Gallup Poll of the Public's Attitudes Toward the Public Schools," *Phi Delta Kappan*, September 2004. Reproduced with permission.

FIGURE 4.16

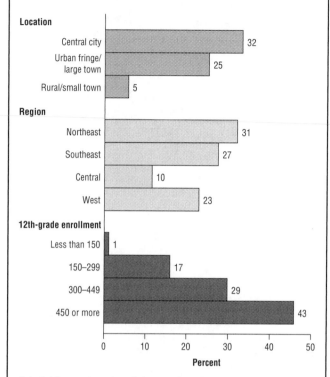

Percentage of students in schools that offer at least four advanced courses each in mathematics, English, science, and foreign language, by location, region, and 12th-grade enrollment, 2000

Note: Detail may not sum to totals because of rounding.

SOURCE: John Wirt, Susan Choy, Patrick Rooney, William Hussar, Stephen Provasnik, and Gillian Hampden-Thompson, "Availability of Advanced Courses: Percentage of Students in Schools That Offer at Least Four Advanced Courses Each in Mathematics, English, Science, and Foreign Language, by Location, Region, and 12th-Grade Enrollment: 2000," in *The Condition of Education, 2005*, NCES 2005-094, U.S. Department of Education, National Center for Education Statistics, Washington, DC, June 2005, http://nces.ed.gov/pubs2005/2005094.pdf (accessed July 26, 2005)

physical education; and foreign language was required in fourteen states. In addition, eleven states required speech or communications classes, twenty-one states required government, and twenty-four states required state, national, or international history.

In the early 2000s school accountability became a major issue of school reform. Many states mandated what children should learn in each grade, developed assessments to measure student achievement, designed school report cards, rated their schools and publicly identified failing schools, assisted low-performing schools with additional funding, and even closed or took over failing schools. Included in the various accountability measures is the high school exit examination.

According to the Council of Chief State School Officers, twenty-nine states were either using high school exit exams or were in the process of developing such tests in 2002. Forty-two percent of the states required the exam for graduation, 20% were developing an exam, and 38% of the states did not require a high school exit exam. (See Figure 4.17.) The CCSSO reported in *Key State Education Policies on PK–12 Education: 2004* that 60% of states would require an exit examination for the class of 2009.

Of the states that require an exit exam prior to graduation, a few differentiate the diplomas according to whether the test was passed or not. Most states initially administer the exit exam in tenth or eleventh grade. This allows time for remediation or other interventions to be provided for students who fail the test the first time. All states with high school exit exams allow students to take the test multiple times.

In 2004, according to the National Center for Education Statistics, nine states tested mathematics, English, science, and social studies; one state tested mathematics, English, and science; ten states tested mathematics and English; one state tested mathematics, English, and computer skills; and thirty-one states did not require a high school exit exam. In 2004 there were five states in the process of phasing in an exam. (See Figure 4.18.)

Proponents of high school exit exams believe that standardized tests are the best way to ensure high standards and accountability. They maintain that tests can communicate what is expected of students and teachers and assess whether progress is being made. Supporters believe that if tests are aligned to a rigorous curriculum, they are the best chance that low-performing students have to get the education they need and to narrow the minority achievement gap.

FIGURE 4.17

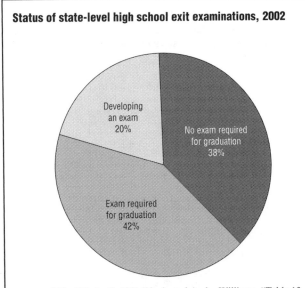

Status of state-level high school exit examinations, 2002

Developing an exam 20%

No exam required for graduation 38%

Exam required for graduation 42%

SOURCE: Abigail Potts, Rolf K. Blank, and Andra Williams, "Table 13. High School Exit Examination Requirement—2002" in *Key State Education Policies on PK–12 Education: 2002*, Council of Chief State School Officers, Washington, DC, 2002. Reproduced with permission.

Those who oppose these tests point out that a single test is not an accurate measure of a student's performance. Opponents claim that these tests put poor and minority students at a disadvantage. A further criticism of "high-stakes" tests is that they push teachers to "teach to" the test, taking too much time away from classroom practices that support true learning.

"The 36th Annual Phi Delta Kappa/Gallup Poll of the Public's Attitude toward the Public Schools" asked members of the American public whether they favored or opposed using a single standardized test in the public schools in their community to determine whether a student should receive a high school diploma. Results were mixed: 51% favored standardized exit exams, while 47% opposed them. (See Table 4.11.)

SCORES ON COLLEGE ENTRANCE TESTS

Students trying to enter most colleges and universities in the United States generally take either the SAT (formerly called the Scholastic Assessment Test) or the American College Test (ACT) as part of their admission requirements. The SAT is the primary admissions test for twenty-two states, mostly in the East and on the West Coast. The ACT is more popular in twenty-eight states in the Midwest, South, and West, where a large percentage of students attend public colleges and universities. Most colleges will accept either the SAT or the ACT. In addition, some schools require three SAT II subject tests.

These two college entrance tests are standardized three-hour tests intended as an assessment of readiness

for college. The SAT measures students' mathematical and verbal reasoning abilities. The ACT is curriculum-based and tests four areas: English, mathematics, reading comprehension, and science reasoning. Students who elect to take these tests usually plan to continue their education beyond high school; therefore, these tests do not profile all high school students.

Performance on the SAT is measured on a scale of 200 to 800. According to the College Board, the mean SAT scores for 2003 were 508 for the verbal section and 518 for the mathematics section. The verbal score was well below the 1972 level (530), while the mathematics score was higher than in 1972, when it was 509. The ACT results are measured on a scale of one to thirty-six. The 2004 average composite ACT score was 20.9.

According to the College Board, about 1.4 million college-bound seniors took the SAT in 2004; the American College Testing Program reports that 1.1 million students took the ACT. The number of students taking both the SAT and the ACT has grown steadily, especially in the early 2000s. In general, the more students taking the tests, the lower the scores will be, because a greater number of test-takers will likely include students who are less academically accomplished.

Trends in Scores

Verbal SAT test scores dropped in the 1970s, 1980s, and early 1990s, and math scores dropped during the 1970s and early 1980s. Observers attributed the decline to the rise in the number of students from lower scholastic achievement levels taking the tests since the 1970s. While that may explain the initial drop, a major part of the decrease also resulted from a decline in performance among the kinds of students who had previously done well in these tests. Although verbal scores remained virtually unchanged from 1995 to 2004, mathematics scores increased slightly starting in the 1990s, leading some officials to be cautiously optimistic. From 2003 to 2004, verbal SAT scores increased one point, and mathematics SAT scores dropped one point.

Gender of Test-Takers

In 2004 females accounted for the majority (53%) of students taking the SAT. Females have historically scored lower than males on college entrance examinations. The SAT was found to over-predict male college grades and under-predict female grades, so in 1995 the SAT was revised, partly to reduce these gender-related differences.

In 2004 female students' mean verbal SAT score was 504, compared to 512 for males, and female test-takers' mean mathematics score was 501, compared to 537 for males. Among ACT-takers, females' 2004 average composite score was 20.9, compared to 21 for males. (See Table 4.12.)

FIGURE 4.18

States with mandatory exit examinations, by subject, and states phasing in exit examinations, by date, 2004

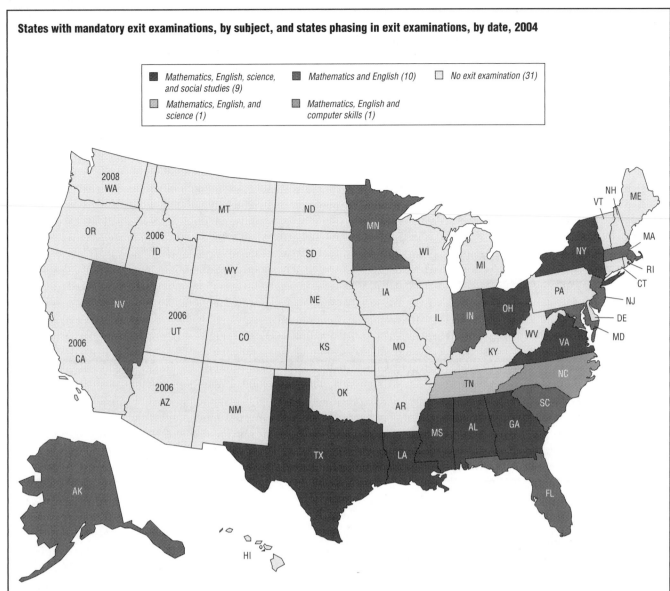

Note: States labeled with years are scheduled to institute exit examinations in the year shown.

SOURCE: John Wirt, Susan Choy, Patrick Rooney, William Hussar, Stephen Provasnik, and Gillian Hampden-Thompson, "Exit Examinations: States with Mandatory Exit Examinations, by Subject, and States Phasing in Exit Examinations, by Date: 2004," in *The Condition of Education, 2005*, NCES 2005-094, U.S. Department of Education, National Center for Education Statistics, Washington, DC, June 2005, http://nces.ed.gov/pubs2005/2005094.pdf (accessed July 26, 2005)

Race and Ethnicity of Test-Takers

According to the College Board, in 2004 white students accounted for nearly two-thirds (63%) of those taking the SAT, although the proportion of minority test-takers has risen steadily from 13% in 1973 to about 37% in 2004. African-American students made up 12%; Asian-American students 10%; Hispanic students 10%; and Native American students about 1%. Four percent of test-takers classified themselves as "other" in the race/ethnicity category.

Gains have been made since 1991, but overall SAT scores for minorities (with the exception of Asian-

American students) still lagged behind the scores of white students. White students averaged 528 on the verbal section and 531 on the mathematics section in 2004, an increase of eight points and twelve points, respectively, since 1994. African-American students scored 430 on the verbal component and 427 on the mathematics. These scores were two points and six points higher, respectively, than those of 1994. So while scores for African-Americans have increased, the gap between African-Americans and whites has nevertheless widened. In 2004 the average scores of Hispanic, Latino, Mexican-American, and Puerto Rican students ranged from 451 to 461 on the verbal section and from 452 to 465 on the

TABLE 4.11

Public opinion on whether a single standardized test in public schools should determine if students receive high school diplomas, 2004

DO YOU FAVOR OR OPPOSE USING A SINGLE STANDARDIZED TEST IN THE PUBLIC SCHOOLS IN YOUR COMMUNITY TO DETERMINE WHETHER A STUDENT SHOULD RECEIVE A HIGH SCHOOL DIPLOMA?

	National totals %	No children in school %	Public school parents %
Favor	51	50	52
Oppose	47	47	45
Don't know	2	3	3

SOURCE: Lowell C. Rose and Alec M. Gallup, "Table 21. Do you favor or oppose using a single standardized test in the public schools in your community to determine whether a student should receive a high school diploma?," in "The 36th Annual Phi Delta Kappa/Gallup Poll of the Public's Attitudes Toward the Public Schools," *Phi Delta Kappan*, September 2004. Reproduced with permission.

TABLE 4.12

National average ACT composite score by gender, 1994–2004

	1994	1995	1996	1997	1998	1999	2000	2001	2002	2003	2004
Males	20.9	21.0	21.0	21.1	21.2	21.1	21.2	21.1	20.9	21.0	21.0
Females	20.7	20.7	20.8	20.8	20.9	20.9	20.9	20.9	20.7	20.8	20.9

SOURCE: The American College Testing Program, "National Average ACT Composite Score by Gender, 1994–2004," in *2004 ACT National and State Scores*, http://www.act.org/news/data/04/charts/text.html (accessed July 26, 2005). Reproduced with permission.

TABLE 4.13

Average ACT composite score by race/ethnic group, 2004

African American/Black	17.1
American Indian/Alaska Native	18.8
Caucasian American/White	21.8
Mexican American/Chicano	18.4
Asian American/Pacific Islander	21.9
Puerto Rican/Hispanic	18.8
Other	19.4
Multiracial	20.9
Prefer not to respond	22
No response	20.7

SOURCE: The American College Testing Program, "Average ACT Composite Score by Race/Ethnic Group, 2004," in *2004 ACT National and State Scores*, http://www.act.org/news/data/04/charts/text.html (accessed July 26, 2005). Reproduced with permission.

mathematics section, up from the 1994 span of scores, which were 444 to 460 for verbal and 442 to 464 for mathematics.

According to the American College Testing program, for those taking the ACT in 2004 the mean composite score of white students was 21.8. For Asian/Pacific Islander students it was 21.9, while scores for Hispanics (18.4 to 18.8), Native American/Alaska Indians (18.8), and African-Americans (17.1) were lower. (See Table 4.13.)

CHAPTER 5
NATIONAL POLICIES FOR IMPROVEMENT

A CALL TO REFORM

A Nation at Risk (Washington, DC, 1983), a report prepared by the National Commission on Excellence in Education, proved to be a "wake-up call" on the state of the U.S. educational system. It warned of a "rising tide of mediocrity that threatens our very future as a nation and as a people." As a result, educators, lawmakers, and governors began earnest efforts to improve schools. The report recommended, among other things, a longer school year, a tougher curriculum, and stronger teacher-training programs. It specifically expressed alarm at the deterioration of academics at the secondary school level.

To improve the situation, the report recommended that no student should graduate from high school without completing four years of English; three years each of mathematics, science, and social studies; one-half year of computer science; and, for college-bound students, two years of a foreign language. *A Nation at Risk* was the beginning of an educational reform movement that has continued into the twenty-first century. The fact that it was still relevant more than twenty years later speaks to how influential it was and is; it is rare for a policy document to survive through several presidential administrations.

NATIONAL EDUCATION GOALS FOR THE YEAR 2000

At the first Education Summit held in Charlottesville, Virginia, in 1989, President George H. W. Bush and the nation's state governors established six National Education Goals to be achieved by the year 2000. The bipartisan National Education Goals Panel was created in 1990 to oversee and report on the progress toward these national goals. The panel was made up of governors, members of Congress, state legislators, and members appointed by the president. Expressing the continued concern of the nation, Congress passed the Goals 2000: Educate America Act (P.L. 103-227), signed on March 31, 1994, by President Bill Clinton. The Act reemphasized the National Education Goals and added two more goals.

The eight goals included preparing children so they are ready to learn by the time they start school (Goal 1); greater levels of high school completion (Goal 2); student achievement (Goal 3); teacher education and professional development (Goal 4); ensuring that U.S. students are first in the world in mathematics and science (Goal 5); increasing adult literacy and lifelong learning (Goal 6); safe, disciplined, and alcohol- and drug-free schools (Goal 7); and parental participation in the schools (Goal 8).

Did We Reach the Goals?

While many schools responded to the challenge first issued in 1989, the Goals panel concluded in its 1992 report that any gains had been modest. In November 1995 the panel reported that results to that point had been disappointing. Although the nation was halfway to the target year (2000), it was far from reaching its education goals. In its 1999 report, the panel found that, of the fifty-three national measures established to gauge progress toward the goals, twelve areas showed improvement, eleven were unchanged, and five had worsened. The remaining twenty-five national measures were either not recorded or only showed baseline (current status) measurements.

In 2000, 2001, and 2002 the panel released reports that examined, for selected indicators in each goal, which states were showing progress, which were not changing, and which had declined. In general, results were mixed. Improvement was made in Goal 1, "Ready to Learn," Goal 2, "School Completion," and Goal 5, "Mathematics and Science." Progress was uneven on Goal 3, "Student Achievement and Citizenship," and Goal 4, "Teacher Education and Development." There was no change in Goal 6, "Adult Literacy and Learning," Goal 7, "Safe, Disciplined, and Alcohol- and Drug-Free Schools," and Goal 8, "Parental Participation."

Goals Not Considered a Failure

In 2002 Congress dissolved the National Education Goals Panel, and no additional reports have been released. In spite of the inability of America's schools to completely reach any of the eight National Education Goals, both Republican and Democratic politicians credited the goals with setting high standards.

THE ELEMENTARY AND SECONDARY EDUCATION ACT

The Elementary and Secondary Education Act of 1965 (ESEA, P.L. 89-10) authorized grants for elementary and secondary school programs for children of low-income families; school library resources, textbooks, and other instructional materials for school children; supplementary educational centers and services; strengthening state education agencies; and educational research and research training. Once established, federal legislation is reviewed, revised, and reauthorized by Congress and the president as time goes by. In the case of ESEA, amendments were added in 1968 with the passage of P.L. 90-247, which modified existing programs, authorized support of regional centers for education of handicapped children, model centers and services for deaf-blind children, recruitment of personnel and dissemination of information on education of the handicapped; technical assistance to education in rural areas; support of dropout prevention projects; and support of bilingual education programs.

In 1994 ESEA was reauthorized by the Improving America's Schools Act (P.L. 103-382). The legislation included Title I, the federal government's largest program providing educational assistance to disadvantaged children; professional development and technical assistance programs; a safe and drug-free schools and communities provision; and provisions promoting school equity. In 1995 the Elementary and Secondary Education Act was updated by Public Law 104-5, which amended Part A of Title IX relating to Native American education, provided a technical amendment, and incorporated other changes.

THE NO CHILD LEFT BEHIND ACT

On January 8, 2002, President George W. Bush signed into law the No Child Left Behind Act (NCLB; P.L. 107-110), a major reform of the Elementary and Secondary Education Act of 1965. NCLB focuses on increasing accountability for results, implementing programs that are based on scientific research, expanding parental options, and increasing local control and flexibility.

Accountability for Results

Under NCLB, every state is required to set standards for grade-level achievement and to develop a system to measure the progress of all students and subgroups of students in meeting those state-determined grade-level standards. According to the U.S. Department of Education in *A Guide to Education and "No Child Left Behind"* (http://www.ed.gov/nclb/overview/intro/guide/), in 2005 funding to support the development and implementation of state assessments was $410 million.

NCLB created standards in each state for what a child should know and learn in reading and mathematics in grades three through eight. Student progress and achievement are measured according to tests based upon those state standards and given to every child, every year. The results are available in annual report cards on school performance and on statewide progress. Statewide reports present performance data classified by race, ethnicity, gender, and other criteria to demonstrate student achievement overall and to chart progress in closing the achievement gap between disadvantaged students and other groups of students. A sample of students in each state participates in the fourth- and eighth-grade National Assessment of Educational Progress (NAEP) in reading and mathematics every other year. (See Table 4.1 in Chapter 4.) States that fail to meet the standards set by NCLB can have their federal funding reduced. Individual schools that fail to live up to the NCLB can also lose students and funding.

Reading First

Under the NCLB, federal funding for reading programs was increased from $286 million in fiscal year (FY) 2001 to more than $1.4 billion in FY 2005. The goal of the Reading First initiative is for every child to be able to read by the end of grade three. Awards are made to states, which then make competitive sub-grants to local communities to identify students at risk and to provide training to elementary school teachers on reading instruction. The Early Reading First program awards grants to Local Education Agencies (LEAs) to support language, literacy, and pre-reading development in preschool age children.

Flexibility at the State and Local Level

NCLB reduced the overall number of ESEA programs at the U.S. Department of Education from fifty-five to forty-five. Up to 50% of the federal dollars school districts receive can be transferred among several education programs without separate approval. All fifty states can transfer up to 50% of the federal non–Title I state activity funds among ESEA programs without advance approval. Local school officials serving rural schools were also given more flexibility in how federal funds are used in their districts.

School Choice and Charter Schools

NCLB created options for public school choice. Parents with children in failing schools are allowed to transfer their child to a better-performing public or charter school immediately after a school is identified as failing. Federal Title I funds (approximately $500 to $1,000 per child) can be used to provide supplemental educational services—including tutoring, after school services, and summer school programs—for children in failing schools. NCLB provides financial assistance for the planning, design, and initial implementation of charter schools, as well as for evaluating the effects of such schools. According to the U.S. Department of Education in *A Guide to Education and "No Child Left Behind,"* support for charter schools and choice options was $504 million in 2005.

Teacher Quality Program

NCLB requires states to put highly qualified teachers in every public school classroom by 2005–06. To be considered "highly qualified," a teacher must hold a bachelor's degree and certification or licensure to teach in the state of his or her employment and have proven knowledge in the subject he or she teaches. Teachers in charter schools do not have to be certified or licensed if the state does not require it.

The Eisenhower Professional Development and Class Size Reduction programs were combined to create the new Teacher and Principal Training and Recruiting Fund (Title II). States and local districts are permitted to use this funding for staff development for their public school teachers, principals, and administrators. The purpose of the fund is to increase student academic achievement by providing support for states and districts so they can meet the requirements for highly qualified teachers. In addition to funding professional development, states and school districts are allowed to use their grants for reforming teacher certification or licensure requirements; alternative certification; tenure reform; merit-based teacher performance systems; bonus pay for teachers in high-need subject areas and in high-poverty schools and districts; and mentoring programs. According to the U.S. Department of Education, support for the program in training, recruitment incentives, loan forgiveness, and tax relief was $5.1 billion in 2005.

English Proficiency

NCLB consolidated the U.S. Department of Education's bilingual and immigrant education programs. The new federal program focuses on helping students who are Limited English Proficient (LEP) learn English. States and school districts are held accountable for making annual increases in English proficiency from the previous year. States set performance objectives to ensure that LEP children achieve English fluency after they have attended school in the United States for three consecutive years. States that do not meet their performance objectives for LEP students could lose up to 10% of the administrative portion of their funding for all ESEA state-administered formula grant programs. The U.S. Department of Education reported in *A Guide to Education and "No Child Left Behind"* that 2005 funding for English language acquisition programs was $681 million.

Local Education Agencies and NCLB

According to the U.S. Department of Education, in addition to focusing on school accountability measures and consequences, NCLB increases attention on the performance of Local Education Agencies (LEAs), emphasizing their important leadership role in school improvement. An LEA is a board of education or other local school authority having administrative control and direction of public education in a county, town, or school district. The law requires State Education Agencies (SEAs) to conduct an annual review of LEAs to ensure that they are making adequate progress. The state and LEAs are required to comply with the requirements of NCLB as a condition of receiving federal funding under Title I of the Elementary and Secondary Education Act. As a provision of NCLB, states must establish accountability performance criteria for determining whether LEAs have made "adequate yearly progress." LEAs that fail to make adequate yearly progress are required to undertake remedial measures, including school improvement plans, corrective action plans, restructuring plans, and other measures.

Status of the NCLB Goals

NCLB identified a total of forty elements in seven key areas:

- Standards and Assessments
- Accountability
- School Improvement
- Safe Schools
- Supplemental Services
- Report Card
- Teacher Quality

In *ECS Report to the Nation: State Implementation of the No Child Left Behind Act* (Kathy Christie, Mary Fulton, William Paul Wanker, Education Commission of the States, Denver, CO, July 2004), the states are categorized according to whether they "appear to be on track," "appear to be partially on track," or "do not appear to be on track" for meeting the requirements of NCLB.

According to the Education Commission of the States (ECS), in 2004 all fifty states had met or were partially on track to meeting half of the forty requirements, which was an

11% increase from 2003. All but two states and the District of Columbia had met or were partially on track to meeting 75% of the requirements, and five states (Connecticut, Kentucky, New York, Oklahoma, and Pennsylvania) had met or were partially on track to meeting all forty NCLB requirements.

The ECS also found that many states were having difficulty with some elements in the teacher quality key area. Fewer than half of the states were on track to making sure technical assistance was provided to low-performing schools. States did not have the technology infrastructure in place to collect, analyze, and report data at the state, district, and school levels.

The ECS made several recommendations, including that NCLB should be embraced as a civil rights issue, in terms of focusing on narrowing the achievement gap that persists in U.S. schools; performance growth of all students, not just low-performing students, should be guaranteed; adequate yearly progress should be analyzed to ensure that it gives a more accurate picture of student performance; the highly qualified teacher requirements should be strengthened; and state departments of education and local school districts may require additional resources to help them assist schools that need improvement.

Standards and Assessments

For the first key area, standards and assessments, there are eleven elements. The elements include reading standards, mathematics standards, science standards, yearly assessments in reading/language arts, yearly assessments in mathematics, yearly assessments in science, assessment of English language proficiency, inclusion of English language learners in the assessment, inclusion of students with disabilities in the assessment, inclusion of migrant students in the assessment, and reporting results not just for all students combined, but for subgroups within the student population. The number of states "on track" ranged from twenty-nine for annual assessments in mathematics, to forty-eight for science standards. All states were either "on track" or "partially on track" in reaching reading standards, mathematics standards, science standards, annual assessments in reading/language arts, annual assessments in mathematics, inclusion of English language learners, inclusion of students with disabilities, and inclusion of migrant students.

Accountability

The second area is accountability, known as Adequate Yearly Progress (AYP). According to the U.S. Department of Education, AYP requires the same high standards for all students, and it must be calculated in a way that is statistically valid and reliable. It must include separate annual measures of achievement, and all stu-

dents must show continuous and significant academic growth. This area includes:

- A single statewide accountability system for tracking results

- All students and schools must be included in the system

- Continuous growth to 100% proficiency

- A yearly determination of whether there is Adequate Yearly Progress

- Accountability measures in place for all groups of students (racial, ethnic, economically disadvantaged, disabled, and Limited English Proficient)

- The measures must be based on academic achievement and graduation rate, and one other measure must be included

- There must be separate objectives for mathematics and reading

- 95% of students in all groups of students must be assessed

The ECS found that the number of states "on track" in the area of accountability ranged from thirty-three for continuous growth to 100% proficiency to forty-six for requiring accountability for all subgroups. "Continuous growth to 100% proficiency," according to the U.S. Department of Education, is "growth in student achievement that is continuous and substantial, such that all students are proficient in reading/language arts and mathematics no later than 2013–2014"

School Improvement

Another key area of NCLB is school improvement. According to the U.S. Department of Education, one element of school improvement is "timely identification." States are required to identify schools that are in need of improvement, take corrective action at those schools before the beginning of the school year, and make sure that districts notify parents. A second element within school improvement is "technical assistance." States must provide technical assistance to schools identified as in need of improvement, corrective action, or restructuring. A third element in school improvement is called "public school choice." The state must allow students at schools that do not make adequate yearly progress for two consecutive years to transfer to another school that has not been identified as needing improvement.

The fourth element of school improvement is "rewards and sanctions." States must have a policy for rewarding and penalizing schools, based on whether they are making adequate yearly progress. Fifth is "school recognition." The state must have financial, academic, or other distinguished school programs for recognizing schools that have closed the achievement gap, made significant gains on student performance, or exceeded adequate yearly progress. "School restructuring" is the sixth element in school improvement. The state must have alternative school governance options in place, which include charter schools, private management companies, or turning over a school that needs improvement to the state for operation. The seventh element is "corrective action for Local Education Agencies." The state must have a process in place for taking corrective action against LEAs that operate schools in need of improvement. The actions include reducing funding, implementing a new curriculum, replacing personnel, arranging for alternative governance of the school, appointing someone to replace the superintendent and school board, abolishing or restructuring the LEA, or allowing students to transfer to a higher-performing school.

According to the ECS, in 2004 the number of states "on track" ranged from twenty-three for technical assistance to thirty-eight for school recognition and school restructuring. There were fourteen states that did "not appear to be on track," plus two that have an unknown status in establishing a policy for taking corrective action against LEAs. For timely identification and public school choice, one state in each element did "not appear to be on track."

Safe Schools

Under NCLB, there are three elements that make up safe schools: having criteria in place for safe schools; a transfer policy for students who attend unsafe schools; and a transfer policy for victims of violent crimes. The ECS reported that all states were "on track" or "partially on track" to ensuring safe schools in 2004. Fifty states had criteria for unsafe schools, and forty-nine had transfer policies for students in unsafe schools and for victims of violent crime.

Supplemental Services

According to the U.S. Department of Education, supplemental services means having tutoring and other academic enrichment available, often in reading, language arts, or mathematics. The supplemental services area of NCLB includes four elements: criteria for supplemental services; a list of approved supplemental services providers; monitoring supplemental services providers; and implementation of supplemental services. According to the ECS, the number of states "on track" for the key area supplemental services in 2004 ranged from thirty-one for implementation of supplemental services to forty-eight for having criteria for supplemental services. Twelve states did "not appear to be on track" in monitoring supplemental service providers.

Report Card

The report card key area contains only one element: the state report card. This means that the state prepares and disseminates an annual state report card that includes all required information set by NCLB. Only one state did "did not appear to be on track," in 2004 while nineteen states appeared to be "on the right track." Thirty-one states appeared to be "partially on track for this measure."

Under NCLB, annual state report cards must provide performance data by race/ethnicity, gender, economically disadvantaged status, English language learners, disability, and migrant status. Many states report student data by demographic characteristics, but most do not report achievement data this way. For states that do report achievement data by demographic characteristics, it is more common at the state than the local level.

Teacher Quality

In the last key area, teacher quality, there are five elements. The elements include having a definition of a high-quality teacher; requiring the teacher to be competent in the subject matter taught; having a competency test for new elementary school teachers; having a highly qualified teacher in every classroom; and having high-quality professional development available to teachers. The number of states "on track" ranged from zero for having a highly qualified teacher in every classroom and for high-quality professional development, to forty-three for having a competency test for new elementary teachers. Fifty states (not including the District of Columbia) appeared to be "partially on track" in having a highly qualified teacher in every classroom.

REACTIONS TO THE NO CHILD LEFT BEHIND ACT

According to the ECS, NCLB has generated responses ranging from strong support to skepticism to outright opposition. Common complaints about the law include that it is underfunded, inflexible, focuses too much on high-stakes testing, is too ambitious in terms of improvement in mathematics and science proficiency, and does not differentiate between urban and rural districts. Proponents of the legislation believe that NCLB ensures success for all students, that education is a civil right, and that high-quality schools are vital to the U.S. economy.

The American Federation of Teachers (AFT), a labor union representing teachers, paraprofessionals, and school-related personnel, expressed concern that the law's mechanism for holding schools accountable—the key area called adequate yearly progress (AYP)—does not accurately distinguish between effective and ineffective schools. In "NCLB: Its Problems, Its Promise" (July 2004), the AFT asserted its support for the principles of education improvement that underlie NCLB, but identified shortcomings with its implementation. In addition to problems with AYP measurements, the AFT considered the teacher quality provision unrealistic in its requirements for teachers in such areas as special education, vocational education, and bilingual education. The AFT also maintained that intervention is necessary to raise student achievement in struggling schools, but considered NCLB's sanctions in this key area ineffective. Finally, the AFT contended that the goals identified by NCLB cannot be realized without additional funding.

The National Education Association (NEA), the nation's largest education union with 2.7 million members, has expressed concerns similar to those of the AFT. On its Web site (http://www.nea.org/esea/index.html), the NEA describes the goals of the legislation, including having high standards and expectations for every child, as "laudable," but concludes that in its current form NCLB is "seriously flawed and underfunded." According to the NEA, NCLB focuses too much on punishments rather than on assistance, on mandates rather than on support for proven practices, and on standardized testing rather than on teacher-led, classroom-focused solutions. The organization recommends a "fix and fund" approach to addressing the law's shortcomings.

In the *Peabody Journal of Education* (vol. 80, no. 2, "Federalism Reconsidered: The Case of the No Child Left Behind Act"), Julia E. Koppich wrote in "A Tale of Two Approaches—The AFT, the NEA, and NCLB" that neither the American Federation of Teachers nor the NEA supported the new legislation initially, but after it was passed, the two organizations had different views. The NEA focused on publicly opposing the law. The AFT took a more careful and less predictable approach to the legislation. The author concludes that these differing strategies fit the patterns of both organizations' reactions to most educational reform efforts since the 1980s. In "Gubernatorial Reactions to No Child Left Behind: Politics, Pressure, and Educational Reform," Lance D. Fusarelli found that although there is some opposition to specific provisions of NCLB, a large majority of state governors in the United States support the goals of the legislation. Fusarelli wrote that there are four reasons for this: consistency with state-level education reform, the law's use by governors to encourage change within schools, the novelty of NCLB, and concerns about sanctions from the federal government.

The International Reading Association (IRA), an organization of reading teachers, surveyed more than 1,500 of its members about NCLB in 2004. The survey asked about seven issues related to NCLB, including the benefits of NCLB, funding, implementation, assessment, outcomes, sanctions, and teacher qualification requirements. According to results released by the IRA in February 2005, the opinions of its members were mixed, with many respondents having either strongly positive or strongly negative

views about specific provisions of NCLB. The majority (more than 70%) of members supported the basic premises of the law. However, about the same proportion (more than 70%) had misgivings about how the law had been implemented and whether funding was adequate.

During spring 2004 the Public Education Network (PEN), an organization working to advance public school reform in low-income communities, held public hearings in eight states. The organization also conducted a survey about NCLB and received 12,000 responses. Fifty-nine percent of respondents identified themselves as teachers; other respondents included school administrators, parents, students, and community members. From the hearings and surveys, PEN found that public concerns about NCLB, particularly about funding, were mainly due to many years of underfunding of education by the states. PEN also reported that parents and other community members were not well informed about school progress. PEN reported that many Americans do not understand the public education system, yet still there was strong support for public schools. PEN recommended improving communication with the public about schools and education. PEN also found that some people were more worried about avoiding the provisions of NCLB than about using the law to address problems in the public schools. PEN continued to hold public forums throughout the fall and winter of 2005–06, and surveyed visitors to its Web site (http://www.publiceducation.org/) on matters related to NCLB.

Public Opinions about NCLB

"The 36th Annual Phi Delta Kappa/Gallup Poll of the Public's Attitudes toward the Public Schools" (http://www.pdkintl.org/kappan/k0409pol.htm) asked a series of questions related to the No Child Left Behind Act. When asked how much, if anything, they knew about NCLB, only 31% of respondents in 2004 said they knew a great deal or a fair amount. More than one-quarter (28%) responded that they knew nothing at all, and 40% knew very little. (See Table 5.1.)

Respondents were asked whether they had a favorable or unfavorable opinion of the Act. In 2004 nearly one-quarter (24%) had a very favorable or somewhat favorable impression. More than half (55%) responded that they did not know enough about NCLB to say, and 20% had a very unfavorable or somewhat unfavorable view. (See Table 5.2.)

When asked whether a single statewide test of students could accurately indicate whether a school needs improvement, more than two-thirds (67%) answered no, while 31% answered yes. (See Table 5.3.)

Respondents were asked if a test covering only English and math would provide a fair picture of whether a school in the community is or is not in need of improvement, or if the test should be based on other subjects also.

TABLE 5.1

How much the public knows about the No Child Left Behind Act, 2004

NOW, HERE ARE A FEW QUESTIONS ABOUT THE NO CHILD LEFT BEHIND ACT. HOW MUCH, IF ANYTHING, WOULD YOU SAY YOU KNOW ABOUT THE NO CHILD LEFT BEHIND ACT—THE FEDERAL EDUCATION BILL THAT WAS PASSED BY CONGRESS IN 2001—A GREAT DEAL, A FAIR AMOUNT, VERY LITTLE, OR NOTHING AT ALL?

	National totals		No children in school		Public school parents	
	'04 %	'03 %	'04 %	'03 %	'04 %	'03 %
Great deal + fair amount	31	24	28	25	37	22
A great deal	7	6	6	5	8	7
A fair amount	24	18	22	20	29	15
Very little	40	40	41	37	38	44
Nothing at all	28	36	30	38	24	34
Don't know	1	*	1	*	1	*
Very little + nothing at all	68	76	71	75	62	78

*Less than one-half of 1%.

SOURCE: Lowell C. Rose and Alec M. Gallup, "Table 6. Now, here are a few questions about the No Child Left Behind Act. How much, if anything, would you say you know about the No Child Left Behind Act—the federal education bill that was passed by Congress in 2001—a great deal, a fair amount, very little, or nothing at all?," in "The 36th Annual Phi Delta Kappa/Gallup Poll of the Public's Attitudes Toward the Public Schools," *Phi Delta Kappan*, September 2004. Reproduced with permission.

The majority (83%) replied that the test should include other subjects, while 16% believed that a test covering English and math would provide an adequate picture of school performance. (See Table 5.4.)

In 2004 most (80%) of those surveyed responded that they would prefer to have additional efforts made in their child's present school if the school was identified as being in need of improvement, rather than transferring the child to a school identified as not in need of improvement, which was favored by 16% of respondents. (See Table 5.5.)

When asked if they favored or opposed test scores reported separately by students' race/ethnicity, disability status, English-speaking ability, and poverty level, 42% favored this requirement of NCLB, and 52% opposed reporting test scores by these demographic categories.

The public was asked whether the standardized test scores of special education students should be included with the test scores of all other students in determining whether a school is in need of improvement. More than half (57%) believed that standardized test scores of special education students should not be included, and 39% responded that the standardized test scores of special education students should be included with the test scores of all other students in determining whether a school is in need of improvement. (See Table 5.6.)

Respondents were asked about the likelihood of having highly qualified teachers in every classroom at schools in their community by 2005–06. More than half (56%) believed that accomplishment of this goal was very likely or somewhat likely, and 42% believed that it was not very likely or not at all likely. (See Table 5.7.)

In 2004 the public was asked how much NCLB would help to improve student achievement at public schools in their community. Slightly more than half (51%) responded that NCLB would help a great deal or a fair amount, slightly less than one-third believed that NCLB would not help very much or would not help at all, and the remaining 17% said that they did not know how much NCLB would help to improve student achievement at public schools in their community. (See Table 5.8.)

TABLE 5.2

Public opinion on the No Child Left Behind Act, 2004

FROM WHAT YOU KNOW OR HAVE HEARD OR READ ABOUT THE NO CHILD LEFT BEHIND ACT, DO YOU HAVE A VERY FAVORABLE, SOMEWHAT FAVORABLE, SOMEWHAT UNFAVORABLE, OR VERY UNFAVORABLE OPINION OF THE ACT—OR DON'T YOU KNOW ENOUGH ABOUT IT TO SAY?

	National totals		Those knowing great deal	Those knowing fair amount	Those knowing very little	Those knowing nothing at all
	'04 %	'03 %	'04 %	'04 %	'04 %	'04 %
Very favorable + somewhat favorable	24	18	50	47	19	5
Very favorable	7	5	27	9	5	2
Somewhat favorable	17	13	23	38	14	3
Somewhat unfavorable	12	7	10	26	11	1
Very unfavorable	8	6	31	11	6	3
Don't know enough to say	55	69	8	14	64	89
Don't know	1	*	1	2	*	2
Somewhat unfavorable + very unfavorable	20	13	41	37	17	4

*Less than one-half of 1%.

SOURCE: Lowell C. Rose and Alec M. Gallup, "Table 7. From what you know about the No Child Left Behind Act, do you have a very favorable, some what favorable, somewhat unfavorable, or very unfavorable opinion of the act—or don't you know enough about it to say?," in "The 36th Annual Phi Delta Kappa/ Gallup Poll of the Public's Attitudes Toward the Public Schools," *Phi Delta Kappan*, September 2004. Reproduced with permission.

TABLE 5.3

Public opinion on whether a single standardized test provides a fair picture of schools needing improvement, 2004

ACCORDING TO THE NCLB ACT, DETERMINING WHETHER A PUBLIC SCHOOL IS OR IS NOT IN NEED OF IMPROVEMENT WILL BE BASED ON THE PERFORMANCE OF ITS STUDENTS ON A SINGLE STATEWIDE TEST. IN YOUR OPINION, WILL A SINGLE TEST PROVIDE A FAIR PICTURE OF WHETHER OR NOT A SCHOOL NEEDS IMPROVEMENT?

| | National totals | | No children in school | | Public school parents | | Those knowing great deal/ fair amount | Those knowing very little/ nothing at all |
	'04 %	'03 %	'04 %	'03 %	'04 %	'03 %	'04 %	'04 %
Yes	31	32	33	32	28	31	28	32
No	67	66	64	67	70	66	71	65
Don't know	2	2	3	1	2	3	1	3

SOURCE: Lowell C. Rose and Alec M. Gallup, "Table 8. According to the NCLB Act, determining whether a public school is or is not in need of improvement will be based on the performance of its students on a single statewide test. In your opinion, will a single test provide a fair picture of whether or not a school needs improvement?," in "The 36th Annual Phi Delta Kappa/Gallup Poll of the Public's Attitudes Toward the Public Schools," *Phi Delta Kappan*, September 2004. Reproduced with permission.

TABLE 5.4

Public opinion on whether tests to determine which schools are in need of improvement should be based only on English and math, or on other subjects, 2004

ACCORDING TO THE NCLB ACT, THE STATEWIDE TESTS OF STUDENTS' PERFORMANCE WILL BE DEVOTED TO ENGLISH AND MATH ONLY. DO YOU THINK A TEST COVERING ONLY ENGLISH AND MATH WOULD PROVIDE A FAIR PICTURE OF WHETHER A SCHOOL IN YOUR COMMUNITY IS OR IS NOT IN NEED OF IMPROVEMENT, OR SHOULD THE TEST BE BASED ON OTHER SUBJECTS ALSO?

| | National totals | | No children in school | | Public school parents | | Those knowing great deal/ fair amount | Those knowing very little/ nothing at all |
	'04 %	'03 %	'04 %	'03 %	'04 %	'03 %	'04 %	'04 %
Test covering only English and math would provide a fair picture of whether a school is in need of improvement	16	15	15	14	18	18	20	14
Test should be based on other subjects also	83	83	84	84	81	81	79	85
Don't know	1	2	1	2	1	1	1	1

SOURCE: Lowell C. Rose and Alec M. Gallup, "Table 9. According to the NCLB Act, the statewide tests of students' performance will be devoted to English and math only. Do you think a test covering only English and math would provide a fair picture of whether a school in your community is or is not in need of improvement, or should the test be based on other subjects also?," in "The 36th Annual Phi Delta Kappa/Gallup Poll of the Public's Attitudes Toward the Public Schools," *Phi Delta Kappan*, September 2004. Reproduced with permission.

TABLE 5.5

Public opinion on whether parents prefer to transfer children who attend schools in need of improvement, or to have additional efforts made at the children's present school, 2004

ASSUME YOU HAD A CHILD ATTENDING A SCHOOL IDENTIFIED AS IN NEED OF IMPROVEMENT BY THE NCLB ACT. WHICH WOULD YOU PREFER, TO TRANSFER YOUR CHILD TO A SCHOOL IDENTIFIED AS NOT IN NEED OF IMPROVEMENT OR TO HAVE ADDITIONAL EFFORTS MADE IN YOUR CHILD'S PRESENT SCHOOL TO HELP HIM OR HER ACHIEVE?

| | National totals | | No children in school | | Public school parents | | Those knowing great deal/ fair amount | Those knowing very little/ nothing at all |
	'04 %	'03 %	'04 %	'03 %	'04 %	'03 %	'04 %	'04 %
To transfer child to school identified as not in need of improvement	16	25	16	24	14	25	18	15
To have additional efforts made in child's present school	80	74	79	75	85	74	81	80
Don't know	4	1	5	1	1	1	1	5

SOURCE: Lowell C. Rose and Alec M. Gallup, "Table 12. Assume you had a child attending a school identified as in need of improvement by the NCLB Act. Which would you prefer, to transfer your child to a school identified as NOT in need of improvement or to have additional efforts made in your child's present school to help him or her achieve?," in "The 36th Annual Phi Delta Kappa/Gallup Poll of the Public's Attitudes Toward the Public Schools," *Phi Delta Kappan*, September 2004. Reproduced with permission.

TABLE 5.6

Public opinion on whether special education students' scores on standardized tests should be included when determining which schools are in need of improvement, 2004

IN YOUR OPINION, SHOULD THE STANDARDIZED TEST SCORES OF SPECIAL EDUCATION STUDENTS BE INCLUDED WITH THE TEST SCORES OF ALL OTHER STUDENTS IN DETERMINING WHETHER A SCHOOL IS IN NEED OF IMPROVEMENT UNDER NCLB OR NOT?

	National totals %	No children in school %	Public school parents %
Yes, should	39	40	40
No, should not	57	56	57
Don't know	4	4	3

SOURCE: Lowell C. Rose and Alec M. Gallup, "Table 16. In your opinion, should the standardized test scores of special education students be included with the test scores of all other students in determining whether a school is in need of improvement under NCLB or not?," in "The 36th Annual Phi Delta Kappa/Gallup Poll of the Public's Attitudes Toward the Public Schools," *Phi Delta Kappan*, September 2004. Reproduced with permission.

TABLE 5.7

Public opinion about whether having a highly qualified teacher in each classroom will happen by the end of the 2005–06 school year, 2004

NCLB REQUIRES THAT THERE BE A HIGHLY QUALIFIED TEACHER IN EACH CLASSROOM BY THE END OF THE 2005-06 SCHOOL YEAR. WHAT DO YOU THINK IS THE LIKELIHOOD OF THIS HAPPENING IN THE PUBLIC SCHOOLS IN YOUR COMMUNITY BY THAT TIME?

	National totals %	No children in school %	Public school parents %	Those knowing great deal/ fair amount %	Those knowing very little/ nothing at all %
Very likely	19	17	24	26	17
Somewhat likely	37	36	41	37	37
Not very likely	31	33	25	25	34
Not at all likely	11	11	10	12	10
Don't know	2	3	*	*	2

*Less than one-half of 1%.

SOURCE: Lowell C. Rose and Alec M. Gallup, "Table 18. NCLB requires that there be a highly qualified teacher in each classroom by the end of the 2005–06 school year. What do you think is the likelihood of this happening in the public schools in your community by that time?," in "The 36th Annual Phi Delta Kappa/Gallup Poll of the Public's Attitudes Toward the Public Schools," *Phi Delta Kappan*, September 2004. Reproduced with permission.

TABLE 5.8

Public opinion on whether the No Child Left Behind Act will improve student achievement, 2004

FROM WHAT YOU HAVE SEEN OR HEARD ABOUT THE NO CHILD LEFT BEHIND ACT, HOW MUCH DO YOU THINK IT WILL HELP TO IMPROVE STUDENT ACHIEVEMENT IN THE PUBLIC SCHOOLS IN YOUR COMMUNITY?

	National totals %	No children in school %	Public school parents %	Those knowing great deal/ fair amount %	Those knowing very little/ nothing at all %
Great deal + fair amount	51	49	57	53	51
A great deal	21	19	25	20	21
A fair amount	30	30	32	33	30
Not very much	23	23	21	32	19
Not at all	9	11	7	13	8
Don't know	17	17	15	2	22
Not very much + not at all	32	34	28	45	27

SOURCE: Lowell C. Rose and Alec M. Gallup, "Table 19. From what you have seen or heard about the No Child Left Behind Act, how much do you think it will help to improve student achievement in the public schools in your community?," in "The 36th Annual Phi Delta Kappa/Gallup Poll of the Public's Attitudes Toward the Public Schools," *Phi Delta Kappan*, September 2004. Reproduced with permission.

CHAPTER 6
STUDENTS AT RISK

WHAT DOES "AT RISK" MEAN?

In *America's Children at Risk* (September 1997), the U.S. Bureau of the Census identified six indicators of risk to children's welfare. These included poverty, welfare dependence, absent parents, single-parent families, unwed mothers, and parents who have not completed high school. Children who grow up with one or more of these conditions may be statistically at greater risk of dropping out of school, being unemployed, or, for girls, becoming teenage mothers.

AT-RISK CHILDREN

In school at-risk children are those who face significant obstacles, such as poverty or cultural and language barriers, that make it difficult for them to succeed academically. According to the U.S. Census Bureau, in 2004 the poverty threshold for a family of four was $19,307. The poverty rate for children under age eighteen was 17.8% in 2004. The proportion of poor varied by race and ethnicity. In 2004 the percentage of African-American children who were living in poverty was 33.6%, and the percentage of Hispanic children living in poverty was 28.9%. By comparison, 10.5% of white children were living in poverty in 2004.

Families headed by only one parent were more likely to be living below the poverty level in 2004. While 5.5% of American households headed by married couples lived below the poverty level in 2004, 13.5% of households headed by fathers alone and 28.4% of households headed by mothers alone lived in poverty. Among whites, 3.9% of married-couple families lived in poverty, compared to 10.6% of families headed by a single father and 20.9% of households headed by single mothers. For African-Americans, the percentages were 9.1% for married-couple families, 21% for male-headed households, and 37.6% for female-headed households; for Hispanics, the proportions were 14.7 % for married-couple households,

15.9% for households headed by a single male and 38.9% for female-headed households.

At-risk students with language barriers are classified as Linguistically Isolated (LI), Limited English Proficient (LEP), or English Language Learners (ELL). LI students are those in homes where no person over thirteen years of age speaks proficient English. LEP indicates those who have difficulty reading, writing, or understanding English. The majority of LEP students are Hispanic.

Parents, educators, and government officials generally agree that disadvantaged children often need special help to prepare them for school, and both public and private services are available. Title I grants are allocated to states and school districts on the basis of their numbers of children from low-income families. According to the U.S. Government Accountability Office in *Title I Funding: Poor Children Benefit Though Funding Per Poor Child Differs* (January 2002), about half of the nation's 7,174 small school districts (those with fewer than 1,000 children enrolled) had 35% of their school population eligible for free or reduced-price meals in 2000. A full 9% of both small and large school districts (those having a student enrollment of at least 20,000) had between 75% and 100% of students eligible for assistance. About 60% of the 7,121 medium-sized districts in the United States (those having an enrollment between 1,000 and 20,000) had up to one-third of their students eligible for free or reduced-price meals.

Alternative schools and programs serve students who are at risk of dropping out of school. According to the National Center for Education Statistics, in 2000–01 nearly 40% of public school districts had alternative schools and programs. Programs were more common in large districts, where 95% had them, than in smaller districts, where only 26% had them. Urban schools were more likely to have an alternative program than rural districts, with 66% of urban schools having them versus

35% of rural schools. Alternative schools were more common in the Southeast (80% of Southeastern schools had them) than in any other region.

MIDDLE SCHOOL AND JUNIOR HIGH— HIGH-RISK YEARS

Schools vary in how they define a "middle" student, but generally a middle school or junior high can include any grades from five through eight. Although there is no exact definition, middle schools usually serve students in either grades five or six through grade eight. Some districts have junior high schools instead of middle schools. Junior high school most often encompasses grades seven and eight.

The Carnegie Council on Adolescent Development published *Turning Points* (Report of the Task Force on Education and Youth Adolescents, New York) in 1989, which highlighted the importance of children's transition during the middle grades. The report sparked debate and additional research on the middle school years, including *Great Transitions: Preparing Adolescents for a New Century* (Carnegie Council on Adolescent Development, New York, 1995). These publications and other research pointed out that the organization and curriculum of middle and junior high schools are often inconsistent with students' intellectual, emotional, and interpersonal needs. For many young people, starting middle school or junior high means leaving the neighborhood elementary school to be thrust into a much larger, usually more impersonal, environment some distance from home.

The Carnegie Council's research concluded that the middle school curriculum does not encourage critical, complex thinking. To help remedy this, the Council encourages the creation of learning teams, a core academic curriculum, the elimination of tracking (sorting students according to their ability level into homogeneous classes, rather than placing them in classes containing a mixture of ability levels), and the hiring of teachers who have been specifically trained to teach in the middle grades. In 1998 the Center for Collaborative Education in Boston (CCE) began to develop a school reform design that would be based on the research and work of the preceding nine years. In 1999 the U.S. Department of Education awarded grants to seven organizations to develop models of school reform. This support, along with funding from private foundations, meant research continued on the issue. In *Turning Points 2000* (Teacher's College Press, New York, 2000), Anthony Jackson and Gayle Davis examined the progress being made and the experiences of middle school teachers and administrators. *Turning Points 2000* builds on the original *Turning Points*, with added emphasis on improving curriculum, assessment, and instruction.

The *Turning Points* model includes seven points for middle-grades school reform: rigorous standards and curriculum, equitable and excellent instruction, preparation and support of expert teachers, schools organized into small units and instructional teams, democratic governance, a healthy learning environment, and schools linked with parents and communities. According to the National Forum to Accelerate Middle Grades Reform, in 2005 seventy-one schools in thirteen states (California, Colorado, Florida, Idaho, Illinois, Massachusetts, Missouri, New York, North Carolina, Rhode Island, Pennsylvania, Vermont, and Wisconsin) were implementing the *Turning Points* model.

The National Forum to Accelerate Middle School Reform reports that in Illinois there was a rise in student achievement and fewer student behavior problems, and in Massachusetts middle schools the Turning Points schools demonstrated gains in the Massachusetts Educational Assessment Program.

According to the RAND corporation (Rand Education, "Problems and Promise of the American Middle School," Rand Research Brief, Santa Monica, California, 2004), in spite of these reform efforts, middle schools continue to face challenges. The transitions required of young people by a separate middle school may cause problems that affect students' development and academic achievement. RAND recommends that states and school districts consider alternatives to the grades six-to-eight structure.

According to *Programs and Practices in K–8 Schools: Do They Meet the Educational Needs of Young Adolescents?* (C. Kenneth McEwin, Thomas S. Dickinson, and Michael G. Jacobson, National Middle School Association, Westerville, Ohio, 2004), Cincinnati and Cleveland, Ohio; Minneapolis, Minnesota; Philadelphia, Pennsylvania; Memphis, Tennessee; Baltimore, Maryland; and Milwaukee, Wisconsin, all have plans to transition students from middle schools to K–8 schools. There is no data yet on whether students in K–8 schools perform better than those in middle schools.

DROPPING OUT

Trends in Dropout Rates

According to the National Center for Education Statistics, in general, high school dropout rates have declined since 1960. The total status dropout rate for people sixteen through twenty-four years of age was 27.2% in 1960, 14.1% in 1980, 12.1% in 1990, and 10.7% in 2001. (Status dropouts are people who are not enrolled in school and who are not high school graduates or holders of General Educational Development [GED] diplomas.)

Historically, Hispanic students have had significantly higher dropout rates than either whites or African-Americans. In 1980 white students had a dropout rate of 11.4%; African-American students, 19.1%; and Hispanic students, 35.2%. By 2001 the estimated rate for whites was 7.3%, 10.9% for African-Americans, and 27% for Hispanics.

The Costs of Dropping Out

Young people who drop out before finishing high school usually pay a high price. Dropouts have a much harder time making the transition from school to work and economic independence. The employment rates of high school graduates and GED holders have consistently been higher than those of dropouts. According to the National Center for Education Statistics, in 2002 the proportion of females ages sixteen to twenty-four who did not complete high school and were unemployed was 17.9%, compared to 12.3% of high school graduates and 5.1% of four-year college graduates. For male dropouts, 18.7% were unemployed, compared to 12.7% of high school graduates and 6.9% of those with bachelor's degrees. (See Table 6.1.)

TABLE 6.1

Unemployment rate of persons age 16 and over, by demographic characteristics, 2000–2002

Sex, race/ethnicity, and educational attainment	Percent unemployed, 2000[a]				Percent unemployed, 2001[a]				Percent unemployed, 2002[a]			
	16- to 24-year-olds[b]				16- to 24-year-olds[b]				16- to 24-year-olds[b]			
	Total	16 to 19 years	20 to 24 years	25 years old and over	Total	16 to 19 years	20 to 24 years	25 years old and over	Total	16 to 19 years	20 to 24 years	25 years old and over
1	2	3	4	5	6	7	8	9	10	11	12	13
All persons												
All education levels	9.3	13.1	7.2	3.0	10.6	14.7	8.3	3.7	12.0	16.5	9.7	4.6
Less than high school completion	15.1	15.6	13.8	6.3	16.7	17.3	15.3	7.2	18.4	19.0	17.0	8.4
High school completion, no college	9.4	11.6	8.4	3.4	10.7	13.3	9.5	4.2	12.6	15.9	11.1	5.3
Some college, no degree	5.5	6.7	5.1	2.9	6.4	8.1	6.0	3.5	7.7	9.2	7.3	4.8
Associate degree	3.3	—	3.3	2.3	4.5	—	4.4	2.9	7.2	—	7.1	4.0
Bachelor's degree or higher	4.3	—	4.3	1.7	5.7	—	5.7	2.3	5.8	—	5.8	2.9
Men												
All education levels	9.7	14.0	7.3	2.8	11.4	16.0	9.0	3.6	12.8	18.1	10.2	4.7
Less than high school completion	14.9	16.5	11.7	5.4	17.1	18.7	14.2	6.4	18.7	20.8	15.1	7.8
High school completion, no college	9.2	11.6	8.2	3.4	10.8	13.1	9.9	4.3	12.7	16.4	11.3	5.4
Some college, no degree	5.7	7.3	5.3	2.7	7.0	9.2	6.5	3.4	8.1	9.8	7.8	4.7
Associate degree	3.3	—	3.1	2.3	5.4	—	5.3	3.1	8.0	—	7.6	4.3
Bachelor's degree or higher	4.4	—	4.5	1.5	6.7	—	6.7	2.2	6.9	—	7.0	3.0
Women												
All education levels	8.9	12.1	7.1	3.2	9.6	13.4	7.5	3.7	11.1	14.9	9.1	4.6
Less than high school completion	15.3	14.5	18.4	7.8	16.0	15.5	17.6	8.6	17.9	17.0	20.7	9.5
High school completion, no college	9.5	11.5	8.5	3.5	10.5	13.4	9.1	4.0	12.3	15.4	10.9	5.1
Some college, no degree	5.3	6.3	4.9	3.0	5.9	7.3	5.5	3.6	7.3	8.8	6.8	5.0
Associate degree	3.3	—	3.4	2.4	3.9	—	3.9	2.7	6.7	—	6.6	3.7
Bachelor's degree or higher	4.2	—	4.2	1.8	5.0	—	5.0	2.3	5.1	—	5.0	2.8
White, non-Hispanic												
All education levels	7.4	10.4	5.5	2.4	8.6	11.7	6.7	3.0	9.8	13.5	7.7	3.9
Less than high school completion	12.7	12.6	13.2	5.2	13.9	13.8	14.3	5.8	15.6	15.4	16.4	7.5
High school completion, no college	7.2	9.0	6.3	2.8	9.0	10.4	8.3	3.5	10.5	13.2	9.2	4.5
Some college, no degree	4.5	5.3	4.2	2.5	5.2	6.7	4.8	3.1	6.3	8.0	5.8	4.2
Associate degree	3.1	—	3.0	2.0	4.4	—	4.3	2.4	6.0	—	5.6	3.5
Bachelor's degree or higher	3.9	—	4.0	1.5	5.4	—	5.4	2.0	5.3	—	5.2	2.7
Black, non-Hispanic												
All education levels	18.5	24.9	15.3	5.4	20.7	29.8	16.4	6.2	22.7	30.1	19.3	7.7
Less than high school completion	29.7	28.5	32.2	10.5	33.0	33.7	31.8	11.9	35.0	34.9	35.2	13.6
High school completion, no college	18.6	23.9	16.7	6.5	19.5	27.1	17.0	7.5	22.6	28.0	20.7	8.8
Some college, no degree	10.0	12.1	9.6	4.2	12.2	16.4	11.4	5.0	14.6	15.7	14.4	6.9
Associate degree	6.7	—	6.8	3.5	8.3	—	8.4	4.8	13.3	—	13.6	6.0
Bachelor's degree or higher	5.9	—	6.1	2.5	7.5	—	7.6	2.6	4.9	—	5.0	4.2

TABLE 6.1

Unemployment rate of persons age 16 and over, by demographic characteristics, 2000–2002 [CONTINUED]

Sex, race/ethnicity, and educational attainment	Percent unemployed, 2000[a]				Percent unemployed, 2001[a]				Percent unemployed, 2002[a]			
	16- to 24-year-olds[b]				16- to 24-year-olds[b]				16- to 24-year-olds[b]			
	Total	16 to 19 years	20 to 24 years	25 years old and over	Total	16 to 19 years	20 to 24 years	25 years old and over	Total	16 to 19 years	20 to 24 years	25 years old and over
1	2	3	4	5	6	7	8	9	10	11	12	13
Hispanic origin[c]												
All education levels	10.3	16.6	7.5	4.4	11.1	17.7	8.1	5.3	12.9	20.0	9.9	6.1
Less than high school completion	14.1	19.9	9.5	6.2	14.8	20.0	10.8	7.4	16.7	22.9	12.2	7.7
High school completion, no college	8.9	12.5	7.8	3.9	9.4	16.4	7.2	4.5	11.4	17.3	9.5	5.9
Some college, no degree	6.3	10.5	5.1	3.3	7.4	9.3	6.8	3.8	8.6	11.9	7.9	5.7
Associate degree	2.1	—	2.2	2.8	1.6	—	1.7	3.8	7.5	—	6.9	5.0
Bachelor's degree or higher	3.9	—	4.0	2.2	5.3	—	5.3	3.6	8.4	—	8.5	3.4

— Not available.

[a]The unemployment rate is the percent of individuals in the labor force who are not working and who made specific efforts to find employment sometime during the prior 4 weeks. The labor force includes both employed and unemployed persons.

[b]Excludes persons enrolled in school.

[c]Persons of Hispanic origin may be of any race.

Note: Some data have been revised from previously published figures.

SOURCE: Thomas D. Snyder, Alexandra G. Tan, and Charlene M. Hoffman, "Table 380. Unemployment Rate of Persons 16 Years Old and Over, by Age, Sex, Race/Ethnicity, and Educational Attainment, 2000, 2001, and 2002," in *Digest of Education Statistics, 2003*, NCES 2005-025, U.S. Department of Education, National Center for Education Statistics, Washington, DC, December 2004, http://nces.ed.gov/programs/digest/d03/tables/dt380.asp (accessed July 26, 2005)

Minority students who drop out are at even higher economic risk. In 2002 the proportion of African-American high school dropouts ages sixteen to twenty-four who were unemployed was 35%, while 16.7% of Hispanic dropouts ages sixteen to twenty-four were unemployed. In comparison, 15.6% of white dropouts in the same age range were unemployed in 2002. (See Table 6.1.)

People without high school diplomas tend to earn considerably less than those with more education. According to the National Center for Education Statistics, in 2000 the median income (half earned more; half earned less) of males ages twenty-five and over who attended high school but did not graduate was $21,365, which is 70% of the annual median earnings of male high school graduates ($30,665). Females with less than a high school education earned $12,753, 69% of the earnings of females who finished high school ($18,393).

Many significant consequences of dropping out of school cannot be measured statistically. Some of those who drop out may experience lifelong poverty. Some who are poorly prepared to compete in society may turn to crime or substance abuse. Some become teenage parents without the ability to offer their children more than they had, possibly contributing to a cycle of dependence. Furthermore, the U.S. economy is deprived of the literate, technically trained, and dedicated workers it needs to compete internationally. Finally, those without a high school diploma generally do not have the opportunities available to the more highly educated.

Factors Related to Dropping Out

Prepared by the National Center for Education Statistics, the National Education Longitudinal Study of 1988 (NELS:88) studied students from the eighth grade through their high school years and beyond. Follow-up surveys were done in 1990, 1992, 1994, and 2000.

The earlier studies found that school-related reasons were usually given for dropping out, such as "did not like school," "failing in school," "could not get along with teachers," or "school expulsion and suspension." Other reasons the students gave were family or job-related, such as "pregnancy or became a parent," "got married," or "found a job." The U.S. Department of Education, in *Dropout Rates in the United States: 1992*, states that "dropping out is a process, not an event" and the reasons given by students "may not be the true causes but rationalizations or simplifications of more complex circumstances."

In a 2002 report based on the NELS, *Coming of Age in the 1990s: The Eighth-Grade Class of 1988 Twelve Years Later*, the National Center for Education Statistics found that the decision to drop out of high school was related to educational experiences before high school, in addition to personal and family background characteristics. Students who exhibited high mathematics achievement, attended a private school, or participated in extracurricular activities in eighth grade were more likely to complete high school than students who lacked those academic characteristics. Students from disadvantaged backgrounds (low income, parents who did not attend college, single-parent households, having an older sibling who dropped out of high school, spending three or more hours home alone after school per day, or being an LEP student) were more likely to drop out of school than students from more advantaged backgrounds.

According to *High School Students at Risk: The Challenge of Dropouts and Pushouts*, (Lucy Hood, Carnegie Corporation of New York, New York, 2004), several factors decrease the likelihood that students will drop out of high school, including being engaged in what they are learning; having the right teacher in the classroom; fewer students in classes; and smaller, more personal, academically rigorous school environments.

"DETACHED YOUTH"

Some young people drop out not only from school, but also from work. The Federal Interagency Forum on Child and Family Statistics applies the term "detached youth" to people ages sixteen to nineteen "who are neither enrolled in school nor working." The proportion of youth fitting this description is one measure of the number of young people who are at risk. Since 1980 this has been a persistent problem; however, there has been a downward trend in the proportion of youth neither enrolled nor working. Most of the decline in this proportion has occurred among young females.

According to the Federal Interagency Forum on Child and Family Statistics, in an average week during the 2004 school year about 8% of youths ages sixteen to nineteen were neither enrolled in school nor working. In 1991, 13% of young females were neither in school nor working; by 2004 this proportion had decreased to 8%. However, young females continued to be slightly more detached from these activities than young males.

African-American and Hispanic youth are more likely to be detached from school and work than white youth. In 2004, 12% of Hispanic youth and 10% of African-American youth were neither in school nor working, compared with 6% of white youth and 6% of youth of other races. (See Figure 6.1.)

Older youth, ages eighteen to nineteen, are more than three times as likely to be detached from these activities as youth ages sixteen to seventeen. In 2004, 13% of youth ages eighteen to nineteen were neither enrolled in school nor working compared with 3% of youth ages sixteen to seventeen.

NATIONAL STUDIES ON ADOLESCENT HEALTH

The behavioral choices teens make can put their health and success in life at risk. Both the Adolescent Health Program at the University of Minnesota (in Minneapolis) and the Centers for Disease Control and Prevention (CDC)

FIGURE 6.1

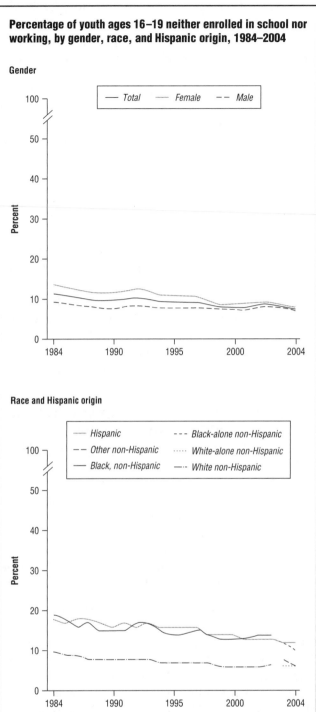

Percentage of youth ages 16–19 neither enrolled in school nor working, by gender, race, and Hispanic origin, 1984–2004

SOURCE: Federal Interagency Forum on Child and Family Statistics, "Table ED6. Percentage of Youth Ages 16–19 Neither Enrolled in School Nor Working, by Gender, Race, and Hispanic Origin, 1984–2004," in *America's Children: Key National Indicators of Well-Being, 2005*, Federal Interagency Forum on Child and Family Statistics, Washington, DC, July 2005, http://www.childstats.gov/americaschildren/edu6.asp (accessed August 10, 2005)

monitor teen risk behaviors. The Adolescent Health Program conducts the National Longitudinal Study on Adolescent Health (Add Health), and the CDC prepares the annual Youth Risk Behavior Surveillance study.

The Add Health study, as reported in "Protecting Adolescents from Harm" (Michael D. Resnick et al., *Journal of the American Medical Association*, vol. 278, no. 10, September 10, 1997), found certain conditions in the home to be statistically associated with risk behaviors. For example, access to guns in the home was linked to suicidal tendencies and violence, and access to addictive substances at home was related to teens' use of cigarettes, alcohol, and marijuana. Working twenty hours or more a week was linked to emotional distress and use of cigarettes, alcohol, and marijuana.

On the other hand, adolescents who felt strongly connected to family and school were protected to some extent against health-risk behaviors. Parental disapproval of early sexual activity was associated with later onset of sexual activity, and parental expectations of school achievement were linked to lower levels of risk behavior. The presence of parents before school, after school, at dinner, and at bedtime was associated with lower levels of emotional distress, suicidal thoughts, and suicide attempts. Feeling "connected" at school also was associated with lower levels of these behaviors.

MONITORING THE FUTURE AND YOUTH RISK BEHAVIOR SURVEILLANCE STUDIES

Funded by the National Institute on Drug Abuse (NIDA) in Washington, D.C., the Institute for Social Research at the University of Michigan conducts an annual survey of substance use among students called Monitoring the Future ("Overall Teen Drug Use Continues Gradual Decline; But Use of Inhalants Rises," Lloyd D. Johnston, Patrick M. O'Malley, Jerald G. Bachman, and John E. Schulenberg, National Institute on Drug Abuse, Bethesda, MD, December 2004).

The CDC also reported on risk behaviors among young people in *Youth Risk Behavior Surveillance— United States, 2003* (Jo Anne Grunbaum, Laura Kann, Steven A. Kinchen, James Ross, Joseph Hawkins, Richard Lowry, William Harris, Tim McManus, David Chyen, and Janet Collins, *CDC Surveillance Summaries*, MMWR 2004, vol. 53, no. SS-2, May 21, 2004).

Attitudes toward Drugs

According to the Monitoring the Future survey (MTF), in 2004 fewer students considered substance use extremely dangerous than in 1991. The proportions of those who saw great risk in the use of marijuana decreased significantly in all grades between 1991 and 2004; only 22% of tenth graders in 2004 said that trying marijuana once or twice was very risky, down from 30% in 1991. In 2004 the proportion (68.4%) of tenth graders who saw great risk in smoking one or more packs of cigarettes a day had increased from

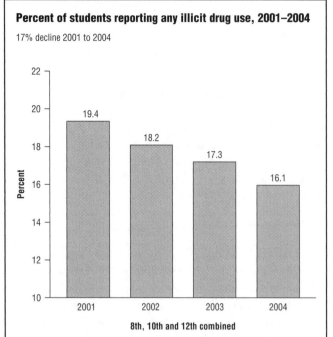

FIGURE 6.2

Percent of students reporting any illicit drug use, 2001–2004

17% decline 2001 to 2004

8th, 10th and 12th combined

SOURCE: Lloyd D. Johnston, Patrick M. O'Malley, Jerald G. Bachman, and John E. Schulenberg, "Percent of Students Reporting Any Illicit Drug Use has Decreased," in *2004 Monitoring the Future Fact Sheet*, National Institute on Drug Abuse, Bethesda, MD, August 2003, http:// www.nida.nih.gov/Newsroom/04/2004MTFFactSheets.pdf (accessed July 26, 2005) Source: University of Michigan, "Monitoring the Future Study, 2004."

1991, when it was 60.3%. All students perceived daily drinking and binge drinking as less risky than they did in 1991. A slightly higher proportion of eighth-grade students considered using heroin dangerous in 2004 than in 1995, when heroin was first added to the survey.

Use of Drugs during the Past Month

Good news from the Monitoring the Future survey (MTF) is that there was a 17% decrease from 2001 to 2004 in the proportion of students who reported any illicit drug use during the past month. With eighth, tenth, and twelfth graders combined, 16.1% reported that they had used illicit drugs in the past month, compared to 19.4% in 2001. (See Figure 6.2.)

Drug Use at School

According to the National Center for Education Statistics and the Bureau of Justice Statistics, about 29% of high school students reported that illegal drugs were made available to them on school property in 2003. Male high school students were more likely than females to report that drugs were made available to them on school property during the previous twelve months. Nearly one-third of males (32%) and one-quarter of female students (25%) reported that illegal drugs were offered, sold, or given to them at school. (See Figure 6.3.)

FIGURE 6.3

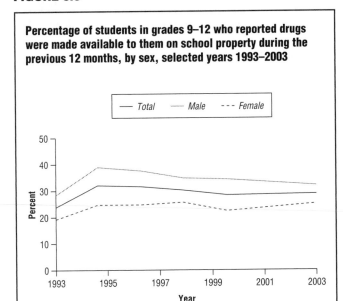

Percentage of students in grades 9–12 who reported drugs were made available to them on school property during the previous 12 months, by sex, selected years 1993–2003

Note: "On school property" was not defined for survey respondents.

SOURCE: Jill F. DeVoe, Katharin Peter, Phillip Kaufman, Sally A. Ruddy, Amanda Miller, Margaret Noonan, Thomas D. Snyder, and Katrina Baum, "Figure 19.1. Percentage of Students in Grades 9–12 Who Reported Drugs Were Made Available to Them on School Property During the Previous 12 Months, by Sex: Selected Years, 1993–2003," in *Indicators of School Crime and Safety: 2004*, NCES 2005-02/NCJ 205290, U.S. Department of Education, National Center for Educational Statistics and U.S. Department of Justice, Bureau of Justice Statistics, Washington, DC, November 2004, http://nces.ed.gov/pubs2005/2005002.pdf (accessed July 26, 2005).

The National Center for Education Statistics and the Bureau of Justice Statistics reported that in 2003 grade level did not make a difference in the percentage of students who reported that drugs were made available to them at school. About 30% of ninth, eleventh, and twelfth graders and 29% of tenth graders reported that drugs were offered, sold, or given to them at school. There was a difference in proportion between students of various racial or ethnic backgrounds. Hispanic students (37%) were more likely to report that drugs were made available to them at school than were Asian-American (23%), African-American (23%), Native American (31%), or white students (28%).

Marijuana

According to the Monitoring the Future survey, in 2004 the proportion of eighth-grade students who reported having used marijuana at least once during their lifetimes was 16.3%, with 35.1% of tenth graders and 45.7% of twelfth graders reporting using marijuana at least once. These rates represented increases from 1991, when 10.2% of eighth graders, 23.4% of tenth graders, and 36.7% of twelfth graders said they had used marijuana at least once in their lives, but they had slightly decreased from 2003, when 17.5% of eighth graders, 36.4% of tenth graders, and 46.1% of twelfth graders said they had used marijuana at least once in their lives.

Inhalants

The Monitoring the Future survey reports that the proportion of eighth, tenth, and twelfth graders who used inhalants, such as glues, solvents, and aerosols, peaked in 1995 and then declined for nearly two decades. By 2004, however, MTF survey results showed that inhalant abuse—especially among eighth graders—had increased significantly. Inhalants are most often used in the earlier grade levels. In 2004, 17.3% of eighth graders reported using an inhalant during their lifetimes, compared to 12.4% of tenth graders and 10.9% of twelfth graders. Because most inhalants are common household products, they are readily available, and young people may not understand that they are potentially lethal.

Alcohol

According to the CDC's Youth Risk Behavior Surveillance study, from 1993 to 2003 the proportion of high school students who reported using alcohol at school declined slightly. Students were much less likely to use alcohol on school property than elsewhere. In 2003, 5.2% of high school students reported drinking alcohol on school property. (See Table 6.2.)

The Monitoring the Future survey reports that in 2004 the proportion of eighth graders who said they had tried alcohol in their lifetimes was 43.9%, with 64.2% of tenth graders and 76.8% of twelfth graders reporting this same behavior. When asked if they had been drunk in their lives, 19.9% of eighth graders, 42.3% of tenth graders, and 60.3% of twelfth graders reported that they had.

In 2004 female students were more likely to report drinking flavored alcohol during the past month than males. About 16% of female eighth graders, 26% of tenth graders, and 33% of twelfth graders reported drinking flavored alcohol, compared to 13%, 25%, and 29%, respectively, for males.

Tobacco Use among Middle and High School Students

According to the MTF survey, cigarette smoking among high school students declined slowly but steadily from 1975 to the early 1990s, but the rates grew during the mid-1990s. The rates began to drop significantly again from 1997 to 2004. The proportion of students who reported using cigarettes during their lifetimes was 27.9% for eighth graders, 40.7% for tenth graders, and 52.8% for twelfth graders in 2004.

In 2004 about two-thirds of students believed that smoking one or more packs of cigarettes a day represented a great risk, which represents an increase in every grade from 1991, when the proportions were closer to one-half. Though students in higher grades were more likely to say that there was "great risk" in smoking one or more packs a day, students in the younger grades were somewhat more likely than seniors to "disapprove" of daily cigarette smoking.

TABLE 6.2

Percentage of high school students who used tobacco and drank alcohol on school property, by sex, race/ethnicity, and grade, 2003

Category	Cigarette use on school property[a]			Smokeless tobacco use on school property[b]			Alcohol use on school property[c]		
	Female %	Male %	Total %	Female %	Male %	Total %	Female %	Male %	Total %
Race/ethnicity									
White[d]	9.6	8.2	8.9	3.3	9.9	6.7	3.2	4.5	3.9
Black[d]	3.5	8.4	5.9	1.8	3.2	2.5	3.8	7.9	5.8
Hispanic	5.8	6.2	6.0	2.6	4.6	3.6	7.9	7.4	7.6
Grade									
9	7.7	7.3	7.5	4.4	6.0	5.2	5.2	5.1	5.1
10	8.0	7.5	7.7	2.6	7.7	5.2	5.0	6.1	5.6
11	8.4	8.1	8.2	3.2	10.8	7.1	3.5	6.4	5.0
12	5.9	10.5	8.3	2.3	10.1	6.3	2.6	6.5	4.5
Total	**7.6**	**8.2**	**8.0**	**3.3**	**8.5**	**5.9**	**4.2**	**6.0**	**5.2**

[a]Smoked cigarettes on ≥1 of the 30 days preceding the survey.
[b]Used chewing tobacco, snuff, or dip ≥1 of the 30 days preceding the survey.
[c]Drank one or more drinks of alcohol on ≥1 of the 30 days preceding the survey.
[d]Non-Hispanic.

SOURCE: Jo Anne Grunbaum, Laura Kann, Steve Kinchen, James Ross, Joseph Hawkins, Richard Lowry, William A. Harris, Tim McManus, David Chyen, and Janet Collins, "Table 38. Percentage of High School Students Who Used Tobacco and Drank Alcohol on School Property, by Sex, Race/Ethnicity, and Grade—United States, Youth Risk Behavior Survey, 2003," in "Youth Risk Behavior Surveillance—United States, 2003," *Surveillance Summaries, MMWR,* vol. 53, no.SS-02, May 21, 2004, http://www.cdc.gov/mmwr/preview/mmwrhtml/ss5302a1.htm#tab38 (accessed July 26, 2005)

In 2004 white eighth graders (10%), tenth graders (18.7%), and twelfth graders (28.2%) and Hispanic eighth graders (10.1%), tenth graders (13.9%), and seniors (18.5%) were more likely than African-American eighth graders (6.9%), tenth graders (9.2%), and twelfth graders (10.1%) to have smoked cigarettes at least once in the thirty days preceding the MTF survey.

Not surprisingly, in 2004 seniors were more likely to be daily (15.6%) smokers than were eighth graders (4.4%). Females in grade eight were more likely to have smoked in the past month (9.9%) than males (8.3%), but in tenth and twelfth grades females were slightly less likely than males to have smoked in the past thirty days. Among tenth graders, 15.7% of females had smoked in the past month, compared to 16.2% of males. Just over 24% of females who were seniors had smoked in the prior thirty days, while 25.3% of males had smoked during that time.

Sexual Activity

Great Transitions: Preparing Adolescents for a New Century (Carnegie Council on Adolescent Development, New York, 1995) pointed out that the age of first intercourse declined during the years between 1965 and 1995. Since that time the proportion of students who reported having initiated sexual intercourse before thirteen years of age has declined from 9% in 1995 to 6.6% in 2001. In its 2003 Youth Risk Behavior Surveillance, the CDC reported that 4.2% of females and 10.4% of males had first experienced sexual intercourse before age thirteen. About one-third (34.3%) of both high school females and males claimed they were currently sexually active. The

proportion of females who reported that they had had four or more sexual partners was 11.2%; the proportion of males, was 17.5%. Older students tended to be more sexually active than younger students, with 48.9% of high school seniors stating that they were currently sexually active. African-American students (49.8%) were more likely than white (30.8%) or Hispanic (37.1%) students to be sexually active.

TEENAGE PREGNANCY. From 1960 through 1986, the number of live births per 1,000 females ages fifteen to seventeen generally declined. The rate increased during the late 1980s and early 1990s before starting to decline again after 1995. Child Trends reported that in 2003 there were 22.4 live births per 1,000 females ages fifteen to seventeen. (See Table 6.3.)

In 2003 mothers under age twenty accounted for a total of 421,626 live births. Teenagers had a birth rate of 41.7 births per 1,000 females ages fifteen to nineteen. The birthrate was higher among teenagers ages eighteen and nineteen (70.8 per 1,000) than for those ages fifteen to seventeen. (See Table 6.3.) In 2003 the teen birth rate for white teens was 27.5, for African-American teens it was 64.8, and for Hispanic teens it was 82.2.

Most teenage mothers are unmarried and lack the resources to give their children adequate care. The National Center for Health Statistics reported that in 2003 about 82% of all teen births occurred outside of marriage.

AIDS AND OTHER SEXUALLY TRANSMITTED DISEASES. The CDC identifies certain diseases as "notifiable," meaning that state and local medical authorities must

TABLE 6.3

Teen birth rate, selected years, 1940–2003

[Births per 1,000 females]

Ages	1940	1950	1960	1970	1980	1986	1990	1991	1995	2000	2002	2003
15–19	54.1	81.6	89.1	68.3	53.0	50.2	59.9	61.8	56.0	47.7	43.0	41.7
15–17	—	—	43.9	38.8	32.5	30.5	37.5	38.6	35.5	26.9	23.2	22.4
18–19	—	—	166.7	114.7	82.1	79.6	88.6	94.0	87.7	78.1	72.8	70.8

SOURCE: Kerry Franzetta, Erum Ikramullah, Jennifer Manlove, Kristin Anderson Moore, and Elizabeth Terry-Humen, "Teen Birth Rate (Births Per 1,000 Females Ages 15–19, 15–17, and 18–19)," in *Facts at a Glance*, Child Trends, Inc., Washington, DC, March 2005, http://www.childtrends.org/Files/Facts_2005 .pdf (accessed July 26, 2005). Reproduced with permission.

report each occurrence to the CDC. Sexually transmitted diseases (STDs) are included in the notifiable disease list. Human immunodeficiency virus (HIV, the virus that causes AIDS [acquired immunodeficiency syndrome]) is probably the best-known STD, but it is not the most common. Syphilis, chlamydia, and gonorrhea are the three most common STDs reported to the CDC.

Adolescents and young adults are at a higher risk for acquiring STDs than older adults. Chlamydia and gonorrhea are the most common STDs among teenagers. The CDC reported in *Sexually Transmitted Disease Surveillance, 2003* (Centers for Disease Control and Prevention, September 2004) that there were 325,416 cases of chlamydia, 95,269 cases of gonorrhea, and 333 cases of syphilis among those ten to nineteen years of age in 2003. Although antibiotics can cure many STDs, these diseases can still have serious health consequences, including an increase in a victim's risk of contracting HIV if exposed, and females may contract pelvic inflammatory disease, which can lead to infertility.

HIV/AIDS remains the most dangerous STD. Young people who are sexually active and/or inject drugs are at great risk of contracting the virus. The CDC reported that a total of 9,079 people under age twenty-five were living with AIDS in 2003. (See Table 6.4.) Countless more are infected with HIV, the virus that causes AIDS. Because of the long incubation period from the time of infection and the onset of symptoms, many people who develop AIDS in their early twenties were probably infected with HIV as teenagers.

SUICIDE

According to the CDC, 16.9% of high school students in the Youth Risk Behavior Surveillance had seriously considered attempting suicide in the year preceding the survey (2003). More females (21.3%) than males (12.8%) considered attempting suicide. The prevalence was higher among white (16.5%) and Hispanic students (18.1%) than among African-American students (12.5%). Nationwide, 8.5% of students had actually attempted suicide, and 2.9% required medical attention as a result of the suicide attempt.

VIOLENCE IN SCHOOL

At the end of the twentieth century, the issue of violence in schools received attention because of several incidents that garnered tremendous attention, including the Columbine massacre in 1999, when two students murdered a dozen of their classmates and a teacher at their Littleton, Colorado, high school.

Violence in school—threats, physical fights, weapons at school, and the feeling of being unsafe—has increased since 1980. Nonetheless, most students and teachers still report that they feel relatively safe at school. In its 2003 Youth Risk Behavior Surveillance, the CDC found that 5.4% of the students surveyed had missed at least one school day during the thirty days before the survey because they felt too unsafe to go to school. About 3.1% of white students felt too unsafe to go to school, compared to 8.4% of African-American and 9.4% of Hispanic students. Students in ninth grade (6.9%) were more likely than twelfth graders (3.8%) to fear going to school.

Juvenile Offenders

According to the U.S. Department of Justice, serious violent crimes committed by juvenile offenders declined at the end of the twentieth century. However, based on their proportion of the population, juveniles were disproportionately involved in arrests for arson, vandalism, motor vehicle theft, burglary, larceny-theft, robbery, and weapons law violations.

Young people who commit violent crimes are likely to be sent to juvenile detention facilities or even to adult prisons and jails. In any of these facilities, they are much less likely to complete their high school education.

FIGHTS IN SCHOOL. The CDC asked high school students whether they had been in a fight on school property. In 2003 about 12.8% of the students surveyed were in at least one physical fight on school property during the twelve months preceding the survey. Male students (17.1%) were more than twice as likely as females (8%) to have been in a fight. African-American (17.1%) and Hispanic (16.7%) students were more likely than white students (10%) to have been in a fight.

TABLE 6.4

Estimated number of persons living with AIDS, by year and selected characteristics, 1999–2003

	1999	2000	2001	2002	2003
Age as of end of year (years)					
<13	3,034	2,843	2,605	2,335	1,998
13—14	440	517	645	728	768
15—24	4,719	4,991	5,229	5,668	6,313
25—34	60,184	56,686	53,687	51,410	49,906
35—44	141,295	151,180	158,173	163,732	168,322
45—54	77,216	89,461	102,252	115,613	129,311
55—64	19,258	22,922	27,197	32,703	38,997
≥65	5,058	6,132	7,251	8,583	10,310
Race/ethnicity					
White, not Hispanic	119,674	126,162	132,258	139,089	146,544
Black, not Hispanic	126,044	137,524	148,469	160,022	172,278
Hispanic	61,194	66,266	71,034	75,782	80,623
Asian/Pacific Islander	2,484	2,755	3,056	3,414	3,826
American Indian/Alaska Native	1,047	1,166	1,262	1,380	1,498
Transmission category					
Male adult or adolescent					
Male-to-male sexual contact	140,216	150,172	160,076	171,035	182,989
Injection drug use	58,006	61,249	63,723	66,003	68,191
Male-to-male sexual contact and injection drug use	21,667	22,403	23,033	23,690	24,334
Heterosexual contact	20,595	23,478	26,471	29,835	33,324
Other[a]	3,807	3,922	4,062	4,204	4,345
Subtotal	244,291	261,223	277,366	294,767	313,183
Female adult or adolescent					
Injection drug use	25,744	27,317	28,602	29,670	30,710
Heterosexual contact	35,603	40,422	45,097	50,142	55,685
Other[a]	1,746	1,908	2,067	2,239	2,420
Subtotal	63,093	69,647	75,765	82,052	88,815
Child (<13 yrs at diagnosis)					
Perinatal	3,672	3,714	3,763	3,808	3,788
Other[b]	148	145	145	143	139
Subtotal	3,820	3,860	3,908	3,951	3,927
Region of residence					
Northeast	92,741	99,964	105,970	111,506	116,827
Midwest	31,016	33,470	35,725	38,513	41,668
South	115,991	125,396	135,465	146,421	158,962
West	62,300	66,280	69,931	74,253	78,333
U.S. dependencies, possessions, and associated nations	9,157	9,621	9,949	10,077	10,136
Total[c]	**311,205**	**334,731**	**357,040**	**380,771**	**405,926**

Note: These numbers do not represent reported case counts. Rather, these numbers are point estimates, which result from adjustments of reported case counts. The reported case counts are adjusted for reporting delays and for redistribution of cases in persons initially reported without an identified risk factor. The estimates do not include adjustment for incomplete reporting.

[a]Includes hemophilia, blood transfusion, perinatal, and risk factor not reported or not identified.

[b]Includes hemophilia, blood transfusion, and risk factor not reported or not identified.

[c]Includes persons of unknown race or multiple races and persons of unknown sex. Because column totals were calculated independently of the values for the subpopulations, the values in each column may not sum to the column total.

SOURCE: Centers for Disease Control and Prevention, "Table 10. Estimated Number of Persons Living with AIDS, by Year and Selected Characteristics, 1999–2003—United States," in *HIV/AIDS Surveillance Report*, vol. 15, 2003, http://www.cdc.gov/hiv/stats/2003SurveillanceReport/table10.htm (accessed July 26, 2005)

CARRYING A WEAPON. Weapons commonly brought to school include guns, knives, clubs, brass knuckles, razor blades, spiked jewelry, and other objects capable of inflicting harm. The 2003 Youth Risk Behavior Surveillance found that 6.1% of students reported carrying a weapon of some type on school property during the thirty days before the survey. Males (8.9%) were more likely than females (3.1%) to carry weapons at school.

The U.S. Departments of Education and Justice report that during the late 1990s there was a steady decline in the proportion of high school students who reported carrying a weapon to school on one or more days during the previous month. Theft, vandalism, and physical fighting that did not involve a weapon were more common in schools than were more serious incidents.

Juvenile Victims

According to the National Center for Education Statistics and the Bureau of Justice Statistics in *Indicators of School Crime and Safety: 2004* (National Center for Education Statistics, http://www.nces.ed.gov/

FIGURE 6.4

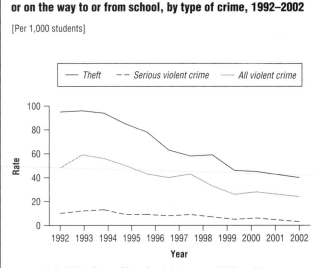

Rate of nonfatal crime against students ages 12–18 at school or on the way to or from school, by type of crime, 1992–2002

[Per 1,000 students]

SOURCE: John Wirt, Susan Choy, Patrick Rooney, William Hussar, Stephen Provasnik, and Gillian Hampden-Thompson, "Trends in Victimization: Rate of Nonfatal Crime Against Students Ages 12–18 at School or On the Way To or From School per 1,000 Students, by Type of Crime: 1992–2002," in *The Condition of Education, 2005*, NCES 2005-094, U.S. Department of Education, National Center for Education Statistics, Washington, DC, June 2005, http://nces.ed.gov/pubs2005/2005094.pdf (accessed July 26, 2005)

FIGURE 6.5

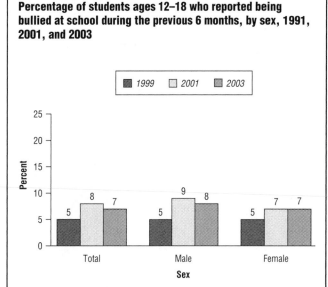

Percentage of students ages 12–18 who reported being bullied at school during the previous 6 months, by sex, 1991, 2001, and 2003

Note: In the 1999 survey, "at school" was defined as in the school building, on the school grounds, or on a school bus. In the 2001 and 2003 surveys, "at school" was defined as in the school building, on school property, on a school bus, or going to and from school. Cognitive interview results suggest that modifications to the definition of "at school" do not have substantial impact on the estimates.

SOURCE: Jill F. DeVoe, Katharin Peter, Phillip Kaufman, Sally A. Ruddy, Amanda Miller, Margaret Noonan, Thomas D. Snyder, and Katrina Baum, "Figure 6.1. Percentage of Students Ages 12–18 Who Reported Being Bullied at School During the Previous 6 Months, by Sex: 1991, 2001, and 2003," in *Indicators of School Crime and Safety: 2004*, NCES 2005-02/NCJ 205290, U.S. Department of Education, National Center for Education Statistics and U.S. Department of Justice, Bureau of Justice Statistics, Washington, DC, November 2004, http://nces.ed.gov/pubs2005/2005002.pdf (accessed July 26, 2005)

pubs2005/2005002.pdf, November 2004), in 2003, 5% of students ages twelve to eighteen reported nonfatal criminal victimization at school during the prior six months. More students reported theft (4%) than violent crimes (1%). Students in grades seven and nine reported more incidents of criminal victimization than students in other grades.

According to the CDC Youth Risk Behavior Surveillance, in 2003 nearly 9.2% of the students surveyed reported that they had been threatened or injured with a weapon at school one or more times in the past twelve months. Males (11.6%) were more likely than females (6.5%) to report this behavior. More ninth graders (12.1%) than tenth graders (9.2%), eleventh graders (7.3%), or twelfth graders (6.3%) reported threats and injuries with weapons.

According to the National Center for Education Statistics, the percentage of students ages twelve to eighteen who report criminal victimization at school or on the way to or from school declined from 1992 to 2002. The crime rates against students at school declined by 58% for theft, 50% for all violent crime, and 70% for serious violent crime. (See Figure 6.4.)

According to the National Center for Education Statistics and the Bureau of Justice Statistics, the percentage of students ages twelve to eighteen who reported being bullied at school during the previous six months increased from 1999 to 2003. About 5% reported being bullied at school in 1999 and 7% in 2003. More males (8%) than females (7%) reported being bullied at school in 2003. (See Figure 6.5.) Sixth graders were most likely to report being bullied in 2003. The proportion of students in grade six who reported being bullied at school was 14% in 2003, up from 11% in 1999. In 2003 more public school students (7%) than private school students (5%) reported being bullied.

CHAPTER 7
ISSUES IN EDUCATION

Schools, like other institutions, face various issues as they grow and attempt to meet the needs of an ever-changing population. In the nineteenth century the common school movement sought to establish education for all that would be paid for by property taxes. In the early twentieth century school advocates debated questions of whether school should be compulsory, whether teachers should use corporal punishment, the best way to train teachers, and school centralization. During the post–World War II "baby boom," concerns included building enough schools and educating enough teachers to fill the need. During the 1960s and beyond, schools faced the challenges of integration and busing. Later came sex and drug education, the role of religion in the classroom, and using ideas from business organizations to restructure schools.

In the twenty-first century American schools continue to face enduring problems and new challenges. Some of the topics under discussion are diversity, higher standards, assessment, accountability, school-choice programs, school funding, safety, discipline, school and classroom size, parental involvement, home-schooling, the achievement gap between demographic groups, and the role of educational technology. There is no clear consensus on how to approach these and other issues, but the passion with which they are debated in contemporary American society gives evidence of their importance.

SCHOOL REFORM MOVEMENTS

In 1957 the "space race" began when the Soviet Union launched *Sputnik I*, the first satellite sent into space. To prevent the nation from falling behind in the technology competition, American leaders called for improved educational techniques and student performance. More than two decades later, the administration of President Ronald Reagan released *A Nation at Risk*

(National Commission on Excellence in Education, Washington, DC, 1983), a report on education in the United States. The report claimed that, instead of responding to the 1957 challenge to raise standards, American education had produced students who actually were scoring lower on performance tests than in 1957. The writers of the report feared that the nation would become less competitive in world markets, causing the economy to suffer.

The report recommended that American education, especially in high school, should primarily focus on academic achievement, with students spending more time in school and working on homework. As a result, most states raised graduation requirements, revised testing and evaluation programs, and improved teacher preparation standards.

Demands for reform continued in 1986 with eight new reports on the state of American education, including *Time for Results* (National Governors' Association, Washington, DC), *A Nation Prepared: Teachers for the 21st Century* (Carnegie Forum on Education and the Economy, Washington, DC), and *What Next? More Leverage for Teachers* (Education Commission of the States, Denver, CO). These publications focused on strategies to improve education, including teacher training and higher salaries, state initiatives to reform education, and school choice. The states followed many of the recommendations issued in the reports, especially in the areas of recruiting and preparing teachers, and in restructuring the organization and management of school systems.

At the Education Summit held in Charlottesville, Virginia, in 1989, President George H. W. Bush and the state governors established six National Education Goals to be met by the year 2000. These goals presented a broad approach to education reform, including providing preschool children sufficient nutrition and health care so they are ready to learn by the time they start school; greater levels of high school completion and student achievement; ensuring that U.S. students are first in the world in mathematics and science; safe, disciplined, and alcohol- and drug-free schools; and improved adult education. In 1994 Congress passed the Goals 2000: Educate America Act (P.L. 103-227), reemphasizing the National Education Goals and adding goals calling for increasing the involvement of parents in schools and providing further professional development for teachers. Progress toward the goals was slow, and in 2002 Congress dissolved the National Education Goals Panel.

Congress passed the Charter School Expansion Act of 1998 (P.L. 105-278), which authorizes State Educational Agencies (SEAs) to use federal funds for planning, designing, and implementing public charter schools and requires Local Education Agencies (LEAs) to use innovative assistance funds for the same purpose. Funding priorities are based on a state's progress toward increasing its number of high-quality charter schools.

The Education Flexibility Partnership Act of 1999 (P.L. 106-25) gives states more freedom in how they spend federal education dollars. To participate in the Ed-Flex Partnership program, states must apply to the Secretary of Education for a waiver from the normal requirements for obtaining federal funds. They may then set up their own programs under which they are held accountable for improved educational results in order to receive continued funding. For example, schools can use federal money intended for science and mathematics teachers on reading programs to boost progress in that area.

The No Child Left Behind Act (NCLB) was signed into law by President George W. Bush in January 2002. The new authorization was a major reform to the Elementary and Secondary Education Act (ESEA) of 1965. NCLB focuses on increasing accountability for results, implementing programs that are based on scientific research, expanding parental options, and increasing the control and flexibility of local school officials. NCLB especially promotes assessment, reading/literacy, teacher quality, school choice, and innovative programs.

The following sections describe some of the approaches developed in recent years in response to the above policy initiatives intended to improve education.

CHARTER SCHOOLS

Charter schools are one element of the school choice movement. They are nonsectarian (not affiliated with any religious groups) public schools that may be exempt from some regulations that apply to regular public schools. Charter schools are related to other aspects of educational reform, including privatization, site-based management, magnet schools, and parental involvement. The idea of

charter schools was first suggested in the 1970s. Albert Shanker, former president of the American Federation of Teachers (AFT), helped promote the idea. In the 1980s Philadelphia piloted several model schools, calling them "charters." In the 1990s Minnesota developed charter schools based on three values: choice, opportunity, and accountability for results.

In charter schools teachers, parents, administrators, community groups, or private corporations design and operate a local school under charter (written contract) from a school district, state education agency, or other public institution. These local schools often have a specific focus, such as mathematics, arts, or science. In some cases charter schools are nearly autonomous (self-directing) and are exempt from many state and district education rules. In other cases the schools operate much like traditional public schools and must apply for certain exemptions, which they may or may not be granted.

Many states find charter schools appealing. Common reasons given for considering alternatives such as charter schools are problems associated with regular public schools, including overcrowded classrooms, district mismanagement or disorganization, low scores on standardized tests, and a high number of students at risk of dropping out of school.

In 1991 only one charter school existed in the United States. According to the *State of the Charter Movement 2005* (Gregg Vanourek, Charter School Leadership Council, May 2005), in 2005 forty states and the District of Columbia had authorized charter schools, and there were an estimated 3,400 charter schools in the country, serving approximately one million students, or about 2% of all students in the nation.

In 2005 more than two-fifths (42%) of charter schools were concentrated in three states (Arizona, California, and Florida), and more than half (54%) of the charter school growth since 2000 had occurred in those three states plus Michigan and Texas.

According to the National Center for Education Statistics, in 2003 most public charter schools (41.2%) were located in the West. About one-quarter each were in the Southeast (24.3%) and Central United States (24.1%). Only 10.4% of charter school students attended schools located in the Northeast. More than half (51.4%) of charter school students attended schools located in central cities in 2003. (See Table 7.1.)

Charter schools tend to be smaller than regular public schools. According to *State of the Charter Movement 2005*, in 2004 median enrollment at charter schools was 250 students. According to the National Center for Education Statistics, in 2003 more than a quarter (28.5%) of students in charter schools attended schools with enrollment of one to 299 students, about one-fifth attended schools with

TABLE 7.1

Students attending public charter schools, by selected school characteristics, 2003

[Percentage distribution]

School characteristic	All public schools		All public charter schools						
			Entity granting school charter				Origin	
	Conventional	Charter	School district	State board of education	Post-secondary institution	State-chartering agency	Newly created school	Pre-existing school
Students served								
All	—	94.8	97.2	87.7	98.4	100.0	95.7	92.9
At-risk	—	4.2[a]	2.8[a]	9.8[a]	*	*	4.0[a]	4.8[a]
Gifted/talented	—	0.9	*	2.5	1.6	*	*	2.3
Enrollment								
1–299	10.9	28.5	31.5[a]	19.7[a]	17.0[a]	78.3	31.5	20.7
300–499	32.0	20.5	12.8[a]	18.9[a]	48.1	21.7	24.5	9.9[a]
500–699	30.1	35.2	36.1[a]	39.2[a]	34.8	*	33.4[a]	40.0
700 or more	27.0	15.9	19.6[a]	22.2[a]	*	*	10.6[a]	29.5
Location								
Central city	28.8	51.4	42.3	67.2	52.4	57.2[a]	53.9	45.7
Urban fringe/large town	41.0	37.4	47.7	21.2[a]	36.4	18.6[a]	35.5	41.9
Rural/small town	30.1	11.2	10.0[a]	11.7[a]	11.2[a]	24.2[a]	10.7[a]	12.4[a]
Region								
Northeast	20.4	10.4	3.4[a]	30.9	0.0	*	14.6	0.8
Southeast	23.7	24.3	36.3	23.7[a]	0.0	*	20.4[a]	33.2[a]
Central	22.2	24.1	9.8	13.7[a]	100.0	*	27.8	15.4[a]
West	33.7	41.2	50.5	31.8	0.0	100.0	37.2	50.6

— Not available.
*Rounds to zero.
[a]Interpret data with caution (estimates are unstable).
Note: Detail may not sum to totals because of rounding.

SOURCE: John Wirt, Susan Choy, Patrick Rooney, William Hussar, Stephen Provasnik, and Gillian Hampden-Thompson, "Table 28–2. Percentage Distribution of Students Attending Public Charter Schools by Type of School, Entity Granting School Charter, Origin of School, and Selected School Characteristics: 2003," in *The Condition of Education, 2005*, NCES 2005-094, U.S. Department of Education, National Center for Education Statistics, Washington, DC, June 2005, http://nces.ed.gov/programs/coe/2005/section4/table.asp?tableID=288 (accessed July 26, 2005)

enrollment of 300 to 499 students, more than one-third (35.2%) attended schools that enrolled 500 to 699 students, and 15.9% of students attended charter schools with 700 or more students. (See Table 7.1.)

The National Center for Education Statistics conducted a pilot study of students in grade four at a sample of charter schools. The study found that in 2003, 48% of fourth-grade charter students were male, and 52% were female. For students in grade four in other public schools, the proportions were 51% and 49%, respectively. Nearly a third (31%) of the charter students were African-American, 45% were white, and 20% were Hispanic. In 2003 more than two-fifths (42%) of charter school students were eligible for a free or reduced-price lunch. (See Figure 7.1.)

Charter schools that target special populations such as at-risk students are increasingly popular. These schools may focus on nontraditional teaching and learning experiences, such as combining academics with work experience or changing the class structure. Some states require a specific number of charter schools to serve this special population.

According to *A Decade of Charter Schools: From Theory to Practice* (Katrina Bulkley and Jennifer Fisler,

CPRE Policy Briefs, University of Pennsylvania, April 2002), about half of charter schools have grade configurations that differ from traditional elementary, middle, and secondary grade organizations. According to Gregg Vanourek in *State of the Charter Movement 2005*, charter school teachers are less likely to be certified than teachers in other public schools, and are more likely to hold master's degrees in such fields as business, arts, and science, as opposed to education. The impact of charter schools on student achievement is uncertain; charter schools as a whole are too new to have established track records. However, parents of students in charter schools, the teachers that work in them, and students who attend them generally are satisfied.

Funding for charter schools varies widely, ranging from direct state funding to funding through the local school district. Since 1994, the U.S. Department of Education has provided grants to support states' charter school efforts, starting with $6 million in fiscal year 1995. In fiscal year 1998 the federal budget appropriated $80 million for charter schools. According to the U.S. Department of Education, in 2005 funding for charter schools and choice options was $504 million.

FIGURE 7.1

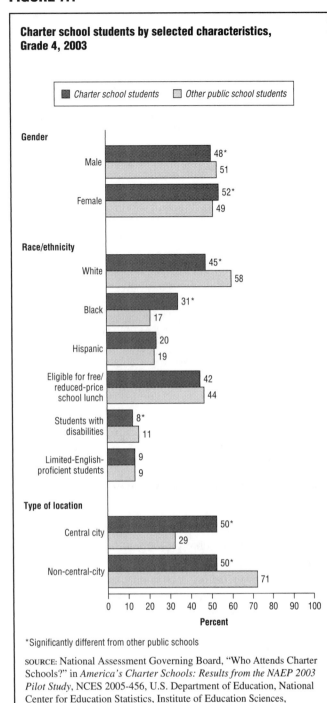

Charter school students by selected characteristics, Grade 4, 2003

■ Charter school students ☐ Other public school students

*Significantly different from other public schools

SOURCE: National Assessment Governing Board, "Who Attends Charter Schools?" in *America's Charter Schools: Results from the NAEP 2003 Pilot Study*, NCES 2005-456, U.S. Department of Education, National Center for Education Statistics, Institute of Education Sciences, Washington, DC, December 2004, http://nces.ed.gov/nationsreportcard/pdf/studies/2005456.pdf (accessed July 26, 2005)

Challenge and Opportunity: The Impact of Charter Schools on School Districts (John Ericson et al., U.S. Department of Education, Washington, DC, June 2001) presented the results of a study of 274 charter schools in Arizona, California, Colorado, Massachusetts, and Michigan. Almost half (47%) of district leaders reported that charter schools had no impact on the district budget; 45% said charter schools had a negative impact. A positive

impact was perceived by 8%, because although enrollment revenues were lost, costs to the district were also less.

FOR-PROFIT SCHOOLS

In some cases school boards and state education offices have turned to "privatizing" their schools, contracting with private corporations to administer one or more local schools. In 2001 the state of Pennsylvania passed a school reform plan to take control of Philadelphia's public schools, privatize the district's leadership positions, and place school operations in the hands of church, business, and other community groups.

Contracts for privatizing services are usually awarded based on bids submitted by the education companies. In general, teachers' unions oppose privatizing schools. The National Education Association (NEA) stated in its 2000–01 resolutions that it opposed education for profit, because there is an inherent conflict between serving the needs of children in an educational setting and serving the needs of stockholders.

According to *State of the Charter Movement 2005*, nearly 90% of charter schools are independently run, rather than managed by educational management companies (EMOs), but the proportion varies by state. In Michigan about 69% of charter schools are operated by a nonprofit or for-profit EMO. In 1998 fifteen states contracted with EMOs, and by 2003 the number had increased to twenty-nine.

The Edison Project

Private, for-profit companies run an estimated 10% of all charter schools. By 2004–05 the Edison Project, the largest private manager of public schools in the country, operated 157 schools in forty-three cities in twenty states, with an enrollment of about 250,000 students. Its program is based on extensive use of high technology, a longer school day and year, and a full-day kindergarten that has an academic program.

Are For-Profit Schools Improving Student Performance?

In the *Seventh Annual Report on School Performance 2003–04* (Edison Schools, New York), the Edison Project stated that Edison schools increased the percentage of student achieving standards by 7.4 percentage points on average from 2002–03 to 2003–04, and that this increase was 1.6 percentage points higher than performance gains in comparable non-Edison schools.

According to the Edison report, the company's schools were closing the achievement gap that exists between African-American and white students; for the ninth consecutive year, parents were very satisfied; and 85% of teachers rated their level of career satisfaction as an A or B, with A being the most popular grade.

In the 1998 AFT *Report on Student Achievement in the Edison Schools* (Washington, DC), researchers studied Edison schools in 1997–98. The AFT reported that the Edison schools used a widely admired reading program for elementary students; that they tended to have motivated parents involved in the schools; and that they attracted donations from outside organizations in addition to public funding. However, the report also noted that class size and teacher turnover rates tend to be high and that years of teaching experience tend to be low. In addition, the report noted that Edison does not measure or report performance in the same way that regular public schools do, but instead presents only the most favorable comparisons and test score gains.

In *A Guide to Recent Studies of School Effectiveness by the Edison Project and the American Federation of Teachers* (Harvard University, Cambridge, MA, May 1998), Paul E. Peterson conducted a review of Edison's 1997 *Annual Report* as well as the AFT report. Peterson stated that the evidence, although not definitive, supported Edison's claims that it was providing more effective schools than were available otherwise to students in Edison's communities.

In another study, Gary Miron and Brooks Applegate compared students at ten Edison Schools with a group of similar students at other schools in *An Evaluation of Student Achievement at Edison Schools Opened in 1995 and 1996* (Western Michigan University, Kalamazoo, MI, December 2000). They concluded that the trends in achievement scores were mixed. The majority of Edison students were achieving at levels no different from students in the group attending conventional public schools.

In 2000 the RAND corporation began an evaluation of Edison Schools, analyzing student achievement and Edison's academic program in a sample of Edison schools. Published in 2005, the report *Inspiration, Perspiration, and Time: Operations and Achievement in Edison Schools* offered statistical analysis of school performance as well as recommendations for Edison managers and for those considering contracting with the firm to educate children within their community. According to the RAND researchers, student achievement gains at Edison Schools matched or exceeded similar improvements in student performance in comparable public schools. The report noted that achievement showed slight declines during the time the Edison methods were being implemented, either as a new school was being started or as a previous school was being converted from conventional management to Edison control. However, by about the fourth or fifth year of operation, Edison students demonstrated higher achievement, particularly in mathematics.

SCHOOL CHOICE AND VOUCHERS

"School choice" allows students to attend schools other than their designated neighborhood school. Families who can afford to move to an area with high-performing schools or send their children to private schools already have school choice; less wealthy families generally do not. The major debate over school choice is whether or not parents should receive some kind of financial assistance from the state or local government to pay school fees if they elect to send their children to private schools.

Parents generally influence which schools their children attend, often locating in an area known for excellent schools. The U.S. Supreme Court, in *Pierce v. Society of Sisters* (286 U.S. 510, 1925), upheld parents' constitutional right to select a church-affiliated or private school. Because "the child is not the mere creature of the state," parents cannot be forced to send their children to public schools. A family is free to choose private education or to leave one school district for another in which it believes the public schools are better. In reality, many people are limited by financial and social restrictions, and moving to another district or enrolling their children in private school may not be possible without financial help.

According to the National Center for Education Statistics, in 1993 about 80% of students attended a public school that was assigned to them based on where they lived. Between 9% and 19% of students attended a public school they had chosen, and between 4% and 10% of students attended a private school. By 1999, 78% or less of students attended a public school that was assigned to them based on where they lived, between 11% and 23% attended a public school they had chosen, and between 5% and 11% attended a private school. Minnesota introduced the first school-choice program in 1987. According to the Alliance for School Choice, in 2005 more than 500,000 children in twelve states were participating in some form of educational choice.

School-choice plans usually follow one of three models:

- The "district-wide" model allows parents to select a public school within their district. Often the district establishes specialty or "magnet" schools (those offering an emphasis on a particular subject area, such as business, science, or the arts) to attract students to different schools.

- The "statewide" model permits students to attend public schools outside their home districts, depending on available space, desegregation requirements, and the students' ability to travel. Typically, when a school district loses students, it also loses state funding, so this plan may not appeal to many school districts.

• The "private school" model, known as the voucher or scholarship plan, is the most controversial. This model allows parents to use public funds to send their children to private schools. As of 2005 only a few school districts offered a voucher plan.

According to the Alliance for School Choice, in Ohio, Wisconsin, and Colorado, voucher programs are means-tested. Poor families who meet specific income criteria can use funds set aside for education by the government to pay for all or part of the tuition at any public, private, or religious school of their choice. In Florida and Colorado parents whose children are doing poorly in school or who attend schools that have been designated as failing can use public funds to send their child to a better performing public, private, or religious school. In Florida parents of children with special educational needs can use public funds to send their children to another public, private, or religious school. In Maine and Vermont parents who live in areas that do not have elementary or secondary schools can send their children to public or non-religious private schools in other areas, using funds provided by the child's home school district.

In Minnesota, Iowa, and Illinois parents can claim a tax credit or tax deduction for educational expenses, including supplies, tutors, and in some cases tuition. Most programs have income caps, which vary from state to state, and limits on the amount a parent can claim. In Florida, Pennsylvania, and Arizona tax-deductible contributions are collected from individuals and corporations that fund scholarship-granting programs. Scholarships are given to children to cover the cost of tutoring and private school tuition. Some programs require that eligible families meet specific income criteria.

Vouchers—Pro and Con

Since about 1990 voucher plans have been a hotly debated political issue. Those favoring voucher programs consider them an equitable means of helping low-income families provide their children with better education. Voucher programs emphasize educational choices rather than requirements dictated by the government. In addition, many believe increased competition will cause public schools to improve or face closure.

Those opposing vouchers believe the plans would only help a few students, leaving most low-income students behind in schools with reduced community commitment. Critics maintain that vouchers weaken public schools by diverting resources from them. The debate becomes even more heated when voucher supporters advocate allowing students to attend religious schools with public voucher funds. A major dimension of that debate concerns whether the use of vouchers at religiously affiliated private schools would violate the First Amendment by directly supporting religious institutions, or whether vouchers avoid such violations by supporting only the children.

Vouchers and the Law

The Court of Appeals for the 6th Circuit in Ohio concluded in December 2000 that there was probable cause that the Cleveland voucher program, which gives low-income students scholarships to attend private secular or religious schools, violated the constitutional separation of church and state and would be found unconstitutional. The court rejected arguments that the Cleveland vouchers were a neutral form of aid to parents that only indirectly benefited religious schools. The ruling was appealed to the U.S. Supreme Court by the state of Ohio as well as by a group of voucher parents and by several religious schools participating in the program, which continued to operate pending the further appeals. The court accepted all three petitions for review but said it would treat them as one case. In late June 2002 the Supreme Court overruled the 6th Circuit and determined that the Cleveland voucher program was legal.

The Wisconsin Supreme Court, in *Jackson v. Benson* (218 Wis.2d 835, 578 N.W.2d 602), ruled that inclusion of religious schools in the Milwaukee Parental Choice Program does not violate U.S. federal or Wisconsin state constitutional prohibitions against government support of religion. The U.S. Supreme Court declined to review the case (119 S. Ct. 467, 1998).

In two related cases (*Bagley v. Raymond School Department* [1999 Me. 60] and *Strout v. Albanese* [No. 98–1986] 1999) brought by parents who wanted reimbursement for the cost of religious schools, the Supreme Judicial Court of Maine and the U.S. Court of Appeals for the 1st Circuit ruled that inclusion of religious schools in the tuition program would be unconstitutional. Maine's "tuitioning" law allows reimbursements to families that send their children from districts lacking public schools to secular private schools. Appeals to the U.S. Supreme Court were filed in both cases. In October 1999 the Court declined without comment or a recorded vote to review either case.

The Arizona Supreme Court, in *Kotterman v. Killian* (972 P.2d 606), upheld the state program allowing a tax credit of up to $500 for individuals making charitable contributions to "school tuition organizations" that provide scholarships to private schools, including religious schools. In October 1999 the U.S. Supreme Court denied review (68 LW 3232).

Do Americans Support School Choice?

The 36th Annual Phi Delta Kappa/Gallup Poll (http://www.pdkintl.org/kappan/k0409pol.htm) asked if respondents favored or opposed allowing students and parents to choose a private school at public expense. The poll found

TABLE 7.2

Public opinion on allowing students to attend a private school at public expense, 2004

DO YOU FAVOR OR OPPOSE ALLOWING STUDENTS AND PARENTS TO CHOOSE A PRIVATE SCHOOL TO ATTEND AT PUBLIC EXPENSE?

	National totals							
	'04 %	'03 %	'02 %	'01 %	'00 %	'99 %	'98 %	'97 %
Favor	42	38	46	34	39	41	44	44
Oppose	54	60	52	62	56	55	50	52
Don't know	4	2	2	4	5	4	6	4

SOURCE: Lowell C. Rose and Alec M. Gallup, "Table 30. Do you favor or oppose allowing students and parents to choose a private school to attend at public expense?," in "The 36th Annual Phi Delta Kappa/Gallup Poll of the Public's Attitudes Toward the Public Schools," *Phi Delta Kappan*, September 2004. Reproduced with permission.

TABLE 7.4

Public opinion on choosing a public, private, or church-related school, if vouchers covered half the price of tuition, 2004

WHAT IF THE VOUCHER COVERED ONLY HALF OF THE TUITION, WHICH DO YOU THINK YOU WOULD CHOOSE?

	National totals		No children in school		Public school parents	
	'04 %	'03 %	'04 %	'03 %	'04 %	'03 %
A public school	46	47	46	45	50	55
A church-related private school	32	34	29	34	34	29
A non-church-related private school	16	17	18	19	11	15
Don't know	6	2	7	2	5	1

SOURCE: Lowell C. Rose and Alec M. Gallup, "Table 32. What if the voucher covered only half of the tuition, which do you think you would choose?," in "The 36th Annual Phi Delta Kappa/Gallup Poll of the Public's Attitudes Toward the Public Schools," *Phi Delta Kappan*, September 2004. Reproduced with permission.

that in 2004 more than half (54%) of Americans did not support allowing parents to choose private schools and receive financial assistance from public funds in order to do so. In contrast, 42% of the survey respondents favored publicly supported school choice. (See Table 7.2.)

The poll asked respondents whether they would choose a public, private, or church-related school if they had a school-age child and were given a voucher that covered the full costs of tuition. Thirty-seven percent said they would choose a public school. More than half (56%) said they would opt out of the public school system: 36% said they would select a church-related private school, and 20% responded that they would choose a non-church-related private school. (See Table 7.3.)

TABLE 7.3

Public opinion on choosing a public, private, or church-related school, if vouchers covered the full price of tuition, 2004

SUPPOSE YOU HAD A SCHOOL-AGE CHILD AND WERE GIVEN A VOUCHER COVERING FULL TUITION THAT WOULD PERMIT YOU TO SEND THAT CHILD TO ANY PUBLIC, PRIVATE, OR CHURCH-RELATED SCHOOL OF YOUR CHOICE. WHICH KIND OF SCHOOL DO YOU THINK YOU WOULD CHOOSE?

	National totals		No children in school		Public school parents	
	'04 %	'03 %	'04 %	'03 %	'04 %	'03 %
A public school	37	35	38	35	38	39
A church-related private school	36	38	33	37	40	38
A non-church-related private school	20	24	22	25	17	21
Don't know	7	3	7	3	5	2

SOURCE: Lowell C. Rose and Alec M. Gallup, "Table 31. Suppose you had a school-age child and were given a voucher covering full tuition that would permit you to send that child to any public, private, or church-related school of your choice. Which kind of school do you think you would choose?," in "The 36th Annual Phi Delta Kappa/Gallup Poll of the Public's Attitudes Toward the Public Schools," *Phi Delta Kappan*, September 2004. Reproduced with permission.

When asked which kind of school they would choose if the voucher covered half the tuition, 46% said they would choose a public school, 32% said they would select a church-related private school, and 16% responded that they would choose a non-church-related private school. (See Table 7.4.)

HOMESCHOOLING

In the 1970s a number of parents, unhappy with public schools, began teaching their children at home. In 1990 the Virginia-based Home School Legal Defense Association (HSLDA) estimated that about 474,000 school-aged children were being taught at home. (The HSLDA provides legal counsel for homeschooling families.) The HSLDA estimates that the rate of growth in homeschooling is 7% to 15% annually. According to the National Center for Education Statistics, there were 850,000 students who were at least partially homeschooled in 1999. By 2003 the number of students who were homeschooled at least part of the time in the United States was more than one million. (See Table 7.5.)

According to the National Center for Education Statistics, in 2003, 31.2% of the children who were homeschooled had parents who cited a concern about the environment of school as the most important reason for doing it; 29.8% had parents who believed religious or moral reasons were most important; and 16.5% had parents who were dissatisfied with academic instruction at conventional schools. (See Table 7.6.)

Based on research data from the late 1990s, the HSLDA reports on its Web site (http://www.hslda.org/) that on average homeschool parents had more education than other parents in the general population, with 88% of homeschooling parents having attended college. Almost

TABLE 7.5

Number and distribution of school-age children who were homeschooled, by amount of time spent in schools, 1999 and 2003

Characteristic	1999			2003		
	Number	Percentage distribution	Home-schooling rate[a]	Number	Percentage distribution	Home-schooling rate[a]
Total	**850,000**	**100.0**	**1.7**	**1,096,000**	**100.0**	**2.2**
Homeschooled entirely	697,000	82.0	100.0	898,000	82.0	100.0
Homeschooled and enrolled in school part time	153,000	18.0	100.0	198,000	18.0	100.0
Enrolled in school less than 9 hours per week	107,000	12.6	100.0	137,000	12.5	100.0
Enrolled in school 9–25 hours per week	46,000	5.4	100.0	61,000	5.6	100.0
Race/ethnicity[b]						
Black	84,000	9.9	1.0	103,000	9.4	1.3
White	640,000	75.3	2.0	843,000	77.0	2.7
Other	49,000	5.8	1.9	91,000	8.3	3.0
Hispanic	77,000	9.1	1.1	59,000	5.3	0.7
Sex						
Male	417,000	49.0	1.6	569,000	51.9	2.2
Female	434,000	51.0	1.8	527,000	48.1	2.1
Number of children in the household						
One child	120,000	14.1	1.5	110,000	10.1	1.4
Two children	207,000	24.4	1.0	306,000	28.0	1.5
Three or more children	523,000	61.6	2.4	679,000	62.0	3.1
Number of parents in the household						
Two parents	683,000	80.4	2.1	886,000	80.8	2.5
One parent	142,000	16.7	0.9	196,000	17.9	1.5
Nonparental guardians	25,000	2.9	1.4	14,000	1.3	0.9
Parents' participation in the labor force						
Two parents, one in labor force	444,000	52.2	4.6	594,000	54.2	5.6
Two parents, both in labor force	237,000	27.9	1.0	274,000	25.0	1.1
One parent in labor force	98,000	11.6	0.7	174,000	15.9	1.4
No parent in labor force	71,000	8.3	1.9	54,000	4.9	1.8
Household income						
$25,000 or less	262,000	30.9	1.6	283,000	25.8	2.3
$25,001–50,000	278,000	32.7	1.8	311,000	28.4	2.4
$50,001–75,000	162,000	19.1	1.9	264,000	24.1	2.4
$75,001 or more	148,000	17.4	1.5	238,000	21.7	1.7
Parents' education						
High school diploma or less	160,000	18.9	0.9	269,000	24.5	1.7
Some college or vocational/technical	287,000	33.7	1.9	338,000	30.8	2.1
Bachelor's degree	213,000	25.1	2.6	274,000	25.0	2.8
Graduate/professional degree	190,000	22.3	2.3	215,000	19.6	2.5

[a]The homeschooling rate is the percentage of the total subgroup that is homeschooled. For example, in 2003, 2.2 percent of all males were homeschooled.
[b]Black includes African American and Hispanic includes Latino. Race categories exclude Hispanic unless specified.
Note: Detail may not sum to totals because of rounding. Homeschooled children are those ages 5–17 educated by their parents full or part time who are in a grade equivalent to kindergarten through 12th grade. Excludes students who were enrolled in public or private school more than 25 hours per week and students who were homeschooled only because of temporary illness.

SOURCE: John Wirt, Susan Choy, Patrick Rooney, William Hussar, Stephen Provasnik, and Gillian Hampden-Thompson, "Homeschooled Students: Number and Distribution of School-Age Children Who Were Homeschooled, by Amount of Time Spent in Schools: 1999 and 2003," in *The Condition of Education, 2005*, NCES 2005-094, U.S. Department of Education, National Center for Education Statistics, Washington, DC, June 2005, http://nces.ed.gov/pubs2005/2005094.pdf (accessed July 26, 2005)

24% of homeschooled students had at least one parent who is a certified teacher. Families who homeschooled had higher median incomes than the median income of all families with children. Homeschool families also were larger than the national average, the majority have three or more children. Only about 6% of homeschooling families were minorities. On average, only 1.6% of homeschooled students in the fourth grade watched three or more hours of television per day.

State Requirements

Homeschooling is legal in all fifty states, but states vary widely in the way they govern homeschooling. Because all states' laws require school attendance, the states have jurisdiction over homeschools. Some states have set up elaborate requirements for homeschools, while others have taken a "hands-off" approach.

Three states—New York, Ohio, and Texas—illustrate the wide variance in homeschool requirements.

TABLE 7.6

Number and percentage of school-age children who were homeschooled, by parents' reasons given for homeschooling, 2003

Reason	Important		Most important	
	Number	Percent[a]	Number	Percentage distribution
A concern about environment of other schools[b]	935,000	85.4	341,000	31.2
A dissatisfaction with academic instruction at other schools	748,000	68.2	180,000	16.5
A desire to provide religious or moral instruction	793,000	72.3	327,000	29.8
Child has a physical or mental health problem	174,000	15.9	71,000	6.5
Child has other special needs	316,000	28.9	79,000	7.2
Other reasons[c]	221,000	20.1	97,000	8.8

[a]Percentages do not sum to 100 percent because respondents could choose more than one reason.
[b]Such as safety, drugs, or negative peer pressure.
[c]Parents homeschool their children for many reasons that are often unique to their family situation. "Other reasons" parents gave for homeschooling include the following: it was the child's choice, to allow parents more control over what child was learning, and to provide more flexibility.
Note: Homeschooled children are those ages 5–17 educated by their parents full or part time who are in a grade equivalent to kindergarten through 12th grade. Excludes students who were enrolled in public or private school more than 25 hours per week and students who were homeschooled only because of temporary illness. Detail may not sum to totals because of rounding.

SOURCE: John Wirt, Susan Choy, Patrick Rooney, William Hussar, Stephen Provasnik, and Gillian Hampden-Thompson, "Table 3–2. Number and Percentage of School-Age Children Who Were Homeschooled, by Parents' Reasons Given as Important and Most Important for Homeschooling: 2003," in *The Condition of Education, 2005*, NCES 2005-094, U.S. Department of Education, National Center for Education Statistics, Washington, DC, June 2005, http://nces.ed.gov/programs/coe/2005/section1/table.asp?tableID=228 (accessed July 26, 2005)

NEW YORK. New York has established extensive requirements for homeschools. Elementary-age students must spend 900 hours per year in class, and those in grades seven through twelve must be in class 990 hours per year. The teacher must be "competent" (no specific credentials required), and each year the superintendent of local schools must receive advance notice of the intent to homeschool. Records of attendance and assessment (including standardized tests) must be filed with the superintendent at specified times. Curriculum is specified by grade level and includes the basics, plus eight other subjects, such as American and New York history, music and art, health, and physical education. Students instructed at home are not awarded high school diplomas.

OHIO. Ohio requires students to spend 900 hours per year in class, and the homeschool teacher must have a high school diploma or equivalent. Each year, advance notice of intent to homeschool and assessment of student performance must be filed with the superintendent of schools. The assessment can be standardized test scores, a written description of progress, or another approved form of assessment. No attendance records are required. The state specifies which subjects must be taught, including the basics and other topics, such as first aid, fine arts, health, and government. Ohio does not award diplomas to students who are homeschooled.

TEXAS. Texas has very few requirements for homeschools, considering them private schools (which are not regulated by the state). The state requires no teacher certification, no advance notice, and no testing or attendance records. The only specified subjects are reading, spelling, grammar, mathematics, and good citizenship. Texas does not award diplomas to students who are homeschooled.

RELIGION IN PUBLIC SCHOOLS

The separation of church and state as outlined in the U.S. Constitution is one of the most widely debated constitutional issues. During the past two decades, controversy has swirled around school prayer, religious baccalaureate services, and other exercises of religious belief within public schools.

The church/state separation clause in the First Amendment was intended to prohibit the establishment of a state religion or the coercion of citizens to belong to a particular group, either religious or antireligious. Contrary to popular belief, the Supreme Court's interpretations of First Amendment rights do not prohibit the private expression of religion in the public school. They do not prevent students from praying at school or in the classroom so long as these activities do not disrupt the school's normal order or instruction. A student may pray either silently or quietly aloud whenever he or she is not actively participating in school activities, such as recitation in class. For example, students may not decide to pray aloud just as the teacher calls on them for an answer in class.

On the other hand, a student may not attempt to turn a class or meeting into a captive audience for a religious service. Public school officials may not legally require prayers during the school day, make them a part of graduation exercises, or organize religious baccalaureate services. Teachers and school administrators may not participate in, encourage, or insist upon student religious or antireligious activities while they are acting in their capacities as representatives of the state. Doing so could be interpreted as coercion or as the establishment of a particular group as a state-sanctioned religion, which violates the First Amendment. Teachers and other school personnel may exercise private religious activity within the boundaries of the First Amendment in faculty lounges or private offices.

Public schools may teach about religion, but they cannot give religious instruction. The study of the Bible and other religious scriptures is permissible as part of literature, history, and social studies classes so that students can understand the contribution of religious ideas and groups to the nation's culture. Students may express their personal religious beliefs in reports, homework, or artwork so long as these meet the goals of the assignments and are appropriate to the topics assigned.

The separation of church and state is very clear in some areas, but it can be ambiguous in others. For example, one of the biggest issues surrounding school vouchers is whether or not state funds, generated from taxes, can be used to pay tuition at parochial (religious) schools. In 1973 the U.S. Supreme Court ruled in *Committee for Public Education and Religious Liberty v. Nyquist* (413 U.S. 756) that doing so would be an unconstitutional mingling of church and state.

The Supreme Court, however, seems to have changed its stance on the necessity for a rigid barrier between public and parochial schools. Five justices criticized a 1985 finding in *Aguilar v. Felton* (473 U.S. 402), which ruled that sending public school teachers to parochial schools to conduct remedial classes was unconstitutional. In 1997 the Court reheard the case, a most unusual procedure. Divided five to four, the Supreme Court, in *Agostini v. Felton* (65 LW 4524, 1997), ruled that "*Aguilar* [is] no longer good law." In reversing *Aguilar* the court declared that

> a federally funded program providing supplemental, remedial instruction to disadvantaged children on a neutral basis is not invalid under the Establishment Clause when such instruction is given on the premises of sectarian schools by government employees pursuant to a program containing safeguards. This carefully constrained program also cannot reasonably be viewed as an endorsement of religion.... The mere circumstance that [an aid recipient] has chosen to use neutrally available state aid to help pay for [a] religious education [does not] confer any message of state endorsement of religion.

Specifically, the Court decided that Title I instructional services may be provided by public school teachers in private schools. Some observers believe the decision may help define future cases concerning state and religion, especially those involving vouchers that could be used to pay for tuition at religious-oriented schools.

The Controversy over the Pledge of Allegiance

In 2001 Michael A. Newdow, an atheist who objected to the Pledge of Allegiance being said in his daughter's school, filed a lawsuit arguing that requiring his daughter to recite the words "under God" in a public school was unconstitutional. In *Elk Grove Unified School District v. Michael A. Newdow* (2002) a panel of the Ninth Circuit court agreed, issuing a 2 to 1 decision that requiring schoolchildren to say the phrase "under God" violates the First Amendment's prohibition of government sponsorship of religion. However, in 2003 the full Ninth Circuit Court of Appeals issued a ninety-day stay, which allowed students in nine Western states to continue saying the Pledge of Allegiance without the words removed, pending a decision by the Supreme Court on whether it would review the case.

The Supreme Court did agree to hear the case, and in 2004 it overturned the Ninth Circuit's original decision, but without ruling on the constitutionality of the Pledge. The Court determined that because Newdow did not have legal custody over his daughter (the child's mother had sole custody), he did not have legal standing to sue the school district on her behalf. This decision effectively kept the phrase "one nation, under God," in the Pledge of Allegiance, but left the door open to future challenges on First Amendment grounds.

Teaching Evolution vs. Teaching Creationism in Schools

The theory of evolution, which argues that life has evolved from simple to complex forms over millions of years, has caused controversy since it was first put forward by Charles Darwin in the nineteenth century. Some people believe that evolution contradicts their religious beliefs that life was created by God, a view known as creationism, and have sought to ban the teaching of evolution and/or have creationism taught in public schools. In 1968 the Supreme Court ruled in *Epperson v. Arkansas* (393 U.S. 97) that bans on teaching evolution in schools violated the Establishment Clause of the U.S. Constitution because their primary purpose was religious. In 1987 the Court used the same reasoning in *Edwards v. Aguillard* (482 U.S. 578) to strike down a Louisiana law that required those who taught evolution to also discuss creation science. Despite these historic rulings, the controversy over teaching evolution and creationism in schools continues. In 1999 the Kansas Board of Education voted to remove the subject of evolution from state standardized tests, but the old science standards were restored in 2001 after the election of a new board. In 2002 the Ohio school board voted to change state science standards, mandating that biology teachers critically analyze evolutionary theory.

Late in 2004 the Dover, Pennsylvania, school board mandated the teaching of "intelligent design," a theory proposing that the universe is so complex that it must have been created by a higher power. In the 2005 case *Kitzmiller v. Dover Area School District*, a group of parents and the American Civil Liberties Union (ACLU) sued the school board for adopting the policy. The lawsuit claimed that the Dover policy violates the Establishment Clause of the First Amendment by promoting a religious doctrine. The school board members who put the intelligent design into the curriculum were voted out of office in November 2005. In December, Judge John Jones ruled that because intelligent design has no scientific basis, it clearly supports the creationist view and therefore violates the Constitution.

A Constitutional Amendment on School Prayer?

Many members of Congress have proposed legislation to amend the constitution specifically to allow prayer in public schools. To date, none of the proposals has passed, but some legislators continue trying. In June 1998 the U.S. House of Representatives voted for the first time since 1971 on a constitutional amendment to restore voluntary school prayer. The measure, the Religious Freedom Amendment, had a majority of voters but not the two-thirds needed to amend the Constitution.

Faith-Based Organizations Providing Services

As part of his education agenda, President George W. Bush proposed using tax dollars to support after-school academic programs provided by faith-based and religious organizations. Through Title I, Part A of the No Child Left Behind Act, faith-based organizations are eligible to apply for approval to provide supplemental educational services to low-income students attending chronically underachieving schools. Federal funds may not be used to support religious practices, such as religious instruction, worship, or prayer. Supported activities include extra help before school, after school, on weekends, or during the summer, in reading, language arts, and mathematics.

TECHNOLOGY IN AMERICAN SCHOOLS

Computer use has become common in American schools. According to the National Center for Education Statistics, 91% of students in nursery school through grade twelve used computers in 2003. Nearly all (97%) students in high school, 95% of students in middle school, 91% of students in elementary school, 80% of children in kindergarten, and 67% of children in nursery school used computers. Equal proportions (91% each) of males and females used computers. Computer use was higher among white students (93%) than African-American (86%) or Hispanic students (85%). More nondisabled (91%) than disabled students (82%) used computers. (See Table 7.7.)

According to the National Center for Education Statistics, 84% of poor children and 93% of those not in poverty used computers in 2003. More children whose parents held bachelor's degrees used computers than children whose parents dropped out of high school (92% versus 82%). The proportion of children in Spanish-only households who used computers was 80%, while 91% of children who lived in households that were not Spanish-only used computers. (See Table 7.7.)

Nearly three-fifths (59%) of students in nursery school through grade twelve used the Internet in 2003, according to the National Center for Education Statistics. More females (61%) than males (58%) used the Internet. Internet use was more common among high school students (80%) than students in middle school (70%), elementary school (50%), kindergarten (32%), or nursery school (23%). Internet use was higher among white students (67%) than

TABLE 7.7

Percentage of children enrolled in grade 12 or below who use computers and the Internet, by child and family/household characteristics, 2003

Characteristic	Number of students (in thousands)	Percent using computers	Percent using the Internet
Total	58,273	91	59
Child characteristics			
Enrollment level			
Nursery school[a]	4,928	67	23
Kindergarten	3,719	80	32
Grade 1–5	20,043	91	50
Grade 6–8	12,522	95	70
Grade 9–12	17,062	97	80
Sex			
Female	28,269	91	61
Male	30,005	91	58
Race/ethnicity[b]			
White, non-Hispanic	35,145	93	67
Hispanic	10,215	85	44
Black, non-Hispanic	8,875	86	47
Asian or Pacific Islander, non-Hispanic	2,116	91	58
American Indian, Aleut, or Eskimo, non-Hispanic	522	88	50
More than one race, non-Hispanic	1,400	92	65
Disability status			
Disabled	646	82	49
Not disabled	47,949	91	61
Family and household characteristics			
Parent educational attainment[c]			
Less than high school credential	5,691	82	37
High school credential	13,804	89	54
Some college	16,548	93	63
Bachelor's degree	8,590	92	67
Some graduate education	10,713	95	73
Household language			
Spanish-only	2,840	80	28
Not Spanish-only	55,434	91	61
Poverty status[d]			
In poverty	10,173	84	40
Not in poverty	39,016	93	66

TABLE 7.7

Percentage of children enrolled in grade 12 or below who use computers and the Internet, by child and family/household characteristics, 2003 [CONTINUED]

Characteristic	Number of students (in thousands)	Percent using computers	Percent using the Internet
Family income			
Under $20,000	8,815	85	41
$20,000–$34,999	9,273	87	50
$35,000–$49,999	7,499	93	62
$50,000–$74,999	9,834	93	66
$75,000 or more	13,769	95	74

ªData on "nursery school" enrollment may not reflect enrollment in all kinds of early childhood programs.
ᵇAmerican Indian includes Alaska Native, black includes African American, Asian or Pacific Islander includes Native Hawaiian, and Hispanic includes Latino.
ᶜParent educational attainment measures the highest level of education of either of the child's parents.
ᵈPoverty status is derived from household size and income. Households with incomes below the poverty threshold for their household size (as currently defined by the U.S. Census Bureau for 2003) were classified as poor. Some households reported incomes in a range that straddles the poverty threshold; these households were classified as poor. The 2003 poverty threshold for a four-person household was $18,810.
Note: Detail may not sum to totals because of rounding or missing data. Population estimates in this table apply to children age 3 and older who are enrolled in nursery school or in grades K–12.

SOURCE: Matthew DeBell, Chris Chapman, and Carol Rohr, "Table 1. Percentage of Children Enrolled in Grade 12 or Below Who Use Computers and the Internet, by Child and Family/Household Characteristics: 2003," in *Issue Brief: Rates of Computer and Internet Use by Children in Nursery School and Students in Kindergarten Through Twelfth Grade: 2003*, NCES 2005-1111, U.S. Department of Education, National Center for Education Statistics, Institute of Education Sciences, Washington, DC, June 2005

African-American (47%) or Hispanic students (44%). More nondisabled (61%) than disabled students (49%) used the Internet. (See Table 7.7.)

According to the National Center for Education Statistics, 40% of poor children and 66% of those not in poverty used the Internet in 2003. More children whose parents held bachelor's degrees used the Internet than children whose parents dropped out of high school (67% versus 37%). The proportion of children in Spanish-only households who used the Internet was 28%, while 61% of children who lived in households that were not Spanish-only used the Internet. (See Table 7.7.)

Distance Learning for Elementary and Secondary Students

According to the National Center for Education Statistics, 8,210 (9%) of the 89,310 schools in the nation had students enrolled in distance education courses. Most (6,250) of the schools were high schools, and most had total enrollments of less than 2,500 students. Schools that had students enrolled in distance learning courses were more common in rural areas than urban or suburban areas. Nearly 37% of the schools were in the Central United States. (See Table 7.8.)

BILINGUAL EDUCATION

According to the National Center for Education Statistics, from 1979 to 2003 the population of school-age children increased by 19%, but the number of children who spoke a language other than English at home or spoke English with difficulty increased by 161%. In 1979 only 9% of all five- to seventeen-year-olds spoke a language other than English at home, and 3% spoke a language other than English at home and spoke English with difficulty. By 2003 those numbers had jumped to 19% and 5%, respectively. (See Figure 7.2.)

According to the National Center for Educational Statistics, in California there were 1.5 million LEP (limited English proficient) students (one-fourth of all students) in 2001–02, while Texas reported more than half a million (one in seven students) receiving LEP services.

When first adopted, bilingual education was intended to offer better education to students (usually poor and recently immigrated to the United States) who did not speak English. The belief was that instructing these students in their native languages—and teaching them English at the same time—would help them overcome the language barriers to successful school achievement.

Some students do not participate in bilingual education, even when it is offered, and in many school districts there is a shortage of bilingual teachers. While it is difficult to measure the effectiveness of bilingual education, many observers believe that children in bilingual programs acquire English at least as well as, and usually better than, children in all-English programs. Others suggest that students in bilingual classes do not learn English more quickly and do not achieve better test scores.

The No Child Left Behind Act consolidated the U.S. Department of Education's bilingual and immigrant education programs. The new federal program focuses on helping LEP students learn English. States and school districts are held accountable for making annual increases in English proficiency from the previous year. States set performance objectives to ensure LEP children achieve English fluency after they have attended school in the United States for three consecutive years. States that do not meet their performance objectives for LEP students could lose up to 10% of the administrative portion of their funding for all ESEA state-administered formula grant programs.

SCHOOL SIZE

The American High School Today: A First Report to Interested Citizens (James Conant, New York: McGraw-Hill, 1959) recommended that in order to be cost effective and to offer a rich curriculum, a secondary school had to have at least 100 students in its graduating class. Conant asserted that the small high school was the most

TABLE 7.8

Number of schools in the nation, and number of schools with students enrolled in distance education courses, by instructional level and district characteristics, 2002–03

District characteristic	Number of schools					Number of schools with students enrolled in distance education courses				
	All instructional levels	Elementary schools	Middle or junior high schools	High schools	Combined or ungraded schools[a]	All instructional levels	Elementary schools	Middle or junior high schools	High schools	Combined or ungraded schools[a]
All public school districts	89,310	50,880	15,520	16,610	6,310	8,210	130	580	6,250	1,250
District enrollment size										
Less than 2,500	30,580	14,300	5,310	7,490	3,480	4,520	40*	190	3,300	990
2,500 to 9,999	26,310	16,130	4,620	4,350	1,200	1,670	20	160	1,360	130
10,000 or more	32,390	20,440	5,590	4,760	1,610	2,020	60	240	1,590	120
Metropolitan status										
Urban	20,400	12,700	3,240	3,090	1,380	960	50*	90	760	60
Suburban	40,430	23,870	7,480	7,010	2,060	2,980	30	280	2,400	270
Rural	28,480	14,310	4,790	6,510	2,870	4,260	40*	210	3,090	920
Region										
Northeast	16,460	10,230	2,750	2,620	860	820	30*	30`	670	100
Southeast	18,840	10,620	3,550	3,390	1,290	1,960	40*	220	1,520	170
Central	25,620	14,410	4,440	4,970	1,810	3,010	40*	150	2,320	510
West	28,390	15,620	4,790	5,630	2,360	2,410	20*	180	1,750	460
Poverty concentration										
Less than 10 percent	27,910	16,720	5,300	4,750	1,140	2,260	30*	200	1,700	330
10 to 19 percent	33,230	18,630	5,980	6,380	2,240	3,390	70*	240	2,560	520
20 percent or more	26,090	15,060	4,080	4,770	2,180	2,420	30	150	1,900	350

*Interpret data with caution. The coefficient of variation is greater than 50 percent.

[a]Combined or ungraded schools are those in which the grades offered in the school span both elementary and secondary grades or that are not divided into grade levels.

Note: Percentages are based on unrounded numbers. There were 3 cases for which district enrollment size was missing and 112 cases for which poverty concentration was missing. Detail may not sum to totals because of rounding or missing data.

SOURCE: J. Carl Setzer, Laurie Lewis, and Bernard Greene, "Table 2. Number of Schools in the Nation, and Number of Schools with Students Enrolled in Distance Education Courses, by Instructional Level and District Characteristics: 2002–03," in *Distance Education Courses for Public Elementary and Secondary School Students: 2002–03*, NCES 2005-010, U.S. Department of Education, National Center for Education Statistics, Institute of Education Sciences, Washington, DC, March 2005, http://nces.ed.gov/pubs2005/2005010.pdf (accessed July 26, 2005)

FIGURE 7.2

Percentage of 5- to 17-year-olds who spoke a language other than English at home and who spoke English with difficulty, various years, 1979–2003

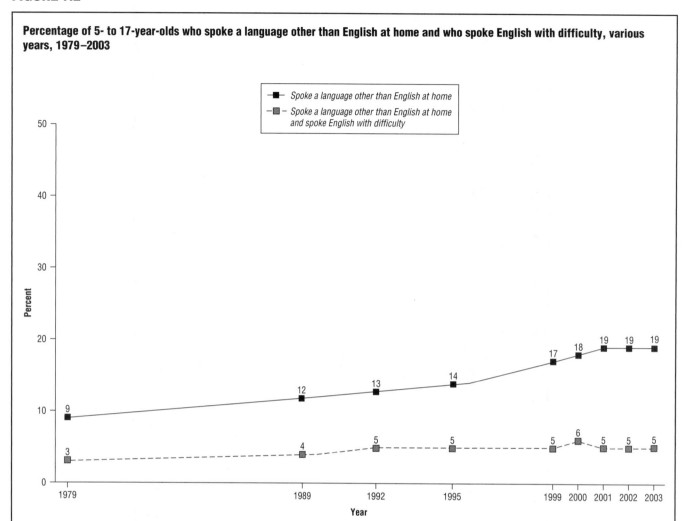

Note: Respondents were asked if each child in the household spoke a language other than English at home. If they answered "yes," they were asked how well each could speak English. Categories used for reporting were "very well," "well," "not well," and "not at all." All those who reported speaking English less than "very well" were considered to have difficulty speaking English. In 1994, the survey methodology for the Current Population Survey (CPS) was changed and weights were adjusted. Spanish-language versions of both the CPS and the American Community Survey (ACS) were available to respondents.

SOURCE: John Wirt, Susan Choy, Patrick Rooney, William Hussar, Stephen Provasnik, and Gillian Hampden-Thompson, "Language Minority: Percentage of 5- to 17-Year-Olds Who Spoke a Language Other Than English at Home and Who Spoke English with Difficulty: Various Years, 1979–2003," in *The Condition of Education, 2005*, NCES 2005-094, U.S. Department of Education, National Center for Education Statistics, Washington, DC, June 2005, http://nces.ed.gov/pubs2005/2005094.pdf (accessed July 26, 2005).

significant problem in education, and that eliminating it should be a top priority. He favored the establishment of larger, comprehensive high schools. This book was influential in reforming schools, and it helped to fuel the consolidation movement. However, the modern high school became considerably larger than Conant advocated; he encouraged creating schools with enrollments of 300 or 400, which would be small by current standards.

According to the National Center for Education Statistics, in 1937–38 there were 119,001 public school districts and 229,394 schools. By 2001–02 the number of districts and schools had decreased to 14,559 and 94,112, respectively. At the same time, enrollments in

schools grew. In 1939–40 public schools enrolled 25.4 million students, and in 2001–02 enrollment was 47.9 million. In 2001–02 the average enrollment at public schools was 520 students per school—477 in elementary schools and 718 in secondary schools. Most (70.4%) public school students attended schools with enrollments of 500 students or more.

The justification for large schools was that they could offer more resources and a better curriculum to students at less cost per student. However, proponents of smaller schools argue that large schools and high enrollment create rigid, impersonal environments that alienate students. They assert that large schools contribute to the high school dropout problem.

Some recent reform efforts have been directed at creating smaller school communities. Advocates of smaller schools suggest that teenagers thrive in more personal settings. Proponents believe that small schools offer individualized education, providing students with more attention and holding them to higher academic standards.

In "School Size, Achievement, and Achievement Gaps" (Bradley J. McMillen, *Education Policy Analysis Archives*, vol. 12, no. 58, October 22, 2004), the author examined the relationship between school size and student achievement. In a study of North Carolina public elementary, middle, and high school students, McMillen found that the achievement gaps existing between certain groups of students were greater in larger schools. In general this was more significant in mathematics than in reading, and it was more pronounced at the high school level.

In the 2002 report *Sizing Things Up*, the opinion research organization Public Agenda found that parents whose children attended small high schools were more likely to say that teachers helped struggling students and that students speak and write well. Parents whose children were in large schools were more likely to report that students were alienated, bullied, and likely to drop out. Teachers in large high schools were more likely to say their schools were overcrowded and more likely to respond that students can fall through the cracks. However, most teachers said that small class size was more important to student achievement than small school size. Both parents and teachers believed that large schools had a more diverse student body. Large numbers of students said there were problems with bullying, cheating, and substance abuse in their school, regardless of the size.

PARENTAL INVOLVEMENT

According to the National Education Association, when parents are involved in their child's education, the child does better in school, and the school the child attends is also improved. The NEA states that three kinds of parental involvement are associated with higher student achievement: organizing a child's time, helping with homework, and discussing what is happening at school. Positive outcomes of parental involvement include improved student achievement, reduced absenteeism, reduced behavior problems, and increased confidence among parents in their children's education.

According to *Parent and Family Involvement in Education 2002–03* (Nancy Vaden-Kiernan, John McManus, and Chris Chapman, U.S. Department of Education, National Center for Education Statistics, Institute of Education Statistics, NCES 2005–043, Washington, DC, May 2005), as students' ages increased, the amount of contact initiated by the school decreased. In 2002–03, 55% of parents of students in grades four and five reported that someone in the school sent a note or e-mail specifically about their child, while for parents of students in grades six through eight the proportion decreased to 49%, with 42% of parents of ninth and tenth graders reporting that the school sent notes or e-mails home.

In 2002–03, according to the National Center for Education Statistics, more parents of students who attended private religious (70%) or secular (63%) schools reporting having served as a volunteer or on a committee than did parents of public school children (38%). The proportion of parents who had attended a general school meeting was higher in households where parents had completed graduate school (93%) or college (93%) than for children whose parents had completed high school (84%) or less than high school (70%).

According to the National Center for Education Statistics, 95% of children in grades kindergarten through twelve had parents who reported they helped with homework in 2002–03, and 85% of children in K–12 had parents who reported that they checked to be sure homework was done. Overall, 90% of students had a place in their homes set aside for doing homework.

CHAPTER 8
TEACHERS

Teachers are the foundation of the education process. A well-designed, challenging curriculum, a first-class facility, and state-of-the-art equipment need motivated and well-trained teachers to complete the equation. Teachers are usually the first to come under fire when test scores and achievement do not meet expectations, and are among the last to be rewarded when things go well. Overall their salaries are considerably lower than those of similarly educated professionals.

A growing number of teachers face situations that would have been inconceivable a generation ago, ranging from lack of respect from students to outright physical attacks. Teachers in inner-city schools particularly bear the brunt of many "school" problems that are often a reflection of society's problems. Despite these challenges, however, the number of teachers is increasing, and a clear majority of teachers are pleased with what they do.

TRENDS IN TEACHER SUPPLY AND DEMAND

According to *Is There Really a Teacher Shortage?* (Richard M. Ingersoll, Center for the Study of Teaching and Policy, Seattle, WA, September 2003), in 2002 teachers made up about 4% of the civilian workforce in the United States. According to the National Center for Education Statistics, the number of classroom teachers in elementary and secondary schools has increased steadily, reaching 3.4 million in 2001, an increase of 36% from 1980. There were nearly three million teachers in public schools in 2001, and 390,000 private school teachers. By 2013 the National Center for Education Statistics projects the number of classroom teachers to increase to 3.6 million—3.2 million public and 411,000 private school teachers.

A Teacher Shortage?

Impacts on teacher supply and demand include: teacher retirement, the region of the country, student enrollment, class size, subject area shortages, turnover rates, the reserve pool of teachers who have already been trained, and school reform efforts. The American Federation of Teachers (AFT) reported in *Survey and Analysis of Teacher Salary Trends 2002* (F. Howard Nelson and Rachel Drown, Washington, DC, 2003) that in general fewer school districts were experiencing considerable shortages than in the past.

According to *Is There Really a Teacher Shortage?*, teacher turnover has been an important factor that impacts the perception of shortages. Between 40% and 50% of new teachers leave the field after five years. Turnover also varies based on the subject. Mathematics, science, and elementary special education teachers have higher rates of turnover than do English and social studies teachers. The type of school impacts turnover as well. Schools with high proportions of impoverished students have higher teacher turnover rates than do schools in wealthier districts. Urban schools have more teacher turnover than suburban or rural schools, and private schools experience more turnover than public schools.

One consequence of teacher shortages is the increased hiring of teachers who are not certified to teach the subject they are assigned. According to *Out-of-Field Teaching and the Limits of Teacher Policy* (Richard M. Ingersoll, Center for the Study of Teaching and Policy, Seattle, WA, September 2003), in 1999–2000 about 38% of seventh- to twelfth-grade mathematics teachers did not have a college major in mathematics, mathematics education, or a related discipline. About one-third of all secondary school English teachers did not have a major or minor in English or a related subject, and more than one-quarter of science teachers did not have a major or minor in one of the sciences or science education.

Most public elementary and secondary teachers (94%) have state-approved teaching certificates. High-poverty schools have fewer certified teachers (90%) than low-poverty schools (96%). Schools with higher levels of minority enrollment have fewer certified teachers (89%)

than schools with low-minority enrollment (96%), and urban schools have fewer certified teachers (92%) than suburban (96%) or rural (95%) schools. Schools that are poor and urban with high minority enrollment have fewer certified teachers (85%) than those that are suburban, serve white students, and are not poor (96%).

According to *Out-of-Field Teaching and the Limits of Teacher Policy*, small schools have more out-of-field teaching than larger schools, and there are more grade seven and eight teachers who are assigned to teach out of field than teachers in grades nine through twelve.

Reasons for Teacher Turnover

Teachers who move to other schools do not represent a loss to the profession, but they are a loss to the schools from which they move. Their departures often require that a replacement be found to fulfill set staffing levels. Overall, Ingersoll found that teachers leave for a variety of reasons, including personal issues (such as caring for family members), school staffing actions (layoffs, school closings, and reorganization), dissatisfaction with teaching, job change (to nonteaching jobs in education or to jobs outside the field of education), and retirement.

Personal reasons, such as departures for family moves, pregnancy and child rearing, or health problems, accounted for 36% of migration (that is, "movers" leaving a teaching job at one school for another) and 44% of attrition ("leavers" giving up the teaching profession entirely).

Pupil-Teacher Ratio

Educators prefer a low ratio of students per teacher, which allows teachers to spend more time with each pupil. According to the National Center for Education Statistics, from 1980 to 2001 the pupil-teacher ratio in elementary and secondary schools declined from 18.6 to 15.8 students per teacher. For public schools, the ratios were 18.7 in 1980 and 15.9 in 2001; in private schools, the ratios were 17.7 and 15.2, respectively. Thus the overall supply of teachers relative to the number of students increased during that time period. This does not mean, however, that all schools were able to find as many well-qualified teachers as they needed.

In fall 2000 Maine, Vermont, and Virginia reported the lowest average pupil-teacher ratio (12.5, 12.1, and 12.5, respectively), while Utah and California reported the highest (21.9 and 20.6, respectively). Some states have laws limiting class sizes, especially in elementary schools. Several other states are involved in developing or are considering similar laws.

CAREER OUTLOOK FOR TEACHERS

According to the Bureau of Labor Statistics (BLS) in *Occupational Outlook 2004–05*, excellent job opportunities will be available over the next decade as many current elementary and secondary teachers reach retirement age. The BLS noted that secondary teachers will be particularly in demand, and opportunities at all levels will be plentiful in states with fast-growing populations, including California, Texas, Georgia, Idaho, Hawaii, Alaska, and New Mexico. According to the BLS, many urban school districts offer good prospects for teachers because of the high turnover experienced in districts with high rates of poverty and overcrowded classrooms. However, rural areas, too, experience high turnover due to their remote locations and low salaries, and offer numerous opportunities for teaching professionals. Subject areas that are considered promising for new teachers include mathematics, chemistry, physics, bilingual education, and foreign languages. In most states, teachers are unionized and have relatively good job security through state tenure laws. Teachers who satisfactorily complete a probationary period are eligible for tenure, which protects them from being fired without a full investigation and due process procedures.

TEACHER EXPERIENCE

The National Center for Education Statistics' Schools and Staffing Survey (SASS) collected cycles of data starting in 1987–88, and then in 1990–91, 1993–94, and 1999–2000. In the 2003 *Condition of Education* (U.S Department of Education, National Center for Education Statistics, Washington, DC, June 2003), the 1999–2000 SASS data was used. During the 1999–2000 school year, 16% of public school teachers had three or fewer years of experience. Nearly one-quarter (23%) of teachers in private schools had three or fewer years of experience. At public schools with more than 75% minority enrollment, 21% of the teachers had three or fewer years of experience. At public schools with less than 10% minority enrollment, 14% of teachers had three or fewer years of experience. More than one-quarter (28%) of teachers had three or fewer years of experience at private schools with more than 75% minority enrollment. For private schools with less than 10% minority enrollment, 20% of teachers had three or fewer years of experience.

SALARIES

Since the mid-1980s there have been great fluctuations in teachers' salaries. As school enrollments fell in the late 1970s and early 1980s, average teachers' salaries (in constant 2002–03 dollars, adjusted for inflation) also declined. According to the National Center for Education Statistics, in 1980–81, teachers' salaries averaged $37,094. From 1982–83 to 1990–91, salaries rose steadily to $44,992, a 21% increase. From 1990–91 to 2002–03, salaries remained comparatively stable. In 2002–03 the average teacher salary was $45,822, a 48% increase over 1959–60 (in constant dollars). Elementary teachers earn slightly less than secondary teachers. (See Table 8.1.) Private schools tend to pay their teachers less than public schools.

TABLE 8.1

Estimated average annual salary of teachers in public elementary and secondary schools, 1959–60 to 2002–03

School year	Current dollars				Ratio of average teachers' salary to earnings per full-time employee	Constant 2002–03 dollars		
	All teachers	Elementary teachers	Secondary teachers	Earnings per full-time employee working for wages or salary*		All teachers	Elementary teachers	Secondary teachers
1	2	3	4	5	6	7	8	9
1959–60	$4,995	$4,815	$5,276	$4,632	1.08	$30,959	$29,844	$32,701
1961–62	5,515	5,340	5,775	4,928	1.12	33,415	32,354	34,990
1963–64	5,995	5,805	6,266	5,373	1.12	35,399	34,278	37,000
1965–66	6,485	6,279	6,761	5,838	1.11	37,013	35,838	38,589
1967–68	7,423	7,208	7,692	6,444	1.15	39,751	38,600	41,192
1969–70	8,626	8,412	8,891	7,334	1.18	41,587	40,555	42,864
1970–71	9,268	9,021	9,568	7,815	1.19	42,489	41,356	43,864
1971–72	9,705	9,424	10,031	8,334	1.16	42,951	41,708	44,394
1972–73	10,174	9,893	10,507	8,858	1.15	43,283	42,087	44,700
1973–74	10,770	10,507	11,077	9,647	1.12	42,067	41,040	43,267
1974–75	11,641	11,334	12,000	10,420	1.12	40,933	39,854	42,196
1975–76	12,600	12,280	12,937	11,218	1.12	41,377	40,326	42,483
1976–77	13,354	12,989	13,776	11,991	1.11	41,436	40,304	42,746
1977–78	14,198	13,845	14,602	12,823	1.11	41,283	40,257	42,458
1978–79	15,032	14,681	15,450	13,822	1.09	39,965	39,031	41,076
1979–80	15,970	15,569	16,459	15,086	1.06	37,463	36,523	38,611
1980–81	17,644	17,230	18,142	16,517	1.07	37,094	36,224	38,141
1981–82	19,274	18,853	19,805	17,863	1.08	37,299	36,484	38,326
1982–83	20,695	20,227	21,291	18,946	1.09	38,399	37,531	39,505
1983–84	21,935	21,487	22,554	19,874	1.10	39,248	38,446	40,355
1984–85	23,600	23,200	24,187	20,815	1.13	40,636	39,947	41,647
1985–86	25,199	24,718	25,846	21,727	1.16	42,173	41,368	43,256
1986–87	26,569	26,057	27,244	22,642	1.17	43,500	42,662	44,605
1987–88	28,034	27,519	28,798	23,698	1.18	44,073	43,263	45,274
1988–89	29,564	29,022	30,218	24,651	1.20	44,426	43,612	45,409
1989–90	31,367	30,832	32,049	25,643	1.22	44,989	44,221	45,967
1990–91	33,084	32,490	33,896	26,791	1.23	44,992	44,184	46,096
1991–92	34,063	33,479	34,827	27,990	1.22	44,885	44,115	45,892
1992–93	35,029	34,350	35,880	29,036	1.21	44,760	43,892	45,847
1993–94	35,737	35,233	36,566	29,778	1.20	44,511	43,884	45,544
1994–95	36,675	36,088	37,523	30,568	1.20	44,407	43,696	45,434
1995–96	37,642	37,138	38,397	31,518	1.19	44,370	43,776	45,260
1996–97	38,443	38,039	39,184	32,735	1.17	44,058	43,595	44,907
1997–98	39,351	39,008	39,945	34,269	1.15	44,308	43,922	44,977
1998–99	40,550	40,097	41,303	35,893	1.13	44,881	44,380	45,715
1999–2000	41,827	41,326	42,571	37,718	1.11	44,996	44,457	45,796
2000–01	43,400	42,937	44,028	39,272	1.11	45,141	44,660	45,794
2001–02	44,683	44,308	45,246	—	—	45,667	45,284	46,243
2002–03	45,822	45,658	46,119	—	—	45,822	45,658	46,119

— Not available.

*Calendar-year data from the U.S. Department of Commerce have been converted to a school-year basis by averaging the two appropriate calendar years in each case. Beginning in 1992–93, data are wage and salary accruals per full-time-equivalent employee.

Note: Constant 2002–03 dollars based on the Consumer Price Index, prepared by the Bureau of Labor Statistics, U.S. Department of Labor. Some data have been revised from previously published figures.

SOURCE: Thomas D. Snyder, Alexandra G. Tan, and Charlene M. Hoffman, "Table 77. Estimated Average Annual Salary of Teachers in Public Elementary and Secondary Schools: 1959–60 to 2002–03," in *Digest of Education Statistics, 2003*, NCES 2005-025, U.S. Department of Education, National Center for Education Statistics, Washington, DC, December 2004, http://nces.ed.gov/programs/digest/d03/tables/dt077.asp (accessed July 26, 2005)

According to the American Federation of Teachers, California had the highest average teachers' salary in 2002–03, at $55,693, followed by Michigan ($54,020), Connecticut ($53,962), New Jersey ($53,872) and the District of Columbia ($53,194). In 2002–03 South Dakota had the lowest average salary ($32,414), followed by Montana ($35,754), Mississippi ($35,135), North Dakota ($33,869) and Oklahoma ($33,277).

Alaska had the highest average beginning salary in 2002–03 ($37,401), followed by New Jersey ($35,673), the District of Columbia ($35,260), New York ($35,259),

and California ($34,805). Montana had the lowest average beginning salary ($23,052), followed by Maine ($24,631), South Dakota ($24,311), North Dakota ($23,591) and Arizona ($23,548).

Comparisons to Selected Other Professionals

According to the BLS in *National Compensation Survey: Occupational Wages in the United States, 2004* (http://www.bls.gov/ncs/ocs/sp/ncbl0727.pdf), the mean hourly earnings (half earned more and half earned less) of full-time elementary school teachers was $32.53, a penny more than full-time secondary teachers in the same survey. The mean number of hours worked per week by full-time elementary school teachers was 36.5 hours, compared with thirty-seven hours for full-time secondary teachers.

Teachers made less per hour than full-time lawyers ($48.63), financial managers ($37.24), and computer systems analysts ($35.17), but also worked fewer hours than people in those professions. The mean number of hours worked per week by full-time lawyers was 41.8; the number for financial managers was 40.5 and for computer systems analysts, 40.1, according to the *National Compensation Survey 2004*. However, teachers earned more per hour in 2004 and worked fewer hours per week than mechanical engineers ($31.68, 40.8 hours), chemists ($30.64, 39.9 hours), or psychologists ($29.00, 38.1 hours).

According to the BLS, the mean hourly earnings of full-time college and university teachers was significantly higher than for elementary and secondary teachers ($41.96) and the workweek longer (39.3 hours). In focused subject areas, college and university teachers were often higher paid than professionals working in those areas. For example, biological sciences teachers at the college level earned $41.76 per hour and worked 40.2 hours per week, while biological and life scientists had mean hourly earnings of $28.09 and worked 39.2 hours per week.

TEACHER AND PRINCIPAL TRAINING AND RECRUITING FUND

The No Child Left Behind Act (see Chapter 5) required states to put highly qualified teachers in every public school classroom by 2005–06. Existing grant programs were combined to create the new Teacher and Principal Training and Recruiting Fund (Title II). States and local districts are permitted to use these funds for staff development for their public school teachers, principals, and administrators. In addition to funding professional development, states and school districts are allowed to use their grants for reforming teacher certification or licensure requirements; alternative certification; tenure reform; merit-based teacher performance systems; bonus pay for teachers in high-need subject areas and in high-poverty schools and districts; and mentoring programs.

Highly qualified teachers must be certified, hold a bachelor's degree, and have passed a state licensing test. Requirements for middle and secondary school teachers are more rigorous for the specific subject matter taught, and experienced teachers are held to higher standards than new teachers.

PUBLIC OPINION ABOUT EXTRA PAY FOR TEACHERS AND ASSESSING THE PERFORMANCE OF TEACHERS

The 36th Annual Phi Delta Kappa/Gallup Poll (http://www.pdkintl.org/kappan/k0409pol.htm, 2004) asked if respondents favored awarding extra pay to public school

TABLE 8.2

Public opinion on awarding extra pay to public school teachers, 2004

I AM GOING TO MENTION SOME POSSIBLE REASONS FOR AWARDING EXTRA PAY TO A PUBLIC SCHOOL TEACHER. AS I READ EACH REASON, WOULD YOU TELL ME WHETHER YOU THINK IT SHOULD BE USED TO DETERMINE WHETHER OR NOT A TEACHER RECEIVES EXTRA PAY?

	Should be used %	Should not be used %	Don't know %
Having an advanced degree such as a master's or a Ph.D.	76	23	1
High evaluations of the teacher by his or her principal and other administrators	70	28	2
Length of his or her teaching experience	71	28	1
High evaluations by other teachers in the teacher's school district	65	33	2
High evaluations by his or her students	64	34	2
High opinions from the parents of his or her students	59	39	2

SOURCE: Lowell C. Rose and Alec M. Gallup, "Table 37. I am going to mention some possible reasons for awarding extra pay to public school teachers. As I read each reason, would you tell me whether you think it should be used to determine whether or not a teacher receives extra pay?," in "The 36th Annual Phi Delta Kappa/Gallup Poll of the Public's Attitudes Toward the Public Schools," *Phi Delta Kappan*, September 2004. Reproduced with permission.

teachers for various reasons. Slightly more than three-quarters (76%) of those surveyed believed that having an advanced degree should be used to determine whether a teacher receives extra pay. The length of teaching experience was favored by 71% of respondents, and nearly as many (70%) believed that high evaluations of the teacher by the school principal or other administrators should be a factor. Nearly two-thirds (65%) favored using high evaluations by other teachers in the school district as a reason to award extra pay, and 64% thought that high evaluations by students should count. Fifty-nine percent of respondents favored high opinions of parents as a reason to award extra pay. (See Table 8.2.)

When asked whether a teacher's ability should be judged on how well his or her students perform on standardized tests, nearly half (49%) responded that it should, and almost as many (47%) believed that it should not. (See Table 8.3.) Applying the same question to school principals in 2004, 47% thought that one measurement of a principal's quality should be based on how well the students in the school perform on standardized tests, and half (50%) responded that this should not be a factor in how the principal's quality is judged. (See Table 8.4.)

CRIMES AGAINST TEACHERS

As shown in Figure 8.1, the average annual rate of crime against teachers is the sum of teacher victimizations for the five years from 1998 to 2002, divided by the sum of the number of teachers during those five

TABLE 8.3

Public opinion on whether teachers' abilities should be measured by how their students perform on standardized tests, 2004

IN YOUR OPINION, SHOULD ONE OF THE MEASUREMENTS OF A TEACHER'S ABILITY BE BASED ON HOW WELL HIS OR HER STUDENTS PERFORM ON STANDARDIZED TESTS OR NOT?

	National totals %	No children in school %	Public school parents %
Yes, should	49	50	49
No, should not	47	45	49
Don't know	4	5	2

SOURCE: Lowell C. Rose and Alec M. Gallup, "Table 22. In your opinion, should one of the measurements of a teacher's ability be based on how well his or her students perform on standardized tests or not?," in "The 36th Annual Phi Delta Kappa/Gallup Poll of the Public's Attitudes Toward the Public Schools," *Phi Delta Kappan*, September 2004. Reproduced with permission.

TABLE 8.4

Public opinion on whether principals' quality should be measured on how students at their schools perform on standardized tests, 2004

HOW ABOUT SCHOOL PRINCIPALS? IN YOUR OPINION, SHOULD ONE OF THE MEASUREMENTS OF A PRINCIPAL'S QUALITY BE BASED ON HOW WELL THE STUDENTS IN HIS OR HER SCHOOL PERFORM ON STANDARDIZED TESTS OR NOT?

	National totals %	No children in school %	Public school parents %
Yes, should	47	47	48
No, should not	50	50	51
Don't know	3	3	1

SOURCE: Lowell C. Rose and Alec M. Gallup, "Table 23. How about school principals? In your opinion, should one of the measurements of a principal's quality be based on how well the students in his or her school perform on standardized tests or not?," in "The 36th Annual Phi Delta Kappa/Gallup Poll of the Public's Attitudes Toward the Public Schools," *Phi Delta Kappan*, September 2004. Reproduced with permission.

years, multiplied by 1,000. From 1998 to 2002, male teachers were more often the victims of violent crimes, with thirty-four violent crimes per 1,000 male teachers and fifteen violent crimes per 1,000 female teachers. Female teachers were more often the victims of theft, with thirty-four incidents of theft per 1,000 female teachers and twenty-three incidents of theft per 1,000 male teachers. Crimes were more common in middle/junior high schools and high schools than in elementary schools. The average annual crime rate was fifty-nine crimes per 1,000 teachers in middle/junior high school, seventy-one crimes per 1,000 teachers in high school, and thirty-eight crimes per 1,000 teachers in elementary school. More crimes occurred in urban schools (sixty-four crimes per 1,000 teachers) than in suburban schools (forty-two crimes per 1,000 teachers). The fewest crimes occurred in rural schools (thirty-four crimes per 1,000 teachers). (See Figure 8.1.)

FIGURE 8.1

Average annual rate of nonfatal crimes against teachers at school, by type of crime and selected teacher and school characteristics, 1998–2002

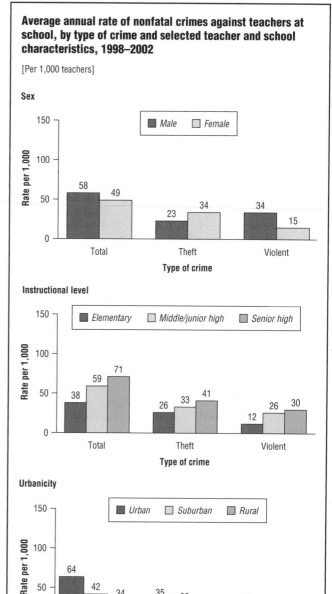

[Per 1,000 teachers]

Note: Violent crimes include rape, sexual assault, robbery, aggravated assault, and simple assault. Total crimes include violent crimes and theft. "At school" includes inside the school building, on school property, at the work site, or while working. For thefts, "while working" is not considered, since thefts of teachers' property kept at school can occur when teachers are not present. The data are aggregated from 1998–2002 due to the small number of teachers in each year's sample. Detail may not sum to totals because of rounding.

SOURCE: Jill F. DeVoe, Katharin Peter, Phillip Kaufman, Sally A. Ruddy, Amanda Miller, Margaret Noonan, Thomas D. Snyder, and Katrina Baum, "Figure 9.1. Average Annual Rate of Nonfatal Crimes Against Teachers at School Per 1,000 Teachers, by Type of Crime and Selected Teacher and School Characteristics: 1998–2002," in *Indicators of School Crime and Safety: 2004*, NCES 2005-02/NCJ 205290, U.S. Department of Education, National Center for Education Statistics and U.S. Department of Justice, Bureau of Justice Statistics, Washington, DC, November 2004, http://nces.ed.gov/pubs2005/2005002.pdf (accessed July 26, 2005)

CHAPTER 9
COLLEGES AND UNIVERSITIES

ENROLLMENT IN COLLEGE

The last half of the twentieth century saw a dramatic increase in the number of high school graduates going on to college. In 1960 only 45% of high school graduates enrolled in college; by 1999, 63% enrolled. Figure 9.1 shows the increase in enrollment at degree-granting colleges and universities by age from 1970 projected to 2013. The enrollment rates have fluctuated from year to year, but the trend has generally been upward and is expected to continue.

The National Center for Education Statistics (NCES) reports that in 2002 a high school diploma was the highest level of education obtained by nearly one-third (32.2%) of the population ages twenty-five and older; 17.8% had earned a bachelor's degree; 17.1% had completed some college; 15.9% were high school dropouts; 8.3% had an associate degree; 6.3% had a master's degree; 1.5% had a professional degree; and 1.2% had a doctoral degree. (See Figure 9.2.)

According to the NCES, in fall 2001 roughly 15.5 million students were enrolled in American colleges and universities, an increase of about 18.5% from the 13.1 million enrolled in 1988. In its middle set of projections, the NCES estimates that college enrollment will reach 18.2 million by 2013. (See Table 9.1.)

Between 1988 and 2001 full-time enrollment grew by 23% (from 7.4 million to 9.1 million) while part-time enrollment increased by 13% (from 5.6 million to 6.3 million). (See Table 9.1.) In 1970 about one-third (32%) of college students attended part-time. By 2001 more than two of every five students (41%) attended part-time. Increased female enrollment has also contributed to the growth in college enrollment. From 1988 to 2001 male enrollment increased by 13% (from six million to 6.8 million), but the number of females enrolled rose by 24% (from seven million to 8.7 million). (See Table 9.1.)

Tuition at most public degree-granting institutions is generally lower than tuition at private institutions. In 2001 far more students were enrolled in public institutions (11.9 million) than in private institutions (3.6 million). (See Table 9.1.)

Older Students

According to the National Center for Education Statistics, during the late 1980s enrollment of nontraditional students (those over thirty years of age) in degree-granting institutions increased faster than enrollment of students under age twenty-two; then between 1993 and 2003 enrollment of students under age twenty-two increased by 23%, while enrollment of people thirty and over increased by 2.5%. The NCES projects continued enrollment increases in degree-granting institutions at all age levels. Between 2002 and 2014, the NCES projects a 16% increase for students aged eighteen to twenty-four, while enrollment of students age thirty-five and older is expected to increase by about 5% (*Projections of Education Statistics to 2014*, National Center for Educational Statistics, http://nces.ed.gov/pubs2005/2005074.pdf).

Minority Enrollment

The enrollment of minority students (non-Hispanic African-Americans, Hispanics, Asians or Pacific Islanders, and Native Americans) in higher education has been rising steadily. Much of the increase can be traced to larger numbers of Hispanic and Asian or Pacific Islander students.

While white students still make up the large majority of college students, the trend is toward more racial and ethnic diversity on campuses. According to the National Center for Education Statistics, in 1976 white students made up 82.6% of higher education enrollment. In 2001 whites accounted for 67.6% of those attending college; African-Americans were 11.6%; Hispanics

FIGURE 9.1

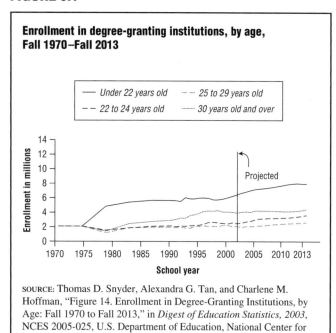

Enrollment in degree-granting institutions, by age, Fall 1970–Fall 2013

— Under 22 years old   ---- 25 to 29 years old
– – 22 to 24 years old   ······ 30 years old and over

Projected

School year

SOURCE: Thomas D. Snyder, Alexandra G. Tan, and Charlene M. Hoffman, "Figure 14. Enrollment in Degree-Granting Institutions, by Age: Fall 1970 to Fall 2013," in *Digest of Education Statistics, 2003*, NCES 2005-025, U.S. Department of Education, National Center for Education Statistics, Washington, DC, December 2004, http://nces.ed .gov/programs/digest/d03/figures/figure_14.asp?popup=1 (accessed July 26, 2005)

FIGURE 9.2

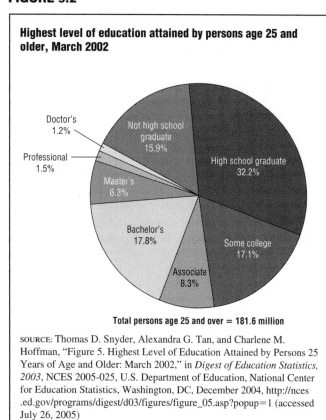

Highest level of education attained by persons age 25 and older, March 2002

Doctor's 1.2%
Professional 1.5%
Not high school graduate 15.9%
High school graduate 32.2%
Master's 6.3%
Bachelor's 17.8%
Some college 17.1%
Associate 8.3%

Total persons age 25 and over = 181.6 million

SOURCE: Thomas D. Snyder, Alexandra G. Tan, and Charlene M. Hoffman, "Figure 5. Highest Level of Education Attained by Persons 25 Years of Age and Older: March 2002," in *Digest of Education Statistics, 2003*, NCES 2005-025, U.S. Department of Education, National Center for Education Statistics, Washington, DC, December 2004, http://nces .ed.gov/programs/digest/d03/figures/figure_05.asp?popup=1 (accessed July 26, 2005)

19% and the number of African-American students by 79%. Other minority groups increased by even higher proportions: Native American enrollment more than doubled, while more than four times as many Hispanics and more than five times as many Asians/Pacific Islanders enrolled. Note that prior to 1995 data were collected for higher education institutions, and they were defined as agencies or associations that were recognized by the U.S. Department of Education. In 1996 the definition was changed slightly, to be four- and two-year degree-granting higher education institutions that participate in Title IV federal financial aid programs.

According to the NCES, in 2002 African-American students were more than twice as likely as Hispanic students to attend an institution where they made up at least 80% of the total enrollment. During fall 2002, 29% of students at degree-granting institutions were minorities. The proportion of minority enrollment was higher at two-year colleges (36%) than at doctoral institutions (24%). (See Figure 9.3.)

The NCES defines institutions as having low-minority enrollments if the proportion of minority students is 20% or less, and institutions as having high-minority enrollments if the proportion of minority students enrolled is 80% or more. In fall 2002 more minority students attended degree-granting institutions with low-minority enrollments than attended high-minority institutions (17% and 13%, respectively). Nearly one-third (31%) of minority students attended four-year degree-granting institutions with high-minority enrollments, while only 4% of minority students attended doctoral degree-granting institutions with high-minority enrollments. One-quarter attended doctoral institutions with low-minority enrollments. (See Figure 9.3.)

International Students

According to the Institute of International Education (IIE) in *Open Doors 2005* (http://opendoors.iienetwork.org/ ?p=69736), 565,039 international students were enrolled at institutions of higher learning in the United States during the 2004–05 school year. This represented a decline of about 1.3% from the previous year's total of 572,509. About 14% of international students were from India (80,466); 11% from China (62,523); 9% from Korea (53,358); 7% from Japan (42,215); and 5% of international students were from Canada (28,140). Another 4.6% were from Taiwan (25,914), and 2.3% were from Mexico (13,063).

Open Doors 2005 also reported that California hosted the largest number of international students (75,032) in 2004–05 and that the University of Southern California, with 6,846 foreign students, had the largest international student population of any college or university in the United States. Business (18% of students) and engineering

were 9.8%; Asians or Pacific Islanders were 6.4%; and Native Americans were 1%. (See Table 9.2.) Between 1976 and 2001 the number of white students grew by

TABLE 9.1

Total enrollment in degree-granting institutions, by sex, attendance status, and control of institution, with alternative projections, Fall 1988–Fall 2013

[In thousands]

Year	Total	Sex		Attendance status		Control	
		Men	Women	Full-time	Part-time	Public	Private
1988	13,055	6,002	7,053	7,437	5,618	10,161	2,894
1989	13,539	6,190	7,349	7,661	5,878	10,578	2,961
1990	13,819	6,284	7,535	7,821	5,998	10,845	2,974
1991	14,359	6,502	7,857	8,115	6,244	11,310	3,049
1992	14,486	6,524	7,963	8,161	6,325	11,385	3,102
1993	14,305	6,427	7,877	8,128	6,177	11,189	3,116
1994	14,279	6,372	7,907	8,138	6,141	11,134	3,145
1995	14,262	6,343	7,919	8,129	6,133	11,092	3,169
1996	14,368	6,353	8,015	8,303	6,065	11,121	3,247
1997	14,502	6,396	8,106	8,438	6,064	11,196	3,306
1998	14,507	6,369	8,138	8,563	5,944	11,138	3,369
1999	14,791	6,491	8,301	8,786	6,005	11,309	3,482
2000	15,312	6,722	8,591	9,010	6,303	11,753	3,560
Middle alternative projections							
2001	15,484	6,801	8,684	9,146	6,338	11,895	3,589
2002	16,102	7,008	9,095	9,590	6,512	12,354	3,749
2003	16,361	7,098	9,263	9,774	6,587	12,546	3,814
2004	16,468	7,144	9,324	9,860	6,608	12,627	3,841
2005	16,679	7,208	9,471	10,008	6,671	12,786	3,893
2006	16,887	7,281	9,606	10,160	6,727	12,942	3,945
2007	17,020	7,342	9,679	10,272	6,749	13,042	3,978
2008	17,168	7,413	9,755	10,400	6,767	13,153	4,015
2009	17,374	7,498	9,876	10,560	6,815	13,308	4,066
2010	17,541	7,561	9,980	10,681	6,860	13,431	4,110
2011	17,724	7,621	10,103	10,795	6,929	13,566	4,158
2012	17,927	7,679	10,248	10,909	7,018	13,716	4,211
2013	18,151	7,734	10,416	11,029	7,122	13,883	4,268
Low alternative projections							
2001	15,484	6,801	8,684	9,146	6,338	11,895	3,589
2002	16,047	6,993	9,054	9,553	6,494	12,435	3,611
2003	16,245	7,065	9,179	9,696	6,549	12,555	3,690
2004	16,330	7,105	9,225	9,764	6,566	12,594	3,737
2005	16,489	7,156	9,333	9,878	6,611	12,693	3,796
2006	16,630	7,210	9,420	9,985	6,645	12,784	3,846
2007	16,723	7,258	9,465	10,068	6,656	12,843	3,880
2008	16,830	7,317	9,513	10,168	6,662	12,915	3,915
2009	16,995	7,390	9,605	10,298	6,697	13,035	3,960
2010	17,140	7,445	9,694	10,404	6,736	13,137	4,002
2011	17,289	7,497	9,792	10,497	6,792	13,245	4,044
2012	17,463	7,550	9,913	10,592	6,870	13,371	4,091
2013	17,671	7,602	10,070	10,703	6,968	13,525	4,146
High alternative projections							
2001	15,484	6,801	8,684	9,146	6,338	11,895	3,589
2002	16,053	6,996	9,057	9,560	6,494	12,367	3,686
2003	16,355	7,094	9,260	9,771	6,584	12,573	3,782
2004	16,552	7,165	9,387	9,913	6,638	12,709	3,843
2005	16,825	7,250	9,575	10,106	6,720	12,907	3,918
2006	17,100	7,342	9,757	10,302	6,798	13,109	3,991
2007	17,317	7,426	9,891	10,469	6,848	13,269	4,048
2008	17,551	7,521	10,030	10,657	6,894	13,443	4,108
2009	17,837	7,627	10,210	10,870	6,967	13,657	4,180
2010	18,068	7,707	10,361	11,035	7,033	13,827	4,241
2011	18,301	7,781	10,520	11,184	7,118	13,999	4,302
2012	18,549	7,853	10,696	11,328	7,221	14,183	4,366
2013	18,809	7,917	10,892	11,471	7,338	14,376	4,433

Note: Detail may not sum to totals because of rounding. Some data have been revised from previously published figures. Data for 1999 were imputed using alternative procedures.

SOURCE: Debra E. Gerald and William J. Hussar, "Table 10. Total Enrollment in Degree-Granting Institutions, by Sex, Attendance Status, and Control of Institution, with Alternative Projections: Fall 1988 to Fall 2013," in *Projections of Education Statistics to 2013*, NCES 2004-013, U.S. Department of Education, National Center for Education Statistics, Washington, DC, October 2003, http://nces.ed.gov/programs/projections/tables/table_10.asp (accessed July 26, 2005)

TABLE 9.2

Total fall enrollment in degree-granting institutions, by demographic characteristics, selected years, 1976–2001

Level of study, sex, and race/ethnicity of student	Inst. of higher ed., in thousands[a] 1976	1980	1990	Degree-granting inst., in thousands[b] 1996	1998	1999	2000	2001	% dist. — Inst. of higher ed.[a] 1976	1980	1990	1996	% dist. — Degree-granting inst.[b] 1998	1999	2000	2001
	2	3	4	5	6	7	8	9	10	11	12	13	14	15	16	17
All students																
Total	10,985.6	12,086.8	13,818.6	14,367.5	14,507.0	14,791.2	15,312.3	15,928.0	100.0	100.0	100.0	100.0	100.0	100.0	100.0	100.0
White, non-Hispanic	9,076.1	9,833.0	10,722.5	10,263.9	10,178.8	10,282.1	10,462.1	10,774.5	82.6	81.4	77.6	71.4	70.2	69.5	68.3	67.6
Total minority	1,690.8	1,948.8	2,704.7	3,637.4	3,884.7	4,020.7	4,321.5	4,588.2	15.4	16.1	19.6	25.3	26.8	27.2	28.2	28.8
Black, non-Hispanic	1,033.0	1,106.8	1,247.0	1,505.6	1,582.9	1,643.2	1,730.3	1,850.4	9.4	9.0	9.0	10.5	10.9	11.1	11.3	11.6
Hispanic	383.8	471.7	782.4	1,166.1	1,257.1	1,319.1	1,461.8	1,560.6	3.5	3.9	5.7	8.1	8.7	8.9	9.5	9.8
Asian or Pacific Islander	197.9	286.4	572.4	828.2	900.5	913.0	978.2	1,019.0	1.8	2.4	4.1	5.8	6.2	6.2	6.4	6.4
American Indian/Alaska Native	76.1	83.9	102.8	137.6	144.2	145.5	151.2	158.2	0.7	0.7	0.7	1.0	1.0	1.0	1.0	1.0
Nonresident alien	218.7	305.0	391.5	466.3	443.5	488.5	528.7	565.3	2.0	2.5	2.8	3.2	3.1	3.3	3.5	3.5
Men	5,794.4	5,868.1	6,283.9	6,352.8	6,369.3	6,490.6	6,721.8	6,960.8	100.0	100.0	100.0	100.0	100.0	100.0	100.0	100.0
White, non-Hispanic	4,813.7	4,772.9	4,861.0	4,552.2	4,499.4	4,551.1	4,634.6	4,762.3	83.1	81.3	77.4	71.7	70.6	70.1	68.9	68.4
Total minority	826.6	884.4	1,176.6	1,533.4	1,615.2	1,663.6	1,789.8	1,881.1	14.3	15.1	18.7	24.1	25.4	25.6	26.6	27.0
Black, non-Hispanic	469.9	463.7	484.7	564.1	584.0	604.2	635.3	672.4	8.1	7.9	7.7	8.9	9.2	9.3	9.5	9.7
Hispanic	209.7	231.6	353.9	506.6	538.6	563.6	627.1	664.2	3.6	3.9	5.6	8.0	8.5	8.7	9.3	9.5
Asian or Pacific Islander	108.4	151.3	294.9	405.5	433.6	437.1	465.9	480.8	1.9	2.6	4.7	6.4	6.8	6.7	6.9	6.9
American Indian/Alaska Native	38.5	37.8	43.1	57.2	59.0	58.6	61.4	63.6	0.7	0.6	0.7	0.9	0.9	0.9	0.9	0.9
Nonresident alien	154.1	210.8	246.3	267.2	254.6	276.0	297.3	317.4	2.7	3.6	3.9	4.2	4.0	4.3	4.4	4.6
Women	5,191.2	6,218.7	7,534.7	8,014.7	8,137.7	8,300.6	8,590.5	8,967.2	100.0	100.0	100.0	100.0	100.0	100.0	100.0	100.0
White, non-Hispanic	4,262.4	5,060.1	5,861.5	5,711.7	5,679.4	5,731.0	5,827.5	6,012.2	82.1	81.4	77.8	71.3	69.8	69.0	67.8	67.0
Total minority	864.2	1,064.4	1,528.1	2,104.0	2,269.4	2,357.2	2,531.7	2,707.1	16.6	17.1	20.3	26.3	27.9	28.4	29.5	30.2
Black, non-Hispanic	563.1	643.0	762.3	941.4	999.0	1,038.9	1,095.0	1,178.0	10.8	10.3	10.1	11.7	12.3	12.5	12.7	13.1
Hispanic	174.1	240.1	428.5	659.5	718.5	755.5	834.7	896.4	3.4	3.9	5.7	8.2	8.8	9.1	9.7	10.0
Asian or Pacific Islander	89.4	135.2	277.5	422.6	466.9	475.8	512.3	538.3	1.7	2.2	3.7	5.3	5.7	5.7	6.0	6.0
American Indian/Alaska Native	37.6	46.1	59.7	80.4	85.1	86.8	89.7	94.5	0.7	0.7	0.8	1.0	1.0	1.0	1.0	1.1
Nonresident alien	64.6	94.2	145.2	199.0	188.9	212.4	231.4	247.8	1.2	1.5	1.9	2.5	2.3	2.6	2.7	2.8
Full-time	6,703.6	7,088.9	7,821.0	8,303.0	8,563.3	8,786.5	9,009.6	9,447.5	100.0	100.0	100.0	100.0	100.0	100.0	100.0	100.0
White, non-Hispanic	5,512.6	5,717.0	6,016.5	5,906.1	6,022.8	6,147.1	6,231.1	6,478.1	82.2	80.6	76.9	71.1	70.3	70.0	69.2	68.6
Total minority	1,030.9	1,137.5	1,514.9	2,046.8	2,193.6	2,263.6	2,368.5	2,530.7	15.4	16.0	19.4	24.7	25.6	25.8	26.3	26.8
Black, non-Hispanic	659.2	685.6	718.3	871.9	917.5	948.1	982.6	1,059.4	9.8	9.7	9.2	10.5	10.7	10.8	10.9	11.2
Hispanic	211.1	247.0	394.7	588.8	636.3	668.5	710.3	761.9	3.1	3.5	5.0	7.1	7.4	7.6	7.9	8.1
Asian or Pacific Islander	117.7	162.0	347.4	508.5	557.0	563.8	591.2	619.9	1.8	2.3	4.4	6.1	6.5	6.4	6.6	6.6
American Indian/Alaska Native	43.0	43.0	54.4	77.5	82.8	83.2	84.4	89.5	0.6	0.6	0.7	0.9	1.0	0.9	0.9	0.9
Nonresident alien	160.0	234.4	289.6	350.1	347.0	375.8	410.0	438.7	2.4	3.3	3.7	4.2	4.1	4.3	4.6	4.6
Part-time	4,282.1	4,997.9	5,997.7	6,064.6	5,943.6	6,004.7	6,302.7	6,480.5	100.0	100.0	100.0	100.0	100.0	100.0	100.0	100.0
White, non-Hispanic	3,563.5	4,116.0	4,706.0	4,357.8	4,156.0	4,135.0	4,231.0	4,296.4	83.2	82.4	78.5	71.9	69.9	68.9	67.1	66.3
Total minority	659.9	811.3	1,189.8	1,590.6	1,691.1	1,757.1	1,953.0	2,057.5	15.4	16.2	19.8	26.2	28.5	29.3	31.0	31.7
Black, non-Hispanic	373.8	421.2	528.7	633.6	665.4	695.1	747.7	791.1	8.7	8.4	8.8	10.4	11.2	11.6	11.9	12.2
Hispanic	172.7	224.8	387.7	577.3	620.8	650.6	751.5	798.7	4.0	4.5	6.5	9.5	10.4	10.8	11.9	12.3
Asian or Pacific Islander	80.2	124.4	225.1	319.6	343.5	349.1	387.1	399.2	1.9	2.5	3.8	5.3	5.8	5.8	6.1	6.2
American Indian/Alaska Native	33.1	40.9	48.4	60.0	61.3	62.3	66.8	68.6	0.8	0.8	0.8	1.0	1.0	1.0	1.1	1.1
Nonresident alien	58.7	70.6	101.8	116.2	96.5	112.7	118.7	126.5	1.4	1.4	1.7	1.9	1.6	1.9	1.9	2.0

TABLE 9.2

Total fall enrollment in degree-granting institutions, by demographic characteristics, selected years, 1976–2001 [CONTINUED]

Level of study, sex, and race/ethnicity of student	Institutions of higher education, in thousands[a]				Degree-granting institutions, in thousands[b]				Percentage distribution of students — Institutions of higher education[a]			Degree-granting institutions[b]				
	1976	1980	1990	1996	1998	1999	2000	2001	1976	1980	1990	1996	1998	1999	2000	2001
1	2	3	4	5	6	7	8	9	10	11	12	13	14	15	16	17
Undergraduate																
Total	**9,419.0**	**10,469.1**	**11,959.1**	**12,326.9**	**12,436.9**	**12,681.2**	**13,155.4**	**13,715.6**	**100.0**	**100.0**	**100.0**	**100.0**	**100.0**	**100.0**	**100.0**	**100.0**
White, non-Hispanic	7,740.5	8,480.7	9,272.6	8,769.5	8,703.6	8,805.7	8,983.5	9,278.7	82.2	81.0	77.5	71.1	70.0	69.4	68.3	67.7
Total minority	1,535.3	1,778.5	2,467.7	3,282.1	3,492.1	3,605.3	3,884.0	4,130.2	16.3	17.0	20.6	26.6	28.1	28.4	29.5	30.1
Black, non-Hispanic	943.4	1,018.8	1,147.2	1,358.6	1,421.7	1,471.9	1,548.9	1,657.1	10.0	9.7	9.6	11.0	11.4	11.6	11.8	12.1
Hispanic	352.9	433.1	724.6	1,079.4	1,159.8	1,214.0	1,351.0	1,444.4	3.7	4.1	6.1	8.8	9.3	9.6	10.3	10.5
Asian or Pacific Islander	169.3	248.7	500.5	717.6	778.3	786.0	845.5	883.9	1.8	2.4	4.2	5.8	6.3	6.2	6.4	6.4
American Indian/Alaska Native	69.7	77.9	95.5	126.5	132.2	133.4	138.5	144.8	0.7	0.7	0.8	1.0	1.1	1.1	1.1	1.1
Nonresident alien	143.2	209.9	218.7	275.3	241.3	270.3	288.0	306.7	1.5	2.0	1.8	2.2	1.9	2.1	2.2	2.2
Men	4,896.8	4,997.4	5,379.8	5,420.7	5,446.1	5,559.5	5,778.3	6,004.4	100.0	100.0	100.0	100.0	100.0	100.0	100.0	100.0
White, non-Hispanic	4,052.2	4,054.9	4,184.4	3,890.8	3,861.8	3,919.7	4,010.1	4,139.6	82.8	81.1	77.8	71.8	70.9	70.5	69.4	68.9
Total minority	748.2	802.7	1,069.3	1,384.1	1,455.5	1,498.0	1,618.0	1,705.9	15.3	16.1	19.9	25.5	26.7	26.9	28.0	28.4
Black, non-Hispanic	430.7	428.2	448.0	513.6	530.2	548.4	577.0	611.7	8.8	8.6	8.3	9.5	9.7	9.9	10.0	10.2
Hispanic	191.7	211.2	326.9	469.2	498.2	520.6	582.6	618.5	3.9	4.2	6.1	8.7	9.1	9.4	10.1	10.3
Asian or Pacific Islander	91.1	128.5	254.5	348.8	373.0	375.0	401.9	417.2	1.9	2.6	4.7	6.4	6.8	6.7	7.0	6.9
American Indian/Alaska Native	34.8	34.8	39.9	52.4	54.2	53.9	56.4	58.5	0.7	0.7	0.7	1.0	1.0	1.0	1.0	1.0
Nonresident alien	96.4	139.8	126.1	145.8	128.8	141.8	150.2	158.9	2.0	2.8	2.3	2.7	2.4	2.6	2.6	2.6
Women	4,522.1	5,471.7	6,579.3	6,906.3	6,990.8	7,121.6	7,377.1	7,711.2	100.0	100.0	100.0	100.0	100.0	100.0	100.0	100.0
White, non-Hispanic	3,688.3	4,425.8	5,088.2	4,878.7	4,841.8	4,886.0	4,973.3	5,139.0	81.6	80.9	77.3	70.6	69.3	68.6	67.4	66.6
Total minority	787.0	975.8	1,398.5	1,898.1	2,036.5	2,107.4	2,266.0	2,424.4	17.4	17.8	21.3	27.5	29.1	29.6	30.7	31.4
Black, non-Hispanic	512.7	590.6	699.2	845.0	891.5	923.5	971.9	1,045.4	11.3	10.8	10.6	12.2	12.8	13.0	13.2	13.6
Hispanic	161.2	221.8	397.6	610.1	661.6	693.4	768.4	825.9	3.6	4.1	6.0	8.8	9.5	9.7	10.4	10.7
Asian or Pacific Islander	78.2	120.2	246.0	368.8	405.3	411.0	443.6	466.7	1.7	2.2	3.7	5.3	5.8	5.8	6.0	6.1
American Indian/Alaska Native	34.9	43.1	55.5	74.1	78.1	79.5	82.1	86.3	0.8	0.8	0.8	1.1	1.1	1.1	1.0	1.1
Nonresident alien	46.8	70.1	92.6	129.5	112.5	128.4	137.8	147.8	1.0	1.3	1.4	1.9	1.6	1.8	1.9	1.9
Graduate																
Total	**1,322.5**	**1,340.9**	**1,586.2**	**1,742.3**	**1,767.6**	**1,806.8**	**1,850.3**	**1,903.7**	**100.0**	**100.0**	**100.0**	**100.0**	**100.0**	**100.0**	**100.0**	**100.0**
White, non-Hispanic	1,115.6	1,104.7	1,228.4	1,272.6	1,254.3	1,256.5	1,258.5	1,275.1	84.4	82.4	77.4	73.0	71.0	69.5	68.0	67.0
Total minority	134.5	144.0	190.5	286.3	318.5	339.8	359.4	378.5	10.2	10.7	12.0	16.4	18.0	18.8	19.4	19.9
Black, non-Hispanic	78.5	75.1	83.9	125.5	138.7	148.7	157.9	169.4	5.9	5.6	5.3	7.2	7.8	8.2	8.5	8.9
Hispanic	26.4	32.1	47.2	72.8	82.9	90.4	95.4	100.5	2.0	2.4	3.0	4.2	4.7	5.0	5.2	5.3
Asian or Pacific Islander	24.5	31.6	53.2	79.1	87.0	90.7	95.8	97.4	1.9	2.4	3.4	4.5	4.9	5.0	5.2	5.1
American Indian/Alaska Native	5.1	5.2	6.2	8.9	9.8	10.0	10.3	11.2	0.4	0.4	0.4	0.5	0.6	0.6	0.6	0.6
Nonresident alien	72.4	92.2	167.3	183.3	194.8	210.6	232.3	250.1	5.5	6.9	10.5	10.5	11.0	11.7	12.6	13.1
Men	707.9	672.2	737.4	759.4	754.3	766.1	779.6	795.7	100.0	100.0	100.0	100.0	100.0	100.0	100.0	100.0
White, non-Hispanic	589.1	538.5	538.8	529.0	510.4	507.4	502.6	503.4	83.2	80.1	73.1	69.7	67.7	66.2	64.5	63.3
Total minority	63.7	65.0	82.1	114.0	122.8	129.3	135.1	138.9	9.0	9.7	11.1	15.0	16.3	16.9	17.3	17.5
Black, non-Hispanic	32.0	28.2	29.3	41.2	44.2	46.7	48.9	51.5	4.5	4.2	4.0	5.4	5.9	6.1	6.3	6.5
Hispanic	14.6	15.7	20.6	29.6	32.6	35.2	36.5	37.8	2.1	2.3	2.8	3.9	4.3	4.6	4.7	4.7
Asian or Pacific Islander	14.4	18.6	29.7	39.7	42.3	43.7	45.8	45.6	2.0	2.8	4.0	5.2	5.6	5.7	5.9	5.7
American Indian/Alaska Native	2.7	2.5	2.6	3.6	3.7	3.7	3.8	4.1	0.4	0.3	0.4	0.5	0.5	0.5	0.5	0.5
Nonresident alien	55.1	68.7	116.4	116.4	121.1	129.4	142.0	153.4	7.8	10.2	15.8	15.3	16.1	16.9	18.2	19.3

TABLE 9.2

Total fall enrollment in degree-granting institutions, by demographic characteristics, selected years, 1976–2001 [CONTINUED]

Level of study, sex, and race/ethnicity of student	Institutions of higher education, in thousands[a]			Degree-granting institutions, in thousands[b]					Percentage distribution of students[a]							
									Institutions of higher education[a]			Degree-granting institutions[b]				
	1976	1980	1990	1996	1998	1999	2000	2001	1976	1980	1990	1996	1998	1999	2000	2001
1	2	3	4	5	6	7	8	9	10	11	12	13	14	15	16	17
Women	614.6	668.7	848.8	982.8	1,013.3	1,040.7	1,070.7	1,108.0	100.0	100.0	100.0	100.0	100.0	100.0	100.0	100.0
White, non-Hispanic	526.5	566.5	689.5	743.6	743.9	749.1	756.0	771.7	85.7	84.7	81.2	75.7	73.4	72.0	70.6	69.6
Total minority	70.8	79.0	108.3	172.3	195.6	210.5	224.4	239.6	11.5	11.8	12.8	17.5	19.3	20.2	21.0	21.6
Black, non-Hispanic	46.5	46.9	54.6	84.3	94.5	102.1	109.0	117.9	7.6	7.0	6.4	8.6	9.3	9.8	10.2	10.6
Hispanic	11.8	16.4	26.6	43.2	50.4	55.2	58.8	62.8	1.9	2.4	3.1	4.4	5.0	5.3	5.5	5.7
Asian or Pacific Islander	10.1	13.0	23.6	39.4	44.8	46.9	50.0	51.8	1.6	1.9	2.8	4.0	4.4	4.5	4.7	4.7
American Indian/ Alaska Native	2.4	2.7	3.6	5.3	6.0	6.3	6.5	7.1	0.4	0.4	0.4	0.5	0.6	0.6	0.6	0.6
Nonresident alien	17.3	23.5	50.9	66.9	73.7	81.1	90.3	96.7	2.8	3.5	6.0	6.8	7.3	7.8	8.4	8.7
First-professional																
Total	244.1	276.8	273.4	298.3	302.5	303.2	306.6	308.6	100.0	100.0	100.0	100.0	100.0	100.0	100.0	100.0
White, non-Hispanic	220.0	247.7	221.5	221.7	220.9	219.9	220.1	220.8	90.1	89.5	81.0	74.3	73.0	72.5	71.8	71.5
Total minority	21.1	26.3	46.5	69.0	74.1	75.6	78.1	79.5	8.6	9.5	17.0	23.1	24.5	24.9	25.5	25.7
Black, non-Hispanic	11.2	12.8	15.9	21.5	22.5	22.5	23.5	23.9	4.6	4.6	5.8	7.2	7.4	7.4	7.7	7.8
Hispanic	4.5	6.5	10.7	13.9	14.4	14.7	15.4	15.6	1.9	2.4	3.9	4.7	4.7	4.9	5.0	5.1
Asian or Pacific Islander	4.1	6.1	18.7	31.4	35.1	36.3	36.8	37.7	1.7	2.2	6.8	10.5	11.6	12.0	12.0	12.2
American Indian/ Alaska Native	1.3	0.8	1.1	2.2	2.2	2.1	2.3	2.1	0.5	0.3	0.4	0.7	0.7	0.7	0.8	0.7
Nonresident alien	3.1	2.9	5.4	7.6	7.4	7.6	8.4	8.4	1.3	1.0	2.0	2.6	2.4	2.5	2.7	2.7
Men	189.6	198.5	166.8	172.7	168.8	165.1	163.9	160.7	100.0	100.0	100.0	100.0	100.0	100.0	100.0	100.0
White, non-Hispanic	172.4	179.5	137.8	132.3	127.2	124.0	122.0	119.3	90.9	90.5	82.6	76.6	75.3	75.1	74.4	74.2
Total minority	14.7	16.7	25.3	35.4	36.9	36.4	36.8	36.3	7.7	8.4	15.1	20.5	21.8	22.0	22.4	22.6
Black, non-Hispanic	7.2	7.4	7.4	9.4	9.5	9.1	9.5	9.3	3.8	3.7	4.4	5.4	5.6	5.5	5.8	5.8
Hispanic	3.5	4.6	6.4	7.7	7.8	7.7	8.0	7.9	1.8	2.3	3.8	4.5	4.6	4.7	4.9	4.9
Asian or Pacific Islander	2.9	4.1	10.8	17.1	18.4	18.4	18.1	18.1	1.5	2.1	6.5	9.9	10.9	11.1	11.1	11.2
American Indian/ Alaska Native	1.0	0.5	0.6	1.2	1.1	1.1	1.2	1.1	0.5	0.3	0.4	0.7	0.7	0.7	0.7	0.7
Nonresident alien	2.5	2.3	3.8	5.1	4.8	4.7	5.1	5.1	1.3	1.1	2.3	2.9	2.8	2.9	3.1	3.2
Women	54.5	78.4	106.6	125.6	133.6	138.1	142.7	148.0	100.0	100.0	100.0	100.0	100.0	100.0	100.0	100.0
White, non-Hispanic	47.6	68.1	83.7	89.4	93.7	95.9	98.1	101.5	87.3	86.9	78.5	71.2	70.1	69.4	68.7	68.6
Total minority	6.4	9.6	21.3	33.6	37.3	39.3	41.3	43.1	11.7	12.3	20.0	26.8	27.9	28.5	28.9	29.1
Black, non-Hispanic	3.9	5.5	8.5	12.1	12.9	13.4	14.0	14.6	7.2	7.0	8.0	9.6	9.7	9.7	9.8	9.9
Hispanic	1.0	1.9	4.3	6.2	6.5	7.0	7.4	7.7	1.9	2.4	4.0	4.9	4.9	5.0	5.2	5.2
Asian or Pacific Islander	1.1	2.0	7.9	14.4	16.8	17.9	18.7	19.7	2.1	2.6	7.4	11.4	12.5	13.0	13.1	13.3
American Indian/ Alaska Native	0.2	0.3	0.5	1.0	1.0	1.0	1.1	1.1	0.4	0.3	0.5	0.8	0.8	0.7	0.8	0.7
Nonresident alien	0.5	0.6	1.6	2.6	2.6	2.9	3.3	3.4	1.0	0.8	1.5	2.0	2.0	2.1	2.3	2.3

[a]Institutions that were accredited by an agency or association that was recognized by the U.S. Department of Education, or recognized directly by the Secretary of Education.

[b]Data are for 4-year and 2-year degree-granting higher education institutions that participated in Title IV federal financial aid programs.

Note: Because of underreporting and nonreporting of racial/ethnic data, some figures are slightly lower than corresponding data in other tables. Data for 1999 were imputed using alternative procedures. Detail may not sum to totals due to rounding.

SOURCE: Thomas D. Snyder, Alexandra G. Tan, and Charlene M. Hoffman, "Table 209. Total Fall Enrollment in Degree-Granting Institutions, by Race/Ethnicity, Sex, Attendance Status, and Level of Study: Selected Years, 1976 to 2001," in *Digest of Education Statistics, 2003*, NCES 2005-025, U.S. Department of Education, National Center for Education Statistics, Washington, DC, December 2004, http://nces.ed.gov/programs/digest/d03/tables/dt209.asp (accessed July 26, 2005)

FIGURE 9.3

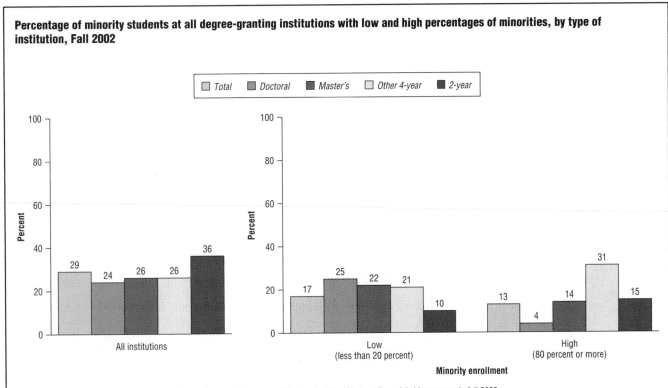

Percentage of minority students at all degree-granting institutions with low and high percentages of minorities, by type of institution, Fall 2002

Note: Data are for 4- and 2-year degree-granting institutions that were participating in Title IV federal financial aid programs in fall 2002.

SOURCE: John Wirt, Susan Choy, Patrick Rooney, William Hussar, Stephen Provasnik, and Gillian Hampden-Thompson, "Minority Enrollment: Percentage of Students Who Were Minorities at All Degree-Granting Institutions with Low and High Percentages of Minorities, by Type of Institution: Fall 2002," in *The Condition of Education, 2005*, NCES 2005-094, U.S. Department of Education, National Center for Education Statistics, Washington, DC, June 2005, http://nces.ed.gov/pubs2005/2005094.pdf (accessed July 26, 2005)

(16%) were the leading areas of study for international students.

Studying Abroad

Many college students from the United States also participate in study abroad programs. According to research published in 2005 by the Institute of International Education (http://opendoors.iienetwork.org/), the number of U.S. students studying abroad had doubled since the early 1990s. The IIE estimated that in 2003–04 there were 191,321 American students studying abroad, which represented a 9.6% increase over the previous year (174,629) and the highest number ever. The IIE, in *Open Doors 2005* (http://opendoors.iienetwork.org/?p=69702), further reported that the number of Americans studying abroad had surged 20% since 2000–01 and suggested that the increase might be due to a growing awareness among American students of the importance of gaining an international perspective. IIE president Allan E. Goodman noted, "Many U.S. campuses now include international education as part of their core educational mission, recognizing that increasing the global competence among the next generation is a national priority and an academic responsibility."

Countries with the largest numbers of Americans enrolled in institutions of higher learning during the 2003–04 school year included Britain (32,237), Italy (21,922), Spain (20,080), France (13,718), Australia (11,418), and Mexico (9,293). The largest number of American students abroad were studying the social sciences (43,258, or 22.6% of U.S. students abroad), followed by business (33,473, or 17.6%), and humanities (25,401, or 13.3%).

PERSISTENCE OF STUDENTS

According to the National Center for Education Statistics, more high school graduates are entering college, and more are eventually graduating. In 1972, 55% of high school graduates entered a postsecondary institution. By 1992 the number had jumped to 77%. Among the 1972 high school graduates who earned more than ten college credits (that is, they did not take one or two courses and drop out of college), 46% earned a bachelor's degree within 8.5 years of their high school graduation. For 1992 high school graduates, 67% had earned a bachelor's degree within 8.5 years of their high school graduation. (See Figure 9.4.) Another way to measure college success is to consider only students who earned at least some of the initial ten credits at a four-year institution, because

FIGURE 9.4

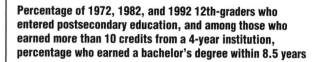

Percentage of 1972, 1982, and 1992 12th-graders who entered postsecondary education, and among those who earned more than 10 credits from a 4-year institution, percentage who earned a bachelor's degree within 8.5 years

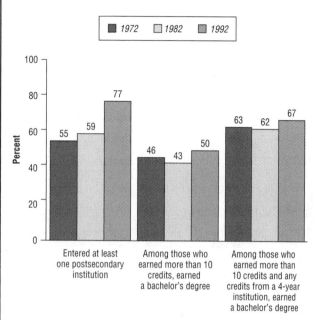

Note: The 8.5 years is relative to the modal high school graduation date (June) for the cohort, not the individual's graduation date. For example, the end point for all the 1992 graduates is the end of 2000.

SOURCE: John Wirt, Susan Choy, Patrick Rooney, William Hussar, Stephen Provasnik, and Gillian Hampden-Thompson, "Access and Persistence: Percentage of 1972, 1982, and 1992 12th-Graders Who Entered Postsecondary Education, and Among Those Who Earned More than 10 Credits or More Than 10 Credits and Any From a 4-Year Institution, Percentage Who Earned a Bachelor's Degree within 8.5 Years," in *The Condition of Education, 2005*, NCES 2005-094, U.S. Department of Education, National Center for Education Statistics, Washington, DC, June 2005, http://nces.ed.gov/pubs2005/2005094.pdf (accessed July 26, 2005)

TABLE 9.3

Total number and percentage of adults taking work-related courses, by type of instructional providers, 2002–03

Instructional provider	Percentage of participants in work-related courses
Total adults participating in work-related courses (in thousands)	68,499
Instructional provider	
Business or industry	51
College/university, vocational/technical school	21
Government agency (federal, state, local)	19
Professional or labor association/organization	19
Other (religious or community organization, tutor, etc.)	8
Elementary/secondary school	6

Note: Some adults took courses from more than one type of provider; therefore, percentages sum to more than 100.

SOURCE: John Wirt, Susan Choy, Stephen Provasnik, Patrick Rooney, Anindita Sen, and Richard Tobin, "Table 7–2. Total Number (in Thousands) and Percentage of Adults Taking Work-Related Courses, by Type of Instructional Providers: 2002–03," in *The Condition of Education, 2004*, NCES 2004-077, U.S. Department of Education, National Center for Education Statistics, Washington, DC, June 2004, http://nces.ed.gov/programs/coe/2004/section1/table.asp?tableID=99 (accessed July 26, 2005)

this may signify that they intended to pursue a bachelor's degree as the goal.

SCHOOL SIZE

Most students go to large colleges and universities. Although about 40% of higher education institutions have enrollments that are under 1,000 students, enrollment at small institutions accounts for less than 5% of total college students in the United States. According to the National Center for Education Statistics, there are 169 higher education institutions that have enrollments over 20,000 students. In fall 2003 the schools with the largest enrollments were Miami-Dade Community College (54,926), the University of Texas at Austin (52,261), Ohio State University, Main Campus (49,676), University of Minnesota, Twin Cities (48,677), and University of Phoenix, Online (48,085).

ADULT EDUCATION

According to the National Center for Education Statistics, in 2002–03, 68.5 million adults participated in work-related courses. The majority (51%) took classes provided by business or industry, and more than two-fifths (21%) took classes at a college, university, or vocational/technical school. Approximately two-fifths (19%) took classes that were provided by a government agency, and another 19% took classes that were offered by a professional or labor organization. Religious or community organizations provided the classes to 8% of the participants, and 6% of adults took them at an elementary or secondary school. (See Table 9.3.)

NUMBER OF SCHOOLS

According to the National Center for Education Statistics, in 2002–03 there were 4,168 degree-granting institutions in the United States—1,712 public and 2,456 private. About 56% (2,324) were four-year institutions, and 44% (1,844) were two-year schools. While most four-year schools were private (1,713, compared to 611 public institutions), most two-year schools were public (1,101, compared to 743 private schools). (See Table 9.4.)

COLLEGES THAT SERVE SPECIFIC POPULATIONS

Women's Colleges

Women's colleges are colleges that identify themselves as having an institutional mission primarily

TABLE 9.4

Degree-granting institutions, by control and type of institution, 1949–50 to 2002–03

Year	All institutions			Public			Private		
	Total	4-year	2-year	Total	4-year	2-year	Total	4-year	2-year
1	2	3	4	5	6	7	8	9	10
	Institutions of higher education[a] excluding branch campuses								
1949–50	1,851	1,327	524	641	344	297	1,210	983	227
1950–51	1,852	1,312	540	636	341	295	1,216	971	245
1951–52	1,832	1,326	506	641	350	291	1,191	976	215
1953–54	1,863	1,345	518	662	369	293	1,201	976	225
1955–56	1,850	1,347	503	650	360	290	1,200	987	213
1956–57	1,878	1,355	523	656	359	297	1,222	996	226
1957–58	1,930	1,390	540	666	366	300	1,264	1,024	240
1958–59	1,947	1,394	553	673	366	307	1,274	1,028	246
1959–60	2,004	1,422	582	695	367	328	1,309	1,055	254
1960–61	2,021	1,431	590	700	368	332	1,321	1,063	258
1961–62	2,033	1,443	590	718	374	344	1,315	1,069	246
1962–63	2,093	1,468	625	740	376	364	1,353	1,092	261
1963–64	2,132	1,499	633	760	386	374	1,372	1,113	259
1964–65	2,175	1,521	654	799	393	406	1,376	1,128	248
1965–66	2,230	1,551	679	821	401	420	1,409	1,150	259
1966–67	2,329	1,577	752	880	403	477	1,449	1,174	275
1967–68	2,374	1,588	786	934	414	520	1,440	1,174	266
1968–69	2,483	1,619	864	1,011	417	594	1,472	1,202	270
1969–70	2,525	1,639	886	1,060	426	634	1,465	1,213	252
1970–71	2,556	1,665	891	1,089	435	654	1,467	1,230	237
1971–72	2,606	1,675	931	1,137	440	697	1,469	1,235	234
1972–73	2,665	1,701	964	1,182	449	733	1,483	1,252	231
1973–74	2,720	1,717	1,003	1,200	440	760	1,520	1,277	243
1974–75	2,747	1,744	1,003	1,214	447	767	1,533	1,297	236
1975–76	2,765	1,767	998	1,219	447	772	1,546	1,320	226
1976–77	2,785	1,783	1,002	1,231	452	779	1,554	1,331	223
1977–78	2,826	1,808	1,018	1,241	454	787	1,585	1,354	231
1978–79	2,954	1,843	1,111	1,308	463	845	1,646	1,380	266
1979–80	2,975	1,863	1,112	1,310	464	846	1,665	1,399	266
1980–81	3,056	1,861	1,195	1,334	465	869	1,722	1,396	[b]326
1981–82	3,083	1,883	1,200	1,340	471	869	1,743	1,412	[b]331
1982–83	3,111	1,887	1,224	1,336	472	864	1,775	1,415	[b]360
1983–84	3,117	1,914	1,203	1,325	474	851	1,792	1,440	352
1984–85	3,146	1,911	1,235	1,329	461	868	1,817	1,450	367
1985–86	3,155	1,915	1,240	1,326	461	865	1,829	1,454	375
	Institutions of higher education, including branch campuses								
1974–75	3,004	1,866	1,138	1,433	537	896	1,571	1,329	242
1975–76	3,026	1,898	1,128	1,442	545	897	1,584	1,353	231
1976–77	3,046	1,913	1,133	1,455	550	905	1,591	1,363	228
1977–78	3,095	1,938	1,157	1,473	552	921	1,622	1,386	236
1978–79	3,134	1,941	1,193	1,474	550	924	1,660	1,391	269
1979–80	3,152	1,957	1,195	1,475	549	926	1,677	1,408	269
1980–81	3,231	1,957	1,274	1,497	552	945	1,734	1,405	[b]329
1981–82	3,253	1,979	1,274	1,498	558	940	1,755	1,421	[b]334
1982–83	3,280	1,984	1,296	1,493	560	933	1,787	1,424	[b]363
1983–84	3,284	2,013	1,271	1,481	565	916	1,803	1,448	355
1984–85	3,331	2,025	1,306	1,501	566	935	1,830	1,459	371
1985–86	3,340	2,029	1,311	1,498	566	932	1,842	1,463	379
1986–87[c]	3,406	2,070	1,336	1,533	573	960	1,873	1,497	376
1987–88[c]	3,587	2,135	1,452	1,591	599	992	1,996	1,536	460
1988–89[c]	3,565	2,129	1,436	1,582	598	984	1,983	1,531	452
1989–90[c]	3,535	2,127	1,408	1,563	595	968	1,972	1,532	440
1990–91[c]	3,559	2,141	1,418	1,567	595	972	1,992	1,546	446
1991–92[c]	3,601	2,157	1,444	1,598	599	999	2,003	1,558	445
1992–93[c]	3,638	2,169	1,469	1,624	600	1,024	2,014	1,569	445
1993–94[c]	3,632	2,190	1,442	1,625	604	1,021	2,007	1,586	421
1994–95[c]	3,688	2,215	1,473	1,641	605	1,036	2,047	1,610	437
1995–96[c]	3,706	2,244	1,462	1,655	608	1,047	2,051	1,636	415

related to promoting and expanding educational opportunities for women. Women's colleges were founded during the late nineteenth century in response to a need for advanced education for women at a time when most institutions of higher education admitted only men.

Most of the independent nonprofit women's colleges that developed at that time were located in the Northeast. As educational opportunities in the South during the nineteenth century were limited to whites, some higher education institutions for African-Americans were formed after the Civil War (1860–65). These institutions

TABLE 9.4

Degree-granting institutions, by control and type of institution, 1949–50 to 2002–03 [CONTINUED]

Year	All institutions			Public			Private		
	Total	4-year	2-year	Total	4-year	2-year	Total	4-year	2-year
1	2	3	4	5	6	7	8	9	10
				Title IV eligible degree-granting institutions					
1996–97	4,009	2,267	1,742	1,702	614	1,088	2,307	1,653	654
1997–98	4,064	2,309	1,755	1,707	615	1,092	2,357	1,694	663
1998–99	4,048	2,335	1,713	1,681	612	1,069	2,367	1,723	644
1999–2000	4,084	2,363	1,721	1,682	614	1,068	2,402	1,749	653
2000–01	4,182	2,450	1,732	1,698	622	1,076	2,484	1,828	656
2001–02	4,197	2,364	1,833	1,713	612	1,101	2,484	1,752	732
2002–03	4,168	2,324	1,844	1,712	611	1,101	2,456	1,713	743

aInstitutions that were accredited by an agency or association that was recognized by the U.S. Department of Education, or recognized directly by the Secretary of Education.
bLarge increases are due to the addition of schools accredited by the Accrediting Commission of Career Schools and Colleges of Technology.
cBecause of revised survey procedures, data are not entirely comparable with figures for earlier years. The number of branch campuses reporting separately has increased since 1986–87.

SOURCE: Thomas D. Snyder, Alexandra G. Tan, and Charlene M. Hoffman, "Table 246. Degree-Granting Institutions, by Control and Type of Institution: 1949–50 to 2002–03," in *Digest of Education Statistics, 2003*, NCES 2005-025, U.S. Department of Education, National Center for Education Statistics, Washington, DC, December 2004, http://nces.ed.gov/programs/digest/d03/tables/dt246.asp (accessed July 26, 2005)

included a few colleges founded especially to serve African-American women, two of which still survive: Bennett College in Greensboro, North Carolina, and Spelman College in Atlanta, Georgia. These are the only African-American women's colleges in the United States today. Various states also developed public higher education institutions open to all women in the state. Three of these colleges still exist: Douglass College, a part of Rutgers University in New Brunswick, New Jersey; Texas Women's University (with branches in Denton, Dallas, and Houston); and the Mississippi University for Women in Columbus, Mississippi.

Currently there are about eighty women's colleges in the United States, down from 200 in 1960. The majority of women's colleges are private four-year institutions, most are independent nonprofit institutions or affiliated with the Roman Catholic Church, and are located in the Northeast. Women's colleges usually have smaller enrollments than other institutions of higher education.

Historically Black Colleges and Universities

Historically Black Colleges and Universities (HBCUs) are accredited institutions of higher learning established before 1964, whose principal mission was to educate African-Americans. The first HBCU was Cheyney University in Pennsylvania, established in 1837, well before the Civil War. At that time, most African-Americans in the nation were still slaves, and the prevailing practice was to limit or prohibit their education.

Richard Humphreys, a Philadelphia Quaker, founded Cheyney University, which began as a high school

and then became a college (Cheyney State College), awarding its first baccalaureate degree in the 1930s, almost 100 years after its founding. Two HBCUs were established in the 1850s: Lincoln University in Pennsylvania (1854) and Wilberforce College in Ohio (1856). Both of these colleges were founded by African-Americans to promote education among other African-Americans.

Another institution whose beginnings go back to the 1850s is now known as the University of the District of Columbia. Miner Normal School was started in 1851 by Myrtilla Miner as a school to train African-American women as teachers. In 1955 this institution united with Wilson Normal School to become D.C. Teachers College. In 1976 D.C. Teachers College, Federal City College, and Washington Technical Institute merged to form today's University of the District of Columbia.

Following the Civil War, educating freed slaves became a top priority of the federal government, the African-American community, and private philanthropic groups. Public support in the various states generally came in the form of land grants for school buildings. Many of the HBCUs founded during this time were religious schools, such as Edward Waters College in Florida (1866), Fisk University in Tennessee (1867), and Talladega College in Alabama (1867). Howard University in Washington, D.C., was also founded in 1867 by an act of the U.S. Congress. The university was established as a coeducational and multiracial private school.

According to the National Center for Education Statistics, in fall 2002 there were 103 HBCUs in the United States; half (50%) were public institutions, and half (50%)

TABLE 9.5

Selected statistics on degree-granting historically black colleges and universities, selected years, 1980–2002

Enrollment, degrees, type of revenues, and type of expenditures	Total	Public			Private		
		Total	4-year	2-year	Total	4-year	2-year
1	2	3	4	5	6	7	8
Number of institutions, fall 2002	103	52	41	11	51	48	3
Total enrollment, fall 1980	**233,557**	**168,217**	**155,085**	**13,132**	**65,340**	**62,924**	**2,416**
Men	106,387	76,994	70,236	6,758	29,393	28,352	1,041
Men, black	81,818	56,435	53,654	2,781	25,383	24,412	971
Women	127,170	91,223	84,849	6,374	35,947	34,572	1,375
Women, black	109,171	75,226	70,582	4,644	33,945	32,589	1,356
Total enrollment, fall 1990	**257,152**	**187,046**	**171,969**	**15,077**	**70,106**	**68,528**	**1,578**
Men	105,157	76,541	70,220	6,321	28,616	28,054	562
Men, black	82,897	57,255	54,041	3,214	25,642	25,198	444
Women	151,995	110,505	101,749	8,756	41,490	40,474	1,016
Women, black	125,785	86,949	80,883	6,066	38,836	38,115	721
Total enrollment, fall 2001	**289,985**	**210,083**	**181,346**	**28,737**	**79,902**	**79,201**	**701**
Men	112,874	81,985	70,261	11,724	30,889	30,721	168
Men, black	90,718	62,603	58,019	4,584	28,115	27,947	168
Women	177,111	128,098	111,085	17,013	49,013	48,480	533
Women, black	147,920	101,751	92,812	8,939	46,169	45,639	530
Full-time enrollment, fall 2001	222,453	150,968	136,040	14,928	71,485	71,084	401
Men	89,688	61,894	55,721	6,173	27,794	27,664	130
Women	132,765	89,074	80,319	8,755	43,691	43,420	271
Part-time enrollment, fall 2001	67,532	59,115	45,306	13,809	8,417	8,117	300
Men	23,186	20,091	14,540	5,551	3,095	3,057	38
Women	44,346	39,024	30,766	8,258	5,322	5,060	262
Earned degrees conferred, 2001–02							
Associate	3,436	3,265	1,034	2,231	171	89	82
Men	1,099	1,044	279	765	55	27	28
Men, black	496	451	94	357	45	18	27
Women	2,337	2,221	755	1,466	116	62	54
Women, black	1,379	1,267	319	948	112	58	54
Bachelor's	28,846	19,101	19,101	*	9,745	9,745	*
Men	10,158	6,936	6,936	*	3,222	3,222	*
Men, black	8,623	5,707	5,707	*	2,916	2,916	*
Women	18,688	12,165	12,165	*	6,523	6,523	*
Women, black	16,499	10,326	10,326	*	6,173	6,173	*
Master's	6,338	5,477	5,477	*	861	861	*
Men	1,773	1,511	1,511	*	262	262	*
Men, black	1,163	975	975	*	188	188	*
Women	4,565	3,966	3,966	*	599	599	*
Women, black	3,298	2,803	2,803	*	495	495	*
First-professional	1,427	531	531	*	896	896	*
Men	617	226	226	*	391	391	*
Men, black	399	106	106	*	293	293	*
Women	810	305	305	*	505	505	*
Women, black	598	202	202	*	396	396	*
Doctor's	364	204	204	*	160	160	*
Men	165	82	82	*	83	83	*
Men, black	108	42	42	*	66	66	*
Women	199	122	122	*	77	77	*
Women, black	148	79	79	*	69	69	*

were private nonprofit colleges. During fall 2001, almost 290,000 students were enrolled. Full-time students outnumbered part-time students by more than three to one. Women made up a majority (61%) of all students at these institutions. Most HBCU students were African-American—84% of the women and 80% of the men. (See Table 9.5.)

Hispanic Serving Institutions

Hispanic Serving Institutions (HSIs) are institutions that have a minimum of 25% Hispanic student enrollment. According to the National Center for Education Statistics, in 2001 there were 334 HSIs in the United States. Total enrollment in 2000–01 at HSIs was 1.7 million students. Fewer than half (45%) were public institutions, less than one-quarter (23%) were private nonprofit colleges, and nearly one-third (32%) were private for-profit organizations.

Native American Colleges

Although Native American and tribal colleges and universities differ widely in their stages of development, they share some similarities. The governing boards of most are made up primarily of Native Americans and Alaska Natives, as are their student bodies. Located in twelve states, most of the tribal colleges are in isolated areas of the nation.

TABLE 9.5

Selected statistics on degree-granting historically black colleges and universities, selected years, 1980–2002 [CONTINUED]

Enrollment, degrees, type of revenues, and type of expenditures	Total	Public			Private		
		Total	4-year	2-year	Total	4-year	2-year
1	2	3	4	5	6	7	8
Financial statistics, 2000–01 in thousands of dollars							
Current-fund revenues	*	$2,865,406	$2,711,332	$154,074	*	*	*
Tuition and fees	*	583,864	551,900	31,964	*	*	*
Federal government	*	499,991	469,679	30,312	*	*	*
State governments	*	1,245,385	1,171,471	73,914	*	*	*
Local governments	*	66,520	57,804	8,715	*	*	*
Private gifts, grants, and contracts	*	48,157	47,864	293	*	*	*
Endowment income	*	8,035	7,973	61	*	*	*
Sales and services	*	367,857	361,299	6,558	*	*	*
Other sources	*	45,597	43,340	2,257	*	*	*
Current-fund expenditures	*	2,803,193	2,657,909	145,283	*	*	*
Educational and general expenditures	*	2,446,802	2,306,989	139,814	*	*	*
Auxiliary enterprises	*	337,645	332,175	5,470	*	*	*
Hospitals	*	0	0	0	*	*	*
Independent operations	*	0	0	0	*	*	*
Other expenditures	*	18,745	18,745	0	*	*	*

*Not applicable.

Note: Historically black colleges and universities are degree-granting institutions established prior to 1964 with the principal mission of educating Black Americans. Federal regulations, 20 U.S. Code, Section 1061 (2), allow for certain exceptions to the founding date. Most institutions are in the southern and border states and were established prior to 1954. Federal, state, and local governments revenue includes appropriations, grants, contracts, and independent operations. Detail may not sum to totals due to rounding.

SOURCE: Thomas D. Snyder, Alexandra G. Tan, and Charlene M. Hoffman, "Table 224. Selected Statistics on Degree-Granting Historically Black Colleges and Universities: 1980, 1990, 2000–01, 2001, and 2001–02," in *Digest of Education Statistics, 2003*, NCES 2005-025, U.S. Department of Education, National Center for Education Statistics, Washington, DC, December 2004, http://nces.ed.gov/programs/digest/d03/tables/dt224.asp (accessed July 26, 2005)

In 2000–01 there were twenty-nine tribal colleges, serving about 13,500 full- and part-time students. All were public institutions, and the enrollment was 467 students on average. One of the major thrusts of the Native American schools is to reinforce traditional cultures and pass them on to coming generations. Their curricula are primarily practical and geared to local needs. Many of them are strongly oriented toward community service.

Most funding for these schools has come from the federal government under the Tribally Controlled College or University Assistance Act (P.L. 95-471). The government pays Native American colleges about $3,000 for each Native American student, almost 40% less than what the average community college receives per student from federal, state, and local sources. Tribal colleges typically do not receive state support because they have been established by sovereign nations and are usually located on federal trust land.

Alliance for Equity in Higher Education

The Alliance for Equity in Higher Education is made up of the Hispanic Association of Colleges and Universities (HACU), the American Indian Higher Education Consortium (AIHEC), and the National Association for Equal Opportunity in Higher Education (NAFEO). It is coordinated by the Institute for Higher Education Policy, a Washington, D.C.–based nonprofit education group. The Alliance represents more than 300 HSIs, HBCUs,

other predominately African-American institutions, and tribal colleges and universities. These colleges educate 42% of all Hispanic students, 24% of African-American students, and 16% of Native American students. However, member institutions serve students of all races and ethnicities; nearly one-quarter of students at NAFEO institutions are non–African-American, more than half of students at HACU institutions are non-Hispanic, and almost two in five students at AIHEC institutions are non–Native American.

The Alliance member colleges provide greater access to low-income and underserved populations, striving to keep tuition affordable. These colleges tend to have higher student success rates among minority students than do traditional colleges.

TRENDS IN DEGREES

Trends in Enrollment by Degree Levels

The National Center for Education Statistics reports that undergraduate enrollment grew from 11.3 million in 1988 to 13.3 million in 2001, an 18% increase. In 2001 women outnumbered men; 56% of those enrolled were women. Enrollment is projected (by mid-range estimates) to reach about 15.6 million by 2013. (See Table 9.6.)

The NCES also notes that between 1988 and 2001 enrollment in graduate schools increased 27%, from 1.5 million to 1.9 million. By 2013 enrollment is projected to reach about 2.2 million, increasing about 17% from 2001.

TABLE 9.6

Total undergraduate enrollment in all degree-granting institutions, by sex, attendance status, and control of institution, with alternative projections, Fall 1988–Fall 2013

[In thousands]

Year	Total	Sex		Attendance status		Control	
		Men	Women	Full-time	Part-time	Public	Private
1988	11,317	5,138	6,179	6,642	4,674	9,103	2,213
1989	11,743	5,311	6,432	6,841	4,902	9,488	2,255
1990	11,959	5,380	6,579	6,976	4,983	9,710	2,250
1991	12,439	5,571	6,868	7,221	5,218	10,148	2,291
1992	12,537	5,582	6,954	7,243	5,293	10,216	2,320
1993	12,324	5,484	6,840	7,179	5,144	10,012	2,312
1994	12,263	5,422	6,840	7,169	5,094	9,945	2,317
1995	12,232	5,401	6,831	7,145	5,086	9,904	2,328
1996	12,327	5,421	6,906	7,299	5,028	9,935	2,392
1997	12,451	5,469	6,982	7,419	5,032	10,007	2,443
1998	12,437	5,446	6,991	7,539	4,898	9,950	2,487
1999	12,681	5,559	7,122	7,735	4,946	10,110	2,571
2000	13,155	5,778	7,377	7,923	5,232	10,539	2,616
Middle alternative projections							
2001	13,300	5,835	7,465	8,054	5,246	10,649	2,651
2002	13,829	6,008	7,821	8,438	5,392	11,058	2,771
2003	14,048	6,085	7,963	8,592	5,456	11,229	2,820
2004	14,146	6,127	8,019	8,668	5,478	11,304	2,842
2005	14,329	6,183	8,146	8,797	5,532	11,447	2,882
2006	14,511	6,248	8,264	8,931	5,580	11,589	2,922
2007	14,634	6,304	8,331	9,033	5,602	11,683	2,951
2008	14,775	6,370	8,405	9,152	5,622	11,790	2,984
2009	14,965	6,448	8,517	9,298	5,667	11,937	3,028
2010	15,109	6,502	8,608	9,403	5,706	12,047	3,062
2011	15,255	6,547	8,708	9,493	5,762	12,161	3,094
2012	15,404	6,586	8,818	9,572	5,832	12,281	3,123
2013	15,568	6,622	8,946	9,657	5,911	12,414	3,154
Low alternative projections							
2001	13,300	5,835	7,465	8,054	5,246	10,649	2,651
2002	13,887	6,015	7,872	8,458	5,429	11,168	2,719
2003	14,037	6,077	7,960	8,567	5,470	11,268	2,769
2004	14,095	6,110	7,985	8,617	5,478	11,299	2,795
2005	14,216	6,151	8,065	8,708	5,508	11,383	2,833
2006	14,328	6,196	8,132	8,797	5,532	11,462	2,866
2007	14,407	6,239	8,168	8,869	5,539	11,517	2,890
2008	14,506	6,293	8,213	8,960	5,546	11,588	2,918
2009	14,656	6,359	8,296	9,078	5,578	11,700	2,956
2010	14,779	6,407	8,372	9,168	5,610	11,792	2,987
2011	14,894	6,445	8,449	9,239	5,655	11,881	3,013
2012	15,018	6,479	8,540	9,303	5,715	11,980	3,038
2013	15,170	6,511	8,658	9,380	5,789	12,102	3,068
High alternative projections							
2001	13,300	5,835	7,465	8,054	5,246	10,649	2,651
2002	13,844	6,014	7,830	8,434	5,409	11,093	2,751
2003	14,078	6,092	7,985	8,604	5,473	11,266	2,812
2004	14,237	6,150	8,086	8,723	5,514	11,384	2,852
2005	14,463	6,222	8,242	8,886	5,578	11,558	2,905
2006	14,696	6,301	8,395	9,056	5,641	11,738	2,959
2007	14,887	6,375	8,512	9,203	5,683	11,884	3,003
2008	15,098	6,461	8,637	9,373	5,725	12,046	3,052
2009	15,354	6,556	8,797	9,564	5,790	12,243	3,110
2010	15,551	6,624	8,927	9,705	5,846	12,395	3,156
2011	15,738	6,682	9,056	9,824	5,914	12,541	3,197
2012	15,923	6,731	9,192	9,929	5,994	12,689	3,234
2013	16,116	6,774	9,342	10,032	6,084	12,844	3,272

Note: Detail may not sum to totals because of rounding. Some data have been revised from previously published figures. Data for 1999 were imputed using alternative procedures.

SOURCE: Debra E. Gerald and William J. Hussar, "Table 19. Total Undergraduate Enrollment in All Degree-Granting Institutions, by Sex, Attendance Status, and Control of Institution, with Alternative Projections: Fall 1988 to Fall 2013," in *Projections of Education Statistics to 2013*, NCES 2004-013, U.S. Department of Education, National Center for Education Statistics, Washington, DC, October 2003, http://nces.ed.gov/programs/projections/tables/table_19.asp (accessed July 26, 2005)

More women (nearly 1.1 million) than men (791,000) were enrolled in graduate programs in 2001. (See Table 9.7.)

Enrollment in first-professional degree programs (medicine, law, dentistry, theology, and others) increased 18% between 1988 and 2001, from 267,000 to 316,000, according to the NCES. In 2001 more men (174,000) than women (142,000) were enrolled in first-professional degree programs. Proportionally, however, the enrollment of women increased from 37.4% in 1988 to 44.9% in 2001. Total enrollment is projected to be 390,000 by 2013, of which 46.6% will be women. (See Table 9.8.)

Trends in Degrees Conferred

According to the NCES in the *Digest of Education Statistics 2003*, the number of associate degrees conferred grew from 481,720 in 1990–91 to 595,133 in 2001–02, a 24% increase. During the same period, bachelor's degrees increased 18%, from 1,094,538 to 1,291,900; master's degrees rose 43%, from 337,168 to 482,118; first-professional degrees increased 12%, from 71,948 to 80,698; and doctoral degrees rose 12%, from 39,294 to 44,160. (See Table 9.9.)

The Federal Interagency Forum on Child and Family Statistics reports that from 1980 to 2004 the percentage of adults earning a bachelor's degree or higher increased from 23% to 28%. Whites ages twenty-five to twenty-nine were more likely than African-Americans or Hispanics to have earned at least a bachelor's degree. In 2004 nearly one-third (32%) of whites, 18% of African-Americans, and 12% of Hispanics in this age group had earned a bachelor's degree or higher. (See Figure 9.5.)

Associate Degrees

In 2001–02, 595,133 students earned associate degrees. (See Table 9.9.) The NCES reports that public institutions accounted for 79% of all associate degrees in 2001–02. At public institutions conferring associate degrees, liberal arts/general studies, business management/administration, and health professions were the most popular areas of study. At private institutions business management/administration was the degree conferred most often, with engineering-related technology and computer and information sciences degrees also being popular. (See Table 9.10.)

Bachelor's Degrees

In 2001–02 students earned 1.3 million bachelor's degrees. Since 1981–82 more bachelor's degrees have been awarded to women than to men. Of the 1.3 million degrees awarded in 2001–02, women earned 742,084 or 57%. (See Table 9.9.) The largest numbers of degrees conferred at public and private institutions included business management/administration, social sciences and history, education, psychology, health and related sciences, and engineering. (See Table 9.10.)

Master's Degrees

The number of master's degrees awarded annually declined during the late 1970s and the early 1980s but began to rise again in the 1984–85 academic year. In 2001–02 the number reached 482,118. The proportion earned by women has steadily increased. In 1970–71 women earned 40% of all master's degrees; in 2001–02 the proportion rose to 57% and is projected to remain around this percentage or slightly higher through 2012–13. (See Table 9.9.) The fields with the greatest numbers of degrees awarded were education and business management/administration. (See Table 9.10.)

Doctoral Degrees

The number of doctorates conferred remained virtually unchanged, at around 33,000, throughout most of the 1970s and early 1980s. Between 1986–87 and 1997–98 the number increased to about 46,000, and it has declined slightly since then. In 2001–02 degrees conferred at this level totaled 44,160. (See Table 9.9.) Generally, men receiving doctoral degrees outnumbered women, but the number of women earning doctorates has more than doubled since the late 1970s. In 2001–02 women earned 46% of all doctoral degrees conferred. The NCES projects that through 2012–13 the proportion will remain about the same or increase slightly. (See Table 9.9.) The majority of doctorates earned in 2001–02 were in education and technical fields such as engineering, the biological/life sciences, and physical sciences/science technologies. (See Table 9.10.)

First-Professional Degrees

According to the NCES, 70,698 first-professional degrees were conferred in 2001–02. There have been large changes in the total number of first-professional degrees (dentistry, medicine, law, and others) awarded to women. There was an almost 700% increase from 1970–71 to 1980–81. (The increase for men during the same period was 49%.) By 2001–02 first-professional degrees earned by women had increased from the 1980–81 figures an additional 99%. Women still lagged behind men, however, earning 47% of all first-professional degrees in 2001–02. Yet this was a marked change from 1970–71, when only 6% of all first-professional degrees went to women. (See Table 9.9.) Women received 38% of dental degrees, 44% of medical degrees, and 48% of all law degrees in 2001–02. (See Table 9.11.)

FACULTY

According to the National Center for Education Statistics, in fall 2001 nearly 3.1 million people were involved in operating the nation's colleges and universities.

TABLE 9.7

Total graduate enrollment in all degree-granting institutions, by sex, attendance status, and control of institution, with alternative projections, Fall 1988–Fall 2013

[In thousands]

Year	Total	Sex		Attendance status		Control	
		Men	Women	Full-time	Part-time	Public	Private
1988	1,472	697	774	553	919	949	522
1989	1,522	710	811	572	949	978	544
1990	1,586	737	849	599	987	1,023	563
1991	1,639	761	878	642	997	1,050	589
1992	1,669	772	896	666	1,003	1,058	611
1993	1,688	771	917	688	1,000	1,064	625
1994	1,721	776	946	706	1,016	1,075	647
1995	1,732	767	965	717	1,015	1,074	659
1996	1,742	759	982	737	1,005	1,069	674
1997	1,753	758	996	752	1,001	1,070	683
1998	1,768	754	1,013	754	1,014	1,067	701
1999	1,807	766	1,041	781	1,026	1,077	730
2000	1,850	780	1,070	813	1,037	1,089	761
Middle alternative projections							
2001	1,868	791	1,077	810	1,058	1,119	749
2002	1,941	817	1,124	855	1,086	1,162	779
2003	1,973	827	1,145	876	1,096	1,181	792
2004	1,980	831	1,149	884	1,095	1,185	795
2005	2,003	836	1,167	899	1,104	1,199	804
2006	2,024	842	1,181	912	1,112	1,211	813
2007	2,032	846	1,185	919	1,112	1,216	816
2008	2,036	850	1,186	926	1,110	1,218	818
2009	2,049	855	1,194	936	1,113	1,226	824
2010	2,067	862	1,205	949	1,118	1,236	831
2011	2,098	873	1,224	967	1,131	1,254	843
2012	2,142	889	1,254	992	1,150	1,281	862
2013	2,193	904	1,288	1,019	1,174	1,311	882
Low alternative projections							
2001	1,868	791	1,077	810	1,058	1,119	749
2002	1,830	791	1,039	797	1,033	1,136	694
2003	1,873	801	1,072	825	1,047	1,153	720
2004	1,898	808	1,090	843	1,056	1,160	739
2005	1,932	817	1,115	862	1,070	1,173	759
2006	1,957	824	1,133	877	1,080	1,183	774
2007	1,970	829	1,140	887	1,083	1,187	783
2008	1,976	833	1,143	894	1,082	1,188	789
2009	1,989	838	1,150	903	1,085	1,193	796
2010	2,007	845	1,161	916	1,091	1,203	804
2011	2,035	856	1,179	932	1,103	1,218	816
2012	2,076	871	1,205	956	1,120	1,242	834
2013	2,125	886	1,238	981	1,143	1,271	854
High alternative projections							
2001	1,868	791	1,077	810	1,058	1,119	749
2002	1,880	798	1,082	828	1,052	1,143	738
2003	1,939	816	1,123	862	1,077	1,171	768
2004	1,972	827	1,145	881	1,090	1,186	785
2005	2,011	838	1,173	904	1,107	1,208	804
2006	2,046	848	1,198	924	1,122	1,227	819
2007	2,068	855	1,213	939	1,129	1,239	829
2008	2,086	863	1,224	953	1,133	1,249	837
2009	2,111	871	1,240	969	1,142	1,263	848
2010	2,138	880	1,258	987	1,152	1,279	859
2011	2,177	893	1,283	1,009	1,167	1,302	875
2012	2,229	911	1,318	1,039	1,190	1,333	896
2013	2,285	928	1,357	1,069	1,216	1,366	919

Note: Detail may not sum to totals because of rounding. Some data have been revised from previously published figures. Data for 1999 were imputed using alternative procedures.

SOURCE: Debra E. Gerald and William J. Hussar, "Table 20. Total Graduate Enrollment in All Degree-Granting Institutions, by Sex, Attendance Status, and Control of Institution, with Alternative Projections: Fall 1988 to Fall 2013," in *Projections of Education Statistics to 2013*, NCES 2004-013, U.S. Department of Education, National Center for Education Statistics, Washington, DC, October 2003, http://nces.ed.gov/programs/projections/tables/table_20.asp (accessed July 26, 2005)

TABLE 9.8

Total first-professional enrollment in all degree-granting institutions, by sex, attendance status, and control of institution, with alternative projections, Fall 1988–Fall 2013

[In thousands]

Year	Total	Sex		Attendance status		Control	
		Men	Women	Full-time	Part-time	Public	Private
1988	267	167	100	241	26	109	158
1989	274	169	106	248	27	113	162
1990	273	167	107	246	28	112	162
1991	281	170	111	252	29	111	169
1992	281	169	112	252	29	111	170
1993	292	173	120	260	33	114	179
1994	295	174	121	263	31	114	181
1995	298	174	124	266	31	115	183
1996	298	173	126	267	31	117	182
1997	298	170	129	267	31	118	180
1998	302	169	134	271	31	121	182
1999	303	165	138	271	33	123	180
2000	307	164	143	274	33	124	183
Middle alternative projections							
2001	316	174	142	282	33	127	189
2002	332	183	149	298	34	134	198
2003	340	186	154	305	34	137	203
2004	342	186	156	308	34	138	204
2005	347	189	159	313	34	140	207
2006	352	191	161	317	35	142	210
2007	355	192	162	320	35	143	211
2008	357	193	163	322	35	144	213
2009	360	195	165	326	35	146	215
2010	365	197	168	330	35	147	217
2011	371	200	171	336	35	150	221
2012	380	204	176	345	36	154	226
2013	390	208	182	354	36	158	232
Low alternative projections							
2001	316	174	142	282	33	127	189
2002	329	187	142	298	31	131	198
2003	335	188	147	303	32	134	201
2004	337	188	150	305	32	135	202
2005	341	189	153	308	33	137	205
2006	345	190	155	311	33	138	206
2007	346	190	156	313	34	139	207
2008	348	191	157	314	34	140	208
2009	350	192	158	316	34	141	209
2010	354	193	161	320	34	143	211
2011	360	196	164	325	34	145	214
2012	368	200	168	333	35	149	219
2013	377	204	173	342	36	153	225
High alternative projections							
2001	316	174	142	282	33	127	189
2002	329	183	146	297	32	132	198
2003	338	186	152	305	33	136	203
2004	344	188	156	310	34	138	205
2005	351	190	160	316	34	141	209
2006	357	193	164	322	35	144	213
2007	362	195	167	327	35	146	216
2008	367	197	169	331	35	148	218
2009	372	200	173	337	35	151	222
2010	378	202	176	343	36	153	225
2011	386	206	180	350	36	157	230
2012	397	211	186	360	37	161	236
2013	408	215	193	370	38	166	242

Note: Detail may not sum to totals because of rounding. Some data have been revised from previously published figures. Data for 1999 were imputed using alternative procedures.

SOURCE: Debra E. Gerald and William J. Hussar, "Table 20. Total First-Professional Enrollment in All Degree-Granting Institutions, by Sex, Attendance Status, and Control of Institution, with Alternative Projections: Fall 1988 to Fall 2013," in *Projections of Education Statistics to 2013*, NCES 2004-013, U.S. Department of Education, National Center for Education Statistics, Washington, DC, October 2003, http://nces.ed.gov/programs/projections/tables/table_21.asp (accessed July 26, 2005).

TABLE 9.9

Earned degrees conferred by degree-granting institutions, by level of degree and sex of student, selected years, 1869–70 to 2012–13

Year	Associate degrees			Bachelor's degrees			Master's degrees			First-professional degrees			Doctor's degrees[a]		
	Total	Men	Women	Total	Men	Women	Total	Men	Women	Total	Men	Women	Total	Men	Women
1	2	3	4	5	6	7	8	9	10	11	12	13	14	15	16
1869–70	—	—	—	9,371[b]	7,993[b]	1,378[b]	0	0	0	c	c	c	1	1	0
1879–80	—	—	—	12,896[b]	10,411[b]	2,485[b]	879	868	11	c	c	c	54	51	3
1889–90	—	—	—	15,539[b]	12,857[b]	2,682[b]	1,015	821	194	c	c	c	149	147	2
1899–1900	—	—	—	27,410[b]	22,173[b]	5,237[b]	1,583	1,280	303	c	c	c	382	359	23
1909–10	—	—	—	37,199[b]	28,762[b]	8,437[b]	2,113	1,555	558	c	c	c	443	399	44
1919–20	—	—	—	48,622[b]	31,980[b]	16,642[b]	4,279	2,985	1,294	c	c	c	615	522	93
1929–30	—	—	—	122,484[b]	73,615[b]	48,869[b]	14,969	8,925	6,044	c	c	c	2,299	1,946	353
1939–40	—	—	—	186,500[b]	109,546[b]	76,954[b]	26,731	16,508	10,223	c	c	c	3,290	2,861	429
1949–50	—	—	—	432,058[b]	328,841[b]	103,217[b]	58,183	41,220	16,963	c	c	c	6,420	5,804	616
1959–60	—	—	—	392,440[b]	254,063[b]	138,377[b]	74,435	50,898	23,537	c	c	c	9,829	8,801	1,028
1960–61	—	—	—	365,174	224,538	140,636	84,609	57,830	26,779	25,253	24,577	676	10,575	9,463	1,112
1961–62	—	—	—	383,961	230,456	153,505	91,418	62,603	28,815	25,607	24,836	771	11,622	10,377	1,245
1962–63	—	—	—	411,420	241,309	170,111	98,684	67,302	31,382	26,590	25,753	837	12,822	11,448	1,374
1963–64	—	—	—	461,266	265,349	195,917	109,183	73,850	35,333	27,209	26,357	852	14,490	12,955	1,535
1964–65	—	—	—	493,757	282,173	211,584	121,167	81,319	39,848	28,290	27,283	1,007	16,467	14,692	1,775
1965–66	111,607	63,779	47,828	520,115	299,287	220,828	140,602	93,081	47,521	30,124	28,982	1,142	18,237	16,121	2,116
1966–67	139,183	78,356	60,827	558,534	322,711	235,823	157,726	103,109	54,617	31,695	30,401	1,294	20,617	18,163	2,454
1967–68	159,441	90,317	69,124	632,289	357,682	274,607	176,749	113,552	63,197	33,939	32,402	1,537	23,089	20,183	2,906
1968–69	183,279	105,661	77,618	728,845	410,595	318,250	193,756	121,531	72,225	35,114	33,595	1,519	26,158	22,722	3,436
1969–70	206,023	117,432	88,591	792,316	451,097	341,219	208,291	125,624	82,667	34,918	33,077	1,841	29,866	25,890	3,976
1970–71	252,311	144,144	108,167	839,730	475,594	364,136	230,509	138,146	92,363	37,946	35,544	2,402	32,107	27,530	4,577
1971–72	292,014	166,227	125,787	887,273	500,590	386,683	251,633	149,550	102,083	43,411	40,723	2,688	33,363	28,090	5,273
1972–73	316,174	175,413	140,761	922,362	518,191	404,171	263,371	154,468	108,903	50,018	46,489	3,529	34,777	28,571	6,206
1973–74	343,924	188,591	155,333	945,776	527,313	418,463	277,033	157,842	119,191	53,816	48,530	5,286	33,816	27,365	6,451
1974–75	360,171	191,017	169,154	922,933	504,841	418,092	292,450	161,570	130,880	55,916	48,956	6,960	34,083	26,817	7,266
1975–76	391,454	209,996	181,458	925,746	504,925	420,821	311,771	167,248	144,523	62,649	52,892	9,757	34,064	26,267	7,797
1976–77	406,377	210,842	195,535	919,549	495,545	424,004	317,164	167,783	149,381	64,359	52,374	11,985	33,232	25,142	8,090
1977–78	412,246	204,718	207,528	921,204	487,347	433,857	311,620	161,212	150,408	66,581	52,270	14,311	32,131	23,658	8,473
1978–79	402,702	192,091	210,611	921,390	477,344	444,046	301,079	153,370	147,709	68,848	52,652	16,196	32,730	23,541	9,189
1979–80	400,910	183,737	217,173	929,417	473,611	455,806	298,081	150,749	147,332	70,131	52,716	17,415	32,615	22,943	9,672
1980–81	416,377	188,638	227,739	935,140	469,883	465,257	295,739	147,043	148,696	71,956	52,792	19,164	32,958	22,711	10,247
1981–82	434,526	196,944	237,582	952,998	473,364	479,634	295,546	145,532	150,014	72,032	52,223	19,809	32,707	22,224	10,483
1982–83	449,620	203,991	245,629	969,510	479,140	490,370	289,921	144,697	145,224	73,054	51,250	21,804	32,775	21,902	10,873
1983–84	452,240	202,704	249,536	974,309	482,319	491,990	284,263	143,595	140,668	74,468	51,378	23,090	33,209	22,064	11,145
1984–85	454,712	202,932	251,780	979,477	482,528	496,949	286,251	143,390	142,861	75,063	50,455	24,608	32,943	21,700	11,243
1985–86	446,047	196,166	249,881	987,823	485,923	501,900	288,567	143,508	145,059	73,910	49,261	24,649	33,653	21,819	11,834
1986–87	436,304	190,839	245,465	991,264	480,782	510,482	289,349	141,269	148,080	71,617	46,523	25,094	34,041	22,061	11,980
1987–88	435,085	190,047	245,038	994,829	477,203	517,626	299,317	145,163	154,154	70,735	45,484	25,251	34,870	22,615	12,255
1988–89	436,764	186,316	250,448	1,018,755	483,346	535,409	310,621	149,354	161,267	70,856	45,046	25,810	35,720	22,648	13,072
1989–90	455,102	191,195	263,907	1,051,344	491,696	559,648	324,301	153,653	170,648	70,988	43,961	27,027	38,371	24,401	13,970
1990–91	481,720	198,634	283,086	1,094,538	504,045	590,493	337,168	156,482	180,686	71,948	43,846	28,102	39,294	24,756	14,538
1991–92	504,231	207,481	296,750	1,136,553	520,811	615,742	352,838	161,842	190,996	74,146	45,071	29,075	40,659	25,557	15,102
1992–93	514,756	211,964	302,792	1,165,178	532,881	632,297	369,585	169,258	200,327	75,387	45,153	30,234	42,132	26,073	16,059
1993–94	530,632	215,261	315,371	1,169,275	532,422	636,853	387,070	176,085	210,985	75,418	44,707	30,711	43,185	26,552	16,633
1994–95	539,691	218,352	321,339	1,160,134	526,131	634,003	397,629	178,598	219,031	75,800	44,853	30,947	44,446	26,916	17,530
1995–96	555,216	219,514	335,702	1,164,792	522,454	642,338	406,301	179,081	227,220	76,734	44,748	31,986	44,652	26,841	17,811
1996–97	571,226	223,948	347,278	1,172,879	520,515	652,364	419,401	180,947	238,454	78,730	45,564	33,166	45,876	27,146	18,730
1997–98	558,555	217,613	340,942	1,184,406	519,956	664,450	430,164	184,375	245,789	78,598	44,911	33,687	46,010	26,664	19,346
1998–99	559,954	218,417	341,537	1,200,303	518,746	681,557	439,986	186,148	253,838	78,439	44,339	34,100	44,077	25,146	18,931
1999–2000	564,933	224,721	340,212	1,237,875	530,367	707,508	457,056	191,792	265,264	80,057	44,239	35,818	44,808	25,028	19,780
2000–01	578,865	231,645	347,220	1,244,171	531,840	712,331	468,476	194,351	274,125	79,707	42,862	36,845	44,904	24,728	20,176
2001–02	595,133	238,109	357,024	1,291,900	549,816	742,084	482,118	199,120	282,998	80,698	42,507	38,191	44,160	23,708	20,452
2002–03[d]	662,000	246,000	416,000	1,311,000	548,000	763,000	492,000	210,000	282,000	80,400	42,300	38,100	43,300	22,900	20,400
2003–04[d]	660,000	243,000	417,000	1,333,000	559,000	774,000	502,000	213,000	289,000	84,400	44,300	40,100	44,200	23,300	20,900
2004–05[d]	669,000	243,000	426,000	1,352,000	578,000	774,000	506,000	213,000	293,000	87,800	46,300	41,500	44,600	23,600	21,000

About 2.1 million (69%) were professional staff, including executives, administrators, and instructors. Almost 31% (951,203) were nonprofessional, such as clerical or secretarial staff, paraprofessionals, and skilled staff, including building maintenance and groundskeepers. (See Table 9.12.)

In fall 2001 approximately 1.5 million men accounted for 47% of all employees at degree-granting institutions, according to the National Center for Education Statistics. The 1.1 million men employed in professional roles comprised more than half (52%) of the professional staff; 644,514 (58%) of the 1.1 million faculty members were men. (See Table 9.12.)

Race/Ethnicity

In 2001, 2.2 million non-Hispanic whites made up more than 72% of all employees at degree-granting institutions. Non-Hispanic African-Americans (309,252)

TABLE 9.9

Earned degrees conferred by degree-granting institutions, by level of degree and sex of student, selected years, 1869–70 to 2012–13

[CONTINUED]

Year	Associate degrees			Bachelor's degrees			Master's degrees			First-professional degrees			Doctor's degrees[a]		
	Total	Men	Women	Total	Men	Women	Total	Men	Women	Total	Men	Women	Total	Men	Women
1	2	3	4	5	6	7	8	9	10	11	12	13	14	15	16
2005–06[d]	675,000	244,000	431,000	1,397,000	584,000	813,000	513,000	215,000	298,000	89,100	47,100	42,000	45,000	23,700	21,300
2006–07[d]	676,000	243,000	433,000	1,413,000	585,000	828,000	519,000	217,000	302,000	90,100	47,300	42,800	45,300	23,800	21,500
2007–08[d]	681,000	244,000	437,000	1,425,000	589,000	836,000	522,000	218,000	304,000	91,300	47,800	43,500	45,600	24,000	21,600
2008–09[d]	684,000	244,000	440,000	1,441,000	594,000	847,000	526,000	219,000	307,000	92,200	48,300	43,900	45,700	24,100	21,600
2009–10[d]	688,000	245,000	443,000	1,456,000	598,000	858,000	530,000	220,000	310,000	92,900	48,600	44,300	45,900	24,200	21,700
2010–11[d]	692,000	246,000	446,000	1,469,000	603,000	866,000	536,000	222,000	314,000	93,600	48,800	44,800	46,200	24,400	21,800
2011–12[d]	696,000	247,000	449,000	1,488,000	610,000	878,000	544,000	224,000	320,000	94,600	49,200	45,400	46,600	24,500	22,100
2012–13[d]	699,000	248,000	451,000	1,509,000	616,000	893,000	556,000	228,000	328,000	95,900	49,600	46,300	47,300	24,700	22,600

— Not available.

[a]Includes Ph.D., Ed.D., and comparable degrees at the doctoral level. Excludes first-professional, such as M.D., D.D.S., and law degrees.

[b]Includes first-professional degrees.

[c]First-professional degrees are included with bachelor's degrees.

[d]Projected.

Note: Data for 1869–70 to 1994–95 are for institutions of higher education. Institutions of higher education were accredited by an agency or association that was recognized by the U.S. Department of Education, or recognized directly by the Secretary of Education. The new degree-granting classification is very similar to the earlier higher education classification, except that it includes some additional institutions, primarily 2-year colleges, and excludes a few higher education institutions that did not award associate or higher degrees. Data for 1998–99 were imputed using alternative procedures. Some data have been revised from previously published figures. Detail may not sum to totals due to rounding.

SOURCE: Thomas D. Snyder, Alexandra G. Tan, and Charlene M. Hoffman, "Table 249. Earned Degrees Conferred by Degree-Granting Institutions, by Level of Degree and Sex of Student: Selected Years, 1869–70 to 2012–13," in *Digest of Education Statistics, 2003*, NCES 2005-025, U.S. Department of Education, National Center for Education Statistics, Washington, DC, December 2004, http://nces.ed.gov/programs/digest/d03/tables/dt249.asp (accessed July 26, 2005)

FIGURE 9.5

Percentage of adults ages 25–29 who have completed a bachelor's or higher degree, by race and Hispanic origin, 1980–2004

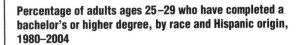

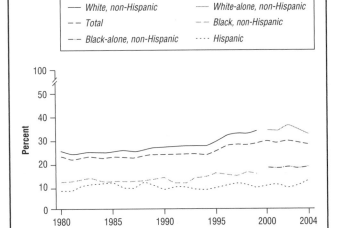

Note: From 1980 to 1999, the 1977 OMB (Office of Management & Budget) Standards for Data on Race and Ethnicity were used to classify persons into one of the following four racial groups: white, black, American Indian or Alaskan Native, or Asian or Pacific Islander. From 2000 to 2003, the revised 1997 OMB standards were used. Persons could select one or more of five racial groups: white, black or African American, American Indian or Alaska Native, Asian, and Native Hawaiian or Other Pacific Islander. Data from 2000 onward are not directly comparable with data from earlier years. In addition, note that data on race and Hispanic origin are collected separately, but are combined for reporting.

SOURCE: Federal Interagency Forum on Child and Family Statistics, "Table ED7. Percentage of Adults Ages 25–29 Who Have Completed a Bachelor's or Higher Degree by Race and Hispanic Origin, 1980–2004," in *America's Children: Key National Indicators of Well-Being, 2005,* Federal Interagency Forum on Child and Family Statistics, Washington, DC, July 2005, http://www.childstats.gov/americaschildren/edu7.asp (accessed August 10, 2005)

accounted for about 10% of employees; Hispanics (157,128) comprised 5%; Asians or Pacific Islanders (148,945) were 5%; and Native Americans (18,423) made up less than 1%. Nonresident aliens (135,026) made up about 4%. (See Table 9.12.)

Salaries

According to the National Center for Education Statistics, average faculty salary decreased during the late 1970s and then recovered during the late 1980s. It remained relatively stable for the next decade and then increased again, starting in the late 1990s. In 1977–78 the average salary for full-time faculty (expressed in 2002–03 dollars) was $57,000, and in 2002–03 it had increased to $62,800. With all benefits included, the average faculty salary was $66,600 in 1977–78 and $78,300 in 2002–03. In 2002–03 the average salary of a full professor was $86,100. For associate and assistant professors, the average salaries were $62,800 and $52,800, respectively, while instructors earned an average of $47,300 and lecturers earned $43,700. (See Table 9.13.)

THE COST OF HIGHER EDUCATION

According to the U.S. Department of Education in *The Condition of Education 2005*, public two- and four-year degree-granting institutions took in $138 billion in education and general revenue in 2000–01. Federal, state, and local governments provided 46% of that sum ($64 billion); tuition and fees at public institutions accounted for 23% ($32 billion) of income; and donations,

TABLE 9.10

Degrees conferred by degree-granting institutions, by control of institution, level of degree, and discipline division, 2001–02

Discipline division	Public institutions				Private institutions			
	Associate degrees	Bachelor's degrees	Master's degrees	Doctor's degrees[a]	Associate degrees	Bachelor's degrees	Master's degrees	Doctor's degrees[a]
1	2	3	4	5	6	7	8	9
Total	471,660	841,512	249,828	27,622	123,473	450,388	232,290	16,538
Agriculture and natural resources[b]	6,135	21,051	3,918	1,146	359	2,302	601	20
Architecture and related programs	353	6,770	2,944	123	90	2,038	1,622	60
Area, ethnic, and cultural studies	85	3,791	807	120	234	2,766	771	96
Biological sciences/life sciences	1,400	39,633	4,123	3,059	117	20,623	2,082	1,430
Business[c]	72,727	164,170	46,580	676	36,184	117,160	74,205	482
Communications	1,695	43,857	2,681	293	1,124	18,934	2,829	81
Communications technologies	1,516	528	110	0	505	582	439	9
Computer and information sciences	14,381	25,873	7,936	448	16,584	21,426	8,177	302
Construction trades	2,216	73	0	0	423	129	9	0
Education	7,927	76,042	75,485	4,798	1,340	30,341	61,094	2,169
Engineering	1,508	44,738	17,632	3,730	216	14,743	8,383	1,465
Engineering-related technologies	17,280	10,367	784	14	15,615	3,750	112	1
English language and literature/letters	813	36,435	5,221	1,066	51	16,727	2,047	380
Foreign languages and literatures	431	10,147	2,080	557	86	5,171	781	286
Health professions and related sciences	65,791	46,272	23,224	2,049	14,097	24,245	20,420	1,474
Home economics and vocational home economics	9,004	15,558	1,569	255	476	2,595	1,047	100
Law and legal studies	3,862	1,106	854	10	2,963	865	3,199	69
Liberal arts and sciences, general studies, and humanities	198,924	27,626	1,112	33	8,239	11,707	1,642	80
Library science	94	73	4,139	43	2	1	974	2
Mathematics	668	8,002	2,659	682	17	4,393	828	276
Mechanics and repairers	7,697	74	0	0	4,389	90	0	0
Multi/interdisciplinary studies	12,972	20,282	1,835	210	232	7,347	1,376	174
Parks, recreation, leisure, and fitness studies	657	15,127	2,189	138	173	5,427	565	13
Philosophy and religion	89	3,842	438	212	45	5,464	896	394
Physical sciences and science technologies	2,224	11,678	3,684	2,693	84	6,173	1,350	1,110
Precision production trades	6,968	356	0	0	3,850	112	2	0
Protective services	15,258	19,037	1,580	46	1,431	6,499	1,355	3
Psychology	1,526	51,095	5,881	1,742	179	25,576	9,007	2,599
Public administration and services	3,007	13,254	15,784	311	316	6,138	9,664	260
R.O.T.C. and military technologies	62	3	0	0	0	0	0	0
Social sciences and history	5,334	86,454	8,773	2,457	259	46,420	5,339	1,445
Theological studies/religious vocations	0	0	0	0	414	7,785	4,952	1,355
Transportation and material moving workers	741	1,649	74	0	418	2,371	635	0
Visual and performing arts	8,262	36,549	5,732	711	12,649	30,224	5,863	403
Not classified by field of study	53	0	0	0	312	264	24	0

[a]Includes Ph.D., Ed.D., and comparable degrees at the doctoral level. Excludes first-professional degrees, such as M.D., D.D.S., and law degrees.
[b]Includes "Agricultural business and production," "Agricultural sciences," and "Conservation and renewable natural resources."
[c]Includes "Business management and administrative services," "Marketing operations/marketing and distribution," and "Consumer and personal services."

SOURCE: Thomas D. Snyder, Alexandra G. Tan, and Charlene M. Hoffman, "Table 257. Degrees Conferred by Degree-Granting Institutions, by Control of Institution, Level of Degree, and Discipline Division, 2001–02" in *Digest of Education Statistics, 2003*, NCES 2005-025, U.S. Department of Education, National Center for Education Statistics, Washington, DC, December 2004, http://nces.ed.gov/programs/digest/d03/tables/dt257.asp (accessed July 26, 2005)

endowments, and government contracts produced another 30% ($42 billion) in 2000–01. Combined spending on post-secondary institutions from both public and private sources averaged $20,358 per student in the United States in 2000, the highest dollar amount in a survey of the thirty countries belonging to the Organization for Economic Co-operation and Development. (See Table 2.8 in Chapter 2.) This figure was up 6% from the $19,220 per student spent in 1999 in the United States, according to the U.S. Department of Education.

What Students Pay

The cost of a college education has been increasing dramatically for some time. In *The Condition of Educa-tion 2005*, the U.S. Department of Education reports that government appropriations per student for public institutions increased 3% from 1969–70 to 2000–01 when adjusted for inflation, but that tuition and fees paid by individuals had increased by 99% during the same period. According to *Trends in College Pricing* (College Board, 2004), in 2004–05, the average residential student paid $14,640 in total costs if he or she attended an in-state, four-year public college, including $5,132 in tuition and fees, $6,222 in room and board, $853 in books and supplies, $774 for transportation, and $1,659 in other costs. At a four-year private college, total costs were $30,295. The West had the lowest tuition rate for public four-year institutions, the Southwest had the lowest

TABLE 9.11

First-professional degrees conferred by degree-granting institutions in dentistry, medicine, and law, selected years, 1949–50 to 2001–02

Year	Dentistry (D.D.S. or D.M.D.)				Medicine (M.D.)				Law (LL.B. or J.D.)			
	Number of institutions conferring degrees	Degrees conferred			Number of institutions conferring degrees	Degrees conferred			Number of institutions conferring degrees	Degrees conferred		
		Total	Men	Women		Total	Men	Women		Total	Men	Women
1	2	3	4	5	6	7	8	9	10	11	12	13
1949–50	40	2,579	2,561	18	72	5,612	5,028	584	—	—	—	—
1951–52	41	2,918	2,895	23	72	6,201	5,871	330	—	—	—	—
1953–54	42	3,102	3,063	39	73	6,712	6,377	335	—	—	—	—
1955–56	42	3,009	2,975	34	73	6,810	6,464	346	131	8,262	7,974	288
1957–58	43	3,065	3,031	34	75	6,816	6,469	347	131	9,394	9,122	272
1959–60	45	3,247	3,221	26	79	7,032	6,645	387	134	9,240	9,010	230
1961–62	46	3,183	3,166	17	81	7,138	6,749	389	134	9,364	9,091	273
1963–64	46	3,180	3,168	12	82	7,303	6,878	425	133	10,679	10,372	307
1965–66	47	3,178	3,146	32	84	7,673	7,170	503	136	13,246	12,776	470
1967–68	48	3,422	3,375	47	85	7,944	7,318	626	138	16,454	15,805	649
1969–70	48	3,718	3,684	34	86	8,314	7,615	699	145	14,916	14,115	801
1970–71	48	3,745	3,703	42	89	8,919	8,110	809	147	17,421	16,181	1,240
1971–72	48	3,862	3,819	43	92	9,253	8,423	830	147	21,764	20,266	1,498
1972–73	51	4,047	3,992	55	97	10,307	9,388	919	152	27,205	25,037	2,168
1973–74	52	4,440	4,355	85	99	11,356	10,093	1,263	151	29,326	25,986	3,340
1974–75	52	4,773	4,627	146	104	12,447	10,818	1,629	154	29,296	24,881	4,415
1975–76	56	5,425	5,187	238	107	13,426	11,252	2,174	166	32,293	26,085	6,208
1976–77	57	5,138	4,764	374	109	13,461	10,891	2,570	169	34,104	26,447	7,657
1977–78	57	5,189	4,623	566	109	14,279	11,210	3,069	169	34,402	25,457	8,945
1978–79	58	5,434	4,794	640	109	14,786	11,381	3,405	175	35,206	25,180	10,026
1979–80	58	5,258	4,558	700	112	14,902	11,416	3,486	179	35,647	24,893	10,754
1980–81	58	5,460	4,672	788	116	15,505	11,672	3,833	176	36,331	24,563	11,768
1981–82	59	5,282	4,467	815	119	15,814	11,867	3,947	180	35,991	23,965	12,026
1982–83	59	5,585	4,631	954	118	15,484	11,350	4,134	177	36,853	23,550	13,303
1983–84	60	5,353	4,302	1,051	119	15,813	11,359	4,454	179	37,012	23,382	13,630
1984–85	59	5,339	4,233	1,106	120	16,041	11,167	4,874	181	37,491	23,070	14,421
1985–86	59	5,046	3,907	1,139	120	15,938	11,022	4,916	181	35,844	21,874	13,970
1986–87	58	4,741	3,603	1,138	121	15,428	10,431	4,997	179	36,056	21,561	14,495
1987–88	57	4,477	3,300	1,177	122	15,358	10,278	5,080	180	35,397	21,067	14,330
1988–89	58	4,265	3,124	1,141	124	15,460	10,310	5,150	182	35,634	21,069	14,565
1989–90	57	4,100	2,834	1,266	124	15,075	9,923	5,152	182	36,485	21,079	15,406
1990–91	55	3,699	2,510	1,189	121	15,043	9,629	5,414	179	37,945	21,643	16,302
1991–92	52	3,593	2,431	1,162	120	15,243	9,796	5,447	177	38,848	22,260	16,588
1992–93	55	3,605	2,383	1,222	122	15,531	9,679	5,852	184	40,302	23,182	17,120

TABLE 9.11

First-professional degrees conferred by degree-granting institutions in dentistry, medicine, and law, selected years, 1949–50 to 2001–02 [CONTINUED]

Year	Dentistry (D.D.S. or D.M.D.)				Medicine (M.D.)				Law (LL.B. or J.D.)			
	Number of institutions conferring degrees	Degrees conferred			Number of institutions conferring degrees	Degrees conferred			Number of institutions conferring degrees	Degrees conferred		
		Total	Men	Women		Total	Men	Women		Total	Men	Women
1	2	3	4	5	6	7	8	9	10	11	12	13
1993–94	53	3,787	2,330	1,457	121	15,368	9,544	5,824	185	40,044	22,826	17,218
1994–95	53	3,897	2,480	1,417	119	15,537	9,507	6,030	183	39,349	22,592	16,757
1995–96	53	3,697	2,374	1,323	119	15,341	9,061	6,280	183	39,828	22,508	17,320
1996–97	52	3,784	2,387	1,397	118	15,571	9,121	6,450	184	40,079	22,548	17,531
1997–98	53	4,032	2,490	1,542	117	15,424	9,006	6,418	185	39,331	21,876	17,455
1998–99	53	4,144	2,674	1,470	118	15,562	8,954	6,608	188	39,167	21,628	17,539
1999–2000	54	4,250	2,547	1,703	118	15,286	8,761	6,525	190	38,152	20,638	17,514
2000–01	54	4,391	2,696	1,695	118	15,403	8,728	6,675	192	37,904	19,981	17,923
2001–02	53	4,239	2,608	1,631	118	15,237	8,469	6,768	192	38,981	20,254	18,727

— Not available.
Note: Data for 1998–99 were imputed using alternative procedures.

SOURCE: Thomas D. Snyder, Alexandra G. Tan, and Charlene M. Hoffman, "Table 259. First-Professional Degrees Conferred by Degree-Granting Institutions in Dentistry, Medicine, and Law, by Number of Institutions Conferring Degrees and Sex of Student: Selected Years, 1949–50 to 2001–02" in *Digest of Education Statistics, 2003*, NCES 2005-025, U.S. Department of Education, National Center for Education Statistics, Washington, DC, December 2004, http://nces.ed.gov/programs/digest/d03/tables/dt259.asp (accessed July 26, 2005)

TABLE 9.12

Employees in degree-granting institutions, by selected characteristics, Fall 2001

Primary occupation, sex, employment status, and type and control of institution	Total	White, non-Hispanic	Black, non-Hispanic	Hispanic	Asian/ Pacific Islander	American Indian/Alaska Native	Non-resident alien	Race/ ethnicity unknown
1	2	3	4	5	6	7	8	9
Total, all institutions	3,083,353	2,232,847	309,252	157,128	148,945	18,423	135,026	81,732
Professional staff	2,132,150	1,600,939	141,535	75,120	111,797	10,831	125,033	66,895
Executive/administrative/managerial	152,038	125,770	14,171	5,412	3,662	910	674	1,439
Faculty (instruction and research)	1,113,183	881,243	61,849	36,376	54,869	5,346	28,949	44,551
Instruction and research assistants	261,136	134,774	9,203	7,869	20,442	1,135	76,188	11,525
Non-faculty professionals	605,793	459,152	56,312	25,463	32,824	3,440	19,222	9,380
Nonprofessional staff	951,203	631,908	167,717	82,008	37,148	7,592	9,993	14,837
Men, total	1,451,773	1,051,988	117,746	68,967	76,269	8,082	84,720	44,001
Professional staff	1,105,053	826,070	57,743	36,080	61,866	5,150	80,231	37,913
Executive/administrative/managerial	79,348	67,150	6,132	2,589	1,909	427	399	742
Faculty (instruction and research)	644,514	509,616	29,831	20,147	35,447	2,852	19,885	26,736
Instruction and research assistants	142,120	67,555	3,611	3,813	11,638	514	48,757	6,232
Non-faculty professionals	239,071	181,749	18,169	9,531	12,872	1,357	11,190	4,203
Nonprofessional staff	346,720	225,918	60,003	32,887	14,403	2,932	4,489	6,088
Women, total	1,631,580	1,180,859	191,506	88,161	72,676	10,341	50,306	37,731
Professional staff	1,027,097	774,869	83,792	39,040	49,931	5,681	44,802	28,982
Executive/administrative/managerial	72,690	58,620	8,039	2,823	1,753	483	275	697
Faculty (instruction and research)	468,669	371,627	32,018	16,229	19,422	2,494	9,064	17,815
Instruction and research assistants	119,016	67,219	5,592	4,056	8,804	621	27,431	5,293
Non-faculty professionals	366,722	277,403	38,143	15,932	19,952	2,083	8,032	5,177
Nonprofessional staff	604,483	405,990	107,714	49,121	22,745	4,660	5,504	8,749
Full-time, total	2,043,208	1,520,204	236,129	112,274	99,844	12,930	42,644	19,183
Professional staff	1,283,684	1,014,658	94,916	46,028	70,717	6,745	37,553	13,067
Executive/administrative/managerial	146,523	121,369	13,720	5,231	3,541	876	634	1,152
Faculty (instruction and research)	617,868	499,557	31,681	18,514	38,026	2,775	20,755	6,560
Non-faculty professionals	519,293	393,732	49,515	22,283	29,150	3,094	16,164	5,355
Nonprofessional staff	759,524	505,546	141,213	66,246	29,127	6,185	5,091	6,116
Part-time, total	1,040,145	712,643	73,123	44,854	49,101	5,493	92,382	62,549
Professional staff	848,466	586,281	46,619	29,092	41,080	4,086	87,480	53,828
Executive/administrative/managerial	5,515	4,401	451	181	121	34	40	287
Faculty (instruction and research)	495,315	381,686	30,168	17,862	16,843	2,571	8,194	37,991
Instruction and research assistants	261,136	134,774	9,203	7,869	20,442	1,135	76,188	11,525
Non-faculty professionals	86,500	65,420	6,797	3,180	3,674	346	3,058	4,025
Nonprofessional staff	191,679	126,362	26,504	15,762	8,021	1,407	4,902	8,721
Public 4-year	1,558,576	1,102,022	153,297	76,737	89,834	10,342	97,978	28,366
Professional staff	1,069,161	775,811	66,408	35,904	69,445	5,911	93,596	22,086
Executive/administrative/managerial	60,245	49,255	6,207	2,148	1,471	346	248	570
Faculty (instruction and research)	438,459	345,636	21,660	12,833	29,045	2,262	19,153	7,870
Instruction and research assistants	218,260	115,345	7,576	6,384	17,156	985	62,683	8,131
Non-faculty professionals	352,197	265,575	30,965	14,539	21,773	2,318	11,512	5,515
Nonprofessional staff	489,415	326,211	86,889	40,833	20,389	4,431	4,382	6,280
Private 4-year	912,924	669,591	96,891	40,320	41,230	2,631	33,798	28,463
Professional staff	627,364	482,505	41,628	18,282	30,652	1,565	29,281	23,451
Executive/administrative/managerial	65,739	55,430	5,541	1,896	1,643	167	405	657
Faculty (instruction and research)	325,713	260,161	16,367	7,688	15,954	796	7,919	16,828
Instruction and research assistants	41,611	18,555	1,485	1,432	3,260	103	13,493	3,283
Non-faculty professionals	194,301	148,359	18,235	7,266	9,795	499	7,464	2,683
Nonprofessional staff	285,560	187,086	55,263	22,038	10,578	1,066	4,517	5,012

tuition rate for private four-year institutions, New England had the highest rate for private four-year institutions, and the Middle states had the highest rate for public four-year institutions. (See Table 9.14.)

Many factors have contributed to the increase in costs at public schools, including declines in government appropriations, increases in instructional and student services costs, and increases in research expenditures. States have raised room and board and tuition costs at once-inexpensive state schools to compensate for declining federal aid. Public schools still remain significantly

less expensive than private schools, but they are not quite the educational bargains that they once were. Private schools attribute their increases to several factors, including higher student aid, increases in salaries and benefits for faculty and staff, higher energy costs, and maintenance of academic programs and libraries.

Financial Assistance for Students

Federal assistance that goes directly to students includes Pell Grants, funds from the Stafford Student Loan Program, and Supplemental Education Opportunity

TABLE 9.12

Employees in degree-granting institutions, by selected characteristics, Fall 2001 [CONTINUED]

Primary occupation, sex, employment status, and type and control of institution	Total	White, non-Hispanic	Black, non-Hispanic	Hispanic	Asian/ Pacific Islander	American Indian/Alaska Native	Non-resident alien	Race/ ethnicity unknown
1	2	3	4	5	6	7	8	9
Public 2-year	578,394	435,674	55,916	38,085	16,889	5,001	3,180	23,649
Professional staff	408,792	321,570	31,089	19,601	10,956	3,103	2,102	20,371
Executive/administrative/managerial	22,566	18,191	2,172	1,231	462	353	16	141
Faculty (instruction and research)	332,665	262,453	22,443	15,154	9,398	2,173	1,844	19,200
Instruction and research assistants	1,215	832	140	51	25	47	11	109
Non-faculty professionals	52,346	40,094	6,334	3,165	1,071	530	231	921
Nonprofessional staff	169,602	114,104	24,827	18,484	5,933	1,898	1,078	3,278
Private 2-year	33,459	25,560	3,148	1,986	992	449	70	1,254
Professional staff	26,833	21,053	2,410	1,333	744	252	54	987
Executive/administrative/managerial	3,488	2,894	251	137	86	44	5	71
Faculty (instruction and research)	16,346	12,993	1,379	701	472	115	33	653
Instruction and research assistants	50	42	2	2	1	0	1	2
Non-faculty professionals	6,949	5,124	778	493	185	93	15	261
Nonprofessional staff	6,626	4,507	738	653	248	197	16	267

SOURCE: Thomas D. Snyder, Alexandra G. Tan, and Charlene M. Hoffman, "Table 228. Employees in Degree-Granting Institutions, by Race/Ethnicity, Primary Occupation, Sex, Employment Status, and Control and Type of Institution: Fall 2001," in *Digest of Education Statistics, 2003*, NCES 2005-025, U.S. Department of Education, National Center for Education Statistics, Washington, DC, December 2004, http://nces.ed.gov/programs/digest/d03/tables/dt228.asp (accessed July 26, 2005)

TABLE 9.13

Average salaries of full–time instructional faculty at degree–granting institutions, selected academic years, 1977–78 to 2002–03

[In constant 2002–03 dollars]

Compensation, salary, and benefits[a]	1977–78	1982–83	1987–88	1992–93	1997–98	2002–03	Percent change 1987–88 to 2002–03
Total compensation	**$66,600**	**$63,100**	**$70,000**	**$72,700**	**$73,500**	**$78,300**	**11.9**
Salary	57,000	52,100	58,400	59,000	59,700	62,800	7.5
Academic rank							
Professor	77,000	68,600	76,800	77,900	79,300	86,100	12.1
Associate professor	58,000	51,800	57,500	58,100	58,600	62,800	9.2
Assistant professor	47,400	42,300	47,400	48,200	48,400	52,800	11.4
Instructor	38,300	34,100	37,200	37,800	38,100	47,300	27.2
Lecturer	44,200	38,500	42,500	40,300	40,900	43,700	2.8
No rank	52,100	46,600	49,600	48,100	49,000	46,500	−6.3
Type of institution							
Doctoral universities	64,600	59,400	67,500	68,600	70,800	75,500	11.9
Master's colleges and universities	55,700	50,300	56,400	55,100	56,000	57,800	2.5
Other 4-year	47,400	44,600	48,800	50,400	50,400	52,700	8.0
2-year	52,200	46,800	50,600	49,300	50,100	51,000	0.8
Fringe benefits	9,600	11,000	11,600	13,700	13,800	15,500	33.6

*Total compensation is the sum of salary and fringe benefits. Salary does not include outside income. Fringe benefits may include, for example, retirement plans, medical/dental plans, group life insurance, other insurance benefits, guaranteed disability income protection, tuition plans (dependent only), housing plans, Social Security taxes, unemployment compensation, worker's compensation, or other benefits.
Note: Full-time instructional faculty on less-than-9-month contracts were excluded. In 2002–03, there were about 3,500 of these faculty, accounting for less than 1 percent of all full-time instructional faculty at degree-granting institutions. Salaries, benefits, and compensation were in constant 2002–03 dollars, which were adjusted by the Consumer Price Index (CPI) from the Bureau of Labor Statistics and rounded to the nearest 100. Detail may not sum to totals because of rounding.

SOURCE: John Wirt, Susan Choy, Patrick Rooney, William Hussar, Stephen Provasnik, and Gillian Hampden-Thompson, "Faculty Salaries: Average Salaries of Full–time Instructional Faculty at Degree–granting Institutions by Academic Rank and Type of Institution, Average Fringe Benefits, and Total Compensation: Selected Academic Years, 1977–78 to 2002–03," in *The Condition of Education, 2005*, NCES 2005-094, U.S. Department of Education, National Center for Education Statistics, Washington, DC, June 2005, http://nces.ed.gov/pubs2005/2005094.pdf (accessed July 26, 2005)

Grants. Colleges or universities also receive assistance, which they in turn pay out to students, through Campus-Based Programs and Perkins Loans. In general, the federal government has shifted its spending from grants to loans.

According to *Trends in Student Aid* (College Board, 2004), aid to all students consisted of 56% loans, 38% grants, 1% work, and 5% tax benefits in 2003–04. For undergraduate students, 44% of aid received was in the form of grants, and almost half (49%) was in the form of

TABLE 9.14

Average student expenses, by College Board region, 2004–2005

	Tuition and fees	Additional out-of-district/ state charges	Books and supplies	Resident			Commuter		
				Room and board	Transpartation	Other costs	Room and board*	Transpartation	Other costs
National									
2-year public	$2,076	$4,037	$773	—	—	—	$5,747	$1,146	$1,608
4-year public	$5,132	$7,291	$853	$6,222	$774	$1,659	$6,177	$1,109	$1,943
4-year private	$20,082		$870	$7,434	$671	$1,238	$6,617	$1,031	$1,524
New England									
2-year public	$3,086	$4,963	$750	—	—	—	$5,914	$1,148	$1,554
4-year public	$6,839	$7,447	$741	$6,677	$518	$1,324	$6,228	$887	$1,468
4-year private	$25,660		$850	$8,851	$494	$1,141	$7,403	$871	$1,178
Middle States									
2-year public	$3,242	$3,555	$770	—	—	—	$5,719	$1,048	$1,407
4-year public	$6,300	$5,796	$828	$7,033	$551	$1,470	$6,121	$839	$1,942
4-year private	$21,439		$855	$8,506	$554	$1,145	$7,341	$953	$1,447
South									
2-year public	$1,953	$4,034	$736	—	—	—	$5,139	$1,435	$1,383
4-year public	$4,143	$8,227	$814	$5,456	$1,009	$1,582	$6,020	$1,222	$1,935
4-year private	$17,317		$859	$6,499	$868	$1,338	$5,968	$1,231	$1,624
Midwest									
2-year public	$2,514	$4,275	$765	—	—	—	$5,137	$1,172	$1,588
4-year public	$6,085	$7,132	$752	$5,776	$646	$1,762	$5,407	$1,063	$1,916
4-year private	$18,690		$850	$6,300	$667	$1,163	$5,796	$1,040	$1,609
Southwest									
2-year public	$1,477	$2,242	$704	$3,445	$774	$1,173	—	$1,300	$1,576
4-year public	$4,569	$6,302	$817	$5,542	$1,122	$1,793	$5,362	$1,409	$1,978
4-year private	$15,867		$876	$5,854	$867	$1,330	$5,320	$1,171	$1,431
West									
2-year public	$1,297	$4,562	$846	—	—	—	$6,485	$935	$1,907
4-year public	$4,130	$9,104	$1,094	$7,709	$876	$1,882	$7,359	$1,087	$2,029
4-year private	$19,998		$985	$7,657	$668	$1,627	$7,246	$903	$1,650

Note: Dashes indicate that the sample was too small to provide meaningful information. Data are enrollment-weighted, with the exception of additional out-of-district (for 2-year public) and out-of-state (for 4-year public) charges, which are unweighted.

*Room and board costs for commuter students are average estimated living expenses for students living off campus but not with parents as reported by institutions in the Annual Survey of Colleges.

SOURCE: College Board, "Table 5. Average Student Expenses, by College Board Region, 2004–2005 (Enrollment-Weighted)," in *Trends in College Pricing, 2004,* Copyright © 2004 by College Board. Reprinted by permission.

loans. Graduate students relied on loans 75% of the time and grants 22% of the time.

According to the College Board, in 2003–04 under-graduate and graduate students received more than $122 billion in financial aid. The largest share of aid was in the form of federal loans, which accounted for more than 47% ($56.8 billion) of the total. Institutional grants made up more than 19% ($23.3 billion) of the total aid to students, and federal Pell Grants made up about 10% ($12.7 billion).

THE BENEFITS OF HIGHER EDUCATION

Regardless of the increases in costs of attendance, the investment in higher education offers impressive returns, and the number of years of school completed by those twenty-five and older steadily increased between 1940 and 2002. (See Figure 9.6.) According to the National Center for Education Statistics, in 2002 median annual income for people twenty-five and older with a bache-

lor's degree or more was nearly twice as much as median annual income among households headed by workers who were high school graduates. (See Figure 9.7.) The unemployment rate of people twenty-five and older with a bachelor's degree or higher in 2002 was 2.9%, compared to 8.4% for people who did not graduate from high school. (See Figure 9.8.)

DISTANCE EDUCATION

Distance education is not a new concept. It started with classes taken by mail (correspondence courses) and by watching teachers' lectures on videos or cable television. Now the term refers to education or training courses delivered to off-campus locations via audio, video, or computer technologies. Distance learning can be used to describe various types of courses, programs, providers, and delivery systems, including online learning.

Distance education is growing rapidly. Many colleges and universities offer online/distance education

FIGURE 9.6

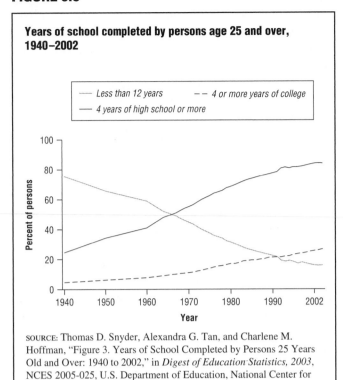

Years of school completed by persons age 25 and over, 1940–2002

SOURCE: Thomas D. Snyder, Alexandra G. Tan, and Charlene M. Hoffman, "Figure 3. Years of School Completed by Persons 25 Years Old and Over: 1940 to 2002," in *Digest of Education Statistics, 2003*, NCES 2005-025, U.S. Department of Education, National Center for Education Statistics, Washington, DC, December 2004, http://nces.ed.gov/programs/digest/d03/figures/figure_03.asp?popup=1 (accessed July 26, 2005)

programs. Enrollment, number of courses, and degrees offered are increasing. Schools usually team up with course management system vendors, which provide the software platforms for online courses. Other schools enter into corporate-university joint ventures run by hybrid content providers that offer courses and programs designed by individual faculty members at universities. Purely "virtual" universities also exist. Generally, these distance education providers offer undergraduate and graduate degrees, and enrollment ranges from a few hundred students to more than 20,000.

According to the National Center for Education Statistics, in 2000–01 enrollment in distance education courses had nearly doubled since 1997–98. More than half (57%) of the institutions in the sample offered distance education courses in 2000–01, up from 34% in 1997–98. While the majority of public two-year and four-year institutions (90% and 89%, respectively) offered distance education, it was less common at private four-year institutions (39%) in 2000–01. In 2000–01 more than three-quarters (76%—2,350,000 of 3,077,000) of the enrollments in distance learning programs were at the undergraduate level. (See Table 9.15.)

SUBSTANCE ABUSE AMONG COLLEGE STUDENTS

Illicit Drug Use

Monitoring the Future: National Survey Results on Drug Use, 1975–2003, Volume II: College Students and Adults Ages 19–45 (National Institute on Drug Abuse,

FIGURE 9.7

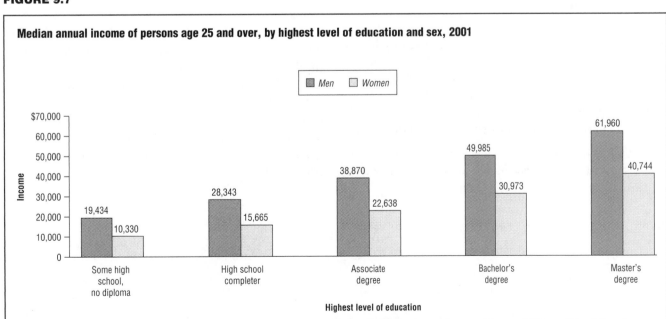

Median annual income of persons age 25 and over, by highest level of education and sex, 2001

SOURCE: Thomas D. Snyder, Alexandra G. Tan, and Charlene M. Hoffman, "Figure 25. Median Annual Income of Persons 25 Years Old and Over, by Highest Level of Education and Sex: 2001," in *Digest of Education Statistics, 2003*, NCES 2005-025, U.S. Department of Education, National Center for Education Statistics, Washington, DC, December 2004, http://nces.ed.gov/programs/digest/d03/figures/figure_25.asp?popup=1 (accessed July 26, 2005)

FIGURE 9.8

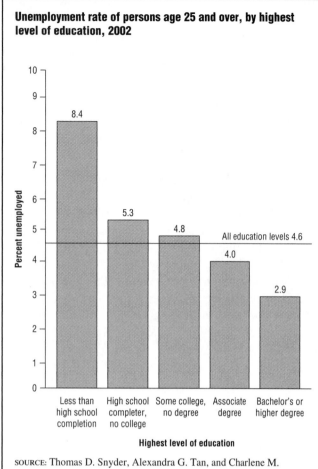

Unemployment rate of persons age 25 and over, by highest level of education, 2002

SOURCE: Thomas D. Snyder, Alexandra G. Tan, and Charlene M. Hoffman, "Figure 23. Unemployment Rate of Persons 25 Years Old and Over, by Highest Level of Education: 2002," in *Digest of Education Statistics, 2003*, NCES 2005-025, U.S. Department of Education, National Center for Education Statistics, Washington, DC, December 2004, http://nces.ed.gov/programs/digest/d03/figures/figure_23.asp?popup=1 (accessed July 26, 2005)

illicit drug use in 2003 (36.5%, compared to 33% for young adults ages nineteen to twenty-eight). College students also reported a greater prevalence of drug use in the thirty days prior to the survey than did their nonstudent peers (21.4% versus 19.9%). Annual prevalence means using a drug at any time within the year preceding the survey; thirty-day prevalence refers to using a drug in the thirty days prior to the survey. Drug use among college students has generally increased since 1991.

In 2003 more than one-third of college students (33.7%) reported that they had used marijuana at some time during the previous year, compared to 29% of nonstudents. Fewer students used cocaine (5.4%) than did their nonstudent peers (6.6%). Use of cocaine within the previous year increased for both college students and young adults not in college. Heroin use remained under 1% among both students and nonstudents in 2003.

Alcohol Use

College students who responded to the 2003 survey were slightly less likely to have used alcohol in the past year than their nonstudent peers (81.7%, compared to 83.3%). The high incidence of heavy or "binge" drinking (five or more drinks in a row in the past two weeks) among college students has been an important issue in recent years. In 2003 about 38.5% of college students reported bouts of heavy drinking in the previous two weeks, compared to 35.8% of nonstudent young adults. Binge drinking has not fluctuated much among either group since 1991.

Tobacco Use

According to *Monitoring the Future,* full-time college students were less likely than other people in the same age group to be regular smokers. In 2002 nearly 16% of college students reported smoking daily, down from 19% in 1999. About 8% reported smoking half a pack or more per day. About 21% of nonstudents in the same age group reported smoking daily, while 14% said they smoked half a pack or more a day.

Bethesda, MD, September 2004) was prepared by Lloyd D. Johnston, Patrick M. O'Malley, Jerald G. Bachman, and John E. Schulenberg at the University of Michigan. The survey of drug use among college students covers full-time students, one to four years out of high school, who were enrolled in two- or four-year institutions.

Compared to their nonstudent peers, college students showed a somewhat higher annual prevalence of

TABLE 9.15

Distance education institutions and enrollment, by level and type of institution, 1997–98 and 2000–01

Type of institution	Total number of institutions	Number of institutions offering distance education courses	Total number of enrollments in all distance education courses	Number of enrollments in college-level, credit-granting distance education courses		
				Undergraduate and graduate levels	Undergraduate courses	Graduate/ first-professional courses
			1997–98			
All institutions	5,010	1,680	1,661,000	1,364,000	1,082,000	281,000
Public 2-year	1,230	760	714,000	691,000	691,000	*
Public 4-year	610	480	711,000	453,000	290,000	163,000
Private 4-year	2,050	390	222,000	209,000	91,000	118,000
			2000–01			
All institutions	4,130	2,320	3,077,000	2,876,000	2,350,000	510,000
Public 2-year	1,070	960	1,472,000	1,436,000	1,435,000	*
Public 4-year	620	550	945,000	888,000	566,000	308,000
Private 4-year	1,800	710	589,000	480,000	278,000	202,000

*Reporting standards not met (too few cases).

Note: The sample for the 1997–98 survey consisted of 2- and 4-year postsecondary institutions (both higher education and postsecondary institutions) in the 50 states and the District of Columbia. The 2000–01 survey consisted of 2- and 4-year Title IV-eligible, degree-granting institutions in the 50 states and the District of Columbia. The change was made because NCES (National Center for Education Statistics) shifted the way in which it categorizes postsecondary institutions. Data for private 2-year institutions are not reported in a separate category because too few private 2-year institutions in the sample offered distance education courses to make reliable estimates. Data for private 2-year institutions are included in the totals. Enrollments may include duplicated counts of students because institutions were instructed to count a student enrolled in multiple courses for each course in which that student was enrolled. Detail may not sum to totals because of rounding, missing data, or because too few cases were reported for a reliable estimate for private 2-year institutions.

SOURCE: John Wirt, Susan Choy, Stephen Provasnik, Patrick Rooney, Anindita Sen, and Richard Tobin, "Table 32–1. Total Number of Institutions That Offered Distance Education Courses, Total Number of Enrollments in All Distance Education Courses, and the Number of Enrollments in College-Level, Credit-Granting Distance Education Courses, by Level and Type of Institution: 1997–98 and 2000–01," in *The Condition of Education, 2004*, NCES 2004-077, U.S. Department of Education, National Center for Education Statistics, Washington, DC, June 2004, http://nces.ed.gov/programs/coe/2004/section5/table.asp?tableID=86 (accessed July 26, 2005)

CHAPTER 10
PUBLIC OPINIONS ABOUT EDUCATION

Every year Phi Delta Kappa, the professional education fraternity, publishes a survey of the American public on education issues. This annual examination is considered one of the best measurements of current American attitudes toward education. Except where otherwise noted, the information in this chapter comes from "The 36th Annual Phi Delta Kappa/Gallup Poll of the Public's Attitudes toward the Public Schools" (Lowell C. Rose and Alec M. Gallup, *Phi Delta Kappan*, September 2004).

Keep in mind that these are surveys of people's opinions and feelings about public education, which may or may not coincide with facts about the nation's schools. Instead, the survey results illustrate trends in current American thought on educational subjects.

BIGGEST PROBLEMS FACING LOCAL PUBLIC SCHOOLS

Since Phi Delta Kappa began surveying the public's opinions about education in 1969, discipline has been at or near the top of the list of concerns. According to the U.S. Department of Education, based on data from Phi Delta Kappa/Gallup, between 1969 and 1985 (with the exception of 1971, when the top issue was finances), discipline was the most frequently mentioned problem. Drug abuse by students replaced discipline as the top concern from 1986 through 1991, and in 1992 drugs tied with lack of proper financial support, at 22% each. In 1993 lack of proper financial support was clearly the number-one concern, with 21% mentioning it as the biggest concern for public schools in their communities. In 1994 lack of discipline tied with fighting/violence/gangs, and in 1995 lack of discipline was back on top. Drug abuse edged out discipline as the top concern of 1996. In 1998 and 1999 lack of discipline, violence in schools, and lack of financial support were the top three concerns. In

2000 the public identified two problems as top concerns: lack of financial support and lack of discipline. The same two concerns topped the poll in 2001 as well. Fighting/violence/gangs and overcrowded schools tied for second place in 2001. (See Table 10.1.) Figure 10.1 shows trends in the public's attitudes about specific problems in schools from 1980 to 2003.

In 2002 lack of financial support topped the list of the public's concerns, with lack of discipline and overcrowding tied for second place. The top two concerns in 2003 were lack of financial support and lack of discipline, with overcrowding coming in third. Again in 2004 lack of financial support was cited most often as the biggest problem facing public schools, with lack of discipline, and overcrowding tied for second place. (See Table 10.2.)

GRADING THE SCHOOLS

Every year the Phi Delta Kappa survey asks respondents to grade the public schools on the same scale used to grade students. In general, the survey has found for many years that the respondents' ties to local schools influence the way they rank them. For example, people generally give their children's schools a higher grade than the schools in the community as a whole, and local community schools are generally given higher grades than is the nation's school system as a whole. (See Table 10.3.)

Overall, the 2004 survey found that almost half (47%) of those surveyed believed the schools in their communities deserved an A or B grade. (See Table 10.4.) Most (61%) public school parents awarded an A or B grade to the public schools in their community. When asked to grade the school attended by their own oldest children, a majority (70%) of public school parents awarded an A or a B. (See Table 10.5.)

TABLE 10.1

Items most frequently cited by the general public as a major problem facing local public schools, selected years 1970–2003

Problem	Percent																		
	1970	1975	1980	1985	1989	1990	1991	1992	1993	1994	1995	1996	1997	1998	1999	2000	2001	2002	2003
1	2	3	4	5	6	7	8	9	10	11	12	13	14	15	16	17	18	19	20
Lack of discipline	18	23	26	25	19	19	20	17	15	18	15	15	15	14	18	15	15	17	16
Lack of financial support	17	14	10	9	13	13	18	22	21	13	11	13	15	12	9	18	15	23	25
Fighting/violence/gangs	—	—	—	—	—	—	—	9	13	18	9	14	12	15	11	11	10	9	4
Use of drugs	11	9	14	18	34	38	22	22	16	11	7	16	14	10	8	9	9	13	9
Standards/quality of education	—	—	—	—	—	—	—	—	—	8	4	—	8	6	2	5	—	—	4
Large schools/overcrowding	—	10	7	5	8	7	9	9	8	7	3	8	8	8	8	12	10	17	14
Lack of respect	—	—	—	—	—	—	—	—	—	3	3	2	—	2	2	2	—	—	—
Lack of family structure/ problems of home life	—	—	—	—	—	—	—	—	—	5	3	4	—	—	—	—	—	—	—
Crime/vandalism	—	—	—	—	—	—	—	—	—	4	2	3	—	2	5	5	—	—	—
Getting good teachers	12	11	6	10	7	7	11	5	5	3	2	3	3	5	4	4	6	8	5
Parents' lack of interest	3	2	6	3	6	4	7	5	4	3	2	—	—	2	4	4	—	—	—
Poor curriculum/standards	6	5	11	11	8	8	10	9	9	3	2	3	—	1	2	2	—	—	—
Pupils' lack of interest/truancy	—	3	5	5	3	6	5	3	4	3	2	5	6	5	2	—	—	—	—
Integration/segregation/ racial discrimination	17	15	10	4	4	5	5	4	4	3	2	2	—	—	—	—	—	—	—
Management of funds/ programs	—	—	—	—	—	—	—	—	—	—	2	—	—	—	—	—	—	—	—
Moral standards	—	—	—	2	3	3	3	4	3	—	—	—	—	2	2	—	—	—	—
Low teacher pay	—	—	—	2	4	6	4	3	3	—	—	—	—	2	2	4	—	—	4
Teachers' lack of interest	—	—	6	4	4	4	2	2	—	—	—	—	—	—	—	—	—	—	—
Drinking/alcoholism	—	—	2	3	4	4	2	2	—	—	—	—	—	—	—	—	—	—	—
Lack of proper facilities	11	3	2	1	1	2	—	—	—	—	—	—	—	—	—	—	—	—	—

— Not available.

Note: Respondents were permitted to select multiple or no major problems.

SOURCE: Thomas D. Snyder, Alexandra G. Tan, and Charlene M. Hoffman, "Table 23. Items Most Frequently Cited by the General Public as a Major Problem Facing the Local Public Schools: Selected Years, 1970 to 2003," in *Digest of Education Statistics, 2003*, NCES 2005-025, U.S. Department of Education, National Center for Education Statistics, Washington, DC, December 2004, http://nces.ed.gov/programs/digest/d03/tables/dt023.asp (accessed July 26, 2005)

FIGURE 10.1

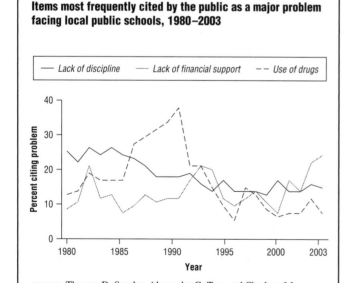

Items most frequently cited by the public as a major problem facing local public schools, 1980–2003

— Lack of discipline   ······ Lack of financial support   – – Use of drugs

SOURCE: Thomas D. Snyder, Alexandra G. Tan, and Charlene M. Hoffman, "Figure 6. Items Most Frequently Cited by the Public as a Major Problem Facing the Local Public Schools, 1980–2003," in *Digest of Education Statistics, 2003*, NCES 2005-025, U.S. Department of Education, National Center for Education Statistics, Washington, DC, December 2004, http://nces.ed.gov/programs/digest/d03/figures/figure _06.asp?popup=1 (accessed July 26, 2005)

Respondents graded the American public school system as a whole much more harshly. Only 26% felt the nation's public schools, overall, deserved A or B grades, while 58% assigned grades of C or D. (See Table 10.6.)

SCHOOL REFORMS

Respondents were asked whether they preferred reforming the existing public schools or finding an alternative to the system. In 2004 nearly two-thirds (66%) said they favored reforming the existing system, while 26% preferred finding an alternative. (See Table 10.7.)

Two-thirds (66%) of respondents favored increasing the mandatory attendance age to eighteen as a way to deal with the school dropout problem (see Table 10.8), and nearly three-quarters opposed eliminating the senior year of high school so that students could get an earlier start on going to college or entering the workforce. (See Table 10.9.)

In 2004 nearly three-quarters (73%) of respondents believed that it is not possible to accurately judge a student's proficiency in English and math on the basis of a single test. (See Table 10.10.) When respondents were asked whether they were concerned that relying on testing for English and math only to judge a school's performance would mean less emphasis on art, music,

TABLE 10.2

Public opinion on school problems, 2004

WHAT DO YOU THINK ARE THE BIGGEST PROBLEMS THE PUBLIC SCHOOLS OF YOUR COMMUNITY MUST DEAL WITH?

	National totals			No children in school			Public school parents		
	'04 %	'03 %	'02 %	'04 %	'03 %	'02 %	'04 %	'03 %	'02 %
Lack of financial support/ funding/money	21	25	23	22	26	23	20	24	23
Lack of discipline, more control	10	16	17	10	17	18	8	13	13
Overcrowded schools	10	14	17	9	12	14	13	16	23
Use of drugs/dope	7	9	13	7	10	14	7	7	11
Fighting/violence/gangs	6	4	9	6	3	9	6	5	9

SOURCE: Lowell C. Rose and Alec M. Gallup, "Table 4. What do you think are the biggest problems the public schools of your community must deal with?," in "The 36th Annual Phi Delta Kappa/Gallup Poll of the Public's Attitudes Toward the Public Schools," *Phi Delta Kappan*, September 2004. Reproduced with permission.

TABLE 10.3

Average grade public would give public schools in their community and in the nation at large, 1974–2003

Year	All adults		No children in school		Public school parents		Private school parents	
	Nation	Local community	Nation	Local community	Nation	Local community	Nation	Local community
1	2	3	4	5	6	7	8	9
1974	—	2.63	—	2.57	—	2.80	—	2.15
1975	—	2.38	—	2.31	—	2.49	—	1.81
1976	—	2.38	—	2.34	—	2.48	—	2.22
1977	—	2.33	—	2.25	—	2.59	—	2.05
1978	—	2.21	—	2.11	—	2.47	—	1.69
1979	—	2.21	—	2.15	—	2.38	—	1.88
1980	—	2.26	—	—	—	—	—	—
1981	1.94	2.20	—	2.12	—	2.36	—	1.88
1982	2.01	2.24	2.04	2.18	2.01	2.35	2.02	2.20
1983	1.91	2.12	1.92	2.10	1.92	2.31	1.82	1.89
1984	2.09	2.36	2.11	2.30	2.11	2.49	2.04	2.17
1985	2.14	2.39	2.16	2.36	2.20	2.44	1.93	2.00
1986	2.13	2.36	—	2.29	—	2.55	—	2.14
1987	2.18	2.44	2.20	2.38	2.22	2.61	2.03	2.01
1988	2.08	2.35	2.02	2.32	2.13	2.48	2.00	2.13
1989	2.01	2.35	1.99	2.27	2.06	2.56	1.93	2.12
1990	1.99	2.29	1.98	2.27	2.03	2.44	1.85	2.09
1991	2.00	2.36	—	—	—	—	—	—
1992	1.93	2.30	1.92	—	1.94	2.73	1.85	—
1993	1.95	2.41	1.97	2.40	1.97	2.48	1.80	2.11
1994	1.95	2.26	1.95	2.16	1.90	2.55	1.86	1.90
1995	1.97	2.28	1.98	2.25	1.93	2.41	1.81	1.85
1996	1.93	2.30	1.91	2.22	2.00	2.56	1.80	1.86
1997	1.97	2.35	1.99	2.27	2.01	2.56	1.99	1.87
1998	1.93	2.41	1.92	2.36	1.96	2.51	1.81	2.20
1999	2.02	2.44	2.03	2.42	1.97	2.56	—	—
2000	1.98	2.47	1.94	2.44	2.05	2.59	—	—
2001	2.01	2.47	2.00	2.42	2.04	2.66	—	—
2002	2.08	2.44	2.08	2.40	2.06	2.61	—	—
2003	2.11	2.41	2.09	2.32	2.16	2.57	—	—

— Not available.
Note: Average based on a scale where A=4, B=3, C=2, D=1, and F=0.

SOURCE: Thomas D. Snyder, Alexandra G. Tan, and Charlene M. Hoffman, "Table 22. Average Grade That the Public Would Give the Public Schools in Their Community and in the Nation at Large: 1974 to 2003," in *Digest of Education Statistics, 2003*, NCES 2005-025, U.S. Department of Education, National Center for Education Statistics, Washington, DC, December 2004, http://nces.ed.gov/programs/digest/d03/tables/dt022.asp (accessed July 26, 2005)

history, and other subjects, the majority (81%) responded that they were concerned a great deal or a fair amount. (See Table 10.11.)

Respondents were asked whether they thought an increased emphasis on English, math, and science at all grade levels would serve all, most, some, or only a few

TABLE 10.4

Public opinion on grading the schools in their community, 2004

STUDENTS ARE OFTEN GIVEN THE GRADES OF A, B, C, D, AND FAIL TO DENOTE THE QUALITY OF THEIR WORK. SUPPOSE THE PUBLIC SCHOOLS THEMSELVES, IN YOUR COMMUNITY, WERE GRADED IN THE SAME WAY. WHAT GRADE WOULD YOU GIVE THE PUBLIC SCHOOLS HERE—A, B, C, D, OR FAIL?

	National totals		No children in school		Public school parents	
	'04 %	'03 %	'04 %	'03 %	'04 %	'03 %
A & B	47	48	42	45	61	55
A	13	11	11	8	17	17
B	34	37	31	37	44	38
C	33	31	37	30	24	31
D	10	10	9	10	10	10
Fail	4	5	3	7	5	3
Don't know	6	6	9	8	*	1

*Less than one-half of 1%.

SOURCE: Lowell C. Rose and Alec M. Gallup, "Table 1. Students are often given the grades of A, B, C, D, and FAIL to denote the quality of their work. Suppose the public schools themselves, in your community, were graded in the same way. What grade would you give the public schools here—A, B, C, D, or FAIL?," in "The 36th Annual Phi Delta Kappa/Gallup Poll of the Public's Attitudes Toward the Public Schools," *Phi Delta Kappan*, September 2004. Reproduced with permission.

TABLE 10.5

Public opinion on grading the school their oldest child attends, 2004

USING THE A, B, C, D, FAIL SCALE AGAIN, WHAT GRADE WOULD YOU GIVE THE SCHOOL YOUR OLDEST CHILD ATTENDS?

	Public school parents	
	'04 %	'03 %
A & B	70	68
A	24	29
B	46	39
C	16	20
D	8	8
Fail	4	4
Don't know	2	*

*Less than one-half of 1%.

SOURCE: Lowell C. Rose and Alec M. Gallup, "Table 3. Using the A, B, C, D, FAIL scale again, what grade would you give the school your oldest child attends?," in "The 36th Annual Phi Delta Kappa/Gallup Poll of the Public's Attitudes Toward the Public Schools," *Phi Delta Kappan*, September 2004. Reproduced with permission.

public school students in the community. The responses were about evenly divided between all, most, and some, with 29% believing that the increased emphasis would serve all students, 32% believing that the increased emphasis would serve most students, and 28% believing that the increased emphasis would serve some students. Only 9% of the public believed that the increased emphasis on English, math, and science at all grade levels would serve only a few students. (See Table 10.12.)

TABLE 10.6

Public opinion on grading the schools in the nation, 2004

HOW ABOUT THE PUBLIC SCHOOLS IN THE NATION AS A WHOLE? WHAT GRADE WOULD YOU GIVE THE PUBLIC SCHOOLS NATIONALLY—A, B, C, D, OR FAIL?

	National totals		No children in school		Public school parents	
	'04 %	'03 %	'04 %	'03 %	'04 %	'03 %
A&B	26	26	28	26	22	26
A	2	2	2	1	3	5
B	24	24	26	25	19	21
C	45	52	45	52	44	49
D	13	12	13	11	13	13
Fail	4	3	3	4	6	2
Don't know	12	7	11	7	15	10

SOURCE: Lowell C. Rose and Alec M. Gallup, "Table 2. How about the public schools in the nation as a whole? What grade would you give the public schools nationally—A, B, C, D, or FAIL?," in "The 36th Annual Phi Delta Kappa/Gallup Poll of the Public's Attitudes Toward the Public Schools," *Phi Delta Kappan*, September 2004. Reproduced with permission.

STUDENT FAILURE

In 2004 survey respondents were asked who is most important in determining how well or how poorly students perform in school. Nearly one-half (45%) believed that students' parents are the most important determinant, while 30% cited students' teachers and 22% cited the students themselves. (See Table 10.13.)

In 2004 more than half (55%) of respondents whose children were failing would prefer tutoring provided by teachers in their child's school, and two-fifths (40%) would favor tutoring provided by an outside agency. (See Table 10.14.)

THE ACHIEVEMENT GAP

In 2004 the public was asked several questions related to the academic achievement gap that exists between white and minority students. More than three-quarters (78%) of respondents believed that minority children had the same educational opportunities as white children in their communities in 2004 (see Table 10.15). Seventy-four percent responded that the achievement gap between white and minority students is related mostly to other factors, not to the quality of schooling (see Table 10.16). When asked how important it is to close this gap between groups of students, 64% responded that it is very important to close the gap (see Table 10.17), and more than half (56%) responded that it is the responsibility of the public schools to close the achievement gap between white and minority students. (See Table 10.18.)

When asked about various proposals to close the achievement gap between white and minority children, in 2004 the public strongly favored encouraging parental involvement (97%), providing more instructional time for low performing students (94%), and strengthening

TABLE 10.7

Public opinion on reforming the existing public school system versus finding an alternative to the existing public school system, 2004

IN ORDER TO IMPROVE PUBLIC EDUCATION IN AMERICA, SOME PEOPLE THINK THE FOCUS SHOULD BE ON REFORMING THE EXISTING PUBLIC SCHOOL SYSTEM. OTHERS BELIEVE THE FOCUS SHOULD BE ON FINDING AN ALTERNATIVE TO THE EXISTING PUBLIC SCHOOL SYSTEM. WHICH APPROACH DO YOU THINK IS PREFERABLE—REFORMING THE EXISTING PUBLIC SCHOOL SYSTEM OR FINDING AN ALTERNATIVE TO THE EXISTING PUBLIC SCHOOL SYSTEM?

	National totals					No children in school					Public school parents				
	'04 %	'03 %	'02 %	'01 %	'00 %	'04 %	'03 %	'02 %	'01 %	'00 %	'04 %	'03 %	'02 %	'01 %	'00 %
Reforming existing system	66	73	69	72	59	63	73	69	73	59	72	73	69	73	60
Finding alternative system	26	25	27	24	34	28	24	26	23	34	21	25	27	25	34
Don't know	8	2	4	4	7	9	3	5	4	7	7	2	4	2	6

SOURCE: Lowell C. Rose and Alec M. Gallup, "Table 5. In order to improve public education in America, some people think the focus should be on reforming the existing public school system. Others believe the focus should be on finding an alternative to the existing public school system. Which approach do you think is preferable—reforming the existing public school system or finding an alternative to the existing public school system?," in "The 36th Annual Phi Delta Kappa/Gallup Poll of the Public's Attitudes Toward the Public Schools," *Phi Delta Kappan*, September 2004. Reproduced with permission.

TABLE 10.8

Public opinion on increasing the mandatory school attendance age, 2004

SOME PEOPLE HAVE PROPOSED INCREASING THE MANDATORY ATTENDANCE AGE TO 18 AS A WAY TO DEAL WITH THE SCHOOL DROPOUT PROBLEM. WOULD YOU FAVOR OR OPPOSE INCREASING THE MANDATORY ATTENDANCE AGE TO 18 IN YOUR STATE?

	National totals %	No children in school %	Public school parents %
Favor	66	66	68
Oppose	30	31	28
Don't know	4	3	4

SOURCE: Lowell C. Rose and Alec M. Gallup, "Table 35. Some people have proposed increasing the mandatory attendance age to 18 as a way to deal with the school dropout problem. Would you favor or oppose increasing the mandatory attendance age to 18 in your state?," in "The 36th Annual Phi Delta Kappa/Gallup Poll of the Public's Attitudes Toward the Public Schools," *Phi Delta Kappan*, September 2004. Reproduced with permission.

TABLE 10.9

Public opinion on eliminating the senior year of high school, 2004

SOME PEOPLE HAVE PROPOSED ELIMINATING THE SENIOR YEAR OF HIGH SCHOOL SO THAT STUDENTS COULD GET AN EARLIER START ON GETTING A COLLEGE EDUCATION OR ON ENTERING THE WORK FORCE. WOULD YOU FAVOR OR OPPOSE USING THIS PLAN IN THE HIGH SCHOOLS IN YOUR COMMUNITY?

	National totals %	No children in school %	Public school parents %
Favor	24	23	25
Oppose	74	75	73
Don't know	2	2	2

SOURCE: Lowell C. Rose and Alec M. Gallup, "Table 36. Some people have proposed eliminating the senior year of high school so that students could get an earlier start on getting a college education or on entering the work force. Would you favor or oppose using this plan in the high schools in your community?," in "The 36th Annual Phi Delta Kappa/Gallup Poll of the Public's Attitudes Toward the Public Schools," *Phi Delta Kappan*, September 2004. Reproduced with permission.

remedial programs (92%). Providing free breakfast and free lunch programs (84%), providing state-funded preschool programs (80%), and providing in-school health clinics (76%) were also supported by the majority of respondents. (See Table 10.19.)

TABLE 10.10

Public opinion on whether it is possible to judge a student's proficiency in English and math on a single test, 2004

IN YOUR OPINION, IS IT POSSIBLE OR NOT POSSIBLE TO ACCURATELY JUDGE A STUDENT'S PROFICIENCY IN ENGLISH AND MATH ON THE BASIS OF A SINGLE TEST?

	National totals		No children in school		Public school parents		Those knowing great deal/ fair amount	Those knowing very little/ nothing at all
	'04 %	'03 %	'04 %	'03 %	'04 %	'03 %	'04 %	'04 %
Yes, possible	25	26	26	27	24	22	27	24
No, not possible	73	72	72	71	75	77	72	74
Don't know	2	2	2	2	1	1	1	2

SOURCE: Lowell C. Rose and Alec M. Gallup, "Table 10. In your opinion, is it possible or not possible to accurately judge a student's proficiency in English and math on the basis of a single test?," in "The 36th Annual Phi Delta Kappa/Gallup Poll of the Public's Attitudes Toward the Public Schools," *Phi Delta Kappan*, September 2004. Reproduced with permission.

TABLE 10.11

Public opinion on whether relying on English and math testing to judge a school's performance will lead to less emphasis on other subjects, 2004

HOW MUCH, IF AT ALL, ARE YOU CONCERNED THAT RELYING ON TESTING FOR ENGLISH AND MATH ONLY TO JUDGE A SCHOOL'S PERFORMANCE WILL MEAN LESS EMPHASIS ON ART, MUSIC, HISTORY, AND OTHER SUBJECTS? WOULD YOU SAY YOU ARE CONCERNED A GREAT DEAL, A FAIR AMOUNT, NOT MUCH, OR NOT AT ALL?

	National totals		No children in school		Public school parents		Those knowing great deal/ fair amount	Those knowing very little/ nothing at all
	'04 %	'03 %	'04 %	'03 %	'04 %	'03 %	'04 %	'04 %
A great deal plus a fair amount	81	80	81	80	85	82	84	81
A great deal	37	40	35	38	43	45	42	35
A fair amount	44	40	46	42	42	37	42	46
Not much	13	14	13	13	11	15	10	14
Not at all	4	6	4	7	3	3	4	5
Don't know	2	*	2	*	1	*	2	0

*Less than one-half of 1 %.

SOURCE: Lowell C. Rose and Alec M. Gallup, "Table 11. How much, if at all, are you concerned that relying on testing for English and math only to judge a school's performance will mean less emphasis on art, music, history, and other subjects? Would you say you are concerned a great deal, a fair amount, or not at all?," in "The 36th Annual Phi Delta Kappa/Gallup Poll of the Public's Attitudes Toward the Public Schools," *Phi Delta Kappan*, September 2004. Reproduced with permission.

TABLE 10.12

Public opinion on whether greater emphasis on English, math, and science will serve students' needs, 2004

SOME STATES ARE NOW REQUIRING THE PUBLIC SCHOOLS TO PLACE GREATER EMPHASIS AT ALL GRADE LEVELS ON ENGLISH, MATH, AND SCIENCE. THINKING ABOUT THE NEEDS OF THE PUBLIC SCHOOL STUDENTS IN YOUR COMMUNITY, DO YOU THINK THIS INCREASED EMPHASIS WILL SERVE ALL, MOST, SOME, OR ONLY A FEW OF THESE STUDENTS NEEDS?

	National totals %	No children in school %	Public school parents %
All	29	28	29
Most	32	30	37
Some	28	30	25
Only a few	9	10	6
Don't know	2	2	3

SOURCE: Lowell C. Rose and Alec M. Gallup, "Table 33. Some states are now requiring the public schools to place greater emphasis at all grade levels on English, math, and science. Thinking about the needs of the public school students in your community, do you think this increased emphasis will serve all, most, some, or only a few of these students' needs?," in "The 36th Annual Phi Delta Kappa/Gallup Poll of the Public's Attitudes Toward the Public Schools," *Phi Delta Kappan*, September 2004. Reproduced with permission.

TABLE 10.13

Public opinion on who is most important in determining how well or poorly students perform in school, 2004

IN YOUR OPINION, WHO IS MOST IMPORTANT IN DETERMINING HOW WELL OR HOW POORLY STUDENTS PERFORM IN SCHOOL—THE STUDENTS THEMSELVES, THE STUDENTS' TEACHERS, OR THE STUDENTS' PARENTS?

	National totals %	No children in school %	Public school parents %
Students themselves	22	23	21
Students' teachers	30	31	29
Students' parents	45	42	48
Don't know	3	4	2

SOURCE: Lowell C. Rose and Alec M. Gallup, "Table 29. In your opinion, who is most important in determining how well or how poorly students perform in school—the students themselves, the students' teachers, or the students' parents?," in "The 36th Annual Phi Delta Kappa/Gallup Poll Of the Public's Attitudes Toward the Public Schools," *Phi Delta Kappan*, September 2004. Reproduced with permission.

TABLE 10.14

Public opinion on tutoring, 2004

NOW, LET'S ASSUME THAT YOUR CHILD WAS FAILING IN HIS OR HER SCHOOL. WHICH KIND OF TUTORING WOULD YOU PREFER—TUTORING PROVIDED BY TEACHERS IN YOUR CHILD'S SCHOOL OR TUTORING PROVIDED BY AN OUTSIDE AGENCY THAT YOU WOULD SELECT FROM A STATE-APPROVED LIST?

	National totals		No children in school		Public school parents		Those knowing great deal/ fair amount	Those knowing very little/ nothing at all
	'04 %	'03 %	'04 %	'03 %	'04 %	'03 %	'04 %	'04 %
Tutoring provided by teachers in child's school	55	52	53	52	60	54	53	56
Tutoring provided by outside agency	40	45	42	46	34	42	41	39
Don't know	5	3	5	2	6	4	6	5

SOURCE: Lowell C. Rose and Alec M. Gallup, "Table 13. Now, let's assume that your child was failing in his or her school. Which kind of tutoring would you prefer—tutoring provided by teachers in your child's school or tutoring provided by an outside agency that you would select from a state-approved list?," in "The 36th Annual Phi Delta Kappa/Gallup Poll of the Public's Attitudes Toward the Public Schools," *Phi Delta Kappan*, September 2004. Reproduced with permission.

TABLE 10.15

Public opinion on whether minority children have the same educational opportunities as other children, 2004

IN YOUR OPINION, DO BLACK CHILDREN AND OTHER MINORITY CHILDREN IN YOUR COMMUNITY HAVE THE SAME EDUCATIONAL OPPORTUNITIES AS WHITE CHILDREN?

	National totals			No children in school			Public school parents		
	'04 %	'01 %	'78 %	'04 %	'01 %	'78 %	'04 %	'01 %	'78 %
Yes, the same	78	79	80	76	78	78	82	80	86
No, not the same	20	18	14	22	17	15	16	18	11
Don't know	2	3	6	2	5	7	2	2	3

SOURCE: Lowell C. Rose and Alec M. Gallup, "Table 28. In your opinion, do black children and other minority children in your community have the same educational opportunities as white children?," in "The 36th Annual Phi Delta Kappa/Gallup Poll of the Public's Attitudes Toward the Public Schools," *Phi Delta Kappan*, September 2004. Reproduced with permission.

TABLE 10.16

Public opinion on whether the achievement gap is related to the quality of schooling or to other factors, 2004

IN YOUR OPINION, IS THE ACHIEVEMENT GAP BETWEEN WHITE STUDENTS AND BLACK AND HISPANIC STUDENTS MOSTLY RELATED TO THE QUALITY OF SCHOOLING RECEIVED OR MOSTLY RELATED TO OTHER FACTORS?

	National totals				No children in school				Public school parents			
	'04 %	'03 %	'02 %	'01 %	'04 %	'03 %	'02 %	'01 %	'04 %	'03 %	'02 %	'01 %
Mostly related to quality of schooling received	19	16	29	21	19	15	31	20	20	18	22	22
Mostly related to other factors	74	80	66	73	73	80	64	72	76	80	75	74
Don't know	7	4	5	6	8	5	5	8	4	2	3	4

SOURCE: Lowell C. Rose and Alec M. Gallup, "Table 25. In your opinion, is the achievement gap between white students and black and Hispanic students mostly related to the quality of the schooling received or mostly related to other factors?," in "The 36th Annual Phi Delta Kappa/Gallup Poll of the Public's Attitudes Toward the Public Schools," *Phi Delta Kappan*, September 2004. Reproduced with permission.

TABLE 10.17

Public opinion on the achievement gap, 2004

BLACK AND HISPANIC STUDENTS GENERALLY SCORE LOWER ON STANDARDIZED TESTS THAN WHITE STUDENTS. IN YOUR OPINION, HOW IMPORTANT DO YOU THINK IT IS TO CLOSE THIS ACADEMIC ACHIEVEMENT GAP BETWEEN THESE GROUPS OF STUDENTS?

	National totals				No children in school				Public school parents			
	'04 %	'03 %	'02 %	'01 %	'04 %	'03 %	'02 %	'01 %	'04 %	'03 %	'02 %	'01 %
Very plus somewhat important	88	90	94	88	89	91	93	89	89	88	96	87
Very important	64	71	80	66	65	70	80	66	63	73	80	67
Somewhat important	24	19	14	22	24	21	13	23	26	15	16	20
Not too important	5	5	2	5	4	5	2	5	3	4	2	5
Not at all important	5	4	3	5	5	3	4	4	7	7	1	6
Don't know	2	1	1	2	2	1	1	2	1	1	1	2

SOURCE: Lowell C. Rose and Alec M. Gallup, "Table 24. Black and Hispanic students generally score lower on standardized tests than white students. In your opinion, how important do you think it is to close this academic achievement gap between these groups of students?," in "The 36th Annual Phi Delta Kappa/Gallup Poll of the Public's Attitudes Toward the Public Schools," *Phi Delta Kappan*, September 2004. Reproduced with permission.

TABLE 10.18

Public opinion on whether it is the public schools' responsibility to close the achievement gap, 2004

IN YOUR OPINION, IS IT THE RESPONSIBILITY OF THE PUBLIC SCHOOLS TO CLOSE THE ACHIEVEMENT GAP BETWEEN WHITE STUDENTS AND BLACK AND HISPANIC STUDENTS OR NOT?

	National totals		No children in school		Public school parents	
	'04 %	'01 %	'04 %	'01 %	'04 %	'01 %
Yes, it is	56	55	56	56	56	53
No, it is not	40	41	39	39	41	45
Don't know	4	4	5	5	3	2

SOURCE: Lowell C. Rose and Alec M. Gallup, "Table 26. In your opinion, is it the responsibility of the public schools to close the achievement gap between white students and black and Hispanic students or not?," in "The 36th Annual Phi Delta Kappa/Gallup Poll of the Public's Attitudes Toward the Public Schools," *Phi Delta Kappan*, September 2004. Reproduced with permission.

TABLE 10.19

Public opinion on various proposals to close the achievement gap, 2004

NUMEROUS PROPOSALS HAVE BEEN SUGGESTED AS WAYS TO CLOSE THE ACHIEVEMENT GAP BETWEEN WHITE, BLACK, AND HISPANIC STUDENTS. AS I MENTION SOME OF THESE PROPOSALS, ONE AT A TIME, WOULD YOU TELL ME WHETHER YOU WOULD FAVOR OR OPPOSE IT AS A WAY TO CLOSE THE ACHIEVEMENT GAP.

	Favor %	Oppose %	Don't know %
Encourage more parent involvement	97	2	1
Provide more instructional time for low-performing students	94	5	1
Strengthen remedial programs for low-performing students	92	6	2
Provide free breakfast and free lunch programs as needed	84	15	1
Provide state-funded preschool programs	80	18	2
Provide in-school health clinics	76	21	3

SOURCE: Lowell C. Rose and Alec M. Gallup, "Table 27. Numerous proposals have been suggested as ways to close the achievement gap between white, black, and Hispanic students. As I mention some of these proposals, one at a time, would you tell me whether you would favor or oppose it as a way to close the achievement gap?," in "The 36th Annual Phi Delta Kappa/Gallup Poll of the Public's Attitudes Toward the Public Schools," *Phi Delta Kappan*, September 2004. Reproduced with permission.

IMPORTANT NAMES AND ADDRESSES

Alliance for School Choice
5080 North 40th St., Ste. 375
Phoenix, AZ 85018
(602) 468-0900
FAX: (602) 468-0920
URL: http://
www.allianceforschoolchoice.org/

American Association for Employment in Education
3040 Riverside Dr., Ste. 125
Columbus, OH 43221
(614) 485-1111
FAX: (614) 485-9609
E-mail: aaee@osu.edu
URL: http://www.aaee.org/

American College Testing (ACT)
500 ACT Dr.
P.O. Box 168
Iowa City, IA 52243-0168
(319) 337-1000
URL: http://www.act.org/

American Federation of Teachers (AFT) AFL-CIO
555 New Jersey Ave. NW
Washington, DC 20001
(202) 879-4400
URL: http://www.aft.org/

Child Trends
4301 Connecticut Ave. NW, Ste. 100
Washington, DC 20008
(202) 572-6000
FAX: (202) 362-8420
URL: http://www.childtrends.org/

College Board (SAT)
45 Columbus Ave.
New York, NY 10023-6992
(212) 713-8000
URL: http://www.collegeboard.com/

Council of Chief State School Officers
One Massachusetts Ave. NW, Ste. 700
Washington, DC 20001-1431

(202) 336-7000
FAX: (202) 408-8072
URL: http://www.ccsso.org/

Council of the Great City Schools
1301 Pennsylvania Ave. NW, Ste. 702
Washington, DC 20004
(202) 393-2427
FAX: (202) 393-2400
URL: http://www.cgcs.org/

Education Commission of the States
700 Broadway, #1200
Denver, CO 80203-3460
(303) 299-3600
FAX: (303) 296-8332
E-mail: ecs@ecs.org
URL: http://www.ecs.org/

Educational Testing Service Corporate Headquarters
Rosedale Rd.
Princeton, NJ 08541
(609) 921-9000
FAX: (609) 734-5410
URL: http://www.ets.org/

Home School Legal Defense Association
P.O. Box 3000
Purcellville, VA 20134-9000
(540) 338-5600
FAX: (540) 338-2733
E-mail: info@hslda.org
URL: http://www.hslda.org/

Institute of International Education
809 United Nations Plaza
New York, NY 10017-3580
(212) 984-5400
FAX: (212) 984-5452
URL: http://www.iie.org/

National Education Association (NEA)
1201 16th St. NW
Washington, DC 20036-3290
(202) 833-4000

FAX: (202) 822-7974
URL: http://www.nea.org/

National Forum to Accelerate Middle-Grades Reform
P.O. Box 11346
Champaign, IL 61826-1346
E-mail: dtkasak@gmail.com
URL: http://www.mgforum.org/

National Teacher Recruitment Clearinghouse/Recruiting New Teachers, Inc. (RNT)
385 Concord Ave., Ste. 103
Belmont, MA 02478
(617) 489-6000
FAX: (617) 489-6005
E-mail: rnt@rnt.org
URL: http://www.recruitingteachers.org/
channels/clearinghouse/

Phi Delta Kappa International
408 North Union St.
P.O. Box 789
Bloomington, IN 47402-0789
(812) 339-1156 or 1-800-766-1156
FAX: (812) 339-0018
E-mail: information@pdkintl.org
URL: http://www.pdkintl.org/

U.S. Department of Education
400 Maryland Ave. SW
Washington, DC 20202
1-800-USA-LEARN
FAX: (202) 401-0689
URL: http://www.ed.gov/

U.S. Department of Education National Center for Education Statistics
1990 K St. NW
Washington, DC 20006
(202) 502-7300
URL: http://nces.ed.gov/

RESOURCES

The National Center for Education Statistics (NCES) of the U.S. Department of Education (Washington, DC) is a valuable source of information about the state of education in America. Its two annual publications, *Digest of Education Statistics* and *The Condition of Education*, provide a detailed compilation of education statistics from pre-kindergarten through graduate school.

Many other NCES publications were of major assistance in the preparation of this book: *The Nation's Report Card: An Introduction to the National Assessment for Educational Progress (NAEP)*; *NAEP 2004 Trends in Academic Progress: Three Decades of Student Performance in Reading and Mathematics Findings in Brief*; *NAEP 2004 Trends in Academic Progress: Three Decades of Student Performance in Reading and Mathematics*; *The Nation's Report Card: Geography Highlights 2001*; *The Nation's Report Card: U.S. History Highlights 2001*; *The Nation's Report Card: Science 2000*; and *The Nation's Report Card: Writing 2002*.

Also from the NCES: *National Education Longitudinal Study of 1988*; *Overview and Inventory of State Education Reforms: 1990 to 2000* (2003); *Projections of Education Statistics to 2013*; *Financing Education So That No Child Is Left Behind: Determining the Costs of Improving Student Performance*; *Parent and Family Involvement in Education 2002–03*; *Coming of Age in the 1990s: The Eighth-Grade Class of 1988 Twelve Years Later*; *America's Charter Schools: Results from the NAEP 2003 Pilot Study*; *Issue Brief: Rates of Computer and Internet Use by Children in Nursery School and Students in Kindergarten through Twelfth Grade: 2003*; *Distance Education Courses for Public Elementary and Secondary School Students: 2002–03*; *Revenues and Expenditures for Public Elementary and Secondary Education: School Year 2002–03*; and *Public Elementary and Secondary Students, Staff, Schools, and School Districts: School Year 2002–03*.

Other offices at the U.S. Department of Education publish valuable reports that were consulted for this book, including *To Assure the Free Appropriate Public Education of All Children with Disabilities*; *24th Annual Report to Congress on the Implementation of the Individuals with Disabilities Act* (2002); *Challenge and Opportunity: The Impact of Charter Schools on School Districts* (2001); and *A Guide to Education and "No Child Left Behind"* (2004).

The National Education Goals Panel (Washington, DC) published *Raising Achievement and Reducing Gaps: Reporting Progress toward Goals for Academic Achievement* (2001).

The U.S. Government Accountability Office (GAO; Washington, DC) has published numerous studies on American education, including *Special Education: Federal Actions Can Assist States in Improving Postsecondary Outcomes for Youth* (2003).

The U.S. Department of Justice (Washington, DC) monitors the problem of crime and violence among the school-age population. A publication produced by the Department of Justice in collaboration with the U.S. Department of Education was used in this book: *Indicators of School Crime and Safety: 2004*. U.S. Census Bureau (Washington, DC) publications were also consulted, including *Income, Poverty, and Health Insurance Coverage in the United States: 2003*.

The Centers for Disease Control and Prevention (CDC; Atlanta, GA) published *HIV/AIDS Surveillance Report* (2003) and *Youth Risk Behavior Surveillance— United States, 2003*, in *CDC Surveillance Summaries* (2004). Dr. Lloyd Johnston of the University of Michigan's Institute for Social Research, with support from the National Institute on Drug Abuse (NIDA), annually performs the *Monitoring the Future* study, an in-depth survey of drug use among high school and college students. The U.S. Department of Health and Human Services, Administration for Children and Families, produced the *Head Start Fact Sheet* (2005).

Other important sources of information include the National Commission on Excellence in Education's *A Nation at Risk* (1983); the National Governor's Association *Time for Results*; the Education Commission of the States' *ECS Report to the Nation: State Implementation of the No Child Left Behind Act* (2004) and *What Next? More Leverage for Teachers*; and the Council of Chief State School Officers' *Key State Education Policies on PK–12 Education* (Washington, DC, 2004).

Also referenced was *America's Children: Key National Indicators of Well-Being* (2004), a report in an annual series prepared by the Interagency Forum on Child and Family Statistics, which provided statistics on early childhood education and "detached youth." Child Trends, in its 2005 *Facts at a Glance* (Washington, DC), published data on teen pregnancy and births.

The Carnegie Council on Adolescent Development printed *Turning Points* (Report of the Task Force on Education and Youth Adolescents, New York, 1989), *High School Students at Risk: The Challenge of Dropouts and Pushouts*, (Carnegie Corporation of New York, 2004), as well as *Great Transitions: Preparing Adolescents for a New Century* (1995). *A Nation Prepared: Teachers for the 21st Century* (Carnegie Forum on Education and the Economy, Washington, DC) and *Turning Points 2000* (Teacher's College Press, New York, 2000) were also referenced for this book, as was The RAND Corporation's *Research Brief: Problems and Promise of the American Middle School* (Rand Education, Santa Monica, CA, 2004).

The American High School Today: A First Report to Interested Citizens (McGraw-Hill, New York, 1959), the Public Agenda report *Sizing Things Up* (2002), and *School Size, Achievement, and Achievement Gaps* (Education Policy Analysis Archives, 2004) were used for information on school size.

Richard M. Ingersoll, in *Is There Really a Teacher Shortage?* (Center for the Study of Teaching and Policy, Seattle, WA, 2003), reported on his study of teacher attrition and migration.

The Consortium for Policy Research in Education published *A Decade of Charter Schools: From Theory to Practice* (Graduate School of Education, University of Pennsylvania, 2002). Also consulted was *State of the Charter Movement 2005* (Charter School Leadership Council, 2005).

Tennessee Initiative for Gifted Education Reform produced the *National Survey on the State Governance of K12 Gifted and Talented Education* (2002).

Phi Delta Kappa, a national teachers' fraternity, publishes numerous reports on the condition of education in the United States, including *The 36th Annual Phi Delta Kappa/Gallup Poll of the Public's Attitudes toward the Public Schools* (*Phi Delta Kappas*, 2004).

The College Board (New York) produced *2004 College Bound Seniors: A Profile of SAT Program Test Takers*; *Trends in College Pricing* (2004); and *Trends in Student Aid* (2004), which were consulted for this book, as were materials from the American College Testing Program's *2004 ACT National and State Scores*.

The American Federation of Teachers (AFT) was a valuable source of information on teacher salaries in *AFT Public Employees Compensation Survey* and *Survey and Analysis of Teacher Salary Trends 2002*. Further information on the teaching profession and salaries was published by the U.S. Department of Labor Bureau of Labor Statistics (Washington, DC) in *Occupational Outlook Handbook, 2004–2005* and *National Compensation Survey: Occupational Wages in the United States, July 2004* (August 2005).

The Institute for International Education's *Open Doors* (2004 and 2005) provided data on international students in the United States, and on American students studying abroad.

The *Seventh Annual Report on School Performance 2003–04* (Edison Schools, New York); the 1998 AFT report *Student Achievement in Edison Schools* (Washington, DC); *A Guide to Recent Studies of School Effectiveness by the Edison Project and the American Federation of Teachers* (Harvard University, Cambridge, MA, May 1998); and *An Evaluation of Student Achievement in Edison Schools Opened in 1995 and 1996* (Western Michigan University, Kalamazoo, MI, 2000) were used to summarize information on for-profit schools.

Finally, numerous Web sites were consulted for this book, including those of the National Education Association; the National Forum to Accelerate Middle School Reform; the Alliance for School Choice; the Home School Legal Defense Association; and National Teacher Recruitment Clearinghouse. Information on these and other organizations can be found in "Important Names and Addresses."

INDEX

special education student standards, 48–49, 48t, 49t, 91(t5.6)

standardized tests as measure of principal ability, 125(t8.4)

standardized tests as measure of teacher ability, 125(t8.3)

student failure, 158

student performance, 158, 160t, 160(t10.10), 160(t10.13)

tutoring, 161(t10.14)

Public schools

Carnegie unit requirements, 78t

diversity, 14

enrollment and finances by type of locale, 18t–19t

enrollment by race/ethnicity, 21t–22t

enrollment by type and size of school, 20t

enrollment changes by state, 17f

expenditures, 27f

geographic enrollment trends, 13

high school enrollment, 2

per-pupil expenditures, 34t–35t

performance standards for special education students, 48–49, 48t, 49t

preprimary programs, 36t

public opinion on grading, 155–156, 157(t10.3), 158t

public opinion on problems facing, 155, 156f, 156t, 157(t10.2)

pupil/teacher ratio, 22–23

religion in, 113–115

revenue sources, 24f, 25t–26t

size, 13

supplementary program participation, 45t–46t

Pupil/teacher ratio, 22–23, 33t, 122

R

Race/ethnicity

achievement gap, 158–159, 161(t10.16), 162t

AIDS, 102t

at-risk students, 93

Carnegie unit requirements, 78t

charter school students, 107, 108f

college entrance test scores, 81–82, 82(t4.13)

colleges serving specific populations, 136–138, 137t–138t

computer and Internet use, 115t–116t

computers in schools, 115

detached youth, 97

diversity in public schools, 14

dropout rates, 52, 54f, 94–96

early childhood activities, 66t

educational attainment, 1, 2, 3t–5t, 6

employees in degree-granting institutions, 148t–149t

enrollment, 7t–8t

faculty, higher education, 143–144

fights in school, 101

gender and educational attainment, 6

Head Start program, 55

high school dropouts, 53t

higher education enrollment, 127–128, 130t–132t

illicit drug use, 99

inclusion programs for disabled children, 47–48

Individuals with Disabilities Education Act, students served by, 48f

National Assessment of Educational Progress geography scores, 74

National Assessment of Educational Progress history scores, 74–75

National Assessment of Educational Progress mathematics scores, 69, 70

National Assessment of Educational Progress reading scores, 63, 64, 64t, 65t

National Assessment of Educational Progress science scores, 73

National Assessment of Educational Progress writing achievement levels, 73–74

poverty, 14, 23t–24t

preschool programs, 24

public school enrollment, 21t–22t

safety, students' feelings of, 101

smoking and alcohol use, 100, 100t

special education students, 44

suicide, 101

unemployment rates, 95t–96t

See also Minorities

Raymond School Department, Bagley v. (1999), 110

Reading

daily reading habits, 65–66

National Assessment of Educational Progress tests, 62–67, 63f, 64t, 65t, 68f

No Child Left Behind Act, 84

for pleasure, 65, 66–67, 68(f4.4)

Religion

church and state, separation of, 110

in public schools, 113–115

Report cards, state, 87

Revenues, 17, 18t–19t, 24f, 25t–26t

Rural areas, 13

S

Safety, school, 87, 101

Salaries. *See* Earnings and salaries

SAT, 80–82

School accountability

exit exams, 79

No Child Left Behind Act, 85

See also Schools in need of improvement

School choice, 85, 109–111, 111t, 114

School improvement, 49t, 86–87, 90t, 91(t5.6)

School performance, public opinion on judging, 160(t10.11)

School prayer, 115

School reform

middle schools and at-risk students, 94

public opinion, 156–158, 159(t10.7)

reform movement, 83–84, 105–106

school size, 119

Schools in need of improvement, 49t, 86–87, 90t, 91(t5.6)

Science

advanced courses, 79f

high school exit examinations, 81f

high school graduation requirements, 77(f4.14), 78t, 79t

National Assessment of Educational Progress scores, 72–73

public opinion on emphasis on, 160(t10.12)

Trends in International Mathematics and Science Study scores, by country, 76t

Sexual activity, 100–101, 101t

Shanker, Albert, 106

Shortage, teacher, 121–122

Size, school, 13, 20t, 116, 118–119, 134

Smoking, 99–100, 100t, 152

Social studies, 77(f4.15), 78t, 81f

Society of Sisters, Pierce v. (1925), 109

Spanish-speaking students, 115t–116t, 116

See also Limited English proficiency students

Special education

disabled children, 41, 44

disabled students, high school completion and dropout rates, 52t

early education, 49

economically disadvantaged students, 51–53

education services by educational environment and disability type, 47t

exiting, 49, 50f, 51t

homeless children, 55

inclusion programs, 44, 47–48

Individuals with Disabilities Education Act, students served by, 48f

Limited English proficiency students, 53

migrant children, 54

performance standards, 48–49, 48t, 49t, 91(t5.6)

students served by disability type, 42t–43t

Standardized tests

in need of improvement in schools, 90t, 91(t5.6)